S0-AIN-828

GRAVEYARDS
of CHICAGO

The People, History,
Art, and Lore of
Cook County Cemeteries

MATT HUCKE
URSULA BIELSKI

Second Edition

LAKE CLAREMONT PRESS

an imprint of Everything Goes Media
Chicago ▪ Milwaukee

Graveyards of Chicago:
The People, History, Art, and Lore of Cook County Cemeteries
Matt Hucke and Ursula Bielski

Published November 2013 by:

LAKE CLAREMONT PRESS

An imprint of Everything Goes Media, LLC
lcp@lakeclaremont.com
www.lakeclaremont.com

Copyright © 2013 by Matt Hucke and Ursula Bielski

All rights reserved. No part of this book may be reproduced or transmitted in any form or by any means, electronic or mechanical, including photocopying, recording, or by any information storage or retrieval system without written permission from the publisher, except for the inclusion of brief quotations in a review.

Publisher's Cataloging-In-Publication Data
(Prepared by The Donohue Group, Inc.)

Hucke, Matt.
   Graveyards of Chicago : the people, history, art, and lore of Cook County cemeteries / Matt Hucke and Ursula Bielski. -- 2nd ed.

   p. : ill. ; cm.

   Includes bibliographical references and index.
   ISBN: 978-1-893121-21-8

   1. Cemeteries--Illinois--Cook County--History--Miscellanea.   2. Cook County (Ill.)--History, Local--Miscellanea.   3. Cook County (Ill.)--Biography--Miscellanea.   4. Cemeteries--Illinois--Chicago--History--Miscellanea.   5. Chicago (Ill.)--Biography--Miscellanea. I. Bielski, Ursula. II. Title.

F547.C7 H84 2013
977.3/1
2013939706

18 17 16 15 14 13   10 9 8 7 6 5 4 3 2 1
Design by Todd Petersen.
All photos by Matt Hucke unless credited otherwise.

For my apprentice graveyard explorers,
Kenna-Elysia Jones and Leila-Harper Jones.
May you love, honor, and protect these sacred spaces.
—M. H.

For the dead of Bachelors Grove,
and all the neglected and forgotten dead.
—U.B.

TABLE OF CONTENTS

INTRODUCTIONS

By Matt Hucke

As a newcomer to this city in 1993, I devoured every piece of writing I could find on its history and culture, fascinated to be in a place where so much had occurred. One of the first books in my collection, *Sweet Home Chicago*,[1] included a list of Chicago's *other* top ten attractions—not touristy places like the Field Museum or Sears Tower or Wrigley Field, but places one could visit for free without having to deal with the crowds: the Maxwell Street Market, the view from the Ravenswood "L," that sort of thing. One of these was Graceland Cemetery. The chapter opened with a photo of the pyramidal Schoenhofen mausoleum at Graceland, further engaging my interest.

Thus, within about a month or two of arriving here, I took the Red Line to the Sheridan Road stop and visited Graceland for the first time. I was unprepared—I didn't know where anything was in the cemetery (the office was closed on a Sunday, so no map was available)—and I didn't even have a camera then. Looking for the millionaires whose enormous tombs had been described in the book, I ended up on the wrong side of the cemetery and instead found a most unusual monument: a glass box with a remarkably lifelike statue of a young girl inside.

Although considerably impressed by my encounter with Inez (more on her later), I did not visit any cemeteries again for a few years, being more concerned with attending university and then going to my first real job. In my spare time I read *alt.folklore.ghost-stories*, a Usenet newsgroup (a type of online forum that predated websites), and the discussion there eventually included stories of Bachelor's Grove.

---

[1] Sherry Kent, Mary Szpur, with Tem Horwitz. *Sweet Home Chicago: The Real City Guide, 3rd Edition* (Chicago: Chicago Review Press, 1987).

I was intrigued. This tiny graveyard in the southwest suburbs was said to be one of the most haunted locations in the country, if not the world, and I now lived within driving distance of it. I had always been fascinated with ghosts, and this seemed to be the perfect opportunity to witness a haunting firsthand. In the autumn of 1995, I set forth to explore the haunted graveyard. I drove nearly two hours, then walked along a path through the woods to the small abandoned cemetery. I thought that, at last, I would see a ghost. My anticipation grew as the cemetery came into sight, my heart pounding. I stepped through a hole in the fence, and then... nothing happened. I left, disappointed, after less than an hour. But I had taken some pictures, at least, with a camera I'd borrowed from roommate Craig Brozefsky.

A few months later, I happened to drive past Rosehill, and looking for a quiet place to relax, ventured inside. I explored the area around the statue of Leonard Volk and was repeatedly surprised by the diversity, quality, and ingenuity of the monuments and mausoleums there. Rosehill possessed charm, character, and atmosphere—it was every bit as beautiful as Graceland, if not so well known. I decided then that I should begin regular trips to Chicago cemeteries until I had seen them all. In the following weeks I returned, with the borrowed camera, to Graceland, Rosehill, Jewish Graceland, and Calvary.

In August 1996 I created the website *Graveyards of Chicago*. At the time, I worked as system administrator at a small Internet service provider, and had configured web servers for hundreds of clients, but had no site of my own. I decided to create one in order to learn the technology, and thought showcasing my rapidly-growing photo collection would be an excellent project. Searching for available domain names, my first few choices—involving the word *cemeteries*—were taken already, but *graveyards.com* was available, so I registered it and got to work.

With dozens of unexplored cemeteries (or *graveyards*, a term that I suddenly found myself preferring due to the simple accident of which Internet domain name I'd found available) around the city, I had plenty of exploring to do, and the site grew rapidly. Those were joyous days, when I knew I could at any time find something new to explore less than an hour's drive from home. I visited Resurrection, site of a world-famous ghost story, and Forest Home and Mount Carmel. I returned the borrowed camera I'd used for the first few trips, upgrading to a Samsung point-and-shoot model with a zoom lens, and after that my first SLR, a Canon Rebel S.

About a year later, my work was noticed by Ursula Bielski, author of the soon-to-be-published *Chicago Haunts: Ghostly Lore of the Windy City*; she asked to use several of my photos for the book. Fittingly enough, Inez at Graceland, the monument that had so amazed me in 1993, was chosen for the cover.

It was shortly after this that publisher Sharon Woodhouse suggested a *Graveyards of Chicago* book. Young and inexperienced as I was, I had no idea how to begin. Ursula stepped in and provided her considerable research and writing skills to accompany my photos. In November 1999, our shared vision became reality—the first edition of *Graveyards of Chicago* was published and well-distributed. Unknown to us then, it would become a local favorite and continue to sell for over 12 years.

Then, with Chicago graveyards finally getting the attention they deserved, I began to widen my focus. Having thoroughly explored the famous cemeteries around Chicago, I looked for new locations further and further out. I pored over printed maps, seeking tiny, little-known graveyards on the fringes of Cook County, and then Lake and Will and DuPage counties, wanting to visit them all.

Around 2003 two technological advances completely changed my methods. One of these was GPS, Global Positioning System, now readily available to the public. With a hand-held receiver, all I needed was a pair of numbers to locate any graveyard in the country—and the published listings of the U.S. Geological Survey provided plenty of these, including sites that mapmakers had overlooked. Loading their list into a database on *graveyards.com*, I'd print lists of all the cemeteries in a given area and then drive between them, watching the numbers on my entry-level GPS receiver change as I got closer to the destination.

The other innovation was digital photography. At about the

same time, digital SLRs went mainstream with the introduction of the Nikon D100. Up to that point, I'd been limited by the cost of film and processing, about 40 cents a shot. At some smaller cemeteries, I had previously taken only five to ten photos, total; even at wonderful huge sites like Graceland and Forest Home I generally would get fewer than 50 pictures in a day. Now, there was essentially no limit, and I could revisit sites and monuments that I'd overlooked simply due to cost.

In 2003 and 2004 I returned to many of the Chicago cemeteries that I'd already explored, seeking to explore and photograph them more thoroughly. (Most of the photos in this edition are from this time period, using the Nikon D100.) I gained a new appreciation for sites that I'd previously dismissed as "kind of ordinary," now aware that even a tiny cemetery had a wealth of beauty and uniqueness for those who took the time to look.

But about this time, I was also discovering that many graveyards had changed in just a few years, generally not for the better.

Monuments had been damaged or destroyed. At Jewish Graceland, a marble portrait of a woman had vanished from the side of her granite monument (how I wish I'd shot a close-up when I could!). At Forest Home, a statue of a World War I soldier had gone AWOL, and the management had—regrettably, due to structural failure—demolished their 90-year-old river bridges. Gates at Jewish Waldheim had been torn down, for visitors' safety. Urns at several locations had snapped off at their narrow bases. Inscriptions had become less readable as acid rain ate at the soft marble. Metal thieves had made off with priceless works of art.

Though caretakers do what they can to slow the process, our cemeteries are crumbling. Those who love places of art, history, and beauty must do what we can to document what is there, before it is lost forever.

The present work is intended to celebrate graveyards, cemeteries, mausoleums, and columbaria of all types—any place set aside to permanently house the remains of the dead. In *The Last Great Necessity*, author David Charles Sloane divides American cemeteries into these classifications:

Frontier graves refer to burials of pioneers, more or less at the site of their death, with simple or no markers. Early Chicago undoubtedly had many such sites, but they are now lost.

Homestead graveyards are those parcels of a family's property intentionally (but informally) set aside as a graveyard. Examples would be the Haase/Zimmerman graves at Forest Home (before it became a public cemetery), Andreas von Zirngibl's solitary South Side grave, Sauerbier-Burkhardt Cemetery near Crestwood. These often grow to include graves from multiple families or a whole village.

Churchyards began as land near a church designated for burials, such as St. James at Sag Bridge, St. Henry in Rogers Park, and numerous suburban sites. For a more unusual example, see the Church of the Holy Comforter. Some churchyards have lost the church building, as when the building is demolished after a congregation relocates, declines in numbers, or merges with another. Examples of this include the now-destroyed St. Johannes at O'Hare and St. James in Sauk Village. Entombments may also be inside the church itself, though this is less common in America than in Europe. St. Sava's in Libertyville is a good local example.

Potter's fields are cemeteries for burial of the poor, with minimal or no markers. Cook County maintained such a site near Oak Forest Hospital, but now contracts with commercial cemeteries to provide this service. The Cook County Poor Farm Cemetery at Dunning is an example.

City cemeteries generally have a rectangular, grid-based layout and simple landscaping, but contain a variety of upright monuments in the common styles of the area. They're usually owned, at least originally, by a municipality. Many suburban cemeteries are of this type: Elk Grove, Hazel Green, Wheeling City Cemetery, Town of Maine. In addition, many of the smaller religious cemeteries are similar in layout and monument types: Wunder's, Jewish Graceland, St. Boniface, St. Peter & St. Paul in Skokie.

Rural cemeteries were commercial ventures, lavishly landscaped Victorian-era cemeteries intended to showcase the natural beauty of the site, originally outside city limits. Monuments at these locations are extraordinarily varied and as elaborate as owners could afford. Community mausoleums are often present. Examples include Graceland, Rosehill, Forest Home. There are a few religious examples as well, such as Calvary, Mount Olivet, Mount Carmel, and Mount Mayriv, which used the same design techniques, though to a lesser degree.

Lawn-park cemeteries, a later development, are similar to rural cemeteries, but designed to have more open and park-like surroundings and less visual clutter. There are upright family monuments but with flat or pillow markers for individual headstones. Examples include Mount Hope, Montrose, Oak Hill, Oak Ridge, Memorial Park in Skokie. Many larger archdiocesan Catholic cemeteries share this style as well, such as Resurrection, Holy Cross, and Queen of Heaven.

Memorial parks typically contain flat markers only, perhaps surrounding cemetery-owned central monuments or "features." In many newer cemeteries of this type, these feature monuments are exactly the same as those found in other cemeteries—"The Lord's Prayer," "Babyland," and "Christ in the Garden" statues are simply ordered from suppliers rather than specifically designed for that site. Local examples are Burr Oak, Restvale, Cedar Park, Chapel Hill Gardens, and Sunset Memorial Lawns. Alternatively, markers may rise a few inches above ground but be uniform in size, as at Acacia Park.

To Sloane's list I would add a few more basic cemetery types:

Military cemeteries are established and maintained by the federal government, local examples being Fort Sheridan Post Cemetery in Lake County and Abraham Lincoln National Cemetery near Joliet. Monuments are almost exclusively government issue, arranged in precise rows.

Institutional cemeteries are characterized by rows of nearly-identical markers, often cast from concrete, sometimes with numbers instead of names, usually ordered by date of death. These are typically made in the institution's own workshop, by other inmates or patients. Examples include Altenheim Old People's Home Cemetery, the state hospital cemeteries near Elgin and Kankakee, and the Illinois State Prison cemetery at Crest Hill.

Native American burial grounds have no monuments, save for mounds of earth. Few such sites survive in the Chicago area. Robinson Woods is one. Others have been incorporated into later cemeteries such as at Forest Home and Oak Wood in Joliet.

Independent mausoleums or columbaria indicate a community mausoleum, not within the grounds of a cemetery. There are no such facilities in Chicago, though other cities (Portland and San Francisco, for example) have them.

"*To see his monument look around you*" graves, drawing inspiration from Sir Christopher Wren, have revered community leaders buried at the centers of the institutions they served. Examples include the Rockefeller Chapel at the University of Chicago, containing the ashes of most of the university's past presidents, and the burial of the founder of the University of Illinois at Urbana-Champaign a few yards off the central quadrangle.

Every cemetery is, of course, unique, and may have characteristics of several of these basic types, making classification sometimes difficult.

By Ursula Bielski

My friend Karl, who I met in Cook County's Bachelors Grove Cemetery, has a specific ritual he practices whenever he enters the Grove, a place that has become a second home to him. Before taking any photos or speaking to anyone who may also be visiting, he does *the circuit.* That is, he traverses the circle that rings the burial ground, calling out hellos to the dead there, asking how all have been, and even commenting on the weather, as one might when visiting any friends or family or meeting neighbors in the street. When he goes a week or two without a visit, there's a real sense of urgency he feels, of neglecting real people, real friends in his life.

A fellow advocate of the dead of the Grove, Rick (who calls himself "the Ghost of Bachelors Grove"), visits most every single day, picking up trash as therapy after three neurological operations, convinced that it is these visits that have saved him from sure demise.

Then there is Angie, head of the Illinois chapter of the Association for Gravestone Studies, who I recently watched, at a party, as she let her dinner get cold and stand uneaten for a solid two and a half hours as she passionately talked to a fellow cemetery enthusiast about the need for greater preservation efforts across the state.

Without a doubt, Karl, Rick, Angie, and countless other *taphophiles*—cemetery enthusiasts—feel a tremendous sense of stewardship for the dead, a duty to their legacy and their lingering contributions to who we are, what we do, and where we take this world of ours.

Such taphophiles have come out of the closet by the millions since the publication of the first edition of *Graveyards of Chicago* in 1999, when times still hadn't changed much since my high school days in the 1980s. Back then, I was called "morbid" and "disturbed" by teachers and staff, who called a parent-teacher conference with my mortified mother after I elected to do my 1985 history project on Chicago's Graceland Cemetery, now commonly recognized as one of the most important historical and artistic sites in the city. Today, Graceland Cemetery is one of the most common topics covered by students in the Chicago history fairs where I now sometimes serve as a guest judge. No matter how many times I see these projects, I can't help but smile to see how far we taphophiles have come.

Today, it's downright trendy to like cemeteries. Local burial grounds offer not only cemetery walks, with local historical societies leading tours of the graves of influential founders, but even cemetery runs, charitable events sponsored by local athletic clubs or schools, like the Resurrection Mary 5K that culminates through the gates of Resurrection Cemetery, home of Chicago's favorite phantom.

I myself credit the majority of the new found freedom of cemetery enthusiasts to co-author Matt Hucke, whose groundbreaking effort, *www.graveyards.com* (and the first edition of this book, its companion), was like the sun coming out on the legions of us, across generations and around the world, who had loved the "morbid" world of the dead in hushed clusters our whole lives. If you, like me, blessed Matt's work then, wait till you get a load of him now. For while the first edition of *Graveyards of Chicago* showcased a large selection of Matt's beautiful photographs, but very little of his text, this edition also gives Matt his voice: indeed, the majority of the updates in this edition are his own. Like me, I know you will find that the man behind the photographs is a stunning and engaging writer. It was a pleasure to step back and to watch him run with this project, something I know he wanted to expand on since its original edition was *completed*, which neither of us—incidentally—ever thought it was. His joy in discovery, and in sharing each bit of new knowledge, was contagious throughout the revision, and I know the reader will find it so as well.

But taphophiles should brace themselves, too, as they turn the page and begin this volume, for this past Chicago decade has ushered in not only sunshine but also longer shadows. In fact, these years have brought some of the most shocking developments imaginable in cemetery culture and news—especially in Chicago and the larger Cook County.

Artist and Northwestern University professor Pamela Bannos sent shockwaves through the city with the revelations of her longtime independent research on the site of the old City Cemetery grounds in Lincoln Park. Far from the scattering of corpses we had been raised to believe still resided there, Bannos disclosed, in heart-breaking detail, that upwards of 13,000 bodies still remain under the baseball fields and running tracks of one of the city's most well-known neighborhoods. She also made it plainly known that the City had long been aware of the gradual discovery of these bodies, over many years, during the development of the park structures, Lincoln Park Zoo, and the Chicago History Museum. Her story, broken in several popular newspapers, left us speechless.

St. Johannes Cemetery, originally established amid the orchards northwest of the city limits, found the living family members of its inhabitants in tears, crushed in a legal battle with the City of Chicago, as the City gave descendants the eviction notice for their loved ones, aiming to build a new runway through the longtime graves. At the end of the long fight, the majority of the graves were reinterred in a local burial ground, having moved from behind the Fed Ex hangar at O'Hare to a ramshackle gathering behind the waterslide at the community swimming pool.

The destitute of the Dunning Poor Farm and Insane Asylum cemeteries finally got their memorial park near Narragansett and Irving Park roads, gathering the scores of bodies found during breakup of the Dunning land for development in the 1990s, but the knowledge of tens of thousands of unaccounted-for graves and the lax upkeep of the existing ones has led to more discontent than peace. Historians believe that approximately 38,000 bodies still lie under the shopping, housing, and industrial complexes that surround the present-day Read-Dunning Memorial Park.

Worst of all were the atrocities discovered at Burr Oak Cemetery in south suburban Worth, where cemetery workers were found to have been reselling graves by the hundreds for an untold number of years, dumping disinterred remains in a literal garbage heap on the grounds, among them some of the greatest lights of Chicago's African-American heritage. A study of the records indicated that more than 140,000 people were buried at Burr Oak, though the site has space for only 130,000 graves. At the lowest and saddest moment in Cook County cemetery history, the sheriff declared the entire site a crime scene.

So where do we go from here?

I have a colleague who shakes his head at the work we try to do at Bachelors Grove Cemetery, a one-acre, abandoned and vandalized cemetery lost out in the woods of the Cook County Forest Preserves. "Let Mother Nature take it back," he says, "there's nothing you can do to help the dead." My friend points to the good we can do by helping the poor and distraught, doing well for the living, furthering justice, fostering peace. I see his point. Tending to the dead takes a lot of energy. In a largely thankless, exhausting effort, sometimes it seems even the dead themselves are working against you.

As a so-called ghost hunter, it's been interesting to see, on the other hand and over the years, a peculiar phenomenon. When commemoration of the dead doesn't happen, or when it falls away, the dead speak. We see it on a grand scale, at places like the site of the Iroquois Theatre Fire in Chicago, where the smell of smoke and the crying of children are still experienced on a nightly basis, more than a century after that dreadful winter afternoon when 602 Chicagoans lost their lives on Randolph Street. Most paranormal researchers will tell you it's because there is no memorial there: no plaque, no statue, nothing to remind us that they suffered and died at this place. We see it on a humble scale, in the story of Chicago's most famous and active ghost, Resurrection Mary, who—coincidence?—has no headstone on her grave at Resurrection Cemetery. Week after week, night after night, year after year, men still see her, wandering along Archer Road on Chicago's South Side, trying to find a way home.

Whether you believe in ghosts or not, the absence of honor for the dead brings nothing but disruption and trouble for the living. A place for the dead in our history and memory—and in our physical world—is essential for our present and for our future, laying to rest, whether in broken and abandoned acreages or among pristine and perfect hills, our broken and perfected dreams as well.

When I sing at the funeral masses at my beloved St. Benedict Church on Chicago's North Side, I always take note in my heart of where the bereaved are going as the mass concludes and the priest says the final words of the Rite of Catholic Burial. As the incense rises sweetly above the casket, the celebrant turns to the family of the dead and invites them to make their way to the cemetery: "In peace, now, let us take our brother (or sister) to his (her) place of rest."

It is, for Catholics, for Christians, a happy moment—at least on paper—the moment the body has completed its long or short years on Earth, its sufferings and joys, its purpose. The body held the soul we loved, and it did the work of love, so we take it now, in awe, to its final home in the physical world.

It may, in fact, be weeks, months, or years until the loved ones make peace with the death. For some, because of long held arguments, sudden death, or other issues, the peace may never come at all.

The family members may visit the grave every week for months or years or generations—or never again after the funeral afternoon.

The family may take a passionate interest in the place of the dead in their family tree, or it may be a hundred years before a descendant cares to find a place for the deceased in a long-worked family genealogy puzzle.

For the famous, the "celebrated," the death may bring a stepping back and a surmising of influence, of impact, of genius, of cunning, of wealth, of benevolence, or of a thousand other traits. For the poor and disenfranchised, there may be no one at all to even stand by.

But to whatever graves the dead go—in casket or columbarium, to mantel or mountainside—with prayers or opening pitches (scattered at Wrigley Field at the Cubs opener perhaps), whether we fight for funds to restore their wrecked tombstones in the woods or walk in awe among their marble columns at Graceland on Sunday afternoon, whether they are remembered with regular visits or rare ones, we are called in some way to be sure that the respect of the dead goes on. That the memory of the dead goes on. That talk of the dead goes on.

We always wish the dead to rest in peace, but the underlying wish is that we may live in it.

CITY
CEMETERIES

Columbarium at Bohemian National Cemetery.

CITY NORTH

William Kimball monument at Graceland Cemetery.

CHICAGO CITY CEMETERY

Lincoln Park, east of Clark Street,
between North and Armitage avenues, Chicago

It seems that nearly every Chicagoan, and many a tourist for that matter, is aware that native businessman **Ira Couch** (1806–1857) is dead, though almost no one knows exactly who he was, what he did, or why his tomb stands in the middle of Lincoln Park. For generations, drivers along the park's rich sweep of green have ogled the hotelkeeper and realtor's somber tomb with a mixture of keen curiosity and frank unease, wondering at the explanation for this odd ornament affixed in the backyard of the Chicago History Museum.

Unknown to many natives and most tourists is the fact that the public playground that is today's Lincoln Park was once the civic cemetery. This aptly named Chicago City Cemetery stretched from

The immovable mausoleum of hotelier Ira Couch (1806–1857) serves as the most visible indication of Lincoln Park's former role as City Cemetery, its right to remain on the spot guaranteed by court decision. The ornamental iron fence is a twenty-first-century reproduction of the original.

present day Armitage Avenue south to the then city limits at North Avenue, providing plots to the departed prairie-dwellers of earliest Chicago. Most of these were later disinterred and relocated to various sites around the city upon the closing of City Cemetery around 1870. When this mass evacuation began, the Couch family reportedly rallied and appealed to officials to let the tomb remain due to the cost of transporting the mausoleum to another site. In time, the city consented, and so the Couch tomb remains, though many historians believe that Ira Couch is actually interred in Rosehill Cemetery, along with the rest of the clan.

Before the establishment of City Cemetery, Chicago had made some poor decisions concerning the question of burial. The area's first homesteaders along the river had buried their kin in their backyards, leading to a few surprises later on when the downtown area was dug up to lay the foundations for skyscrapers and other developments. In addition, the Chicago River sometimes played tricks on the bereaved who might bid farewell to their loved ones only to watch them floating by on the waterway some time later, having been purged from their graves after a particularly heavy rain. Further, the two cemeteries that were finally established in 1835—a Protestant one at Chicago and Michigan avenues and a Catholic one near 23rd Street and Calumet Avenue—were both situated squarely on the lakeshore, leading to the frequent unearthing of caskets. When population increases added to the inadequacy of the funerary system, the city selected acreage at Clark Street and North Avenue on which to found Chicago City Cemetery. Simultaneously, the Roman Catholic Diocese of Chicago secured for its faithful a portion of property between Dearborn and State streets, south of North Avenue. Though none of this land was exactly towering above the water table, any of it was preferable to the shaky sepulchers of the earliest burial grounds. The transfer of bodies to the new sites began at once.

Scarcely a decade after the opening of the new cemeteries, however, Chicagoans began to loudly complain about them. Besides the overcrowding resulting from both population growth and a string of cholera epidemics, echoes of earlier days could be heard in the fear that inadequate burials were leading to increased disease and contamination of the water. Fueling this near panic was the fact that the city morgue, as well as a holding building for epidemic victims, the so-called Pest House, were both located on the Chicago City Cemetery grounds. By the mid-1850s, concerned congregations and families were beginning to bury their loved ones at "safer," outlying sites such as Graceland, Rosehill, Calvary, and Oak Woods. By the early 1870s, City Cemetery was closed.

After all the unpleasant lessons had been learned, Chicago went about its business, secure in the belief that Lincoln Park's posh property was virtually corpse-free, except for the tomb of Mr. Couch and the unmarked grave of **David Kennison** (1736–1852), who claimed to be a 116-year-old Boston Tea Party survivor. But a far different story would someday come to light, after smoldering for generations just under the surface.

During an interview with researcher Pamela Bannos around the year 2000, Lester Fisher, erstwhile director of Lincoln Park Zoo, which stands on the old cemetery property, talked of a casket be-

Near Lincoln Park Zoo, this boulder placed in 1903 commemorates David Kennison (1736 –1852), buried somewhere nearby. On arriving in Chicago in 1845, he claimed to be a 109-year-old last survivor of the Boston Tea Party. Though the story was absurd, the citizens of the young frontier town were thrilled to have a celebrity. His funeral included 40,000 mourners, a brass band, and an appearance by the mayor.

ing found in 1962 when the foundation was dug for the familiar red barn at the "Farm in the Zoo" exhibit on the zoo's west end. When the City gave no response to requests for direction for dealing with the remains, zoo administration directed the reburial of the remains where they had been found. The remains were reinterred, concrete was poured, and the barn built on top, where it stands (and where the remains lie) today.

In 1970, bones were found during the building of an addition to the Chicago Historical Society, today the Chicago History Museum, at North Avenue and Clark Street. Then, again, in 1998 the remains of 81 corpses were discovered during excavation for the museum's parking lot, just north of the La Salle Street extension to Lake Shore Drive.

Adhering to the Human Skeletal Remains Protection Act, an archaeologist was contacted to work with the museum on a proper excavation of the remains. Archaeologist David Keene found bone fragments in initial soil samples of the area, and so the Illinois Historic Preservation Agency blessed the excavation project with a permit. The excavated were sent to the collections of the Illinois State Museum in Springfield and painstakingly catalogued. The corpses, which all were only partial, were found to belong to 81 different individuals. Along with the skeletons discovered, Keene's team also uncovered a Fisk metallic buried case with a corpse inside.

One of the central reasons for the prevalence of abandoned graves was the destruction of markers in the Great Fire of 1871. At that time, many grave markers were made of wood, called "head boards." History abounds with stories of panicked Chicagoans seeking refuge from the fire in the open graves of the slowly transitioning property, carrying with them their scant but cherished property, which was yet eventually abandoned to the flames.

In *The Great Conflagration*, written immediately after the fire, James W. Sheehan and George P. Upton painted a graphic picture of the devastation at City Cemetery:

Into these grave yards many fugitives had fled during that Sunday night and Monday morning. ... The occupants were of all classes. Strong men, hard working able bodied men; weak and delicate women; many of the occupants of fashionable dens of vice; refined and cultivated women; merchants, lawyers and bankers; servant men and women, but the great bulk were the families of small tradesmen, and working people of the neighborhood. Of course there were troops of children, all huddled in groups, with backs to the fire, to protect their eyes from the blinding smoke and consuming heat. Incessantly there fell among them the flying sparks and cinders. In vain did these poor fugitives seek to cover their packages of clothing with sand. The fire would fall upon them and set them ablaze. At last the fire approached them; it seized upon the long wooden sidewalks of the streets beyond, and with the speed of lightning traversed block after block, encircling every place with a cordon of fire. The fences one after another caught, the twigs, and scattered lumber, with here and there a house, a stable, or a shed seemed to furnish food enough to carry that fire along. At last it reached the grave yard, the fences caught and blazed; the heat prepared everything for the advancing column of fire. Group after group fled before the flame; the straw beds, chairs, tables, the trunks, the bundles of clothes and the household goods, soon were on fire; head board after head board blazed as a brazen mirror reflecting light. The little fences around the burial lots, the scanty trees and shrubbery all took fire, and each fed the rapacious flames. The living had to abandon even the desolate grave yard, and the fire swept from the earth everything that was consumable. Stout trees were burned down below the ordinary level of the soil in which they grew. These cemeteries before the fire were desolate—one half the dead having been disinterred, and the monuments and valuable adornments removed, and now came the fire to make desolation more desolate, not a vestige remains of anything in these silent cities of the dead save the blackened embers of the once erect grave signs, and of the little property carried there for safety and then overtaken and consumed by the insatiable fire.

...There are no strangers here. There are no ceremonies. The cement of a kindred sorrow has done its work. ...At last the raging sea sweeps by to the northward, following the line of houses, and the most reckless or courageous ... lie down upon the graves to sleep—the queerest camp that ever gathered under heaven.

At two o'clock came the blessed rain ....

In recent years, artist and researcher Pamela Bannos publicly shared the tireless work she had done for years on the history of City Cemetery. Her expansive "Hidden Truths" project has revealed some staggering discrepancies between the longstanding records and beliefs, and the reality of the truth. For generations, historians put the numbers of forgotten graves in Lincoln Park at around one thousand. Bannos discovered that, from the estimated 35,000 burials in City Cemetery (and the adjoining Catholic Cemetery), there were approximately 14,500 disinterments of marked graves, along with about 8,000 bodies from the potter's field, the latter of which were moved to Oak Woods and the Cook County Poor Farm Cemetery (Dunning).

Left behind, then, in Lincoln Park, would be an estimated 13,000 unmarked graves.

GRACELAND CEMETERY
4001 North Clark Street, Chicago
gracelandcemetery.org
Established 1860

When real estate investor Thomas B. Bryan founded Graceland Cemetery in 1860, the now-bustling neighborhood was practically wilderness. Over the years, a number of architects and designers worked to civilize this 120-acre enclosure in typical Chicago fashion. Bryan's nephew, Bryan Lathrop, served as president of the cemetery for a number of years and was enchanted by naturalism. As a result, architects William Le Baron Jenney and Ossian Cole Simonds were hired to enhance the grounds. Simonds was so taken with the project that he ended up turning his professional attention fully towards landscape design. Through the work he did at Graceland and afterward, Simonds anticipated the gracious natural appreciation of the Prairie School artists.

At Graceland, not only the landscape can be credited to Chicago's architectural geniuses. More obvious contributions can be found in the several buildings and monuments on the property. Visitors enter gates designed by acclaimed local firm Holabird & Roche, who also created the administration building and waiting room near the entrance, as well as the cemetery's chapel, which includes the city's oldest crematorium, circa 1893.

Graceland's original entrance gate was constructed in August 1860. This impressive stone archway was set a few feet behind the columns that form the present entrance, and included a central carriageway over which spanned a Gothic arch with *Graceland* written along the curve. The arch was set into a triangular gable,[2] at the top of which projected a small turret. Attached to the arch on one side were the office and waiting rooms, and on the other side, a receiving vault. Greenhouses were soon added on its west side, where the present-day office stands.[3]

A second entrance and office were added in 1883, on the eastern edge of the cemetery at Buena Avenue, incorporating a train station that permitted access from the Chicago and Evanston Railway.[4] The eastern office

The cemetery's chapel, as it appeared about 2005. The section with the ivy-covered gable at far left is the original Holabird & Roche chapel, built in 1888. The long wall in the center is the 1934 addition, and the windows at right are part of a section added in 1958. The two additions were recently demolished, restoring the chapel exterior to its original appearance.

[2] The center portion of the entrance was very similar to the one at Calvary in Evanston. See that chapter for a photo.

[3] Christopher Vernon, *Graceland Cemetery: A Design History* (Amherst, MA: University of Massachusetts Press, 2011), 55, 170.

[4] Vernon, *Graceland Cemetery*, 142–143.

and train station stood next to Lake Hazelmere, one of three artificial bodies of water within the cemetery. This now-vanished lake was about half the size of Lake Willowmere, the only one of the three still present.

By 1896, an increase in the number of visitors required that the main (southwest) entrance be widened and a larger office constructed.[5] The archway, office, and vault were demolished and replaced with an entirely new design. The new entrance

An artificial island in Lake Willowmere, originally intended to be left wild, instead became a memorial for the architect of the White City and author of the 1909 *Plan of Chicago*, Daniel Hudson Burnham (1846–1912). Burnham is remembered today as the source of the oft-quoted words, "Make no little plans. They have no magic to stir men's blood."

consisted of two square columns of rough-cut red Waupaca granite blocks, each with a pyramidal cap. Between them was an elaborate bronze fence with three movable gates, two of them pedestrian-sized, flanking the large central carriage entrance. Photographs show that at some later date, the granite columns were repositioned inwards, such that the pedestrian gates were outside the columns rather than between them. To the south, a new office was constructed, far more spacious than before, roofed with red clay tiles in the Spanish style.

The popularity of the Buena Avenue entrance on the east inspired the placement of a new chapel nearby in 1888.[6] Holabird & Roche designed the granite chapel in the new Arts & Crafts style, eschewing the Gothic style that had been popular only a few years before. The chapel was expanded in 1934, with the interior of the original structure converted to a lobby for the much larger new wing that stretched to the north. In 1958 it was expanded yet again. In 2006

[5] Ibid., 169.
[6] Ibid., 163.

the additional segments were demolished, reducing the chapel to its original size and providing more land for burials and columbarium walls.[7] The chapel interior was refinished in warm, dark woods, with columbarium niches set into the walls. These changes delighted some admirers of the cemetery and saddened others. The chapel was now restored to a design much more like that intended by the original architects, but a long, beautiful, ivy-covered wall had been lost.

The Buena Avenue entrance and railway station were demolished about 1950, and the landscaping around it simplified to permit more space for burials.[8] Today there is only a long unbroken concrete wall on the eastern perimeter. By 1968, Lake Hazelmere, which lay just north of the defunct Buena Avenue station, was filled in. The groundskeepers' equipment shed now occupies much of the former lake's footprint.[9] The third water body at Graceland, the tiny Lotus Pond in the southeast corner, had disappeared far earlier, filled in and reclaimed for burial space as early as 1897.

A walk through Graceland will bring the visitor in close contact with thousands of Chicago's most influential personalities, including some of the city's earliest residents and most aggressive civic leaders.

John Kinzie (1763–1828), the much-maligned first white settler of the Chicago area, was taken ill with apoplexy on January 6, 1828, while living with his family at the home of John Beaubien, just south of Fort Dearborn. He was originally buried north of the river. Later, however, his body was disinterred and transferred first to the old North Side cemetery, then to City Cemetery, and finally to its current location at Graceland, miles north of the fledgling settlement he had known.

A Quebec native, Kinzie was born several years before the American Revolution, traveling in adulthood to the prairie along the southwestern shores of Lake Michigan and settling across the river from Fort Dearborn. The Kinzies occupied the homestead originally built by Jean Baptiste DuSable, the first true permanent settler of the

[7] "Chapel," Graceland Cemetery, http://www.gracelandcemetery.org/pages/chapel.html.

[8] Vernon, *Graceland Cemetery*, 181.

[9] "Map of Graceland Cemetery, 1884," reproduced in Vernon, *Graceland Cemetery*, 116 and 118.

area, where they lived until the Fort Dearborn Massacre of 1812. By fleeing to Michigan, they escaped the fate of their fellow settlers and soldiers who were butchered on the sands. Several years later, Kinzie returned to the site to reclaim his land and resume his trade.

Chicago's first wheeler-dealer died in 1828. But the Chicago he left behind had only just begun. The relentless business sense of Kinzie was echoed in the lives of hundreds of entrepreneurs who followed his lead in exploiting the rich resources, geographical and human, of the burgeoning city on the lake. A good number of those empire builders join Kinzie at Graceland.

Chicago women were among the first in America to be smitten with a new concept in shopping, the department store, flocking to bustling State Street to patronize a remarkable retail institution, the darling of merchandising king **Marshall Field** (1834–1906). Guiding the venture to the top as the largest wholesale and retail dry goods dealer in the world, Field became the richest man in Chicago, worth an estimated $120 million.

Field's final days were filled with sorrow after the shooting of his only son, **Marshall Field II** (1865–1905), in November 1905. Ruled an accidental death by the coroner, rumors nevertheless spread that it was either a suicide or the result of a brawl in the Everleigh Club, a luxurious brothel of local infamy. The elder Marshall Field never recovered from his grief, died of pneumonia three months later, and went to his rest at Graceland, where he reposes with four generations of Fields. His monument was created by noted sculptor Daniel Chester French, who later designed the Lincoln Memorial in Washington, D.C.

Maine-bred piano and organ manufacturer **William Kimball** (1828–1904) began his life in Chicago as a traveling salesman intrigued by the opportunity offered by this burgeoning metropolis. Anticipating a lively future here for the arts, Kimball settled in Chicago and set up a piano and organ dealership. His success led him to open an organ factory, and demand soon added pianos to his list of products. He was successful enough to be counted among the cream of Chicago society, living out his days in a million-dollar mansion at the corner of 18th Street and Prairie Avenue, in the heart of the city's most exclusive residential district.

Philip D. Armour (1832–1901), one of Chicago's meat-packing giants, created his empire by selling canned pork to the Union Army during the Civil War. In 1875, he moved his Milwaukee-based business to Chicago, where he began shipping fresh meat across the country in refrigerated train cars and exporting canned meat to the entire world. Armour was a very religious man, and after a particularly moving sermon by Reverend Frank Gunsaulus entitled *If I Had a Million Dollars*, he gave the good preacher $1 million to fund a school, the Armour Institute, now known as the Illinois Institute of Technology (IIT). His Grace-land monument is an immense rectangular solid of grey granite on a three-tiered base.

George Mortimer Pullman (1831–1897) was buried securely by a family terrified that his body would be snatched by the railroad emperor's incensed ex-employees, most of whom had lost their jobs at the end of the infamous 1894 Pullman Strike. Dying only three years after the event, which was forcefully settled by federal troops, Pullman's body was encased in a coffin, sealed in a block of concrete, and covered with an extra ton of concrete and railroad ties. Over this extraordinarily well-protected corpse rises a mighty Corinthian column flanked by curving stone benches, a monument designed by Solon Beman, architect of the company

The spectacular tomb of William Wallace Kimball (1828–1904) features an open colonnade surrounding this kneeling angel, watching over crypts set into the floor, the entire structure made of brilliant white marble. Kimball was founder of the Kimball Piano Company, the world's leading piano and organ manufacturer.

town of Pullman (later annexed to the South Side of Chicago).

Ironically, the body of a beloved liberator was given the same protection as that of a hated oppressor: President Lincoln is likewise entombed in a block of reinforced concrete in downstate Springfield. This is no coincidence, for Robert Todd Lincoln, son of the murdered president, was a Pullman Company executive, succeeding George Pullman as company president. The lessons he learned protecting his employer's body served, a few years later, to protect his father as well.[10]

The Goodman Family monument provides a dramatic overlook that beckons visitors to spend a few moments gazing across the halcyon waters of Lake Willowmere. Lumber mogul William Goodman had the family mausoleum designed by architect friend, Howard Van Doren Shaw, upon the death of Goodman's son, **Kenneth Sawyer Goodman** (1883–1918). A playwright in training for a lieutenant's commission with the United States Navy, 35-year-old Kenneth was fatally stricken with influenza during the 1918 epidemic. Along with commissioning the handsome monument in his son's honor, Goodman also hired Shaw to create a memorial theater in the same style, the renowned Goodman Theatre in the Loop.

There is no debating the most prestigious cemetery in Chi-

The monument of railroad tycoon George Mortimer Pullman (1831–1897), though quite beautiful on the surface, is more famous for what lies beneath. A tyrannical employer who drove his employees to desperation, Pullman was so hated that extreme measures were taken to protect his corpse from vengeance: His lead coffin, within a steel vault, was embedded in a block of concrete reinforced with railroad ties.

---

[10] Thanks to John Martine for informing us of this connection.

cago—Graceland—or the most prestigious site in that cemetery: the hilltop shrine to the memory of the Palmers. In death, as in life, **Potter Palmer** (1826–1902) and **Bertha Honoré Palmer** (1850–1918) bought themselves the center of attention. They rest beneath a breathtaking Greco-Roman temple, also overlooking Lake Willowmere, that remains the last word in eternal digs, at least in Chicago. Hailing from New York, Palmer moved his dry-goods shop to Chicago's bustling Lake Street district. His concept of the money-back guarantee caused a sensation and won him a legion of loyal customers. Palmer was the originator of the now-widespread motto of businesses everywhere: *The customer is always right.* After accumulating a king's ransom in profits, Palmer sold his store to Marshall Field and Levi Leiter, choosing to focus his efforts on real estate.

With the money to back up his wildest dreams, Palmer bought a street, State Street, aiming to create an entirely new business district. First, he widened the thoroughfare, then put up new buildings along its length, setting as its jewel a gorgeous luxury hotel. Dubbing it the Palmer House, Potter presented the hotel to new wife, Bertha, on the occasion of their marriage in 1871. A good year for weddings in Chicago, it was a poor one for real estate investments, and the Palmers watched

Young playwright Kenneth Sawyer Goodman (1883–1918) died in an influenza pandemic. His father, lumber tycoon William Goodman, established the Goodman Theatre in his memory, and also erected a mausoleum best appreciated from across the water.

their new commercial strip burn to the ground with the rest of the city in the Great Chicago Fire. Among the buildings destroyed was Palmer's new marble palace of commerce, a two-year-old building that he leased to Marshall Field. Still inspired, still loaded, and with the aid of the largest loan ever given to an individual at the time, Potter rebuilt everything, including the hotel, whose opulent elegance put its lavish predecessor to shame.

Once he had moved the center of Chicago business, Palmer set his sights on moving the center of its society, from Prairie Avenue on the near South Side, to the North Side stretch of Lake Shore Drive at Oak Street where he erected the now-demolished Palmer Mansion. Among the house's peculiarities: the exterior doors had no knobs on the outside, for there would always be plenty of servants on hand to let the family back in.

One of the most photographed mausoleums at Graceland is the strangely eclectic tomb of the Schoenhofen family, a monstrous pyramid structure that houses the remains of German immigrant

Potter Palmer (1826–1902), at one time Chicago's richest citizen, owned much of State Street in the nineteenth century, including the opulent Palmer House Hotel and a department store that he later sold to Marshall Field. The Palmer tomb is the largest private cemetery memorial in Chicago.

and master brewer, **Peter Schoenhofen** (1827–1893). The family became the victims of one of Chicago's most heated cases of property seizure when authorities discovered that the Schoenhofens retained and encouraged their Germanic ties. As a result, the family's possessions were whisked away. Schoenhofen's tomb, which combines Egyptian and Christian symbols, was designed by architect Richard Schmidt in 1893,[11] based on a similar pyramid in Milan, Italy.[12] Similar structures can be found in other American cities, including Brooklyn and New Orleans, all manifestations of the Victorian passion for Egyptology.

The richly carved granite sarcophagi of Potter Palmer and wife Bertha Honoré Palmer (1849–1918) lay side by side under the roof of their immense tomb. Considered the queen of Chicago society, Bertha Palmer lived in a mansion that became the center of the "Gold Coast" on North Lake Shore Drive, as other millionaires sold their South Side mansions to move to the newly fashionable district. The sarcophagi, suitable for American royalty, include such Victorian flourishes as flowered garlands and inverted torches—a symbol of mourning.

East of Schoenhofen's monument, near the equipment shed that stands on the footprint of the now-defunct Lake Hazelmere, stands an enormous mausoleum, the height of a two-story building. This is the second burial site of discount department store owner **Ernst Johann Lehmann** (1849–1900), who had originally been buried in an

---

[11] "Monuments and Their Makers," Graceland Cemetery, http://www.gracelandcemetery.org/pages/monuments.html.

[12] Peggy McDowell and Richard E. Meyer, *The Revival Styles in American Memorial Art* (Bowling Green, Ohio: Bowling Green State University Popular Press, 1994), 144.

even grander mausoleum at German Waldheim (Forest Home), but was moved to Graceland in 1920.[13] Lehmann's original mausoleum was an open structure of columns supporting a massive stone roof, with lions flanking the steps and burial crypts in the basement. The second Lehmann tomb, though large, is of a much more conventional design. The original mausoleum still stands at Forest Home, empty and stripped of its owner's name.

Not only business leaders rest at Graceland. The cemetery also gathers an impressive array of local public heroes. During his time in office, Illinois governor **John Peter Altgeld** (1847–1902) played a high-profile role in Chicago's unfolding history. First, Altgeld was highly criticized and even burned in effigy after his pardoning of the so-called Haymarket martyrs.[14] Undaunted by public opinion, he went on to defend the Pullman strikers the very next year, urging President Cleveland to refrain from breaking up the strike with federal troops. For his humanitarian efforts, Altgeld was himself branded an anarchist, a designation that guaranteed the end of his political career.

The pyramidal monument of brewer Peter Schoenhofen (1827–1893), with a sphinx guarding the door, was inspired by the surge of Egyptian archaeological discoveries that captured the popular imagination in the late nineteenth century. To make it a bit less pagan in its appearance, an angel was added as well.

Charles Wacker (1856–1929) was a driving force behind the establishment of architect Daniel Burnham's 1909 *Plan of Chicago*, which laid out the city on a grid, conceived traffic-relieving bi-lev-

---

[13] Historical Society of Oak Park and River Forest, *Nature's Choicest Spot: A Guide to Forest Home and German Waldheim Cemeteries* (Oak Park, IL: Historical Society of Oak Park and River Forest, 1998), 57.

[14] See Forest Home chapter for the Haymarket story.

eled streets around the downtown area, and arranged for the design of a group of large, scattered parks strung together by boulevards. Wacker served as chairman of the Plan Commission, laboring long and hard for the dollars and dedicated to making it a reality. When the Plan went through, Wacker's struggle was commemorated by the city, who named the new double-decker bank of the Chicago River after the man who had made this remarkable street and the rest of the *Plan of Chicago* possible.

Graceland also boasts some of the most beautiful funerary art in the world. A popular and atypical example is the knight standing guard over the plot of *Chicago Daily News* publisher **Victor Lawson** (1850–1925). Designed by renowned sculptor Lorado Taft, the piece, entitled *Crusader*, was considered a fitting memorial to the humanitarian newspaperman, known for his creation and use of the foreign correspondent as a valuable news resource. This beautiful rendering bears no name, but is inscribed with Lawson's belief that *Above All Things Truth Beareth Away the Victory.*

Without question, Graceland's most familiar, and most photographed, memorial is another of Taft's masterpieces: the cloaked bronze rendering of *Eternal Silence*, popularly christened "The Statue of Death." Standing sentinel over **Dexter Graves** (1789–1844), a hotel owner and early settler, and his family, the figure has been called striking, haunting, frightening, morbid, imposing, foreboding. And rumor still has it that an unflinching gaze into its shrouded eyes will grant the beholder a vision of the afterworld.

The ashes of architect **William Le Baron Jenney** (1832–1907) were scattered on his wife's plot, next to *Eternal Silence*. Known as "Father of the Skyscraper," Jenney grew frustrated by the height limitations imposed by load-bearing walls. He thus masterminded the skeleton frame and first used the concept in designing the Home Insurance Building, which, at ten stories, towered over the intersection of LaSalle and Adams streets when it was built in 1884. Unfortunately, the pioneer structure was demolished in 1931, but modern architecture is everywhere, especially in Chicago, haunted by its memory. For one hundred years, nothing marked the gravesite of this eminent individual, until in 2007 an innovative monument was placed on the spot—a set of six flat granite markers, separated by gutters of a few inches wide, together forming an image of a skyscraper's steel frame.

Not only a memorial ground for local legends, Graceland boasts many national and international heroes as well. Farming was revolutionized when **Cyrus Hall McCormick** (1809–1894) invented a machine that combined the separate tasks of earlier harvesters into one device. This reaper led farmers to more than double their crop sizes and made McCormick a fortune. A Virginia native, Cyrus inherited the impetus toward invention from his father, who himself worked for many years, in vain, to create a mechanical reaper. When the younger McCormick finally got it right, he patented the device and began producing copies of it in 1837. Over the next ten years, the popularity of the machine was so great that McCormick decided to build a factory in Chicago. He further boosted sales by sending door-to-door salesmen to peddle the reaper. A written guarantee and the promise of easy assembly won McCormick many customers, as well as a place among the great inventors cited as exemplifiers of American ingenuity and the country's trial-and-error system of development.

Lorado Taft's bronze sculpture *Eternal Silence* is easily Graceland's best-known monument. According to local legend, a visitor looking into the hooded statue's eyes would receive a vision of their own death. The eerie figure, appropriately enough, stands at the grave of a man named "Graves": Dexter Graves (1789–1844), leader of a group of pioneers from Ohio who settled in Chicago in 1831.

Glasgow-born **Allan Pinkerton** (1819–1884) immigrated while in his twenties to the growing Chicago area and settled down to work as a barrel maker. At some point during this modest career, Pinkerton nabbed a gang of counterfeiters. An appreciative public saw fit to elect him sheriff, and so the dedicated Scotsman took the first step down a remarkable road.

In 1850, Pinkerton organized Pinkerton's National Detective Agency, becoming the first ever private detective. He was also appointed to the position of city detective in his adopted hometown. When Pinkerton recovered a burgled cache of money for the Adams Express Co. he won much adulation. Far greater praise, however, came in 1861, when the enterprising private eye uncovered a plot to murder Abraham Lincoln. Pinkerton went on to support Lincoln's government throughout the Civil War, organizing the U.S. Army's Secret Service. Just before his death in 1884, he published *Thirty Years a Detective*, in which he chronicled the unique experiences of his singular profession.

Joining Pinkerton at Graceland is top Pinkerton employee and Civil War personality **Timothy Webster** (1821–1862), who was hanged in Virginia after being convicted as a spy for the Union, and **Kate Warne** (1833–1868), the country's first female detective, who died of pneumonia after a short but distinguished career. Near their graves is that of **Vincent Starrett** (1886–1974), *Chicago Tribune* columnist and founding member of The Baker Street Irregulars, the oldest and most prestigious of the many societies devoted to the appreciation of Sherlock Holmes.

Eighth Chief Justice of the United States, **Melville Weston Fuller** (1833–1910), was the first such appointee to have academic legal training, having attended Harvard Law School for one year during the mid–nineteenth century. After one term in the Illinois Legislature and a number of minor statewide Democratic Party positions, Fuller was offered several appointments by President Grover Cleveland until finally agreeing to take the helm of the Supreme Court. In this role, he administered the oath of office to Presidents-elect McKinley, in 1897, and Taft, in 1909. His greatest legacy is the phrase inscribed across the architrave of the Supreme Court Building, *Equal Justice Under Law*, originally written as "equal and impar-

Behind the chapel is the plot of Allan Pinkerton (1819–1884), private detective. His firm's logo, the "all-seeing eye," was the origin of the term "private eye." Also buried in his plot are two early Pinkerton employees, Timothy Webster and Kate Wame, who worked covertly as spies against the Confederacy under Pinkerton's direction.

tial justice under the law" in one of Chief Justice Fuller's opinions.

Alongside these early Chicago powerhouses, rest several Chicago mayors, including **Joseph Medill** (1823–1899), who won election on the "Fireproof" ticket; **Hempstead Washburne** (1852–1919), Chicago mayor and son of U.S. secretary of state Elihu B. Washburne (buried in Galena, Illinois); and wartime mayor **Francis Sherman** (1805–1870), buried next to a limestone obelisk with his son, Brigadier General **Francis Trowbridge Sherman** (1825–1905).

Sports historians and fans will search in vain for a stone commemorating the first black world heavyweight champion, **Jack Johnson** (1878–1946). When Johnson won the championship in 1908, angry whites were desperate to find someone, an elusive "Great White Hope," to reclaim the title. Enraged by Johnson's marriage to a white woman, the champ's enemies jeered him until 1915, when Johnson lost the title to Jess Willard. The devoted husband bought his wife, Etta, a plot in Graceland, marked by a large monument inscribed with their surname. But while Mrs. Johnson's grave is clearly identified, the prizefighter himself rests beside her in anonymity, despite offers of fans to put up a marker.

For visible recognition of the fight game, look to the headstone of **Robert Fitzsimmons** (1862–1917), another boxing superstar, this one famous for his signature uppercut punch. An English native raised in New Zealand, Fitzsimmons held titles in three divisions, winning the middleweight title in 1891, the heavyweight title in 1897, and the light-heavyweight title in 1903. After his death, many new fans were won over by the endearing photos affixed to Fitzsimmons's flush stone, inscribed by his wife to *My Beloved Husband... World Champion.*

A whimsical stone baseball commemorates the life of **William A. Hulbert** (1832–1882), founder of the National League, who would be overjoyed to hear the sound of the crowds on the wind blowing out from Wrigley Field just a few blocks away.

One of the most obviously represented of Graceland's diverse cultural groups is that of the architects who designed many of the site's most acclaimed mausoleums and markers, including their own. The mausoleum of **Martin Ryerson** (1818–1887) was commissioned to architect Louis Henri Sullivan, who had envisioned a number of office buildings for the lumber merchant. Hulking and unornamented, the Ryerson structure seems nothing like its neighbor, the Getty Tomb, though this landmark was also designed by Sullivan for Ryerson's partner, **Henry Harrison Getty** (1838–1920). Of this masterpiece of ornamentation, no lesser critic than Frank Lloyd Wright remarked,

"Outside the realm of music, what finer requiem?"

Though he made priceless contributions to architecture and design, and left Chicago a thousand times more beautiful for his efforts, **Louis Sullivan** (1856–1924) joined his clients in Graceland with little more than his funeral suit to show for his work. At the time of his death, Sullivan's genius had fallen out of fashion, as popular taste reverted to classical styles. The prodigious architect received only one commission in his last year of life, and his estate did not allow for even a grave marker.[15] Those faithful to the beloved architect,

---

[15] Sullivan's business partner, Dankmar Adler, had died more than 20 years before and was given a magnificent memorial—a column from one of his own buildings. See Zion Gardens entry for details.

however, later furnished his lot with a fitting headstone, designed by Thomas Tallmadge, who invented the term *Chicago School* in writing of the city's influential architects. In creating this tangible tribute to a true master, Tallmadge achieved a perfect reflection of Sullivan's work, embossing a large impressive stone with a profile of the architectural giant, along with an intricate geometric design characteristic of and derived from Sullivan's own renderings. The sides of the boulder-like stone are finely chiseled, demonstrating the harmony of the modern skyscraper with the natural world.

An adjacent section holds the grave of **Richard Nickel** (1928–1972), an architecture photographer who was accidentally killed during the demolition of the Chicago Stock Exchange while trying to preserve Sullivan's work. Nickel's friends chose to place him here, in the orbit of the man whose work he admired so much.

The "Less is More" philosophy of **Ludwig Mies van der Rohe** (1886–1969) echoes for eternity through the utilitarian marker designed by his grandson, architect Dirk Lohan, an unpolished slab of black granite bearing only his bluntly-chiseled name. **László Moholy-Nagy** (1895–1946), founder of the Chicago-based New Bauhaus, is buried beneath a nondescript flush stone near the cemetery chapel. Nearby, architect **Marion Mahony Griffin** (1871–1962) took Moholy-Nagy one step further: her grave is actually unmarked. A disciple of

Called "a symphony in stone," Louis Sullivan's masterful tomb for Carrie Eliza Getty and Henry Harrison Getty is considered one of the finest works of funerary art of the modern age, registered as a Chicago Landmark and a National Historic Place.

Frank Lloyd Wright and member of the "Prairie School," Mahony was one of the first licensed female architects in the world. And, one more Prairie School architect rests in peace here, **Dwight Perkins** (1867–1941), who aided in the establishment of the Forest Preserve District of Cook County.

Architect **Daniel Hudson Burnham** (1846–1912), creator of the universally acclaimed 1909 *Plan of Chicago*, is buried with his family on the little island afloat in Lake Willowmere, their graves accessible to all by a newly-restored bridge. One of the most influential of the city's many architectural giants, Burnham designed a number of remarkable Chicago buildings, including the Reliance Building and the landmark department store of Marshall Field & Co., and planned the legendary White City for the Columbian Exposition of 1893. Yet he is most lauded today for saving Chicago's lakefront from commercial and residential development. Even now, the miles of open, public shoreline, lined with parks, a zoo, museums, bicycle trails, a golf course, even a bird sanctuary, bear testimony to the unfathomable foresight of Burnham's design. Because of his plan, Lake Michigan has remained the mysterious and intimate center of Chicago's identity.

The grave of Burnham's business partner, **John Wellborn Root** (1850–1891), is marked by a massive Celtic cross, uncharacteristically traditional except for a giveaway inset near the base, which bears Root's drawing of the entrance to the now-demolished Phoenix Building. Though most of Burnham & Root's work has disappeared from Chicago's landscape, two of their structures remain favorites among architecture aficionados: the Rookery at 209 South LaSalle Street and the Monadnock Building at Dearborn Street and Jackson Boulevard. The latter marked the end of one engineering road. At 16 stories, it is the tallest building that could be designed using the old load-bearing walls.

Near Root is the massive pink granite monument of architect **Peirce Anderson** (1870–1924), inset with a bronze carving of the deceased's face. Anderson worked with Daniel Burnham before helping to found the architectural firm of Graham, Anderson, Probst &

White. The only inscription this stunning grave marker bears is Anderson's name cut into the bronze in tiny lettering, easily overlooked.

A final destination here for architecture fans is the grave of thoroughly modern designer, **Fazlur Rahman Khan** (1929–1982), whose work with Skidmore, Owings & Merrill brought both the Sears Tower (now the Willis Tower) and John Hancock Building to Chicago's dramatic skyline.

The west side of the cemetery boasts a wonderfully picturesque row of in-ground mausoleums, all about the same size, built from three different colors of granite. Slightly north of these is an obelisk commemorating two Chicago mayors, father and son. **Carter Henry Harrison** (1825–1893), a cousin of presidents William Henry Harrison and Benjamin Harrison, was a two-term United States congressman, then mayor of Chicago from 1879 to 1887. He did not run for re-election at the end of his four terms, instead retiring from politics to manage his businesses including his newspaper, the *Chicago Times*. In 1893, he candidated for mayor once again, winning an unprecedented fifth term. On October 28 of that year the newly re-elected mayor was shot dead in his own home by a deranged newspaper distributor who had supported Harrison's campaign and therefore felt that Harrison owed him an appointment. Though defended by Clarence Darrow, the killer was found guilty and hanged within a year.

Four years later, the murdered mayor's son **Carter Henry Harrison, Jr.** (1860–1953) was elected to the same office his father had held, becoming the city's thirtieth mayor, the first to be born in Chicago. Also elected to five terms, the younger Harrison was mayor for twelve years—though with a six-year gap separating them—the longest span of any mayor up to that time. Chicago history buffs best remember Harrison for his order to shut down the Everleigh Club, the city's leading brothel, which had attracted national attention after publishing a pamphlet advertising their services. Living to the advanced age of 93, Carter Harrison's life in Chicago encompassed the years of the Civil War, both World Wars, the Prohibition Era, and the founding of *Playboy Magazine*. He wrote two autobiographies, *Stormy Years* and *Growing Up With Chicago*. Harrison died on Christmas

Day, 1953.

Located not far from the Carter Harrisons is the monument that has, more than any other memorial at Graceland, evoked much discussion in recent years on various Internet forums devoted to graveyards or ghostly phenomena. The little girl in the glass box, so-called **"Inez Clarke,"** has delighted visitors for

Carter Henry Harrison I (1825–1893), the World's Fair mayor who was assassinated in his own home, and his son Carter Henry Harrison II (1860–1953), both of whom were elected mayor of Chicago five times.

over a century. The white marble statue portrays a six-year-old girl sitting on a rustic wooden chair, one hand resting comfortably on a parasol, her hat leaning casually against her other shoulder, looking straight ahead with a slight smile. The artwork is of the highest quality, with every detail lovingly rendered, down to the lace of her dress, the bows on her shoes, and the pupils of her eyes—and thanks to the glass box having been placed over the sculpture before it began to significantly deteriorate, all of this detail remains crisp and intact to the present day.

Such a superb monument deserves a good story, and naturally one was invented to fit. Young Inez, it is said, was killed by a bolt of lightning during a family picnic. Or, perhaps, she had been locked out of her house as punishment, and then the storm arose. Her ghost now roams the part of the cemetery near the grave, the stories continue. A young girl in Victorian dress has been spotted over the years laughing and playing there. And, due to the nature of her tragic demise, she has a special fear of summer storms—on such occasions, the statue is said to disappear entirely from its box, various night watchmen over the years finding it empty.

There is, however, no evidence to support the story of a lightning strike killing a young girl on August 1, 1880—an unusual event that surely would have been in the newspapers. And, strangely enough, no "Inez Clarke" appears in the cemetery records either. The statue itself gives her name as *INEZ* (it's carved a few inches beneath her feet), and the pedestal says *Daughter of J.N. & M.C. Clarke, Born Sep 20 1873, Died Aug 1 1880*. The bronze plaque on the base gives the names of John and Mary Clarke as well. But who is Inez Clarke?

Some have speculated that there never was an Inez, that the monument was not meant to depict a living person but was rather an advertisement for the stone-carving prowess of sculptor Andrew Gagel (whose name appears on the rear of the statue), that it had been erected in a then-unused section of the cemetery and simply left there permanently, its original purpose forgotten when the plot was sold. This theory has its flaws as well. Why would the pedestal state that a "Daughter of..." was buried there when no such person existed? Indeed, if it was merely an advertisement, the sculptor's name and business address would have been a much more sensible use of that space.

One of Chicago's best-loved cemetery monuments is the statue of six-year-old Inez Briggs (1873–1880), popularly known by her stepfather's name of Clarke. Legend has it that she was killed in a thunderstorm and her ghost has been seen running and playing in the cemetery.

Cemetery records do indicate that a child was buried in that spot, in August 1880, but that *his* name was Amos Briggs. No "Inez Clarke" exists in Graceland's records at all.

In 2009, Chicago historian John Binder unraveled the mystery.[16] There never was an Inez Clarke, who died at the age of six in 1880, but there was an **Inez Briggs**, who died on exactly the day specified, August 1, 1880,[17] of diphtheria. She was six years old, and her death certificate stated that she would be buried at Graceland, though the name Inez Briggs doesn't appear in the cemetery records either. This could be a simple transcription error. When spoken aloud, the names "Inez" and "Amos" are not all that different. One might speculate that when the statue was delivered, a year after Inez had been buried under the wrong name, neither the family nor the cemetery management noticed that the name on the monument didn't match the one in the books.

Records from the 1880 U.S. census corroborate Binder's theory. Inez Briggs, clearly identified as a female, aged 7 ("close enough for government work," as they say), was living with her grandparents, David and Jenny Rothrock. And, buried in the same plot at Graceland, their monuments intact and easily read, are David and Jane Rothrock, with years of birth that agree with that census entry to within a year or two.[18]

Mary McClure was Jane Rothrock's daughter. In 1872 she married Wilber Briggs, father of Inez, but by 1880 Briggs was gone and Mary had remarried John Clarke. Clarke, according to city directories, was then living at the same address as the Rothrocks on what is now the 800 block of West Armitage,[19] across the street from the building where Charlie Trotter would operate a world-class restaurant for 25 years. John Clarke was not Inez's natural father, but he called her "daughter" on the monument—leading to more than a century of confusion.

By any name, it's a superb monument.

---

[16] Mark Konkol, "Ghost story back from the dead—Phantom girl stories were debunked—but records may give tale new life," *Chicago Sun-Times*, October 30, 2009.

[17] "Illinois, Cook County Deaths 1878–1922," Index. FamilySearch, Salt Lake City, Utah, 2010. Illinois Department of Public Health. "Birth and Death Records, 1916–present," Division of Vital Records, Springfield, Illinois.

[18] Mark Masek, "Chicago Remains to Be Seen—Inez Clarke," Cemetery Guide, http://www.cemeteryguide.com/inezclarke.html.

[19] Konkol, "Ghost Story Back from the Dead."

THE CEMETERY LADY

Universally acknowledged as the foremost authority on Chicago cemeteries, **Helen Sclair** (1930–2009) was known as "The Cemetery Lady," appearing frequently on local television and interviewed by reporters whenever cemetery happenings made the news. Her decades of research and expertise paved the way for those of us who followed.

Helen Sclair was born Helen Young in 1930. While she was still a child, her mother died, and it was in part due to visiting her mother's grave in southern Illinois that she developed a lifelong interest in cemeteries and burial customs.[1] Her father, Irvin Young, also had a unique place in Chicago history. A missionary in Africa, needing to raise funds for his church, he captured a gorilla for the Lincoln Park Zoo, "Bushman,"[2] who remained there for 20 years, a star attraction.

Helen Young worked for her father's manufacturing company and later became a teacher in the Chicago Public Schools system, mostly teaching at Gladstone Elementary, a career that spanned 30 years.[3]

It was shortly after the death of Helen's second husband, Marvin Sclair, in 1975, that her interest in cemeteries was rekindled when she passed by Lincoln Park and pondered its history as a graveyard.[4] She began to seriously research the subject, researching city records and newspaper archives, collecting a mountain of cemetery memorabilia—news clippings, memorial cards, cemetery and mortuary advertisements, casket and

---

[1] Trevor Jensen, "Helen Sclair: 1930–2009: Authority on Cemeteries," *Chicago Tribune*, December 20, 2009.

[2] John Martine, "A Tribute to Helen Sclair," in *Markers XXVII* (Greenfield, MA: The Association for Gravestone Studies, 2011), 6.

[3] Jensen, "Helen Sclair."

[4] "Cemetery Talk is a Lively Topic: Mt. Greenwood Hosts Mourning Expert," *Chicago Tribune*, October 5, 2003.

monument catalogs.[5] In 1991 her research led to a greatly improved understanding of the earliest Chicago cemeteries in Lincoln Park.[6]

As an active member of the Association for Gravestone Studies, Sclair frequently contributed to their publications and was instrumental in organizing their 1994 conference in Elmhurst, Illinois, authoring a booklet given to participants with historical details and self-guided tours of area cemeteries, a resource that also proved invaluable to the authors of the present work.

For ten years or more, Sclair lectured on cemeteries and mourning customs at the Newberry Library, and occasionally at other locations such as a cemetery chapel.[7] Her lectures were popular and well-received, serious but injected with her sense of humor as well.

In 2002, health problems made the climb to her fourth-floor Lincoln Park apartment difficult. Sclair found a perfect new home: the caretaker's cottage on the grounds of Bohemian National Cemetery.[8] She moved in with her impressive collection of funerary literature and memorabilia. The collection extended beyond printed matter and included such eclectic and rare objects as a death mask of John Dillinger, mourning ribbons worn by members of fraternal orders, a commemorative black-bordered handkerchief from the funeral of King Edward VII, a wicker casket, skull candies, and Halloween decor of every kind.[9]

Sclair continued to be "an advocate for the dead," always ready to answer the questions of a reporter—or of a young graveyard explorer seeking to follow her path. Whenever

[5] "The Cemetery Lady," The Newberry, http://newberrylibrary.tumblr.com/ post/34703867175/the-cemetery-lady.

[6] Jensen, "Helen Sclair."

[7] "Cemetery Talk is a Lively Topic."

[8] Jensen, "Helen Sclair."

[9] Martine, "A Tribute to Helen Sclair," 6–7.

Chicago police uncovered decades-old skeletal remains in a Lincoln Park basement, a quick phone call to Helen would let them know if that skeleton had a perfectly natural right to be there—or not.[10]

While living on the grounds of Bohemian National Cemetery, Sclair chose a grave for herself in the same place. She designed her own monument, which she delighted in showing to friends who came to visit.[11] On December 16, 2009, she died at a rehab center while recovering from surgery.[12] Her ashes (she had always disliked the portmanteau *cremains*, cremated + remains) were buried next to her monument at Bohemian. Of Barre grey granite, the upper portion reads *Helen A. Sclair—The Cemetery Lady—1930–2009*, and on the base: *An Advocate for the Dead*.

Monument of "Cemetery Lady" Helen Sclair, of her
own design, at Bohemian National Cemetery.
(*Photo courtesy of John Martine*)

[10] Martine, "A Tribute to Helen Sclair," 7.
[11] Martine, "A Tribute to Helen Sclair," 8.
[12] Jensen, "Helen Sclair."

JEWISH GRACELAND AND HEBREW BENEVOLENT CEMETERIES

3919 North Clark Street, Chicago
Established 1854

Chicago's first Jewish congregation, organized in 1847, was *Kehilath Anshe Maariv,* the "Congregation of the Men of the West," consisting principally of immigrants from a handful of neighboring villages in Bavaria. Their original graveyard no longer survives. The graves were relocated not once but twice—first from the lakefront to Belmont and Clark, then finally to Mount Mayriv Cemetery in Dunning (today known as Zion Gardens). The oldest extant Jewish cemeteries in Chicago are the four tiny graveyards sharing a five-acre plot of land on North Clark Street, adjacent to Wunder's Lutheran Cemetery, a block away from prestigious and posh Graceland. The project began with a $600 land purchase by the Hebrew Benevolent Society of Chicago (HBSC), a charitable organization formed in 1851 by Jewish businessmen to provide aid to the sick and burial for the growing community's dead.[20]

Though the first Jewish settlers were almost exclusively Bavarian, later waves of immigrants in the 1850s came from lands further east, including Prussia and Poland, with differing cultural and religious traditions. Dissatisfied with the Bavarian flavor of *Kehilath Anshe Maariv* (KAM), these later arrivals formed a new congregation, *Kehilath B'nai Sholom,* "Congregation of the Children of Peace," in 1852.[21] The new congregation was closely linked with HBSC—one of its earliest presidents was HBSC co-founder David Witkowsky. *B'nai Sholom* purchased a part of Hebrew Benevolent Cemetery for their own use and, thus, the site was now two graveyards.[22]

---

[20] Irving Cutler, *The Jews of Chicago: From Shtetl to Suburb* (Urbana, IL: University of Illinois Press, 1996), 10.

[21] Cutler, *Jews of Chicago*, 15.

[22] Mark Mandle, "Development, Decline and Renewal of Old Jewish Cemetery," *Jewish Historical Society Newsletter*, June 1986, JewishGen, http://www.jewishgen.org/jgsi/grace-hist.htm.

The cemetery complex opened in 1854 with the interment of **Ida Kohn** on the sixth of August that year.[23] The second burial was that of **Emanuel Frank**, notable for the circumstances of his death—at dusk, the nearsighted Frank walked off the end of the Lake Street drawbridge while it was still in the process of closing, falling into the Chicago River.[24]

In 1856 some B'nai Sholom congregants formed another charitable organization and purchased the southernmost portion of the Clark Street site. *Chevra Gemilath Chassodim Ubikkur Cholim*, the "Society of Benevolence and Relief of the Sick," was a German-speaking group dedicated to compassionate works, with much the same aims as HBSC itself. Internal schisms caused the group to disintegrate in 1861. Finally, the northernmost parcel of land was sold to an unaffiliated congregation, B'nai Zion, from the far north neighborhood of Rogers Park.

Thus, the tiny plot, less than five acres, had been divided into four independent cemeteries, each a narrow strip of land extending the length of one block east from Clark Street, each with its own entrance on Clark. From north to south, the order is *B'nai Zion, B'nai Shalom*, HBSC, and *Chevra Kadisha*[25]—this last, which means "Holy Society," being a successor to the defunct Society of Benevolence. Together, these cemeteries became commonly known as "Jewish Graceland," or alternately, "Hebrew Cemetery."

In 1893, the author of *Chicago: The Garden City* observed that the cemeteries were "well-kept" and "show tender care." At that time, the groundskeeper was a Christian, a Swede named Neiglick, who worked without wages, instead supporting himself entirely through the sale of flowers and landscaping services to individual lot-holders.[26]

The convoluted ownership situation of the cemeteries led to severe financial and maintenance problems in the late twentieth century. Congregation B'nai Sholom merged with Temple Israel

[23] Andreas Simon, *Chicago, the Garden City: Its Magnificent Parks, Boulevards, and Cemeteries* (Chicago: The Franz Gindele Printing Co, 1893), 140.

[24] Mandle, "Development, Decline and Renewal."

[25] "Hebrew Benevolent Society and Jewish Graceland Indexing Project," Jewish Gen, http://www.jewishgen.org/jgsi/graceland.htm.

[26] Simon, *Chicago, the Garden City*, 147.

Entrance to Hebrew Benevolent Society Cemetery, which occupies the two center lots.

in 1906, then Isaiah Temple in 1924,[27] eventually rejoining KAM, from which it had originally split in 1852. Hebrew Benevolent Society declined in numbers until it had "no active members" by the 1980s.[28] The Society of Benevolence had lasted only a few years, and its cemetery was purchased in the 1950s by Laurent Clody, owner of the flower shop across the street,[29] whose family had maintained the cemetery since the 1920s.[30]

The cemeteries had been established with the intention that the families of those buried there would contribute to the upkeep. This did not happen as expected, as descendants moved away from Chicago, stopped visiting, or simply ignored requests for payment. The congregations were left with the bill. On the death of Laurent Clody, his cemetery passed to his niece Charlotte Wells and her husband Ronald, who became caretakers of the other cemeteries under agreement with those owners.[31]

[27] "History of Our Congregation," KAM Isaiah Israel, http://kamii.org/node/44.

[28] Michael Arndt, "Graveyard Buried in Troubles: Hebrew Cemetery Plagued by Vandals, Money Shortage," *Chicago Tribune*, September 16, 1985.

[29] "Bandit Killed; 3 Wounded in Holdup Battle: Robber Killed in Battle for Florists' Mother's Day Receipts," *Chicago Daily Tribune*, May 9, 1932. The story is about an armed robbery at "Clody the Florist" at 3900 N. Clark, in which Laurent Clody (1897–1970) and his father Edward defended their substantial Mother's Day receipts against a gang of four armed robbers, killing one. The Clodys were hailed as heroes. The two buildings housing their flower shop, across from the cemetery, are still intact and are presently home of a theatre group, Teatro Luna.

[30] Arndt, "Graveyard Buried in Troubles."

[31] Ibid.

Vandalism of the site was rampant throughout the 1970s and early 80s. Ronald Wells reported in 1977 that $10,000 of damage had been done, with the maintenance shed repeatedly broken into, tools stolen, hoses cut, and monuments toppled.[32] Yet the money coming in from the congregations was insufficient to repair the damage, according to Wells,[33] and conditions led some family members to refuse to pay maintenance fees even as they complained to the press. About 1979, due to a dispute over the fees, Congregation *B'nai Zion* stopped paying the Wells's company, which in turn discontinued work in that section.[34]

Vandals and drunks had easy access during the night, for at that time no fence separated Jewish Graceland from Wunder's. The caretakers regularly found the cemetery strewn with beer bottles and cans and other trash. Monuments were knocked over, some of them repeatedly. Worst of all, the door of the Hyman mausoleum was broken down and a coffin opened, the vandals throwing bones on the ground as they picnicked inside the vault. Swastikas were painted on the mausoleum and on other monuments.[35]

In 1985, Hans Spear, a retired German-American resident of Chicago whose brother had been killed by the Nazis, began to organize a clean-up of Jewish Graceland. Howard Eiseman, president of the Hebrew Benevolent Society, sought new ways to protect and restore the site. Though the Society barely clung to life, Eiseman was able to use its investments to provide $10,000 for a barbed-wire-topped fence on the cemetery's north side, cutting off the vandals' preferred means of entry. Hans Spear campaigned for donations from the public, and KAM Isaiah Israel provided funds for repairs as well. The Jewish Genealogical Society organized efforts to document and catalog the burials.[36] In September 1987, Eiseman, Spear, and Rabbi Perelmutter of KAM Isaiah Israel held a re-dedication ceremony with 50 participants, who gathered around a pile of broken

---

[32] "Cemetery Faces More Vandalism, Alderman Says," *Chicago Tribune*, August 18, 1977.
[33] Ibid.
[34] Arndt, "Graveyard Buried in Troubles."
[35] Arndt, "Graveyard Buried in Troubles."
[36] Michael Arndt, "Hebrew Cemetery Turns a New Face to the Past," *Chicago Tribune*, January 9, 1987.

and illegible monuments and offered prayers.[37]

The cemeteries' troubles were far from over, however. In 1993 the *Chevra Kadisha* and *B'nai Zion* sections were purchased by a former funeral home employee known as Alexander Lichtenstadt-Partin. Partin had been released from prison only a few years before, having been convicted in 1985 of "indecent liberties with a child"[38] after allegedly fondling a 14-year-old boy.[39] He had also been accused by a state regulatory board of practicing medicine without a license.[40] Claiming he wanted to maintain the cemeteries because his relatives were buried there, he proceeded to attempt several schemes to profit from the land. He proposed a pet cemetery on the site, sending faxes advertising the idea to veterinarians. He buried two of his own dogs there, a move that outraged Jewish community leaders. Hebrew Benevolent Society, owner of the two sections between Partin's properties, threatened an injunction.

With the kibosh put on the pet cemetery idea, Partin raised money by charging admission for Halloween parties in the cemetery and (unsuccessfully) marketed gravesites to non-Jews. He abandoned maintenance and allowed the cemetery to fall into disrepair and neglect, prompting the local alderman to call in city inspectors. Saplings and thick brush grew from the graves. Helen Sclair, Chicago's foremost cemetery historian, described the site in 2007 as "a slum for the dead."[41]

Most outrageous of all, however, was Partin's attempt in 2002 to sell the property for $2.25 million for development of condominiums.[42] This plan caused such outcry that in 2007 the Illinois Senate

---

[37] Andrew Martin, "The Resurrection of a Cemetery; Group Gathers to Give Thanks for Facelift of Jewish Site," *Chicago Tribune*, September 28, 1987.

[38] Jodi S. Cohen, "Jewish Leaders Protest Pet-Burial Plan at Cemetery North Side. Site Needs Help, Its Owner Says," *Chicago Tribune*, October 14, 1998.

[39] Noreen S. Ahmed-Ullah, "Jewish Cemetery's New Owner Plans for Renewal; Deal Revives Community Interest in Historical Burial Ground with Curious Past," *Chicago Tribune*, May 13, 2007.

[40] Andrew Zajac, "Descendants Key to Cemetery Fate," *Chicago Tribune*, February 11, 2002.

[41] Mark Brown, "Owner of Jewish Graceland Lets Cemetery Fall Apart," *Chicago Sun-Times*, March 18, 2007.

[42] Zajac, "Descendants Key."

passed a bill to forbid anyone convicted of a child sex offense from owning a cemetery. With that bill seemingly likely to become law, Partin finally gave up the land, selling it in April of 2007.

The new owner was Doris Weiss-Evon, an artist who had long been familiar with the site, having once lived in the caretaker's house at Wunder's Cemetery and who had often visited Jewish Graceland to sketch and reflect.[43] Weiss-Evon, who had bought the cemeteries with the help of unnamed benefactors, intended to repair the damage caused by more than a decade of neglect, and ensure that it would remain a Jewish cemetery.

In this, she has been successful. The cemeteries operated by her Jewish Graceland and Lakeview Cemetery Company, at north and south,[44] have been cleaned up, with brush cleared away and monuments righted. These parcels are as beautiful and well-kept as the Hebrew Benevolent Society's cemeteries in the middle. Under the care of someone who has long loved the site, Jewish Graceland's long struggle with disrepair and neglect appears to finally be at an end.

Though each of the four cemeteries once had its own entrance on Clark Street, only one of these survives today in more or less its nineteenth-century form: two columns, square in cross section, support a decorative iron gate with a smaller pedestrian entrance to one side. Immediately south of this entrance stood a small red brick building until it was torn down in the early 2000s. A stone panel set into the front wall was inscribed *Hebrew Benevolent Society Cemetery*. This was removed during the building's demolition and now stands upright in the middle of the empty space where the building had been, *Founded 1851* having been added to the inscription.[45]

Inside the cemetery complex, long concrete walkways extend east from the front fence, and it is not immediately obvious where the boundaries between sections lie, though during the Partin years it was clearer, as those cemeteries were neglected while Hebrew Benevolent Society's sections were better kept. Coping—low stone curbing

---

[43] Ahmed-Ullah, "Jewish Cemetery's New Owner."

[44] "JUF: Guide to Jewish Living: Jewish Graceland and Lakeview Cemetery Company," Jewish United Fun, http://www.juf.org/guide/detail.aspx?id=19026.

[45] However, as was said earlier, the first burials did not take place until 1854.

The family lot of Hannah and Samuel Meyer, just inside the gate, included four shafts of varying sizes for members of the family, though it suffered much damage in the 1990s.

surrounding a plot—is plentiful here, though most other cemeteries disallow it to ease maintenance. The monuments are of a pleasing variety of styles, including tablets, obelisks, pedestal tombs, and slant or pillow headstones. Plots are spacious. The cemeteries look nothing like the more densely packed contemporaneous Jewish cemeteries at Waldheim and Oak Woods, nor do they have any of the porcelain portraits so common there. Indeed, if not for the Hebrew lettering, these would look more like a typical Lutheran cemetery.

Near the site of the former office is the **Meyer** plot, where four columns once stood on pedestals to mark the graves of the family. The children's columns are of grey granite and comparatively short. Behind them stood the red granite columns of **Samuel Meyer** (1829–1910) and **Hannah Meyer** (1833–1888). Samuel Meyer's column and pedestal were about twice the size of his wife's. The pedestal itself is taller than a man and its granite shaft stretched up into the treetop. Between this author's visits in 1996 and 1998, this stately column fell to the ground. A few years later it had been dragged to the rear of the cemetery and left lying in a pile of rubble. Hannah Meyer's column, though much smaller in size, was more notable for its adornment—attached to the front of the red granite shaft was a white marble panel bearing the image of her face in relief. This, too, was lost between 1996 and 1998, only a discolored spot remaining where it had previously been attached. A poem on her pedestal begins, *Honest and true was she; no better wife, no better mother could be.*

And she will keep her place, until we see her heavenly face.

Sarcophagus-shaped monuments of Patrick Harvey and Bertha Harvey Hirsch, once covered with ivy, now cleared. Patrick Harvey collapsed and died of heat exhaustion after marching in a parade.

Behind the Meyer plot, surrounded with coping, are the twin sarcophagi of **Patrick Harvey** (1844–1897) and **Bertha Harvey Hirsch** (1848–1918). Patrick Harvey, a plumber, collapsed and died of heat exhaustion while marching with the Knights Templar in the first Logan Day parade,[46] a parade of 16,000 to honor General John A. Logan, founder of Memorial Day.[47] Thickly covered with ivy in the early 1990s, a photograph of their monuments served as the original title image on the main page of *graveyards.com*.

Further east in the Hebrew Benevolent Society Cemetery, side-by-side monuments both feature carved portraits, though these have suffered from the elements. On the side of a grey granite pedestal is affixed a marble portrait of **Samuel Salkey** (1830–1888), though the upper half of his face is now missing. A few feet away is a monument similar in size and shape, but made entirely of white marble, with a faint, badly weathered relief carving of a man's face recognizable on the east side. It is of **Colonel Marcus M. Spiegel** (1829–1864), commander of the 120th Ohio Volunteer Infantry in the Union Army, one of the first Jews to reach the rank of colonel. He was mortally

---

[46] "One Marcher is Dead: Patrick Harvey Overcome in Ranks and Dies in a Cab," *Chicago Daily Tribune*, July 23, 1897.

[47] Adriana Schroeder, "Preserving the Legacy of John A. Logan, Founder of Memorial Day," readMedia, http://readme.readmedia.com/Preserving-the-Legacy-of-John-A-Logan-Founder-of-Memorial-Day/2404254.

wounded in Louisiana in 1864. A book of his letters was published posthumously as *A Jewish Colonel in the Civil War: Marcus M. Spiegel of the Ohio Volunteers.*

Hannah Greenebaum Solomon (1858–1942) is buried in her family plot alongside an obelisk. Solomon and her sister were the first Jewish women elected to the Chicago Woman's Club, an upper-class social and civic service club. At the World's Columbian Exposition of 1893, the Jewish Women's Congress organized for the fair opted to form a more permanent organization, creating the National Council of Jewish Women. Hannah Solomon was unanimously elected its first president.

At the rear of the cemetery stands the sole mausoleum here, the **Nathan and Rachel Hyman** tomb, erected in 1928, later the target of vandals. To deter a recurrence of this shocking crime, the bronze door was removed in the late 1990s and replaced with a solid slab of granite.

The cemeteries to the north and south, long neglected, were roped off for safety for several years after their purchase, as restoration and cleanup work took place.[48] Today, these sections are once again in fine condition, no longer set apart from the Hebrew Benevolent Cemetery in between.

WUNDER'S CEMETERY

3963 North Clark Street, Chicago
fspauls.org
Established 1859

As the movement to abolish City Cemetery was building momentum, First Saint Paul's Evangelical Lutheran Church procured a cemetery for their congregation on Clark Street north of the growing city.

48 Ropes visible in Google Street View, May 2009, and Find a Grave, June 2011, http://www.findagrave.com.

"First German Lutheran Cemetery," as it was then called,[49] was established in 1859 through the efforts of First Saint Paul's pastor, Dr. Heinrich Wunder. The cemetery was co-owned by a daughter congregation, First Immanuel Lutheran Church, until the mid-1980s, but is now owned and operated solely by First St. Paul's. Founded in 1846, First St. Paul's is the oldest Lutheran congregation in Chicago.[50]

As early as 1893, during Wunder's extraordinarily lengthy pastorate, First German Lutheran Cemetery became commonly known as "Wunder's Cemetery."[51] It was officially incorporated as the "German Evangelical Lutheran Cemetery Association" in 1912.[52] In 1919, six years after Pastor Wunder's death, the cemetery was officially renamed in his honor.[53]

Wunder's Cemetery is located immediately south of Graceland, across Irving Park Road. The 14.5-acre cemetery is roughly shaped like a reversed letter "L," with the east portion extending south behind the much smaller Jewish Graceland and Hebrew Benevolent cemeteries. A typical Chicago-style yellow brick two-flat at the northwest corner of the property serves as the cemetery office, and has entrances both on the public sidewalk and within the cemetery itself. A single road runs through the cemetery, proceeding east from the entrance towards the maintenance building in the back, then continuing south before doubling back to run parallel with itself until reaching Clark Street again. Perhaps due to the nuisance of baseball fans seeking parking within a few blocks of Wrigley Field, signs posted by both entrances sternly warn that parking is allowed only when visiting a gravesite or the cemetery office.

For the most part, monuments display the range of typical nineteenth-century styles. Obelisks are found in both marble and granite. Stone urns, some sculpted to depict cloth drapery, stand on

[49] "Wunder's Cemetery," First Saint Paul's Evangelical Lutheran Church, http://fspauls.org/ wunder_s_cemetery.

[50] Jayne Wysch Kegley, Superintendent, Wunder's Cemetery, personal communication, April 11, 2000.

[51] Simon, Chicago, the Garden City, 144. Simon calls it "Wunder's Church-Yard" and "Wunder's cemetery," not using the then-official name "First German Lutheran" at all.

[52] "Wunder's Cemetery."

[53] Kegley, 2000.

large square-sectioned pedestals. Black-letter typography reminds the visitor that this is a German cemetery. Some of the older marble monuments bear inscriptions in a delicate script that is now all but unreadable.

Andreas Simon in 1893 provided a translation for one of these: "Wanderer, stand still! Here rests in God a true husband and father, who had to lose his life in his calling as fireman." These words memorialized **John Streming**, who was "killed at a fire on South Water Street, June 8th, 1865, while on duty."[54] The marble obelisk of **Gustav Sprengel**, also near the entrance, is truncated by design, with a tasseled cloth in place of the pyramidal cap. Carved roses frame the name on the front of the base.

Near the north fence, a sad-eyed girl stands holding a dove, a wide-brimmed hat on the ground at her feet. Buried here are not one, but three children: Bertha, William, and Frederick, children of **William & Johanna Gruel**.

The cemetery's most visually stunning monument is next to the main road, a work of fine art equaling anything found at Graceland or Rosehill. Encased in a transparent box is a marble statue of two kneeling women in diaphanous dresses, their heads bowed, one clutching the shoulders of the other in apparent grief, her face buried in her companion's neck. Flowers spill from the lap of one, to the other, to the ground. Across the front of the granite base is the black-letter inscription, *Sei getreu bis in den Tod*, "Be faithful unto death."

This monument celebrates the love between two sisters, Margaret and Marie. Upon the death of 48-year-old **Margaret Raithel** (1858–1906), younger sister **Marie** (1863–1930) erected this touching memorial. Marie followed her sister *in den Tod* 24 years later.[55] The soft marble artwork was encased in glass with bronze framing to protect it. In 1993 thieves shattered the glass in order to steal the monument. Although they removed the statue from its pedestal, they ended up abandoning it on the road nearby. Cemetery management

---

[54] Simon, *Chicago, the Garden City*, 144. I have not observed this monument myself and believe it may be lost.

[55] Anne Little, "Unearthing Sociological Trends Through North Side Cemeteries," *Chicago Tribune*, June 4, 1986.

restored the artwork to its base and replaced the glass with durable Lexan.[56] As the Lexan has aged and become less transparent, the enclosure now appears to be filled with mist, giving the statue a dreamy, ethereal quality.

The Raithel sisters' monument was placed in the family plot, next to the more traditional urn-topped marble shaft of their parents, **John N. Raithel** (1821–1889) and **H. Barbara Raithel** (1827–1867). That their mother had died while the sisters were at such young ages, nine and four, perhaps explains their devotion to each other.

Frederick William Krause (1816–1889) is buried beneath

Marie Raithel's touching tribute to her sister Margaret, enclosed in a Lexan box for protection. In recent years the box has become increasingly opaque.

a large and ornate grey granite pedestal, over which stands a traditional depiction of Faith, a woman holding a flower-entwined cross, her other hand pointing heavenward. The granite pedestal, like many others here, has taken on a multi-colored patina from the effects of the air. A white marble obelisk, octagonal in cross-section, with a fringed and tasseled cloth covering the top, pays tribute to **Andrew Drechsler** (1832–1879). **Charles Jorn** (1838–1913) is memorialized with one of the more unusual monuments here, a miniature sarcophagus. The box-like granite stone is intricately carved with scrollwork and leaves on all sides.

Near the south fence stands the cemetery's solitary mausoleum, built from thick granite blocks. The name **Mueller** is visible over the doorway, which has been permanently sealed with concrete blocks. Ivy grows on the front and sides of the mausoleum. A few feet away,

---

[56] Kegley, 2000.

over a fence topped with barbed wire, are the Jewish Graceland cemeteries, which have struggled with neglect and overgrowth through much of their history. For decades there was no fence between the Lutheran and Jewish cemeteries, until one was installed in the late 1980s by the Hebrew Benevolent Society to deter vandalism.

Eponymous pastor **Heinrich Wunder** (1830–1913) is buried with his wife **Emilie** (1844–1897), next to a simple grey granite shaft. Wunder was

Originally called "First German Lutheran Cemetery," the cemetery was officially renamed for longtime pastor Heinrich Wunder in 1919.

the second pastor of First St. Paul's, taking the position in 1851 after the first pastor, Augustus Selle, accepted an appointment in downstate Crete. Pastor Wunder oversaw the creation of the cemetery in 1859, and in 1871 risked his life to retrieve records from his church as it burned in the Great Chicago Fire. He died in December 1913 after having led his congregation for 62 years.[57]

ST. BONIFACE CATHOLIC CEMETERY

4901 North Clark Street, Chicago
www.catholiccemeterieschicago.org
Consecrated 1863

A bit further north of the cemetery cluster at Clark Street and Irving Park Road is another urban ethnic burial ground, this one

---

[57] "Church History," First Saint Paul's Evangelical Lutheran Church, http://fspauls.org/church_history.

founded by German Roman
Catholics.

Like most ethnic populations
of the nineteenth century, Germans harbored intense preju-
dices. In this case, the disdain
of German Catholics for their
Irish brethren led to Germans
refusal to be buried with these
Celtic congregants at the Diocesan cemetery, Calvary, in Evanston. With no other place to send
their dead, German Catholic
congregations at the Diocesan
churches of St. Joseph, St. Francis, St. Michael, St. Boniface, and
St. Peter[58] founded the German
Roman Catholic Saint Boniface
Cemetery Association to provide

This modern monument portrays the
patron saint of the cemetery, Saint
Boniface, who converted early Germans
to Christianity. Behind it is a row of
priests' graves.

burial space and services exclusively for Roman Catholics of German
origin, with any surplus revenue to be used for charitable purposes.
This benevolent policy is evident in the contrast between St. Boniface
and Calvary, the latter of which re-invested surplus funds in itself and,
as a result, boasts one of the metropolitan area's most stunning entrance arches, as opposed to the simple iron entry gate of St. Boniface.

This 36-acre cemetery was platted and consecrated in 1863, and its
first burial took place on October 19 of that year, when nine-day-old
infant **Marie Jung** was laid to rest.[59] The designers favored, for the
most part, a simple no-nonsense rectilinear plan, typical of city cemeteries. Unlike rural cemeteries such as Rosehill or Calvary, there were
no winding roads, water features, or carefully-sculpted landscapes designed to highlight the natural beauty of the site. This has been a simple, functional cemetery from the start. Rows of graves are arranged

---

[58] These are the same five parishes listed in an 1872 *Chicago Tribune* article that described
various facets of the German population of the city.

[59] Simon, *Chicago, the Garden City*, 140.

on a uniform, north-to-south axis with almost no variation.

As the author of *Chicago, the Garden City* observed in 1893, later developments deviated from this strict grid layout. St. Boniface's newer, eastern section incorporated some principles of the park cemetery movement, introducing slight curvature into the roads and dispensing with coping and railings. In these sections, statues are abundant, and you'll see the only two mausoleums in the cemetery.

A receiving vault, now vanished, once stood alongside the cemetery's main road near the original office.[60] In the 1960s, the cemetery was modernized, with the original entrance arch demolished and replaced with an entrance wide enough for easy automotive access. A one-block segment of Ainslie Street, which borders St. Boniface to the north, was closed off, joining St. Boniface to a newly-acquired property where a new chapel and administrative building were constructed.[61]

This granite soldier stands atop a tall pedestal in the northwest corner of the cemetery, the first monument in America to German-American soldiers of the Civil War.

The cemetery commemorates the legend of its namesake with a *cenotaph* (a tomb in memory of someone buried elsewhere) honoring the eighth-century Boniface, who requested permission from Pope Gregory II to convert the pagans of Thuringia (now a state in Germany). Once among them, the missionary priest aimed to demonstrate the authority of the Christian God. Chopping down a tree sacred to Thor, Boniface watched confidently as the pieces of wood fell into the

[60] Simon, *Chicago, the Garden City*, 140.
[61] "St. Boniface Catholic Cemetery," Catholic Cemeteries, Archdiocese of Chicago , http:// www.catholiccemeterieschicago.org/locations.php?id=22.

shape of a cross, underscoring his message of Christian salvation. For his efforts and faith, the missionary won many Germanic converts to the Church, becoming known as the Apostle of Germany. Here in this Chicago cemetery, Boniface's memorial watches over the graves of area priests buried around the marker.[62]

A grey granite statue of a soldier with a rifle atop a 22-foot pedestal in the northwest corner of the cemetery commemorates the *Amerikanischen Bürgerkriege* ("American Civil War"). On the front of the monument, the German inscription memorializes the heroes of the *neuen Vaterland* ("new homeland"). A gift of the St. Boniface Union Soldiers' and Sailors' Monument Association, this was the first monument in America honoring the German-American soldiers of the Civil War. Dedicated on Decoration Day (the precursor to Memorial Day), May 30, 1887, the ceremony was interrupted when the speakers' platform collapsed, injuring a child. The chaos was short-lived and the unveiling proceeded as planned.[63]

Nearby is the monument of the **Ambrosius Maennerchor**, a sculpture of a lyre over a pedestal listing names of members of this men's singing society. The **Klor** memorial features a tall, rough-carved granite cross, at the base of which an angel stands with bowed head. Behind it, what looks like a pile of white marble rubble is in fact a single stone, a monument base apparently missing its upper part. This **Schleicher** monument was carved to look like rough, separate blocks, disguising its solidity.

St. Boniface contains an impressive collection of *rustic monuments*, limestone memorials carved to look like trees. The trees depicted by rustic monuments are always dead, missing their tops, with peeling bark, and every branch cut off, symbolizing the human life that was cut short. Yet even these dead trees teem with other representations of life—the sculptors include ivy, birds, squirrels, mushrooms, ferns, and other small details. Where the bark is peeled back, the artists

---

[62] I believe this section was built on the site of the original receiving vault, but have no documentary evidence of this at present.

[63] "Honoring Dead Heroes. A General Observance by Chicago of Decoration-Day," *Chicago Daily Tribune*, May 31, 1887. The article also includes happenings at other cemeteries, such as the unveiling of Major Drury's monument at Rosehill on the same day, with 10,000 in attendance.

etched the names of the deceased. Some such rustic monuments at St. Boniface are crowned with a fireman's helmet, honoring one who risked his life—or gave his life—for others.

Another form of rustic monument portrays rocks with an anchor, of which several survive at St. Boniface. The white marble monument of **F. Scholer** is one such, its base carved to resemble natural stone against which an anchor lies with a rope connecting it to the marble tree trunk. An anchor typically doesn't indicate that the lot belongs to a seafarer. Rather, it was a symbol of safety and of the hope of Christian salvation.[64]

Hope, with Faith and Charity, are the three "theological virtues," and each may appear allegorically in cemeteries as a female figure. Near the office on the north side of the cemetery, the **J. B. Kopf** monument shows the traditional figure of Faith, as a white marble statue with one hand pointing to heaven, the other hand holding a cross. The letters I.H.S. appear on her cross, as they do on many other monuments. The initials may be read as either *Iesus Hominum Salvator* ("Jesus, Savior of men") or *In Hoc Signo* ("in this sign," i.e., the sign of the cross). Two clasped hands appear at the base of this symbol-rich monument—one disembodied hand adorned by a feminine sleeve, the other wearing a masculine sleeve—signifying a marriage that will continue in eternity.

Sarcophagi are plentiful here. These granite monuments have the shape of a coffin, some even

The marble statue atop the J.B. Kopf monument represents the virtue of Faith, holding a cross entwined in roses and raising one hand toward heaven.

[64] "Catholic Encyclopedia: The Anchor (as Symbol)," New Advent, http://www.newadvent.org/cathen/01462a.htm.

featuring an attached "headstone." Though a casual observer might mistake these for above-ground entombments, they in fact do not contain bodies but are solid stone resting above the grave. These sarcophagi appear individually or in groups of two or more on family plots, usually with a cross carved into the horizontal upper surface. Those that mark the graves of priests are often more richly decorated, additionally adorned with sculpted chalices and vestments.

The monument of **Anton C. Hesing** and **Louise Hesing** has attracted the most acclaim of any at St. Boniface, appearing as a full-page plate in Andreas Simon's 1893 work. The seven-and-a-half foot statue was carved from Westerly grey granite by Chicago-based artist Franz Engelsmann.[65] The statue depicts St. Elizabeth, daughter of a thirteenth-century king of Hungary, who as a child was given in marriage to a prince of Thuringia. When her husband was away in service of the Emperor, flood and famine devastated the land. Elizabeth gave generously to the poor, built a hospital, and tended to the afflicted herself.[66] She is shown here wearing a crown, holding a loaf of bread along with a bundle of roses. The roses recall the miracle that occurred when her returning husband forced open the basket of food she was carrying for the poor, only to find it filled with roses instead.[67] Under the statue of St. Elizabeth, the base of the Hesing monument originally bore two large bronze medallions bearing portraits of Anton and Louise. While Anton's portrait survives, Louise's portrait disappeared decades ago, leaving only a discolored circle of stone to mark its passing.[68]

Like St. Elizabeth, **Louise Lamping Hesing** (~1824–1886) was noted for her charitable works, as one of the founders of St. Vincent's House of Providence, which provided services to the poor and elderly. She died of pneumonia in November 1886; her obituary states that she contracted her fatal illness while attending church. A na-

[65] Simon, *Chicago, the Garden City*, 143.

[66] "Catholic Encyclopedia: St. Elizabeth of Hungary," New Advent, http://www.newadvent.org/cathen/05389a.htm.

[67] Simon, *Chicago, the Garden City*, 143.

[68] Louise's portrait medallion was photographed and appears in Simon's 1893 book, as well as the more recent book *Chicago's Monuments, Markers and Memorials* by Graf and Skorpad.

tive of the now-defunct Grand Duchy of Oldenburg, Louise met her husband-to-be on a ship bound for America, marrying him in Baltimore in 1848.[69] **Anton C. Hesing** (~1823–1895), also a native of Oldenburg, was for more than 30 years a prominent Chicago newspaper editor, president of the *Illinois Staats-Zeitung.* When Hesing suddenly collapsed and died at the age of 73, his fellow journalists attributed his demise to his indignation at political corruption; he had written a strongly-worded editorial only hours before, denouncing an "abominable" ordinance that would transfer control of the city's water system to a private company packed with aldermanic cronies. "What a fearful outrage!" he wrote, "Never have I so seriously felt that I am an old and broken-down man." The manuscript was found on the bedside table next to his body the following morning.[70]

Monument of newspaper editor Anton Hesing and wife Louise. As Louise died before her husband, her name appears on the front of the monument and his name on the side. The circular bronze portrait of Louise has been missing for many years.

The **Link** mausoleum, larger of the two mausoleums at St. Boniface, is a uniquely ornate structure. The grey limestone walls are made of alternating courses of smooth and rusticated blocks, giving it a striped appearance. Projecting corners taper inwards as they rise to meet a pyramidal roof. Red granite columns with foliate limestone capitals stand on either side of the entrance, supporting a pediment from which a winged cherub peers; the date "1894" appears on the bronze door. On pedestals a few feet in front of the tomb stand two

---

[69] "Obituary. Mrs. A.C. Hesing," *Chicago Daily Tribune,* November 14, 1886.

[70] "A. C. Hesing Dead: The Famous German Editor Called Rather Suddenly. Anger Hastens the End," *Chicago Daily Tribune,* April 1, 1895.

marble statues of saints—one, a medieval king, holding a sword and a model church; the other, a pious woman, her hands clasped, standing atop a dragon, crushing its head beneath her feet.

This spectacular tomb was built for carriage-maker **Ferdinand Link** (1829–1908), well in advance of his death. On their fiftieth wedding anniversary in 1902, Link and his wife **Mary Laux Link** (1833–1911)[71] came to the cemetery to dedicate the $10,000 mausoleum, which had then been under construction for eight years.[72] The statues show their patron saints—St. Ferdinand, thirteenth-century king of Castille, and the Virgin Mary, triumphant over the dragon Satan. Having arranged for funerals and even selected coffins years before these became necessary, the well-prepared carriage maker died in February 1908, fourteen years after the date on the mausoleum door.

A rough granite cross marks the grave of one who shaped many

One of only two mausoleums in the cemetery, the tomb of Ferdinand and Mary Link took eight years to construct—the date on the door, 1894, is when the mausoleum was finished and dedicated, with both Links still living. Statues of their namesake saints guard the door.

[71] "Sheahan Family Tree," Ancestry.com, http://www.ancestry.com.
[72] "Death Reaches Waiting Man: Ferdinand Link Built Mausoleum and Paid for Burial," *Chicago Daily Tribune*, February 2, 1908.

Chicago cemeteries, stone-carver **Engelbert Gast** (1850–1914). Trained as a sculptor in his native Fuessen, Bavaria, Gast immigrated to America and here worked under Leonard Wells Volk,[73] assisting with the Lincoln portraits for which Volk is famed. In 1880 he joined Christian Buscher, creating the monument company Buscher & Gast, working from a studio on North Clark Street, just outside the gates of St. Boniface. Gast created many highly detailed and intricate monuments in all of Chicago's most prominent cemeteries; his best-known work is the railroad car monument of George Bangs in Rosehill. In 1906, Engelbert's son Joseph Gast bought Christian Buscher's share of the business; the elder Gast died in 1914. Still a family business, Gast Monuments, Inc., continues to operate today.[74] Erstwhile partner **Christian Buscher** (1852–1926), too, is buried at St. Boniface; he and his wife lie beneath a pair of the sarcophagi described earlier.

The tallest monument at St. Boniface Cemetery features St. Boniface himself. Atop the square-sided marble shaft is a life-size figure of the saint, dressed in robes and a bishop's miter, holding an open book in his hands. More than a century of weathering has softened the details, with his facial features barely discernible from the ground. Below the shaft, the pedestal is richly ornamented, with floral garlands over bas-relief portraits in profile on the sides; this, too, has suffered from the elements. **John Herting** (1818–1881), a prominent Bavarian-born businessman, invested his grocery store earnings in real estate and a number of other businesses, including the Shufeldt Distillery, the German Savings Bank, and the Home Insurance Company, which suffered enormous losses with the Great Chicago Fire of 1871.[75]

A mottled pink and grey granite boulder gives fitting tribute to **Paul Dresser** (1858–1906), author of *On the Banks of the Wabash, Far Away*, state song of Indiana. After a successful career as a composer, Dresser's livelihood disappeared as tastes in popular music

---

[73] Volk is buried at Rosehill.

[74] "History of Gast Monuments, Chicago Memorial Design and Marker Restoration," Gast Monuments, http://www.gastmonuments.com/history.php. See St. Henry Cemetery chapter for the continuation of the Gast story.

[75] "Obituary: John Herting," *Chicago Daily Tribune*, July 9, 1881.

changed. Dying impoverished and depressed, he was buried in an unmarked grave in St. Boniface. In 1922 the Indiana Society of Chicago installed this Wabash River boulder to mark his plot. Brewer **Michael Diversey** (1810–1869), for whom Diversey Parkway was named, is buried here as well;[76] his sprawling, four-story, two-acre "Chicago Brewery" was located next to Chicago's famed Water Tower, and a parcel of land donated by Diversey became the site of St. Michael's Church, Chicago's tallest building before 1885.[77]

The association of parishes that created St. Boniface had an opportunity to repeat their worthy endeavor in 1887, when Heinrich and Maria Wischemeyer presented them with a grant of land on the opposite side of the city—60 acres on 87th street. With the creation of **St. Maria Cemetery** on that location the following year, the German Catholics of the South Side were provided with a cemetery the equal of St. Boniface, closer to home.[78]

A popular monument option at St. Boniface is the granite sarcophagus with attached headstone. Dozens of groups of such monuments may be found here. These are solid structures that do not contain bodies, but instead sit on top of a grave.

---

[76] Phyllis Magida, "To See Art, Find Tranquility, Cemeteries Are for the Living," *Chicago Tribune*, September 6, 1985.

[77] "A Little Background on Our Namesake," Michael Diversey's, http://www.mdtavern.com.

[78] Simon, *Chicago, the Garden City*, 152.

AFTER THE FIRE:
THE TROUBLE WITH CREMAINS

With a cost less than half that of embalming, increasing numbers are choosing the fiery furnace as their postmortem destination. In the United States, cremation is now preferred by over 40 percent[1] of the year's dead, up from a scant four percent in the 1950s, and that figure is expected to reach or exceed 50 percent in the 2020s.

Appropriately, the Cremation Society of North America is evangelizing against the ignorance of Americans who insist on calling that shoe box full of somebody, *ashes.* Indeed, political correctness shakes its finger even in the crematorium: The proper term is *cremains,* thank you very much.

In fact, the fruit of the inferno is not dust but fragments, the knobby, gnarled, and broken bones left behind after the literal vaporization, at 1,800 degrees, of everything else. It is the pulverization of these cremains that yields the powdery substance of popular imagination.

Whether gathered together *au naturel* or ground to smithereens, cremains are indeed remains and, as such, they must go somewhere. A coffin is still the most prevalent container, though the urn is commonly thought to be the most logical.

For those who do choose the urn, the decision making has just begun. A plastic repository may be purchased for about $20. If your budget is a little bigger, the 24K-gold-plated, sapphire-studded ones run $3,500.

What to do with this conversation piece? Bequeath it to your beloved or buy a nook in a columbarium, where you'll reside for eternity within a proper mausoleum.

[1] "Statistics," National Funeral Directors Association, http://nfda.org/media-center/statistics.html. Figure is for the year 2010.

If these choices are too tiresome, forego them. Get yourself scattered instead. If, however, you choose as your burial site a piece of public land, a site in a national park, a river, lake, or beach, don't tell anyone about your plans—most statutes call it littering. For while cremains are perfectly healthy, the idea of them still makes most constituents' skin crawl.

If the urn seems too cramped, and scattering too criminal, there is another legal option. For less than $5,000, Houston-based Celestis, Inc. will happily shoot a portion of your ashes into outer space—as they did for astronaut Gordon Cooper and *Star Trek* creator Gene Roddenberry. There, it is promised, they will orbit the Earth for several years before exploding in a blaze of glory.

ROSEHILL CEMETERY

5800 North Ravenswood Avenue, Chicago
www.rosehillcemetery.com
Established 1859

When Rosehill, the largest nonsectarian cemetery in the Chicago metropolitan area, was established in 1859, the 350-acre site sprawled almost five miles north of the city limits. Funeral parties traveled to it by renting special cars from the Chicago & North Western railroad, which ran a spur line from the heart of the city to the Rosehill gates. Today, the enormous expanse is surrounded by neighborhoods, circumvented by buses and taxis, and generally ignored by local residents, whose primary concern is how to get around the cemetery during rush hour.

Though the name "Rosehill" is a popular one for cemeteries

throughout the country, local legend has it that the name was picked for this cemetery due to another business in early Chicago—"Roe's Hill," the site had originally been called, after local tavern keeper Hiram Roe. Some say that he consented to sell his land only if the cemetery was named in his honor, while other versions of the story have it that it was a simple typographical error that created the modern version of the name.

After the C&NW tracks were elevated around the turn of the century, a new station was built at the Rosehill entrance, along with a casket elevator, whose tower is still visible. Both were designed to harmonize with the cemetery's signature entrance, built five years after its opening. The entry's architect, **W.W. Boyington** (1818–1898), himself an eternal occupant of Rosehill, celebrated the site with a limestone portal of castellated Gothic magnificence, which hinted at his later, now famous design of the Chicago Water Tower. Beyond this gate is a beautifully landscaped rural cemetery with winding roads and five man-made lakes, the work

The castellated Gothic entrance of architect William Boyington, still intact to this day, houses the cemetery's administrative offices. A nearby train station once allowed for trains with a special funeral car, built to accommodate a coffin, to convey mourners directly to the cemetery.

of noted botanist and landscape architect William Saunders[79] (1822–1900). A few years later Saunders would go on to design the grounds of Lincoln's Tomb at Oak Ridge in Springfield and the Soldiers National Cemetery at Gettysburg.[80]

Take a walk through these gates and find yourself among a who's who of Chicago history: Rosehill is home to **Ignaz Schwinn** (1860–1948), bicycle king; **Robert S. Scott**, colleague of Carson and Pirie; **George W. Maher** (1864–1926), architect; **Aaron Montgomery Ward** (1843–1913), mail order pioneer; **Julius Rosenwald** (1862–1932), financial genius behind Sears, Roebuck & Co. and founder of the Museum of Science and Industry; **Richard Warren Sears** (1863–1914) himself; and thousands of other hometown movers and shakers.

Seated statue of Charles J. Hull (1820–1889), best remembered today for the mansion he built—"Hull House," a name that continued when the house was the center of a complex of buildings serving Chicago's immigrant community under the stewardship of Jane Addams.

Just inside the Ravenswood Avenue gates is the larger-than-life statue of **Charles Hull** (1820–1889), whose likeness keeps watch over the graves of his family. One of Chicago's pioneering residents, Hull gained fortune through real estate development and fame when he leased his Halsted Street mansion to progressive activist Jane Addams. Hull House became the first of the nation's so-called settlement houses, a refuge of sorts for the homeless, friendless, poverty-stricken, and uneducated, where everyone from infants to the elderly

---

[79] Alice Sinkevitch, *AIA Guide to Chicago* (Boston: Houghton Mifflin Harcourt, 2004), 471.
[80] "William Saunders," The Cultural Landscape Foundation, http://tclf.org/pioneer/william-saunders. Saunders is buried in Washington, DC.

The Volunteer Firefighters Monument, designed by Leonard Wells Volk, features a helmeted fireman at its summit. A fire hose is wrapped around the bottom of the marble shaft. Tablets in front bear the names of Chicago firefighters who died in the line of duty.

This full-sized statue is a self-portrait of sculptor Leonard Wells Volk (1828–1895), famed for his portrayals of President Lincoln and Senator Douglas. On the cover of the book under his right arm is a bas-relief portrait of his wife Emily Barlow.

could find shelter and food, learn language and other skills, indulge in sport, pursue the arts, and even study for citizenship tests. Addams's ultimate goal was to foster self-sufficiency in a time when the problems of urban life had begun to cause deep social and personal problems for city residents, especially immigrants.

Also deeply involved in the reform movement, and laid to rest not far from the Hull plot, is Evanstonian **Frances Willard** (1839–1898), founder of the Woman's Christian Temperance Union.

Towering near Willard's grave is the **Volunteer Firefighters Monument**, complete with a stone hose wrapped around a 36-foot marker. The first of such memorials in the United States, the 1864 masterpiece pays homage to the volunteer firefighters who died in the great South Water Street Fire of 1857. Renowned Lincoln sculptor **Leonard Volk** (1818–1895) designed the monument and went on to create a self-portrait in stone for placement on his own lot in Rosehill. Viewers of the Chicago-filmed *Backdraft* may recognize a replica of this monument—a stunt double was temporarily installed in Graceland Cemetery for the movie's purposes.

Travelers of Chicago's streets will recognize a number of namesakes here as well: **Hoyne, Wells, Peterson, Kedzie.** Inventors, too, are represented at Rosehill with inhabitants like **A.B. Dick** (1856–1934), originator of the duplicating machine; and **George S. Bangs** (1826–1877), designer of the railway mail car, commemorated with a most unusual monument. Bangs's memorial, designed by skilled stonecutter Engelbert Gast,[81] is a limestone tree trunk with broken branches and peeling bark, like so many other rustic monuments. What sets it apart is at the base, where a wonderfully detailed railway car rests on a segment of track, one end disappearing into a carved tunnel. "United States Post Office Railway" appears on the side of the car, as does a tiny "Letter Box." Bangs's predecessor as superintendent of the postal railway service, **George Buchanan Armstrong** (1822–1871), is also at Rosehill. His monument, too, is decorated with a train car, but one etched in bronze.

George S. Bangs (1826–1877), originator of the railway mail car, is memorialized with a model of his invention. About two feet long, the car protrudes from a tunnel at the base of a tree-shaped monument, sculpted by noted Chicago artist Engelbert Gast.

Deep within the cemetery, a small lake is ringed by prestigious family mausoleums housing the likes of advertising mogul **Leo Burnett** (1891–1971), and the founding families of Harris Bank and Goodrich Tires. Vice-President of the United States

---

[81] See St. Boniface Cemetery entry for more on Gast Monuments.

Charles Gates Dawes (1865–1951), brigadier general and recipient of the Nobel Peace Prize, is entombed on this shore, the only U.S. vice president buried in Cook County. The most eye-catching of these is undoubtedly the Egyptian-styled tomb of Burlington Railroad president **Darius Miller** (1859–1914). While surveying Glacier Park in Montana with his wife and railroad officials, Miller suddenly became ill with appendicitis. Though a team of the best surgeons in the West were rushed to his location by special train, and the operation appeared to go well, he lost consciousness and died a few days later.[82] Miller's sudden death, coupled with his interest in Egyptian architecture, had led some to concoct a story that he was felled by the "Curse of Tutankhamun"—nonsense, of course, as he died years before the Pharaoh's tomb was plundered.[83]

Near this charmed circle, the May Chapel stands sentinel. **Horatio Nelson May** (1843–1898), a real estate speculator and city government official, died suddenly from *the grip* (influenza) while visiting Germany in September 1898. Rather than a more traditional monument, his family endowed a chapel for the use of cemetery visitors. Designed by architect Joseph Silsbee, the chapel features Gothic and Romanesque elements, and a porch with a mosaic ceiling, supported by arches. The interior is a warm space, filled with

The family of Horatio N. May endowed this spectacular chapel, built by architect Joseph Silsbee in 1898. May himself is buried under a simple flat marker a few feet away. Built into the chapel at the rear is a receiving vault, now unused and padlocked.

---

[82] "Darius Miller Dead in West: Burlington Chief Succumbs After Appendicitis Operation," *Chicago Tribune*, August 14, 2914.

[83] Douglas M. Rife, "The Curse of King Tut," Gravely Speaking, http://gravelyspeaking. com/2013/01/09/the-curse-of-king-tut/.

richly carved wood. On the side of the chapel is a receiving vault, no longer used, for the storage of winter corpses until the spring thaw.

In 1867, Dr. I. Chronic, a prestigious German scholar and rabbi, contracted with Rosehill Cemetery for a portion of its holdings, initiating Chicago's first Jewish burials in a non-Jewish cemetery.[84] Sinai Congregation's section, in the south part of the cemetery, is noticeably Jewish in character, with Hebrew writing and symbols on the monuments.

Nearby is the plot where one of Rosehill's better monuments has, sadly, gone missing in recent years. The plot of clothing manufacturer and real estate developer **Morris Vehon** (1867–1950), landscaped by noted architect Jens Jensen, featured a shallow pool before a curved stone bench. At the center of the pool stood a lovely bronze statue of a girl, called "the water nymph" by cemetery fans. This monument was tragically stolen about 2009, leaving only a bare platform. Its ultimate fate is unknown.

Arguably, the single most impressive cemetery experience to be had in the Chicago metropolitan area is the walk through the **Community Mausoleum** at Rosehill, the first ever large-scale communal crypt. Designed in 1914 by **Sidney Lovell** (1867–1938), a noted mausoleum architect who is himself entombed within, the massive structure is a multi-level maze of marble-lined passageways stacked to the ceilings with thousands of dearly departed, including a number of notables from the worlds of retail, law, and politics.

In 1892, **Milton Florsheim** (1868–1936) began making shoes in a small factory at Clinton and Adams streets. Though he focused on a high quality product from the beginning, believing that a fine shoe would sell better than a mediocre one, Florsheim knew that it would take more than a good product to make him a fortune. Investing in this belief, the entrepreneur sought out a number of potential retailers to set up shops across the country which would carry his footwear. While the shoemaker initially sold his product through small-town storefronts, he eventually branched out further, opening retail locations in the largest American cities. These were the first Florsheim

---

[84] Cutler, *The Jews of* Chicago, 25.

Until the day break and the shadows flee away reads the exedra behind this exquisite statue at the grave of developer Morris Vehon.

The largest community mausoleum in Illinois, Rosehill Mausoleum was designed in 1912 by Sidney Lovell. In addition to the architect himself, the mausoleum shelters the remains of two Illinois governors, a number of business magnates, and a popular sportscaster.

shoe shops, which carried the entire line of Florsheim styles and sizes. Florsheim continued to use manufacturing and merchandising innovations to build up his trade, eventually creating a mammoth network of retailers that continues to operate today. His success earned him his hoped-for fortune, and, ultimately, a fitting place of repose among Chicago's other super salesmen.

Also here in the Community Mausoleum are merchandising arch-enemies, **Aaron Montgomery Ward** (1843–1913) and **Richard Warren Sears** (1863–1914), the latter of whom is said to walk the mausoleum hallways, dressed to the nines in white tie and tails. Ghosts or not, illuminated only by the light leaking through the color-drenched panes of Louis Comfort Tiffany, the mausoleum is not for the faint-of-heart. The impressive surroundings, beautiful as they are, are dampened by both the clammy environment and the resulting, telltale scent of formaldehyde. Still, stiffen your lip and set your heart on getting a look at the most gloriously solemn burial site in the mausoleum: the family room of aquarium name-sake, **John G. Shedd** (1850–1926).

A New Hampshire native, Shedd migrated to Chicago in 1850, where he began a long and successful career with Marshall Field & Co., succeeding the department store's founder as company president in 1906. Though he achieved social and financial prominence through his work, Shedd guaranteed himself lasting fame when he spent $3 million on the development of what he dreamed would be the world's largest aquarium. Planned by a conscientious board of directors and built on landfill at the south end of Grant Park, the Shedd Aquarium was completed in 1929 and opened to 20,000 first-day visitors in May 1930.

One of the most intriguing and important aspects of the aquarium was that it was the only inland aquarium to display both freshwater and saltwater varieties of aquatic life. The required sea water was transported via railroad cars, a million gallons at a time, from Key West, Florida. This practice continued on a regular basis for more than 40 years, until the aquarium began simulating seawater in Chicago by a new process.

Though John G. Shedd died in 1926 (four years before his dream aquarium would open), the outstanding directors he had chosen for the project remained loyal to his specifications, contributing to Chicago and the world, and the memory of Shedd, one of the finest showcases of marine life in the world. A little piece of this paradise is silently reflected in the Shedd family room in Rosehill's Community Mausoleum. Before his death, the philanthropist commissioned a one-of-a-kind stained glass window from Tiffany that would bathe his crypt in blue light at sunset. The underwater theme of the family room is echoed in the skylit anteroom: even its chairs are adorned with the fanciful oceanic motifs of seahorses and shells.

Yet with all of the accolades duly lavished on the residents of Rosehill and their sumptuous memorials, perhaps no one grave here is currently more sought after than the mausoleum crypt of the city's beloved baseball broadcaster **Jack Brickhouse** (1916–1998). He rests near Illinois Governor **Richard Ogilvie** (1923–1988), for whom Chicago's downtown train station was named, on the mausoleum's main floor. On the lower level is the more modest crypt of another Illinois governor, **Dwight Green** (1897–1958), notable also as one of the federal prosecutors who sent Al Capone to prison.

Outside this labyrinth and far across the cemetery, claiming the largest lot in Rosehill, is former Chicago mayor **"Long" John Wentworth** (1815–1888). The 6-foot, 6-inch Wentworth served several terms as a Democratic congressman before defecting to the Republican Party, becoming an abolitionist and mayor of Chicago in the 1850s. A friend of President Abraham Lincoln, he was one of the honorary pall bearers when Lincoln's funeral train passed through Chicago. Hogging two-thirds of an acre of this vast burial ground, Wentworth also staked his claim with Rosehill's tallest monument, a 70-foot granite obelisk shooting to the North Side skies. According to the dictates of the deceased, no inscription was to be placed on the marker, so that the curious would ask whose it was. Thus would he be assured a place at the center of conversation for years to come. Later, however, more sensible heads prevailed. The obelisk is now clearly inscribed with Wentworth's name and, for the uninformed, a list of his earthly achievements.

But don't ignore the lesser lights. At Rosehill, as at all cemeteries, every stone has its story, and a number of Chicago mayors have found more understated solace here at Rosehill: **George Bell Swift** (1845–1912), **Roswell Mason** (1805–1892), **Isaac Lawrence Milliken** (1815–1885), **DeWitt Clinton Cregier** (1829–1898), **John Roche** (1844–1904), **Levi Day Boone** (1808–1882), **John Blake Rice** (1809–1874), **Harvey Doolittle Colvin** (1815–1892), **Augustus Garrett** (1801–1848), and acting mayor **Lester Bond** (1829–1903), who held the post for three months while Mayor Medill was convalescing in Europe.

While the Windy City may have been driven by politics, it was made of meat and railroads, and students of its history will want to seek out the grave of local lunchtime hero **Oscar Mayer** (1859–

1955), a sausage titan whose 96-year lifespan speaks well for the health benefits of preserved pork. Visitors at his grave have included the famed Wienermobile. Nearby, buried side-by-side, are water magnates **Otis Ward Hinckley** (1861–1924) and **George Schmitt** (1866–1931), a delivery man and pharmacists' assistant, respectively, who partnered in 1888 to provide clean and fresh-tasting bottled spring water to Chicago businesses.

Untimely deaths have brought many to Rosehill's soil, among them that of **Reinhart Schwimmer** (1900–1929), an eye doctor affiliated with the Moran gang who was killed in the St. Valentine's Day Massacre. Perhaps most poignant, however, is the grave of one of Chicago's most pitied homicide victims. In 1924, 14-year-old **Bobby Franks** was killed by two University of Chicago students, Nathan Leopold and Richard Loeb, who wanted to get some intellectual kicks by committing the perfect crime. The ensuing kidnapping and murder of Franks led to the so-called Trial of the Century, during which the immortal Clarence Darrow successfully argued against the death penalty for Leopold and Loeb, though Loeb was later killed in prison by a fellow inmate.

After his demise, Bobby Franks was buried at Rosehill with the understanding that his lot number would not be given out to the curious. To this day, that information remains confidential. Visitors can find the Franks grave among Rosehill's tens of thousands only by accident, or by a tip-off through the grapevine of local legend.

Almost as heart-wrenching as the murders of youth are the deaths

Considered one of Chicago's finest funerary monuments, this marble sculpture under glass portrays Frances Pearce (d. 1864) and her infant.

of children taken by disease, and the earth of nineteenth-century cemeteries is heavy with such casualties. Still, to the benefit of the modern observer, the unmatched grief of bereaved parents has inspired the commissioning of some of the most meticulous likenesses in funerary art, many of them so delicately detailed that they are encased under glass, such as the panes enclosing the Rosehill monument to young **Lulu Edith Fellows** (~1867–1883), who died at the age of 16. The beauty of the monument underscores the inscribed sentiment: *Many hopes lie buried here.*

Another of Rosehill's glass-encased monuments has won wide artistic acclaim: The breathtaking sculpture of a reclining mother and child commissioned for the graves of **Frances Pearce** (1835–1854) and her infant daughter by grieving widower and father (1811–1877). The monument, designed by Chauncey Ives, was initially placed over the original pair of graves in the old City Cemetery. Upon the reinterment of the remains at Rosehill after City Cemetery closed, a protective glass encasement was added to protect the sculpture, later named the "Best Monument in Chicago" by *Chicago Magazine.*

ST. HENRY CATHOLIC CEMETERY
6346 North Ridge, Chicago
www.catholiccemeterieschicago.org
Consecrated 1863

The only surviving churchyard cemetery in the city of Chicago, this little graveyard occupies about half the space of a city block at Devon and Ridge in Rogers Park, the city's northernmost neighborhood. On this site, the German, Luxembourgian, and Irish parishioners of St. Henry first built a small wood-frame church in 1851, then a second church before 1873,[85] and the present church in 1905. The

---

[85] *The Archdiocese of Chicago: Antecedents and Developments* (Des Plaines, IL: St. Mary's Training School Press, 1920).

cemetery began in 1863.[86]

Designed by ecclesiastical architect Henry J. Schlacks, the red brick church is a stately, neo-Gothic structure. Delicate limestone structures frame the windows, and statues are set in niches on the exterior walls. The towering steeple is off-center, rising from the church's northeast corner. Copper spires decorate the steeple and the gables of the nave and three transepts. The facade of the church extends south, connecting directly to the rectory.

St. Henry Church has long been linked with the adjacent Angel Guardian Orphanage, founded in 1865 by the same five German Catholic parishes that

This small cemetery stretches for about one block behind the Catholic Church at Devon and Ridge, originally German, now serving a Croatian parish.

established St. Boniface Cemetery. The orphanage housed dependent children on its 40-acre campus,[87] with nearly 900 orphan children in residence as late as the 1960s.[88] After the orphanage shut down in 1974, the facilities became the Misericordia Home, which provides services for people with developmental disabilities. The disused church gained a new life in 1982 when it was renovated by the Croatian Catholic Mission and renamed Angel Guardian Croatian Catholic Church, in memory of the orphanage. In 1998 it was renamed again, to Blessed Aloysius Stepinac Croatian Catholic Church.

On the north side of the church stands a World War I memorial, surrounded by flat markers. The limestone sculpture portrays Christ,

---

[86] "St. Henry Catholic Cemetery," Catholic Cemeteries, Archdiocese of Chicago, http://www.catholiccemeterieschicago.org/locations.php?id=26.

[87] Paula F. Pfeffer, "Angel Guardian Orphanage," Encyclopedia of Chicago, http://www.encyclopedia.chicagohistory.org/pages/50.html.

[88] Laura Putre, "History: The Hard-Knock Life," *Chicago Reader*, August 30, 2007.

The World War I memorial, the first such monument in Chicago, features the Prince of Peace blessing a soldier and sailor on the field of battle. Another soldier lies dead at his feet.

his head crowned with thorns, holding a cross. At his sides kneel a soldier and sailor, gazing upwards at their savior and comforter, whose hand rests on the soldier's head. Below them, a dead man is sculpted, mouth agape. The pedestal, of Barre granite, is engraved with a dedication to the Prince of Peace, and names three parishioners of St. Henry's who gave their lives in the Great War. At the base are the dates *1917–1919* and a bronze medallion depicting an eagle, shield, and crossed flags. The monument was designed and carved by Gast Monuments.[89] At its dedication on November 27, 1919, about 70 veterans of the armed forces attended the ceremony. This was the first monument to the Great War erected in Chicago.[90]

The section alongside the church is surrounded by brick walls, but a gap in the rear wall allows one to step into the larger portion of the cemetery. Passing through, the visitor will see obelisks and pedestals supporting crosses and religious statues, the statues severely weathered due to the poor air quality in the city. Next to the brick wall are three small granite sarcophagi, of the same design as those at St. Boniface. Beyond, the ground rises to a level several feet above that of the sidewalk on the other side of the retaining wall, giving the obelisks the illusion of extra height when viewed from the street.

The image of one child buried here now holds the status of a registered trademark. With his little dog Bingo, this boy wearing a dark blue sailor suit and giving a jaunty salute has appeared on countless boxes and bags of caramel-coated popcorn and peanuts.

[89] Bert J. Gast, personal communication, about 1997.
[90] *The Archdiocese of Chicago*.

Robert Muno Rueckheim (1913–1920) was a grandson of Frederick Rueckheim, creator of Cracker Jack.[91] Robert inspired the mascot "Sailor Jack" before his untimely death of pneumonia at the age of seven. For decades, his flat marker was decorated with a ceramic photograph of the child, wearing a sailor suit and cap.[92] This has unfortunately disappeared.

Two generations of monument makers are buried here. **Joseph F. Gast** (1873–1943) was the son of Engelbert Joseph Gast,[93] partner in the Buscher & Gast Company. In 1906 he became head of the company, renaming it the Joseph F. Gast Monumental Works,[94] and it was during his tenure that the company created St. Henry's World War I memorial. He died in 1943 and was buried here, beside his wife Helen M. Gast (~1873–1937). Their son **Bert C. Gast** (1895–1986) is also here, next to the short driveway in the middle of the cemetery. Bert served in World War I, studied at the Art Institute of Chicago, and continued the family business, eventually passing it to his son Bert J. Gast.[95]

Two statues set into the wall of the church succinctly summarize the site's history. One portrays St. Henry himself, the Holy Roman Emperor who is depicted with a model of a church, commemorating his role as the builder of the cathedral at Bamberg, Germany. The other shows an angel accompanied by two small children—an Angel Guardian.

---

[91] See Oak Woods Cemetery entry for more on Frederick Rueckheim.

[92] Dick Griffin, "Cracker Jack's Sweet Smell of Success," *Chicago Tribune*, November 20, 1983. The article states that the portrait on the gravestone was present, though slightly damaged, as of 1983.

[93] The elder Gast, and his colleague Christian Buscher, are buried at St. Boniface.

[94] "History of Gast Monuments, Chicago Memorial Design and Marker Restoration," Gast Monuments, http://www.gastmonuments.com/history.php.

[95] I spoke with Bert J. Gast and Jan Gast about 1997 in their Clark Street workspace. Bert J. Gast died in 2005 and is buried at All Saints.

JUMPIN' THAT TRAIN: LINCOLN'S LAST, LONG HAUL

When the body of President Abraham Lincoln rolled into Chicago on its way to rest in Springfield, Illinois, the city was waiting. Passing through a 40-foot high arch that had cost more than $15,000 to build, the coffin was removed from its rail car and carried through a countless sea of mourners for display. It is estimated that 7,000 Chicago viewers per hour paid their final respects to President Lincoln on May 1, 1865. This spare-no-expense attitude had been reflected as well in the lavish preparations of Baltimore, Harrisburg, Philadelphia, New York, Albany, Buffalo, Cleveland, Columbus, and Indianapolis, each city striving to distinguish itself as the most gracious host of all.

Though the temporary surroundings varied, constant comfort was provided by the funeral car itself. Designed for Lincoln's use by the U.S. Military Railroad System, the car—christened *The United States*—was run for the first time only after his death. Sadly, for the car was the grandest example of railcar construction of its time, complete with 16 wheels, expertly crafted woodwork, etched-glass windows, and upholstered walls. In addition, its wheels were cleverly designed to allow undisrupted travel across the irregularly-spaced rails that remained for years after Lincoln himself signed legislation standardizing the gauge between rails. The president would surely have been tickled.

Even cities not on the funeral route did their best to impress the now-unimpressible president: the mayor of St. Louis, for example, provided the $6,000 hearse, festooned with lavish plumes and striking trim, that awaited Lincoln in Springfield. And many towns along the route erected their own arches over the local railroad tracks in tribute. Perhaps most poignant was the one spanning the rails at Michigan City, Indiana, its epitaph gathering the sentiments of millions:

With Tears We Resign Thee to God and History;
The Purposes of the Almighty are Perfect and Must Prevail.

BOHEMIAN NATIONAL CEMETERY

5255 North Pulaski Road, Chicago
www.bohemiannationalcemeterychicago.org
Established 1877

Beginning in 1877, Bohemian National Cemetery attracted Czech settlers to Chicago's North Park neighborhood. Until that time, the area was occupied almost exclusively by German and Swedish immigrants who planted and harvested vegetables along the fertile shore of the North Branch of the Chicago River.

The cemetery itself began because of an incident in the Chicago Bohemian community in the years after the Great Fire. A woman named Marie Silhanek was denied burial at the available Catholic

The main entrance of the cemetery, a designated landmark, was built in 1893 in the Gothic Revival style. Waiting rooms are on either side of the driveway.

cemeteries, owing to the testimony of Fr. Joseph Molitor of St. James Church, who claimed Silhanek had not made a confession before death. The more than 25,000 members of the city's Bohemian population protested what they viewed as a profound injustice, organizing against the authority of the Church to deny Christian burial to one of their own. By the late 1870s, the Bohemians had gathered enough support to found Bohemian National Cemetery, though the organization created for the task met with much protest from residents of Jefferson Township where the cemetery was to be located. The panicky population, imagining a replay of the disease and decay of the shuttered City Cemetery, urged the cemetery planners to abandon the project or find another site for its development.

Despite all pleas, and even a few unsuccessful lawsuits, Bohemian National Cemetery interred its first body in July of 1877. Since its founding, the cemetery has hosted countless dedication ceremonies commemorating local, national, and international heroes and events. Such events have typically drawn enormous and enthusiastic crowds. Even on ordinary days, a number of points of interest continue to draw sightseers to Bohemian National.

For cemetery and funerary historians, the primary attraction here is the original funeral bell in the cemetery gate. The bell is the only one of such fixtures still remaining in Chicago. Most others have been removed or replaced by modern substitutes.

One of the most popular destinations for non-mourners at Bohemian National is a piece by Czech-American sculptor Albin Polasek, entitled *The Pilgrim* but commonly held to resemble a Grim Reaper, poised as if to enter the Stejskal-Buchal family mausoleum deep inside the cemetery. Cemetery expert Helen Sclair is buried a few feet away.

Also of interest is Section 16, a communal plot occupied by many victims of the 1915 *Eastland* disaster, in which the *Eastland* steamer, loaded to overflowing with Western Electric employees embarking on a picnic cruise from a downtown Chicago River dock, overturned, resulting in the deaths of more than 800 people, including 22 entire families.

Bohemian National is home to the mausoleum of the late mayor

Anton Cermak (1873–1933). Born near Prague in the 1870s, Cermak was raised as a Hussite, a follower of Protestant reformer John Huss. Immigrating to America when Anton was barely a year old, the Cermak family settled near 15th and Canal streets and later spent a number of years in the coal mining community of Braidwood far southwest of Chicago.

It was only with the family's move back to the city, this time to a predominantly Bohemian West Side neighborhood, that Anton began to see the value of a stable home base, especially in the pursuit of political life. The young Cermak made some attempts to succeed at business

This bronze sculpture by Albin Polasek, *The Pilgrim*, is viewed by some as a representation of Death, its face eternally in shadow. The statue is in the Stejskal-Buchal plot, walking toward the family mausoleum.

and soon found himself in the Illinois state legislature for four terms. After serving those terms, Cermak was elected alderman, went on to serve as a court bailiff, and then returned to the post of alderman before being elected president of the Cook County Board of Commissioners in the early 1920s.

From the beginning, Cermak distinguished himself as a nononsense public figure. He was known to settle political debates by inviting opponents to step outside, and he won many advocates by organizing the United Societies for Local Self-Government, which fought for the right of citizens to drink on Sunday. Leading the march against dry ordinances regulating liquor consumption, Cermak's alcoholic activism led the *Chicago Tribune* to label him the wettest man in Chicago. Despite his bawdy style, however, the Democratic Cermak went on to create the most organized political party the city

Assassinated mayor Anton Cermak, as he lay dying in hospital, said to President Roosevelt, "I am glad it was me instead of you."

had ever known. A prototype of efficiency, the party is credited as the first of its kind in the country to use statistical analysis in its strategic planning and performance evaluations.

Cermak's fatal mistake was sending police to rough up Frank Nitti, head of Chicago's most powerful mob. Assassin Giuseppe Zangara shot Cermak while he was on stage in Miami with president-elect Franklin D. Roosevelt. He lingered for a month after the shooting, then died after saying to Roosevelt, "I'm glad it was me instead of you." Whether the gunman's true target was Roosevelt or Cermak is still debated. Cermak's legacy is well memorialized by his revered mausoleum at Bohemian National, which is inscribed with those famous words.

A draw not only for native Chicagoans, Bohemian patriots, too, will find a gold mine at this expansive site. Monuments here commemorate some of the most moving events and influential personalities in Czech history. A monument to **František "Ladimir" Klácel** (1808–1882) was funded by donations from colleagues and admirers of the Bohemian philosopher. Expelled by the Austrian government in the 1860s on charges of radicalism, Klácel had been teaching at the Augustinian Friars School in Brno, Moravia, but was then forced to migrate to the United States. Here, he became a leading force in the Czech Rationalist movement until his death in 1882. Buried in Iowa, his monument in Chicago is a cenotaph.

The **Lidice Memorial** keeps an eternal vigil to the victims of

Adolph Hitler's 1942 attack on the tiny Czech town of Lidice. Staged in retaliation for the assassination of Reinhard Heydrich, Hitler's Chief of the Occupation forces in Czechoslovakia, by Czechoslovakian freedom fighters, the attack brought tanks and bulldozers rolling into the unsuspecting city, eliminating everything in their path. Simultaneously, women and children were evacuated from the city by force, many mothers separated forever from their offspring. Worst of all, the men of Lidice were gathered into a local barnyard and brutally mowed down by machine gun spray. Despite the gruesome response, Heydrich's assassins refused to surrender to Hitler. Amazingly, though one other Czech village suffered a similar fate to that of Lidice, Nazi threats of further retaliation fizzled under the burden of overwhelming negative world opinion. The Bohemian dead had become international heroes.

As the center of Czech nationalism in the United States, Chicago rocked with critical voices raging against the destruction at Lidice. A foundation was organized by *Chicago Sun-Times* publisher, Marshall Field, to raise money for a monument to the Lidice dead, and to rename an American town after the vanquished Bohemian city. The plan reached speedy fruition: A small town outside of Joliet, Illinois, was chosen for erection of the monument and, upon its dedication, the town of Stern Park was rechristened Lidice, though it was later incorporated into Crest Hill. In Chicago, an urn of dirt from the destroyed Czech village was placed on display in the main chapel of the crematorium at Bohemian National Cemetery.

This tiny statue, less than two feet tall, stands in a distant corner of the cemetery. The name on the monument is almost completely worn away.

The Bohemian Soldiers' and Sailors' Monument, today known as the Civil War Veterans Memorial, was designed by artist Joseph Klir. The dedication ceremony in May 1892 was attended by Bohemian community leaders, representatives of the Grand Army of the Republic, and Mayor Carter Henry Harrison.

Entitled *Hiker*, this Spanish-American War Memorial, a bronze figure more than eight feet tall, stands atop an immense red granite boulder. The monument was dedicated in 1926.

A second urn accompanies the Lidice memorial at Bohemian National, this one containing a mixture of soil and ashes from Poland's Osweiscim concentration camp, where hundreds of members of Czechoslovakian *sokols* (gymnastic societies) were executed.

Also greatly represented at Bohemian National are the contributions of Chicago Bohemians to American history. A Civil War Veterans Memorial was dedicated here in 1889 with much fanfare—more than one hundred testimonials, contributed by numerous Czech organizations, were sealed in the marker's cornerstone.

Another patriotic structure is the United Spanish War Veterans Memorial, popularly known as "The Hiker Monument" for its sculpture of an American soldier in Spanish-American War battle gear. The soldier's hulking pedestal is a solid piece of granite, which was transported to Bohemian National from Wausau, Wisconsin. Dedicated in 1926, the entire monument was erected by the Bohemian American Camp No. 30, United Spanish War Veterans.

A fine tradition perseveres at the World War I and II Memorial. An American flag has been flown from the monument's flagpole since its dedication in 1952, but these banners are frequently changed by the cemetery. Over the years, hundreds of veterans' families have donated flags to be flown over the site in honor of their deceased loved ones.

The most celebrated feature at Bohemian National is its indoor columbarium, several rooms with walls lined with niches for the storage of urns of human ashes. In most cemeteries, these niches are enclosed with front panels of granite or marble that are decorated with a simple name plate. Here, frames of iron or bronze support glass panels that allow the contents of each niche to be seen. Urns range from elaborately carved wooden boxes to cardboard cylinders, some of them still marked "temporary container." Most of these niches are

The indoor columbarium at Bohemian National Cemetery is famed for its highly personalized displays, containing urns of every design accompanied by flowers, photographs, and other mementos.

highly decorated and personalized, filled with photographs, artificial flowers, flags, and, in one case, a miniature mausoleum of white marble. The eternal residents of the columbarium exude personality at a fraction of the cost of traditional stone monuments.

At least one final monument deserves commentary—that dedicated simply and powerfully to *Mother*. Also designed by Albin Polasek, the monument was erected in commemoration of the cemetery's fiftieth anniversary and dedicated before a reported audience of 25,000 people. A stirring tribute to an unmatched profession, the memorial sculpture of a woman sheltering her children continues to be a favorite with visitors from around the world.

ST. LUKE CEMETERY

5300 North Pulaski Road, Chicago
www.stlukechicago.org/cemetery
Established 1900

In 1900 a group of Lutheran congregations formed the Saint Lucas Cemetery Association and purchased a 65-acre parcel of land across the road from Bohemian National Cemetery, creating the second Lutheran cemetery in Chicago[96] (after Wunder's). Two years later, an undertaker purchased the land immediately north of Saint Lucas to create the privately owned Montrose Cemetery, thus completing the trio of burial grounds near the Foster and Pulaski intersection.

Over the years, most of the congregations left the Saint Lucas association. The last to depart was Christ Evangelical Lutheran Church of Logan Square, dissolved in the 1980s, leaving only one member congregation, Saint Luke Church[97] at Belmont and Greenview.[98] In 1998 the name of the cemetery was officially changed from

[96] "St. Luke Cemetery: History," Saint Luke Ministries, http://www.stlukechicago.org/cemetery/history.shtml.

[97] "St. Luke Cemetery: History."

[98] "Saint Luke Church," Saint Luke Ministries, http://www.stlukechicago.org/church/.

Saint Lucas to Saint Luke.

Upon entering the cemetery, the visitor's eyes are immediately drawn to the **Waltz Memorial Obelisk**,[99] a unique stainless steel shaft with a slender cross perched on its top. Of the more conventional monuments, the most beautiful and poignant are those of children, several of which are here adorned with angel statues and ceramic portraits.

One in particular stands out, that of **Edna Miriam Paul** (1897–1907). The marble statue atop the granite shaft was carved as a faithful reproduction of the photograph on the front of the monument, depicting the child wearing a lacy dress and a ribbon in her curly hair. At the base of the stone are words similar to those on Lulu Fellows's monument at Rosehill: *Many hopes are buried here.*

Johannes Ernst August Mueller (1858–1917), first pastor of Saint Luke, is buried beneath a cross-shaped monument, its front decorated with cross and crown. Mueller was pastor for 33 years,[100] leading his congregation at the time of the cemetery's founding in 1900.

A new administration building was constructed and dedicated here in 1955. The dedication sermon was given by a visiting pastor from suburban Mount Prospect, Rev. John E. A. Mueller.[101] The younger Mueller had followed his father's calling

Lifelike statue of Edna Miriam Paul (1897–1907), modeled on a photograph affixed to the pedestal.

[99] "Saint Luke Cemetery: History."

[100] John Astley-Cock, "Golden Jubilee to be observed at Saint Luke's: Rev. Mueller's Memory to be Recalled," *Chicago Daily Tribune*, January 21, 1934.

[101] "Set Dedication of St. Lucas Cemetery Unit," *Chicago Daily Tribune*, June 5, 1955.

to become the first pastor of St. Paul Lutheran Church in Mount Prospect.[102]

In the years that followed, unused portions of the cemetery grounds were sold to developers. The southeast corner of the site was sold in 1992, becoming a Jewel-Osco. In 1995 another 14 acres at the rear of the cemetery were sold[103] and a group of five-story condominium buildings built on the site. Some of these have balconies overlooking the cemetery, providing a truly enviable view.

Another section was set aside in 2009 for a different use, tan-

Monument of Johannes E. A. Mueller (1858–1917), longtime pastor of St. Luke church.

gentially related to the cemetery's mission: the "Garden of Saint Francis," a pet cemetery, created on unconsecrated ground within Saint Luke[104] in partnership with the Chicago Pet Funeral Home.[105] This pleasantly naturalistic section features walking trails winding through native Illinois prairie grasses, just a stone's throw away from the Chicago River.

---

[102] "Rev. J. E. A. (John Ernst August) Mueller," Mount Prospect Historical Society, http://www.mtphist.org/rev-j-e-a-john-ernst-august-mueller/. Census documents on ancestry.com show that the St. Paul's pastor (born 1887) was son of the elder John Mueller (occupation given as "minister" in the 1910 census).

[103] "Saint Luke Cemetery: History."

[104] "Saint Luke Cemetery: Pet Cemetery," Saint Luke Ministries, http://www.stlukechicago.org/cemetery/petcemetery.shtml.

[105] "Pet Burial Services," Chicago Pet Funeral Home, http://www.chicagopetfuneralhome.com/services/pet-burial.aspx.

MONTROSE CEMETERY
5400 North Pulaski Road, Chicago
montrosecemetery.com
Established 1902

In the early months of 1935, the Japanese Mutual Aid Society of Chicago formed to fulfill a very short and specific agenda: to purchase a substantial group of cemetery lots for Japanese-Americans and to help with the burial fees for those who died unable to pay. The society chose Montrose Cemetery as their communal burial spot and, by 1937, a mausoleum had been completed at the site.[106]

The formation of the society and the selection of the lots proved foresighted. With the rise of anti-Japanese sentiment during World War II came a proportional increase in the rejection of Japanese-Americans by established cemeteries. In addition, after the closing of the internment camps, more than 20,000 Japanese-Americans settled in the Chicago area. Accordingly, the Japanese population at this cemetery also grew, forcing the expansion of the mausoleum as well as the purchase of lots surrounding the structure.

Montrose Cemetery also has a substantial Serbian-American section and plays host to an astounding array of ethnic populations, including Romany, Indians, Iranians, Puerto Ricans, Mexicans, Cambodians, and others.

The "Everyone is Welcome" policy dates back to the beginnings of the cemetery. German-American funeral home operator Andrew Kircher founded the cemetery in 1902, on rural land north of the city, hiring Ossian Simonds's company to landscape the grounds.[107] Two years later, a most newsworthy burial took place at the young cemetery.

On December 30, 1903, some 600 met their deaths in the brand-

---

[106] Helen Sclair, "Ethnic Cemeteries: Underground Rites," in *Ethnic Chicago: A Multicultural Portrait*, Fourth Edition, ed. Melvin G. Holli and Peter d'A. Jones (Grand Rapids, Michigan: William B. Eerdmans Publishing Company, 1995), 634.

[107] "History," Montrose Cemetery, http://montrosecemetery.com/History.html.

The Japanese Mausoleum, erected in October 1937 by the Japanese Mutual Aid Society, houses the cremated remains of a number of Japanese immigrants.

new, "absolutely fireproof" Iroquois, when a number of deadly circumstances combined to create the worst theater fire in U.S. history. During a matinée performance of *Mr. Bluebeard*, attended mostly by children, an electric arc light malfunctioned and ignited muslin curtains over the stage. With the flames quickly growing beyond the abilities of the crew to douse, the stage manager attempted to lower a heavy asbestos curtain, recently installed as a safety feature meant to separate the audience from backstage fires. The curtain stopped midway down, caught on another piece of equipment, thus rendering it entirely ineffective. The panicked crowd attempted to flee the auditorium, only to find their progress impeded by iron gates that had been installed to prevent patrons from moving from cheaper to more expensive seats. Those who reached the doors found that many of them were locked, or were merely windows designed to look like doors,

The Iroquois Theatre Fire memorial, erected by the Iroquois Memorial Association on land donated by cemetery owner Andrew Kircher, stands over the grave of the fire's only unidentified victim.

or that they opened inwards, and could not be operated with the pressure of the crowd from behind. Many were crushed against the doors, where bodies were later found piled ten layers deep.

When the carnage had ended and the authorities had broken down the doors, over 570 bodies were removed and taken to a temporary morgue at the nearby Marshall Field's store.[108] In the days and months that followed, all of these were identified and claimed by grieving relatives—except one, an adult woman, whom no one could identify, though hundreds viewed the body. After six months in the custody of the county coroner, she was finally buried at Montrose in June 1904, with the words *The Unknown, December 30, 1903* inscribed on her coffin. Andrew Kircher donated his services as undertaker, as well as the grave itself. Five hundred attended her service.[109]

Five years after the disaster, the Iroquois Memorial Association erected the unusual diamond-shaped monument over the grave of the unknown victim. In the years that followed, annual memorial services were held at the site every thirtieth of December.[110]

Nearby stands another extraordinary monument—the life-size statue of **Pastor Gotthilf J. Lambrecht** (1841–1918). Not only is the pastor himself rendered in granite but his customary surroundings are there as well—the balding, sad-eyed minister, dressed in flowing vestments and holding a prayer book, stands next to a full-sized pulpit, on which rests a Bible with a bookmark dangling in front, a cross at its end. At the rear and sides of the platform is a waist-high railing, all of this carved from the same grey granite.

Born in Prussia, Lambrecht immigrated to America shortly after graduating from seminary. After a brief stint in another church in Hoosiers Grove, Reverend Lambrecht became pastor of St. Peter's German Evangelical Lutheran Congregation in 1870,[111] remaining

---

[108] Troy Taylor, "Iroquois Theater Fire," Weird Chicago, http://www.weirdchicago.com/iroquois.html.

[109] "Last Laid at Rest: Only Unidentified Victim of the Iroquois Fire is Buried," *Chicago Daily Tribune*, June 13, 1904.

[110] "Last Laid at Rest."

[111] "History and Ministry of St. Peters UCC," St. Peter's United Church of Christ, http://saintpetes.net/HistoryandMinistryofStPetersUCC.dsp. The church was located at Cortez and Oakley in Rev. Lambrecht's day. At present it is St. Peter's United Church of

there for most of his 52 years as a clergyman. The beloved pastor's epitaph, emblazoned on the face of his stone pulpit, is *Er war ein Bote Gottes* ("He was a Messenger of God").

A distinguished crematorium and chapel building in the classical style graces the grounds at Montrose. Built in 1912, the chapel was designed by architect Fred V. Prather, inspired by the Portico of the Maidens on the Acropolis. A cupola once stood atop the chapel, until this was lost in a 1979 fire. Inside, an anteroom houses niches for ashes and leads to a three-story interior.[112] Two cremation retorts were installed on the lower level. On either side of the building, porticoes about seven feet off the ground house entombments beneath the floors, each one covered with a *ledger*, or grave-length slab of stone.

This remarkable monument, a life-sized granite statue, honors Lutheran pastor Gotthilf Lambrecht (1841–1918), a messenger of God.

Montrose Cemetery remains proudly independent today, owned and operated by the descendants of Andrew Kircher.[113]

Christ at 5450 W. Diversey. Upon his death Gotthilf Lambrecht was succeeded as pastor by his assistant, Henry Lambrecht (no relation).

[112] "History," Montrose Cemetery.

[113] "History," Montrose Cemetery.

CITY WEST

Receiving vault at Union Ridge Cemetery. These temporary tombs would store the remains of those who died during winter, until the ground thawed enough for a grave to be dug.

ALL SAINTS POLISH NATIONAL CATHOLIC CEMETERY

9201 West Higgins Road, Chicago
ascpncc.org
Established 1895

This Higgins Road burial ground was established to serve Chicago-area followers of the so-called Polish National Catholic Church. Since the beginning of Polish immigration to the United States, transplanted Poles had found fault with the American administration of the Roman Catholic Church, believing that its authority was overwhelmingly centered in Irish leaders. In Chicago, **Father Anthony Kozlowski** (1857–1907), assistant pastor of St. Hedwig's in Bucktown, took it upon himself to establish the Church of All Saints to serve potential congregants who felt disenfranchised by the established parish communities. In June of 1895, Fr. Kozlowski, suspended from his position at St. Hedwig's, declared the independence of "All Saints Polish Independent Church." For his efforts,

Cathedral church of All Saints parish, located next to the cemetery.

Kozlowski was ex-communicated by Archbishop Feehan.[114]

The renegade priest forged on, founding the Polish National Catholic Church and winning a devoted legion of followers. In September, the new parish purchased a 30-acre site on Higgins Road for their church. Initially, the land was to be used for a school, but almost immediately it was decided to create a cemetery instead. Father Kozlowski dedicated the cemetery on October 13, 1895. In 1897 he was consecrated a bishop in Bonn, Germany, by a group of bishops acting independently of Rome; this new title gave All Saints Church the status of a cathedral.

Though independent of Rome, All Saints is culturally Catholic, and crucifixes are a favorite monument design.

Bishop Kozlowski died in 1907 and was entombed in a sarcophagus here, with one of his successors eventually buried alongside. Visitors to All Saints Polish National Catholic should note that the cemetery includes a picnic area, one of only a handful of Chicago cemeteries to provide for the ethnic custom of picnicking at the graves of loved ones.

---

[114] "History," All Saints Cathedral Parish, http://ascpncc.org/files/ASC_History.pdf.

SAINT NICHOLAS UKRAINIAN CATHOLIC CEMETERY

8901 West Higgins Road, Chicago
www.stnicholaschicago.org
Established 1925

Though a Catholic Cemetery, this site is not under the jurisdiction of the Roman Church; rather, it belongs to the Ukrainian Greek Catholic Church, an Eastern Rite Catholic Church in full communion with the Holy See.[115] The affiliated parish, St. Nicholas Ukrainian Catholic Cathedral, is the mother church of the Ukrainian Catholic Eparchy (diocese) of Saint Nicholas of Chicago, which comprises the entire Western United States.[116]

Established in 1925, the cemetery serves five Ukrainian Catholic parishes in the metropolitan area. The principal monument, a towering stainless steel cross, was erected in 1940 to commemorate the 950th anniversary of Christianity in Ukraine.[117]

After World War II the Ukrainian population of Chicago grew rapidly, and the cemetery began to fill. By 1994 about 90 percent of the graves were occupied, prompting the Cathedral authorities to

Erected in 1940, this stainless steel cross commemorates 950 years of Ukrainian Christianity.

[115] "Ukrainian Greek Catholic Church," Wikipedia, http://en.wikipedia.org/wiki/Ukrainian_Greek_Catholic_Church.
[116] "Facts & Figures," Saint Nicholas Ukrainian Catholic Eparchy, http://esnucc.org/eparchy/eparchy/facts-figures.
[117] "Our Cemetery," St. Nicholas Ukrainian Catholic Cathedral, http://www.stnicholaschicago.org/#Our_Cemetery.

construct a mausoleum. This was completed by 1996 and dedicated on Memorial Day of that year.[118] At the southeast corner of the cemetery, only a few yards from I-90, it consists of a central chapel over which rises a round dome, itself topped with a smaller onion dome. Two wings, faced with garden crypts, project west and north from the main building, as if to embrace that corner of the cemetery.

The graveyard itself is a stunning sight; the graves are highly decorated, colorful, and lovingly tended. Grave markers emblazoned with suns, crosses, and images of saints are inscribed with epitaphs in English and Ukrainian, the latter in the Cyrillic alphabet. Monuments here are highly individual; they include such things as crosses made from pipe and grave covers of brick amidst the more common granite stones. Even the granite here looks amazing, with many of the inscriptions inked for better contrast.

ST. JOHANNES CEMETERY

O'Hare Airport Property
Established 1837, Removed 2011
www.stjohnsfamilyassistance.com

REST HAVEN CEMETERY

O'Hare Airport Property

Before the age of air travel, these two farmland cemeteries existed where O'Hare International Airport now sprawls. The founding date of St. Johannes, 1837, matches that of southwest suburban St. James-Sag, seeming to tie the two as the oldest Chicago-area cemeteries, though burials at St. James-Sag are assumed to have taken place before that cemetery's official founding.

A wistful sight at Rest Haven is the ruined monument over the grave of three-year-old **Laura Elfring** (1895–1898). The long-decap-

---

[118] "Our Cemetery," St. Nicholas Ukrainian Catholic Cathedral.

itated statue depicts a young girl holding a dove in her left hand. Also especially poignant is the round stone remembering the mere six days of life given to little **Emma Luehring** (May 11, 1903–May 17, 1903).

St. Johannes, located between a run-

Most of Rest Haven Cemetery can be seen in this photograph, taken after the O'Hare Modernization Project had begun.

way and the FedEx hangar, drew many curious visitors because of the churchyard's unique setting, but several spots within the graveyard always grabbed extra attention, including the monument to St. John's **Pastor William Boerner** and a row of four lectern-shaped markers dating to the 1890s. (The church changed from the German St. Johannes to the English St. John's a few decades ago, and both names are used interchangeably, especially when referring to the cemetery.) Also of interest was a large wooden cross at the north end of the cemetery, a twentieth-century addition marking the spot where the church once stood. In the 1950s the church was moved on wheels and stands today near the Bensenville Library at Route 83 and Foster Avenue.

Also drawing attention was the monument to **Henry Kolze**, leader of a prominent area family of innkeepers, town leaders, and abolitionists. Chicagoans may remember stories of Kolze's Electric Grove, where five-cent beer and a gaslit dance floor drew guests to what is now Merrimac Park at Irving Park and Narragansett.

Joining these founders at St. Johannes were the **Dierklings**, blueberry famers who created orchards out of the former prairie here on the site of the United Airlines terminal, and for whom "Orchard Field Airport" was named. Travelers know that ORD is still the airport code for O'Hare, taking its letters from "Orchard Field."

Until the 1950s, residents of this rural area enjoyed quiet visits to their local cemeteries, the nearby airport generally minding its own business. When the city took over the airport, however, officials annexed the land around it, re-naming the field in honor of Chicago World War II veteran, Edward "Butch" O'Hare. The annexed land included the three cemeteries. One of them, Wilmer's Old Settlers Cemetery—a former Native American burial ground—was shuttered, the graves moved in part to adjoining Rest Haven, and others to Oak Ridge in Westmont. The remaining cemeteries (Rest Haven and St. Johannes) soon became decidedly unrestful, but great for plane spotters. Despite the air traffic, the ossuaries continued to operate into the twenty-first century. Then, with the city's ever-growing visions for O'Hare, their existence was once again—and this time fatally—threatened.

In August of 2003, St. Johannes and Rest Haven found themselves at the heart of a brutal legal battle, when the city's O'Hare Modernization Act was passed, seizing the cemetery land for O'Hare Airport expansion. Known as the "cemetery runway," the proposed Runway 10 Center/28 Center was slated to cut right through the old burial grounds, and so plans ensued to contact the families of the deceased with instructions to prepare for disinterment and removal of their loved ones. Almost immediately the St. Johannes Cemetery Alliance was formed, headed by the Reverend Michael Kirchoff, pastor of St. Johannes Church, to stop the seizure and removal. He was joined by the very vocal Bob Sell, a congregant with five generations buried at St. Johannes. At Rest Haven, a different tac-

Also known as St. John's Cemetery, St. Johannes was located only a few hundred feet from O'Hare's runways, allowing for spectacular views of planes about to land.

Planes at the Southwest Cargo Area loomed over the cemetery, just across the access road.

tic was tried when the Native American community attempted to invoke the Native American Grave Protection and Reparation Act to protect the Potawatomi graves believed to have been moved there when Wilmer's was closed.

In 2010, the trial court that heard the lawsuit filed on behalf of the dead awarded the City of Chicago ownership of the St. Johannes property. Despite further appeals with the Appellate Courts, the cemeteries found little sympathy.

As descendants wrung their hands and pushed for legal hope, the city continued to refer critics to the O'Hare Modernization Act, which exempted the city from complying with state laws, including the Illinois Human Skeletal Remains Protection Act, the Illinois Archaeological and Paleontological Resources Protection Act, and even the Illinois Municipal Code.

The cemetery was separated from the airport by a high fence with razor wire at the top.

When the Illinois Supreme Court refused to hear the case on further appeal, the remaining disinterment of the approximately 1,400 burials at St. Johannes resumed. Rest Haven withdrew from the fight after the plan for a cargo bay on the property was scrapped, allowing the burial ground to remain.

The first disinterment had been done in 2009, for the Geils Funeral Home, which had arranged for the Chicora Foundation, an archaeological firm, to conduct the excavations of the burial sites and provide an extensive report on the human and material remains of the burials. These excavations led to much turmoil for family members, as they were informed that coffins had largely rotted, having been buried in an age where vaults were not commonly used, and

This cross identifies the former site of St. Johannes Church. The first church here was constructed in 1849. The second, built in 1873, was moved in 1952 to Route 83 at Foster Avenue. The cross was moved to Eden Memorial Park after the cemetery's destruction.

the remains of their loved ones had substantially mixed with the soil. When other families, then, reached the point of disinterment, heated arguments arose between the city—with its heavy machinery and orders to remove—and family members who wanted to be at the gravesites when the disinterment occurred. Loved ones and descendants wanted to be sure that all soil was removed along with the remains, as well as to hold religious services at the time of the removals.

Another serious issue was where the remains would be relocated. Many pushed for a new cemetery to be opened, so that all the burials could be kept together. Others simply wanted their loved ones moved to family plots at existing cemeteries. Reports arose that the city had been working with Mount Emblem and other cemeteries to push loved ones to move their loved ones before the court battle was settled. Other confusion arose when unrelated cemeteries contacted family members with offers to bury their dead in special sections they were creating for the St. Johannes dead. In the end, the city agreed to efforts to keep as many burials together as possible, and so the Alliance worked with family members to decide on an existing cemetery for reinterment of the burials in a common location. The site chosen was Eden Memorial Park in Schiller Park, which created an "Old St. Johannes" section, featuring the cross and memorial marker from the original airport location, as well as whatever markers could be rescued from the original site. The majority of reinterments occurred at this site or at Mount Emblem, though a good number of family members chose to reinter their loved ones at alternate locations.

The completion of the so-called "cemetery runway" is slated for 2013.

ROBINSON WOODS INDIAN BURIAL GROUND
Robinson Woods North, East River Road at Lawrence Avenue, Chicago

This Native American burial ground is part of the Forest Preserve District of Cook County's far Northwest Side holdings. The burial ground is easily accessed by pulling into the site's own wayside at Lawrence Avenue and East River Road and is subject to the same visitation rules as other FPD property. At one time, travelers on a nearby highway were drawn here by a sign inviting sightseers to "a real Indian cemetery," but today only a Forest Preserve District sign at the wayside along with a battered showcase full of worn and faded documents hint at the wealth of history at this storied site.

Alexander Robinson is also known as Chief Che-Che-Pin-Qua

("Blinking Eye") and was one of the most active and important players in pre-founding Chicago. A leader of the Potawatomi, Ottawa, and Chippewa tribes, Robinson profoundly enhanced relations between the native and early white residents of the city in a time when stresses between them threatened new wars at every turn. Best known for ferrying Anglos to Michigan—and safety—during the time of the 1812 Fort Dearborn Massacre, Robinson was awarded by the Treaty of Prairie du Chien a large segment of land and an annuity for his role in the negotiations. According to Chicago-area archaeologist and Robinson family historian Dan Melone, however, Robinson was also given this land because he helped the government secure the lead mines in Galena, Illinois, thus giving the government control over the mines and the procurement of lead for the production of ammunition.

But the land awarded by the Treaty, a beautiful expanse of woodlands along the Des Plaines River, became the family farmsteads and burial ground. The farmsteads remained into the mid-twentieth century, when the last of the family homes burned in a 1955 fire that led, eventually, to the bulldozing and torching of the remaining farm structures. And while the burials of Robinson, his second

A single red granite boulder, one side smoothed to provide a place for the inscription, is the only monument on the family burial grounds of the Native American chieftain known to Westerners as Alexander Robinson.

wife, Catherine Chevalier, and a number of descendants remain, the original marble and concrete markers have disappeared, replaced by a single stone boulder bearing the story of Alexander Robinson and his ties to this land…and to Chicago and American history. But very little of Robinson's real story is recorded here. And neither is the legend of the family's troubled tenure on this land.

Hailing from the Perth area of Scotland, Robinson's ancestors were Highlanders who traced their genealogy back to a Viking called Ivan the Black, who at one time aspired to invade England. The king caught wind of it and sent his people with money and gifts to try to hold Ivan off. Ivan greeted the King's men, confiscated the booty, and cut off the heads of messengers, sending back a message to their King that read, "Do not ever send a second in command to do the job of a King. The next head rolling will be yours." The King packed up and fled the country leaving Ivan to walk in without a fight.

Unlike his ancestor, Chicago's Robinson became known for his peacemaking, creating and fostering alliances between the native peoples of the prairie and the encroaching white settlers throughout the turbulent nineteenth century. In addition to his work in Chicago, Robinson was called on occasion to Springfield, Illinois, by up-and-coming attorney Abraham Lincoln to consult on various land trials, as Robinson was highly informed about Chicago property and knew all the key players of the day.

Robinson moved among local, state, and national circles with ease. At one point he was hired by the federal government to take 35 men in pursuit of Chief Blackhawk. The team left on the trail of the ferocious leader, trailing him into Wisconsin, where he was brought to his demise along the Mississippi River bluffs.

Though Robinson lived in town (in a home in present-day Schiller Park just recently torn down), his descendants lived a robust life on the land now popularly known as "Robinson Woods." But as they farmed and canned and raised their children, as the rest of their neighbors did, unsavory legends of the Robinson family abounded throughout the first half of the twentieth century. Locals often talked of rowdy parties, drunken brawls, and carousing on the enigmatic

"Indian land." Stories even circulated that debaucherous Indians had burned down the last house during a particularly devilish escapade, or that the City of Chicago had staged a fire to force the ne'er-do-well Robinsons off the site.

Ironically, according to Verlyn "Buzz" Spreeman, authorized historian of the Robinson family (and himself a Robinson descendent), most of the family followed Alexander's lead and did not drink. Robinson himself was a teetotaler and never touched liquor, though he ran the quite prosperous first tavern in Chicago, the inn at Wolf's Point at the mouth of the Chicago River. The only one of the descendants who did drink was one of Robinson's great-grandsons, a colorful character who was often found sleeping in the basement of local homes and businesses, including Schiller Park's Great Escape Restaurant, still in operation today. As for the mysterious conflagration, it was a kitchen fire, started accidentally by an aging Catherine Boettcher, one of Robinson's granddaughters and the last descendent to live on the land.

Along with his abstinence, another surprising fact about Alexander Robinson was that he was a Roman Catholic. During the drafting of the Treaty of Prairie Du Chein in 1829, Robinson tried, without success, to have six sections of North Side Chicago land deeded to the church.

Today, the Robinsons have mysteriously vanished from the land deeded "forever" to the descendants of one of the most influential personalities in Chicago's history. All that remains are a few farm furrows, visible after controlled burns, a rusted section of farm fence here and there, and a boulder to mark the remains of the old family cemetery. Where the tombstones went we may never know, where the property title went is anyone's guess.

Despite the glaring absence of Robinsons here, the preserve and the burial ground are considered extremely sacred ground by the Robinson family descendants and Native Americans as a whole. Both groups ask your profound respect if you visit.

READ-DUNNING MEMORIAL PARK
Belle Plaine Avenue, west of Narragansett Avenue, Chicago
Established 1854

From 1851 through 1910, an expanse of land at Irving Park Road and Narragansett Avenue in the then-suburb of Dunning was utilized by the county as a hospital, tuberculosis sanitarium, insane asylum, and poor farm, with burials from the dead of each institution taking place on the grounds. Though much of the land was built over, use of portions of the land as a mental health facility and children's home has continued into the twenty-first century. The facility today operates under the name of Chicago-Read Mental Health Facility, located on Oak Park Avenue just west of the memorial park, though the complex has come to public scandal time and again, charged with unsanitary conditions, unnecessary restraint of patients, neglect of mentally disabled children, and other atrocities.

As for the larger property of the original asylum, only in recent years were the abandoned portions of the old site unearthed—including human remains—during the break-up of land for the building of Wright College, the Ridgemoor Estates residences, and a shopping complex called Dunning Square.

The complex known for a century as simply "Dunning" was first opened as a county poorhouse in 1851, a place where indigent individuals and families lived and worked an adjoining farm. The Dunning poor farm sprawled over more than 150 acres owned by Peter Ludby, a farmer whose rights to the land were that of a squatter's, circa 1839. Seven years after the poor farm opened, the Cook County Insane Asylum was completed on the acreage, directed by a Dr. D.B. Fonda. From the beginning, under-financing and overcrowding were problems. Despite the inadequate resources, the need for a larger facility became increasingly apparent and, in 1871, the year of the Great Fire, a new structure was completed that was serving around 600 patients by 1885.

Two fires at the hospital, in 1912 and 1923, destroyed great portions of the asylum structures and sent the city into a panic when, each time, a number of inmates escaped from the grounds. New construction soon began to replace the destroyed infirmary buildings and, in the summer of 1912, Cook County transferred the property and institution to the State of Illinois. The name was officially changed to Chicago State Hospital, though, for Chicagoans, the "Dunning" moniker would always remain,

A new entrance arch was erected in 2005 at the site of the once-forgotten Cook County Poor Farm cemetery, now called Read-Dunning Memorial Park.

its name calling up to this day fearful images of the hopelessly insane, retained under the most horrific conditions.

In the late 1980s, Pontarelli Brothers, a prolific Chicago real estate developer, purchased the land with the intention of building a residential community on the old Dunning grounds. When digging began, workers began uncovering human remains in astonishing numbers.

Archaeologists at Loyola University were hired to excavate, and many university students volunteered to assist in the painstaking process. It was revealed that at least three separate cemeteries had occupied the land, containing remains from a variety of sources.

Records had shown that in 1876, 633 bodies were buried at Dunning, including those from hospitals, an orphanage, a house of corrections, and a "home for the friendless." Adding to the burial site were unclaimed victims from the Great Fire and penniless veterans of the Civil War, the dead of the poor farm, and Dunning inmates who had perished as patients. Many among them were the bodies from the potter's field at the original City Cemetery in Lincoln Park, which were reportedly moved to the poor farm after the cem-

Inside the entrance, a large concrete disc with boulders and bronze plaques provides visitors with a history of the site. At its center is a fragment of the dedication stone of the 1884 Cook County Infirmary building, one of several institutions that buried its dead on the site.

etery was closed.

Read-Dunning Memorial Park, the only memorial to the Dunning dead, was built on a three-acre tract of land set aside for re-interment of the remains found at the Dunning site, and today the site is reportedly complete. The final design reveals a snaking pathway through grass, fenced off from surrounding industrial and condominium complexes, connected by seven concrete circles, here and there decorated with artifacts from the old Dunning complex. At its dedication on December 18, 2001, the remains of the 182 disturbed graves were reburied in an official memorial service to dedicate the park.

Visitors to the area and students of history, however, should be aware of the fact that researchers still place the likely body count on the larger Dunning property at around 38,000—all but those 182 moved to Read-Dunning Park presumably plowed under and built over by developers.

IRVING PARK CEMETERY

7777 West Irving Park Road, Chicago
www.irvingparkcemetery.com
Established 1918

Irving Park Cemetery's main entrance and office.

At the western edge of Chicago, where Irving Park Road meets the city limits, three adjacent cemeteries were laid out in the first half of the twentieth century. The first of these was Irving Park Cemetery, a modern, non-denominational lawn park cemetery.

Brothers-with-arms **Frank Gusenberg** (1892–1929) and **Peter Gusenberg** (1889–1929) were buried at this Chicago cemetery after being fatally tommy-gunned in the St. Valentine's Day Massacre. As members of the O'Banion/Weiss/Moran North Side gang, the brothers were a tough pair. In fact, Frank actually lived through the massacre, surviving long enough to make it to the hospital. Riddled with machine gun fire and utterly doomed, he was questioned there by police about the identity of the assailants. But Gusenberg refused to rat. In answer to the pleas of desperate detectives for an identification, Frank replied simply and scowlingly, "I ain't no copper." They would be his last words.

Typical of twentieth-century cemeteries, monuments at Irving Park are almost entirely granite in a variety of colors, surrounded by lawn-level markers. The cemetery also offers above-ground entombment in a garden-crypt mausoleum.

ACACIA PARK CEMETERY
7800 West Irving Park Road, Norridge
Established 1923

Between Irving Park Cemetery and Westlawn Cemetery, at Chicago's city limits on the Northwest Side, is Acacia Park, a memorial park cemetery steeped in Masonic symbolism. Graves are marked by simple granite "pillow" markers, uniform in size, rising about six inches above the ground. The landscape is dominated by two towering grey granite obelisks, set atop small hills and decorated with Masonic symbols in tribute to the cemetery's origins. Before each obelisk is a marble statue of a woman, each next to a broken granite column. One, gazing upwards with a book in her hand, is titled "Faith." The other, leaning on the column, looks down contemplatively while holding a palm frond, symbol of triumph over death.

Between the obelisks is Acacia Park's most remarkable feature: a huge, sprawling mausoleum of classical design, set in a beautifully landscaped formal garden. Marble steps lead down from the level of the cemetery to the sunken garden, where a wide path of reddish-brown pebbles surrounds a fountain. Garden-crypt walls at the rear and sides provide a sense of privacy and solitude, while not impeding

The principal monuments at Acacia Park are two identical obelisks, each atop a small hill. The Masonic square-and-compass symbol appears on the front of each shaft, and marble statues stand in front.

This marble statue stands before one of the two obelisks.

the spectacular view of the mausoleum's facade.

The mausoleum was constructed in 1927 and later rededicated to the memory of cemetery founder and mausoleum builder, **Street Lightfoot** (1880–1955). From the garden, steps lead up to a heavy bronze door between Ionic columns. The main level is clad almost entirely in white marble. At its center, below a skylight, is a large chapel with wooden pews facing a speaker's dais, at the rear of which a marble throne is decorated with the Masonic square and compass emblem. A Masonic Bible stands open on a nearby table. Small private burial chambers are on all sides of the chapel and entrance hall. One of them encloses a free-standing sarcophagus housing **Charles M. Hayes** (1877–1957) and **Ella Mae Hayes** (1880–1958). Charles Hayes was president of the Chicago Motor Club, one of several local motorists' organizations that in 1902 banded together to form the AAA.

Descending to the lower level, the visitor encounters newer sec-

A formal garden provides for a breathtaking view of the mausoleum, built in 1927. Garden-crypt walls are visible at rear and sides.

tions of the mausoleum. With walls and crypt faces fashioned from a variety of colors of marble, and some sections paneled with wood, this level feels warmer and more welcoming than the severely monochromatic upper level. In one crypt on the ground floor is journalist and columnist **Mike Royko** (1932–1997). Another holds **Ral Donner** (1943–1984), singer of "You Don't Know What You've Got (Until You Lose It)." At the very top of the mausoleum is a long, narrow room accessible only by a cramped, ancient elevator, barely large enough to accommodate a coffin. Among those forever secluded here is **Alvah Roebuck** (1864–1948), business partner of Richard Sears.[119]

One marker outside the mausoleum is a favorite among Chicago cemetery explorers: the cenotaph of **Herman Schuenemann** (~1865–1912), the so-called "Christmas Tree Captain," who each December would bring loads of freshly-cut evergreens from Michigan to Chicago, selling them to the public directly from his ship, the *Rouse Simmons*. It was on one such voyage that the three-masted schooner, heavily laden with three to five thousand trees in the hold

---

[119] Sears is entombed in the community mausoleum at Rosehill.

In addition to the mausoleum, the cemetery has a separate columbarium and crematory building. Niches for cremated remains are set into the interior walls.

and on the decks, disappeared in a wintry Lake Michigan gale. It would be almost 60 years before divers found the wreckage.[120] Herman's widow **Barbara Schuenemann** (1865–1933) continued the business until her death. Their story inspired a musical production, *The Christmas Schooner*, which continues to draw crowds in Chicago-area theaters. Though the grave is Barbara's alone, as Herman's body was lost, both names appear on the red granite headstone, along with an illustration of a Christmas tree.

WESTLAWN CEMETERY

7801 West Montrose Avenue, Chicago
westlawncemetery.org
Established 1937

During the latter half of the nineteenth century when Chicago experienced its second wave of Jewish immigration, Jewish cemeteries were characterized by a strict sectionalization of groups, according to membership in various synagogues, fraternities, *Vereins* (societies), or *Landsmanschaften* (compatriot associations). By the 1920s, however, newly-founded burial grounds were following the lead of patrons of

---

[120] Glenn V. Longacre, "The Christmas Tree Ship: Captain Herman E. Schuenemann and the Schooner *Rouse Simmons*," *Prologue Magazine*, Vol. 38. No. 4, Winter 2006.

non-Jewish cemeteries, who were opting for individual or family plots over communal burial based on spiritual or secular affiliations. Westlawn is a good example of this shift in practice: The amply-spaced, individual markers are typically grouped with those of other family members, and the majority of inscriptions are in English.

A number of luminaries of the entertainment industry repose at Westlawn, including some unique contributors to American culture.

In 1924, Chicago's Savoy Ballroom at South Park and Kedzie avenues had fallen on hard times, and in order to draw better crowds, the hall's owners began holding basketball games before the dances. Twenty-four-year-old **Abe Saperstein** (1902–1966) begged the Savoy to sponsor his new team. When they did, he dubbed it the Savoy Big Five. The idea flopped, but the team of Tommy Brookings, William Grant, Lester Johnson, Walter Wright, Inman Jackson, Joe Lillard, William Watson, and Randolph Ramsey wanted to stay together. Saperstein took them on the road in his Model T Ford. They made their debut on January 7, 1927, in Hinckley, Illinois, sporting hand-me-down jerseys emblazoned with *New York*. Later, Saperstein added one more word to the jersey, and a sensation was born: Saperstein's *New York Globetrotters*.

The rest, as they say, is history.

Joining Saperstein at Westlawn is quintessential movie reviewer **Gene Siskel** (1946–1999). Falling victim to complications from a brain tumor, the Chicago-bred personality died in early 1999, leav-

Westlawn's landscaping includes this carefully-sculpted artificial pond, spanned by a graceful white bridge.

A dramatic departure from traditional cemetery ornamentation is this organic-
looking sculpture by Dionicio Rodriguez, called "Shady Rest."

ing behind a legion of filmgoers left to turn to his partner in criticism, Roger Ebert, for reel-time recommendations. Siskel was raised
by his aunt and uncle after his parents died when he was nine years
old. Attending Yale University, the enthusiastic Gene got a job with
the *Chicago Tribune* two years after his graduation in 1967. In the
mid-1970s, Siskel joined forces with Ebert to create the local public
television movie-review program, *Sneak Previews*. After seven years,
the pair sold their concept into syndication when their locally-pop-
ular banter clicked with national
audiences. Carried along by Siskel and Ebert's good-natured
competitive criticism, the show
went on to become a major influence on box-office draws during
the 80s and 90s.

Nightclub owner **Jack Ruby**
(1911–1967) finally eluded the
press here at Westlawn. Ruby
was born and buried in Chicago.

Two days after the shooting of President
Kennedy, a horrified nation watched
Jack Ruby (1911–1967) murder Lee
Harvey Oswald on live TV. He died of
cancer three years later.

In between, he ran numbers for Al Capone's crowd and assassinated Lee Harvey Oswald.

And, playing for the other side on the other side: Westlawn resident **Albert N. "Wallpaper" Wolff** (1903–1998), one of Eliot Ness's legendary crew, whose grave marker identifies him as *Last of the FBI Untouchables*.

TOGETHER FOREVER: THE MANY TIES THAT BIND

The impetus towards group identification is not limited to this life. In fact, perhaps nowhere is the insistence on set-apartedness more obvious than in the modern cemetery.

In Chicago, as elsewhere, religious differences demanded the first divisions. Catholics and Protestants insisted on separate burial grounds during the establishment of the earliest municipal cemeteries. After the closing of these graveyards and the opening of new Catholic, Protestant, Jewish, and non-sectarian sites, ethnic prejudice began to emerge. German Catholics, for example, shuddered at the Irish overtones of the Diocesan cemetery, Calvary, in Evanston, opting instead to establish the burial grounds of St. Boniface and St. Maria as bluntly Germanic. And even within these exclusive enclosures segregation continued, the dead being clustered according to membership in military organizations, singing societies, and other groups. Jewish cemeteries, too, were obsessed with division, erecting rigid gated fences between the sections owned by differing congregations and social groups.

In the so-called non-sectarian cemeteries of Graceland, Rosehill, and Oak Woods, among others, another kind of self-sorting is evident: The class structure of late nineteenth-

and early twentieth-century Chicago could be easily mapped today by simply noting the names of those buried in the posh central sections—encrusted with marble, lavishly landscaped, and refreshed with pools and lakes—and those recorded on the modest markers and closely-crowded flush stones skirting the grounds.

Obvious, too, is the everlasting bond of brotherhood, made tangible at death by the erection of common monuments by the Freemasons, the Order of the Eastern Star, the Woodmen, the Elks, the Odd Fellows, the Rebekah Lodge, and other fraternities and sister organizations.

Careers, too, often set graves apart. Modern cemeteries are rife with group burials of military divisions, police and fire personnel, members of religious orders, railroad workers, and even waiters and bartenders. In west suburban Woodlawn Cemetery, a large section dubbed "Showmen's Rest" is set aside for the burial of circus performers.

Sadly, but because misery loves company, victims of tragedies are sometimes gathered together as well. Witness, for example, the heart-wrenching local cemetery memorials to the Iroquois Theatre fire, the capsizing of the *Eastland* steamer, and the devastating conflagration at Our Lady of the Angels parish school, among too many others. And the new children's sections at many burial grounds—rich with gifts of toys, candy, balloons, and comic books—attest to the particularly poignant commonality of their silent residents.

MOUNT OLIVE CEMETERY

3800 North Narragansett Avenue, Chicago
www.mountolivecemetery.com
Established 1889

The entrance archway, one of few such structures to remain intact. A bell in the tower is rung when funeral processions pass through the gates.

Claiming the largest section of an impressive cemetery complex, Mt. Olive shares a piece of Chicago with the adjacent Zion Gardens Cemetery.

Strollers in late–nineteenth century Mt. Olive will come upon the obsolete railroad grade that once served trains traveling to and from the old Cook County Poor Farm and Insane Asylum, located until 1910 near the area now known as Dunning Square.

Like the entrance arch, the cemetery's original 1889 chapel was built of yellow limestone in a medieval architectural style.

Originally founded for Chicago's Scandinavians, as evidenced by the delightful Viking drinking fountain near the entry arch, the cemetery has more recently hosted the burials of Latvians, Armenians, and other ethnic groups.

While there is no shortage of mourners here, an extremely uncommon glass mausoleum draws many cemetery buffs as well to this eclectic site.

Evidence of the cemetery's Scandinavian heritage is this Viking-themed drinking fountain just inside the entrance, near a monument display.

UNION RIDGE CEMETERY
6700 West Higgins Road, Chicago
Established 1841/1875

Though it was incorporated with the State of Illinois in 1875, Union Ridge's use as a graveyard dates back far further. Pioneer farmer Henry Smith, who donated the land, was the first to be buried here in 1841. Initially called "Smith's Ridge" by mapmakers, due to it being located on a high glacial ridge, the cemetery became Union Ridge when about 67 Civil War soldiers were buried here.[121]

---

[121] Chicago Genealogical Society, "The History of Union Ridge Cemetery," *Union Ridge Cemetery*, 1995.

The original pioneer cemetery makes up the northeast corner of the present cemetery. The southernmost portion, including the site of the present main entrance, was initially a separate cemetery, Norwood Park Cemetery (established 1904). The trustees of the new Norwood Park Cemetery, however, seem to have almost immediately lost interest in the project. By 1913 their sole remaining representative, a Henry Smith descendant who had relocated to Colorado, was looking to sell. The land was then acquired by the Union Ridge Cemetery Association and made a part of Union Ridge Cemetery. A brick chapel and administrative building was built in the newly-acquired south portion of the cemetery in 1916.[122]

The cemetery includes a small receiving vault, built in 1902.

Like the name of the cemetery itself, this cannon at Union Ridge honors veterans of the Civil War, buried in the adjacent plot.

ZION GARDENS CEMETERY
3600 North Narragansett Avenue, Chicago
www.ziongardenscemetery.com

Chicago's earliest Jewish immigrants called themselves "Men of the West," identifying not with their Bavarian homeland but with the new American frontier they had chosen for their future. *Kehilath Anshe Maariv*, "Congregation of the Men of the West," was founded in

---

[122] "The History of Union Ridge Cemetery."

1847 when the Jewish population numbered under a hundred and held its first meetings in a room above a shop.[123] Yet even before the Jewish pioneers had formed their first congregation, they had need for a graveyard. The first Jewish organization of any kind in the frontier town was the Jewish Burial Ground Society, which in 1846 purchased a single acre on the north side of North Avenue near the lake shore, creating Chicago's first Jewish cemetery.[124]

Like the other lakeside cemeteries, this site was inadequate—the harsh winds and ever-shifting sands disturbed the graves. Under the authority of *Kehilath Anshe Maariv* (KAM), which had absorbed the burial ground society, the graveyard was relocated in 1856 to the southwest corner of Belmont and Clark—today a thriving intersection filled with young people out for a night on the town. By 1893 the congregation had moved its dead a second time, to the northwest part of the city, as Mount Mayriv Cemetery.[125]

Mount Mayriv[126] was the first of five adjacent Jewish cemeteries sharing a 50-acre site at Narragansett and Addison in the Dunning community area, immediately south of Mount Olive, a Lutheran cemetery. It was soon joined by other congregations, setting up smaller cemeteries immediately west of Mount Mayriv, and finally by a modern park cemetery, Rosemont Park, at the western edge of the property. The oldest graves, reburials from the earlier cemetery, are thought to be in section F in the northeast corner. Though mostly illegible, at least one of these stones indicates a death date of 1857.[127]

Mount Mayriv, at 20 acres the largest of the five cemeteries, was designed as a rural cemetery with gently curving roads intended to showcase the beauty of the landscape. Plots and monument placement follow the curve of the roadways rather than a uniform grid. Monu-

---

[123] Cutler, *The Jews of Chicago*, 10.

[124] Ibid.

[125] Simon, *Chicago, the Garden City*, 147. Simon described it in 1893 as a 20-acre site, "the cemetery of the *Anshe Mayrive* congregation," located "in Jefferson in the neighborhood of the Cook County Poor House."

[126] The literature almost universally prefers the spelling "Maariv" for the name of the congregation, from the Hebrew word for "west," but the name of the cemetery on the signs is "Mayriv." I have elected to keep both spellings as the respective sources give them.

[127] "Jewish Cemeteries," JewishGen, http://www.jewishgen.org/infofiles/chicago/cemeteries.htm#Rosemont Park.

ments are generally Victorian in design, with urns, obelisks, columns, and funerary symbols such as the sarcophagus and inverted torch.

On the eastern edge of the site, the entrance to Mount Mayriv is flanked by a pair of massive granite blocks with "Mount Mayriv Cemetery" engraved on the face of each, and on top a steel menorah of sleek modern design. To the left of the entrance stands a small office of red brick. Next to the office is a memorial to governor **Henry Horner** (1878–1940). Born as Henry Levy, he took his mother's surname after his parents' divorce, and pursued a career in the law, serving for 18 years as probate court judge. In 1932 Horner campaigned for the governor's office as a Democrat, and upon winning election became the first Jewish governor of Illinois. Though he won a second term in 1936, a heart condition limited his activity for his last two years, during which he tried to fulfill his gubernatorial role as best he could while keeping physical activity limited. He died at his home in Winnetka, where he had gone to rest in the hopes of regaining his strength, and was succeeded in office by Lieutenant Governor John Stelle from downstate Hamilton County.[128]

Governor Horner's funeral was held in an artillery armory on Chicago Avenue, attended by more than 7,500 mourners and dignitaries.[129] President Roosevelt sent a floral wreath. Horner had been a member of Sinai Temple, and its rabbi, Dr. Louis Mann, presided over the funeral alongside other local religious leaders. The governor, a lifelong bachelor, was buried alongside his mother, **Dilah Horner Levy**, in the family plot at Mount Mayriv. One year later, in a public ceremony, a cenotaph was also installed, not at Horner's gravesite, but at the front of the cemetery near the office. The cenotaph is a block of brown South Dakota granite standing before a flag pole,[130] with benches of the same material on either side and a bronze plaque on the front listing Horner's achievements.

Governor Horner's maternal grandparents **Henry Horner** and-

[128] "Gov. Henry Horner Is Dead," *Chicago Daily Tribune*, October 6, 1940.

[129] "7,550 Pay Their Final Tribute to Gov. Horner: Hailed as Martyr to Cause of Good Government," *Chicago Daily Tribune*, October 9, 1940.

[130] "Plan Dedication of Memorial to Horner Sunday," *Chicago Daily Tribune*, October 10, 1941.

Governor Henry Horner's cenotaph was placed in a prominent location near the entrance; his actual grave has a much smaller monument. Behind it, the two menorahs on granite blocks on either side of the entrance may be seen.

Hannah Dernberg Horner[131] are buried around a mighty obelisk, its front decorated by a calligraphic "H" within a wreath. Another obelisk of similar size lies fallen on the ground several sections away: the **Sloss** monument, apparent victim of vandalism or shifting ground, was broken into two pieces, each far too heavy to put back into position without specialized equipment.

The obelisk of millionaire dry-goods merchant **Jacob Rosenberg** (1819–1900),[132] one of the earliest Jewish settlers of Chicago,[133] occupies a prime spot at the exact center of the cemetery, standing in the center of a small circular section from which the other roads radiate. In 1849 he married **Hannah Reese** in Chicago's first Jew-

---

[131] "Cook County, Illinois, Deaths Index, 1878–1922," Ancestry.com, http://www.ancestry. com. The names on Dilah Horner Levy's death record match those surrounding the Horner obelisk.

[132] "Death of Jacob Rosenberg: Pioneer Merchant of Chicago Passes Away," *Chicago Daily Tribune*, March 30, 1900.

[133] Peter Wiernik, *History of the Jews in America: From the Period of the Discovery of the New World to the Present Time*, (New York: The Jewish Press Publishing Company, 1912), 150.

ish wedding.[134] Their son **Joseph Rosenberg**, who predeceased his father in 1891, bequeathed to the city the Rosenberg Fountain in Grant Park, with its bronze statue of water-bearer Hebe. The fountain recalls the younger Rosenberg's days as a newsboy when local merchants would not give him a drink of water. He vowed that if he were to become wealthy, he would provide a fountain from which the newsboys of the city could freely drink.[135]

Other notable monuments include the **Kohn** family memorial, a sarcophagus decorated with ornate scrollwork, garlands, and inverted torches in the finest Victorian funerary tradition, and the **Schoenstadt** mausoleum, sitting on a foundation several steps above ground level, with an intricately detailed arch over its door.

The monument of architect Dankmar Adler, a column from his recently-demolished music hall. Its twin stands at Rosehill.

A two-story red granite column with a Corinthian-inspired capital boasts an impressive history. It was one of two that originally flanked the entrance of the Central Music Hall. It now marks the grave of the architect of that theater, **Dankmar Adler** (1844–1900). Born in Germany, Adler came as a child to Chicago with his father, **Dr. Liebman Adler** (1812–1892), who for nearly 20 years was rabbi of KAM,[136] and who was also buried at this cemetery.[137]

[134] Cutler, *The Jews of Chicago*, 8.

[135] "Rosenberg Fountain (in Grant Park)," Explore Chicago: The City of Chicago's Official Tourism Site, http://www.choosechicago.com/articles/view/WEST-NEAR-SOUTH-NORTH/316/.

[136] Cutler, *The Jews of Chicago*, 174.

[137] "Funeral of Rabbi L. Adler," *Chicago Daily Tribune*, February 1, 1892. The article states

The younger Adler enlisted in the Union Army and was wounded at Chickamauga.[138] He trained as an engineer and architect, working with several partners until beginning his own firm. In 1880 Adler hired Louis Henri Sullivan,[139] making the latter a partner in 1883. It was this collaboration that enabled both men to realize their greatest works. Adler & Sullivan designed and constructed great public buildings that continue to be highly praised today for their originality and aesthetic excellence—among them the Auditorium Building, the Chicago Stock Exchange, and the Wainright Building in St. Louis. Adler and Sullivan were noteworthy also as mentors of their much younger employee, Frank Lloyd Wright, who would go on to great fame of his own, and had nothing but praise for his former employers.

Dankmar Adler died in April 1900, at about the same time as one of his early public buildings, the Central Music Hall, was being demolished to make way for the flagship store of Marshall Field & Company. The columns on either side of the main entrance were rescued by Edwin Walker, a building contractor and limestone quarry owner who had become a friend of Adler when they worked together to build the music hall in 1879. One of these columns, with its original base, was placed at Adler's grave at Mount Mayriv. The other, somewhat modified and with the addition of a large ball on top, decorates Walker's grave at Rosehill.[140]

A much more modest monument marks the grave of influential community organizer **Saul Alinsky** (1909–1972),[141] author of *Rules for Radicals*, a "pragmatic primer" published in 1971 for idealistic young people seeking to change the world, a leftist counterpart to Machiavelli's *The Prince*. Alinsky is widely credited, by people on both

---

"the remains of Rabbi Liebman Adler were born to their last resting place yesterday in the cemetery of the Congregation Kehilath Anshe Maariv, at Dunning."

[138] Cutler, *The Jews of Chicago*, 21.

[139] Sullivan is buried at Graceland.

[140] Norman D. Schwartz, "A Tale of Two Columns," *Chicago Jewish History*, Summer 1995, Chicago Jewish Historical Society, http://chicagojewishhistory.org/pdf/2011/CJH.3.2011_web.pdf.

[141] Phyllis Magida, "To See Art, Find Tranquility, Cemeteries Are for the Living," *Chicago Tribune*, September 6, 1985.

ends of the political spectrum, as a major influence on Chicago-based community organizer, and future U.S. president, Barack Obama.

West of Mount Mayriv are three smaller graveyards, laid out as four parallel rectangles,[142] stacked north to south, spanning roughly the same distance from east to west. The landscape design is simpler than that of Mount Mayriv. Rather than sweeping curvatures, the roads are straight lines that meet at right angles, with the exception of a teardrop-shaped feature in the southern portion. Isaiah Israel (established c. 1886) is the southernmost of these small cemeteries, having an entrance on Addison Street next to the maintenance building. Next, proceeding north, is B'nai B'rith Cemetery (established c. 1887), then Mount Jehoshua (established c. 1899), and finally a second Isaiah Israel section.[143]

Rosemont Park Cemetery (established c. 1933),[144] a modern park-like cemetery filled with polished granite monuments and generously planted with evergreen bushes, occupies the west side of the cemetery group. It, too, has an entrance on Addison, this one spanned with a concrete arch decorated with carved funerary wreaths and the name "ROSEMONT" spanning the facade above the opening. Though this cemetery is more compact than Mount Mayriv, much attention was given to its landscaping, with straight and curving roads forming a generally pleasant pattern that provides for small round or triangular "islands," most of these having a mausoleum at its center.

Barney Ross (1909–1967) was a champion boxer in the 1930s, winning world lightweight and welterweight championships. Retiring from boxing in 1938, he enlisted in the marines and was wounded in battle at Guadalcanal, where he killed 22 of the enemy while rescuing three wounded comrades under heavy fire. For this, he received a Presidential citation, a Silver Star, and a lengthy hospital-

---

[142] A map posted on the Rosemont Park office building, circa 2010, gives the layout of these cemeteries. It is worth nothing that the names of the cemeteries are slightly different on the map, on the sign, and in the press release at the time of the Zion Gardens takeover. I have elected to use names matching those on the map.

[143] Dates are estimates, as given in "Jewish Cemeteries," JewishGen, http://www.jewishgen. org/infofiles/chicago/cemeteries.htm.

[144] JewishGen, http://www.jewishgen.org, a guide to Jewish genealogy in Chicagoland, provides date.

ization that made him a morphine addict. By his own admission he spent $250,000 on drugs in the years that followed. When his wife left him, he realized he had to turn his life around. He beat the addiction and his wife came back. Ross gave talks about defeating addiction and was the subject of a 1957 movie, *Monkey on My Back*.[145]

In April 2011 all five cemeteries on the site were acquired by a group of Waldheim Cemetery executives, who renamed them collectively "Zion Gardens." Under the previous management, investments had not generated sufficient income to maintain the cemeteries, and the principal invested in the trust fund had been depleted to provide for operational costs.[146] With the approval of Illinois Comptroller Judy Baar Topinka, the new owners reorganized with a new trust fund and strict financial controls, ensuring a stable future. They have also announced substantial improvements to the cemetery, including new fencing and a new office, accessible to the disabled, and have introduced the system of affixing stickers to monuments, already in use at Waldheim, to indicate the level of service required.[147] With this new connection to the much larger Waldheim, the future of Zion Gardens seems assured.

---

[145] "Death Claims Ring Champ, Court King: Ross Loses Gallant Fight with Throat Cancer at 57," *Chicago Tribune*, January 19, 1967.

[146] "Rosemont Park Acquired and New Management Announced. Zion Gardens to be Managed by Waldheim Cemetery Company," Business Wire, http://www.businesswire.com/news/home/20110420006394/en/Rosemont-Park-Acquired-Management-Announced.

[147] *Zion Gardens Gazette*, Volume 2, 2012, Zion Gardens Cemetery, http://www.ziongardenscemetery.com/newsletter.php.

CITY SOUTH

Members of the Benevolent Protective Order of Elks held benefit dinners to raise funds for this white bronze statue, once the centerpiece of the "Elk's Rest" section. On the base was written: *The faults of our BROTHERS we will write upon the sands.* As of 2013, the majestic statue is unfortunately no longer present. A smaller bronze elk was recently installed in its place.

OAK WOODS CEMETERY

1035 East 67th Street, Chicago
www.oakwoodscemetery.net
Established 1853

Chicago's historic South Side cemetery was created by a special act of the Illinois General Assembly on February 12, 1853, birthday of future president Abraham Lincoln.[148] The 183-acre tract sits beside Cottage Grove Avenue, spanning from 67th Street to 71st Street.

The six-story Tower of Remembrance is Chicago's tallest mausoleum. On its front, a sculpted man rises toward heaven.

Oak Woods was landscaped by cemetery architect Adolph Strauch,[149] notable as the designer of Spring Grove Cemetery in Cincinnati. Wanting to avoid the perceived clutter of other rural cemeteries, Strauch aimed for a park-like atmosphere, with formal layouts and plenty of open space.[150] The grounds include four manmade lakes, a picturesque English Gothic chapel, a six-story marble-clad mausoleum, lawn crypts, and greenhouses, as well as private family monuments of every kind.

The cemetery is enclosed by a perimeter wall that is concrete for most of its length, save for a section on 67th Street built from dark

---

[148] *Chicago: As We Remember Her* (Chicago: Oak Woods Cemetery Association, 1955), 11.

[149] Helen Sclair, *Greater Chicagoland Cemeteries* (Worcester, MA: Association for Gravestone Studies, 1994).

[150] "Cemeteries—Confederate Mound," U.S. Department of Veterans Affairs, National Cemetery Administration, http://www.cem.va.gov/cems/lots/confederate_mound.asp.

red brick with buttresses rising from the sidewalk, which forms the rear of the maintenance building. At the center of the north wall is the main entrance, consisting of a number of red granite posts supporting an elaborate bronze fence with fleur-de-lis finials on each vertical member. Inside, the cemetery office is immediately visible, as is the chapel building a few dozen yards away. West of the entrance is a small pile of blackened debris. A sign on a short post informs visitors that this is a relic of the original cemetery office, once located in the Loop but destroyed in the Great Chicago Fire of 1871.

The cemetery's chapel and crematory was designed in the English Gothic style by William Carbys Zimmerman to resemble a country church.[151] Built of limestone, the chapel features a tall roof with long sloping sides over the nave, a smaller roof of the same design over the narthex, and smaller versions still over the transepts. The steeple consists of a pyramidal base—echoing the shape of the vestibule roof—with an elongated pyramid rising from its center. Both steeple and vestibule roof are capped with bronze finials. The interior is a space dominated by dark woods, curtains, and hanging bronze lamps, beneath a ceiling of timber-framed white panels.

Near the chapel are the graves of the **parents of General "Black Jack" Pershing**, supreme commander of the American forces in the Great War, though General Pershing himself is absent, having earned a place of honor in Arlington National Cemetery. In an

William Carbys Zimmerman designed the chapel in the English Gothic style, modeled on English country churches. Its exterior has remained essentially unchanged for more than 100 years.

[151] Alice Sinkevitch, *AIA Guide to Chicago* (Houghton Mifflin Harcourt, 2004), 471.

adjacent plot is a monument erected by the Chicago Fire Department to commemorate 15 firemen who died at the World's Columbian Exposition of 1893, an incident known as the Cold Storage Warehouse Fire. The large number of food concessions at the fair required constant supplies of ice, and for this purpose a "Cold Storage Warehouse" was constructed. The five-story refrigerated structure was cooled by ammonia compressors powered by a massive steam engine with enough power to even provide for a skating rink on the top floor. On the afternoon of July 10, 1893, flames were spotted at the top of the flue. Firemen quickly responded, climbing onto the roof to gain access to the flue, but were soon trapped as the fire spread to the roof and cutting off their only escape route. As the flames grew closer, they jumped to their deaths to escape immolation. Seven of these firefighters are buried here at Oak Woods, but the names of all 15 appear on the monument.[152]

Another hero who gave his life in the line of duty is buried in this section. **Cale Cramer** (1850–1887) was the engineer on an express passenger train on the Baltimore & Ohio Railroad, eastbound from Chicago to Philadelphia on the night of July 27,

Cale Cramer's monument, a pile of locomotive parts rendered in limestone, is unique in all the world. Cramer was one of only three fatalities when his train collided with another after entering a siding at full speed due to a vandalized switch. His grateful passengers paid for the monument.

[152] Andy Pearson, "Lessons Learned from the Cold Storage Fire at the Chicago World's Fair of 1893," *The Free Library*, January 1, 2009.

1887.[153] At about ten o'clock that evening, at York Township, Noble County, Indiana, the train entered a siding at an estimated 55 miles per hour. Already present in the siding was a freight train that had stopped there to allow Cramer's express train to pass on the main line. Cramer and his fireman, Edward Coakin, applied the brakes and shut down steam to the engine to reduce speed, but they were unable to bring the train to a complete stop.

At the moment of impact, Cramer and Coakin attempted to jump clear, but both were killed. The fireman of the passenger train escaped successfully, but that train's engineer, William Divine, had his right leg crushed. Though it was amputated immediately, he died later that night. Both engines, and several cars on each train, were completely destroyed,[154] but no passengers were injured.[155]

An investigation on the night of the crash revealed that the switch had not merely been set incorrectly, but had been vandalized. Forty minutes before, it had been in perfect working order and had allowed an excursion train to pass through as usual; but soon after it had been smashed with a club, and the lock was missing. A newspaper account speculated that several tramps who had had an altercation with trainmen earlier that evening were the likely culprits.[156]

In gratitude, the passengers of the No. 46 Express erected a most unusual monument at Oak Woods. Cramer's limestone monument depicts a pile of disassembled steam locomotive parts, including smokestack, boiler, and a large spoked wheel, all of which sit on a length of track, with rails and ties rendered in stone. Two spokes of the wheel are broken, symbolizing death. On one side of the monument, a large rectangular panel depicts an intact engine and coal car, and states that the 37-year-old Cramer "lost his life by

---

[153] "Death in a Collision," *Chicago Daily Tribune*, July 28, 1887. The engineer was identified as "C. Cramer" in the article, and appears as Cale Cramer on the monument, but is given as "Gale Cramer" in several later articles on the incident and in the cemetery's own literature. The *Chicago Tribune* article gives the fireman's name as Kookin. An 1880 census record for a boarding house in Garrett, Indiana, lists a "Cail Cramer," age 29, profession "RR Engineer."

[154] *Albion New Era* (Albion, Indiana), August 3, 1887. The article gives the location of the crash as York siding, between Albion and Cromwell.

[155] "Death in a Collision."

[156] *Albion New Era* (Albion, Indiana), August 3, 1887.

saving the train."

At the end of 1974, another man who died to save strangers was laid to rest near Cramer. The unidentified man, described as "male/white/unknown," in his late twenties, intervened when three teenagers were threatened by a knife-wielding thug in front of the Wilson Men's Hotel, a North Side flophouse. He was stabbed in the chest.[157] With the body lying unidentified and unclaimed for months, a businessman and an unnamed mortuary donated a coffin and a grave in a prime location. As the man's religious affiliation was unknown, a priest, a minister, and a rabbi jointly performed the service.[158]

East of Cramer's section, across the Peaceful Lake, a white marble monument shows a seated woman with an artist's palette and brush, her body shown in profile, melding with the stone backdrop. **Martha Baker** (1871–1911) was educated at the Art Institute of Chicago, where she later lectured. She painted portraits in oils and water colors, and was especially noted for her work in miniature painting. Baker died four days before her fortieth birthday.[159]

Further east is the modest headstone of **Enrico Fermi** (1901–1953). Born in Rome, Fermi became fascinated with physics at a young age and showed remarkable ability. At the age of 24, he became professor of theoretical physics at the University of Rome. By the 1930s he was working on the bombardment of atoms with neutrons, a process that would eventually lead to the discovery of nuclear fission. In 1938 he received the Nobel Prize for his work with nuclear reactions. That same year he immigrated to the United States so that his Jewish wife would be safe from Mussolini's Fascist government. At Columbia University in New York, he conducted the first fission experiments in the United States. By 1942 he was at the University of Chicago, where his team created the first self-sustaining nuclear reaction using a pile of uranium and graphite blocks in a squash court under a disused football stadium.

---

[157] Rick Soll, "He Deserved a Dignified Burial," *Chicago Tribune*, December 31, 1974.

[158] Jeff Lyon, "Fitting Farewell for Dead Hero," *Chicago Tribune*, December 28, 1974.

[159] "A Memorial Exhibition of Works of The Late Martha S. Baker at the Art Institute of Chicago, Oct. 1 to 23, 1912," Art Institute of Chicago, http://www.artic.edu/sites/default/files/libraries/pubs/1912/AIC1912Baker_comb.pdf.

Moving to the secret government laboratory in Los Alamos, New Mexico, Fermi joined the Manhattan Project to further research fission, including its potential use as a weapon. He was present at the first test detonation of an atomic bomb.

The simple marker of Enrico Fermi, winner of the 1938 Nobel Prize in Physics.

In 1953 Fermi died from stomach cancer, one of three of the team who worked on the poorly shielded "Chicago Pile 1" who would later die due to various cancers. His headstone at Oak Woods is a simple slanted marker. Below his name appears the one-word epitaph, *Physicist*.

Music, too, is well-represented at Oak Woods. **Eddie Harris** (1934–1996), world renowned saxophonist, was entombed in a granite sarcophagus with a musical score etched across its face. His *Exodus* was the first jazz single to sell over one million copies.[160] The granite monument of **Maurice Chassagne** (1912–1972) is shaped like an upright piano, complete with pedals, keys, and the words *Music is Heaven!* printed across the score.

Returning to the Peaceful Lake and proceeding southwest along its shore, the visitor comes to the baseball-themed monument of **"Cap" Anson** (1852–1922). Adrian Constantine Anson played ball for several teams before becoming captain of the Chicago White Stockings. His innovative leadership was nationally recognized, as he originated the concept of "spring training." His legacy is tainted, however, by his overt racism, particularly by refusing to play exhibition games against black players. Anson's monument features two bats crossed over a wreath, a ball between them, and the words *He Played the Game*. Unlike the similar grave of Bob Figg at Calvary, Anson's bats are depicted triumphantly upright, not pointed down-

---

[160] Yvonne Harris Burnley, his daughter, personal communication, 2009.

wards in mourning.

Nearby is another of professional baseball's powerful figures, Judge **Kenesaw Mountain Landis** (1866–1944), whose unusual given name commemorates the Civil War battlefield where his father was wounded. A self-educated attorney, Landis worked as secretary to Secretary of State Gresham, then was named federal judge by President Theodore Roosevelt. As judge, Landis became known for taking on big business. In 1920, with professional baseball in disrepute after the Black Sox scandal, Landis was hired by the team owners as the first Commissioner of Baseball. He acted swiftly and decisively to restore the sport's integrity, banning for life the eight Chicago White Sox players who had taken bribes.

A beautiful memorial nearby is that of **George Eastman** (1863–1928), where a bronze statue of a sorrowful woman, a "surrogate mourner," cradles her head on one arm, leaning against a red granite tablet. Eastman was a prominent farmer from Hancock County in Western Illinois.[161]

In a row of mausoleums extending south from here is the tomb of one of Chicago's early mob bosses, **"Big" Jim Colosimo** (1878–1920). Colosimo was an extortionist, a pimp, and a practitioner of "white slavery," luring young girls to the city then forcing them into lives of captivity and prostitution. His nephew Johnny Torrio served as enforcer, and Torrio eventually brought a young Brooklyn thug named Alphonse Capone to work for the Colosimo organization. In 1920, Colosimo was shot dead in his own restaurant—a hit probably arranged by Torrio, who became the next leader of the organization and changed its focus from prostitution to bootlegging.

Archbishop George Mundelein refused to permit the gangster to be buried in a Catholic cemetery—not because of his involvement in murder or prostitution, but because he had been divorced. Instead, he was entombed at the non-sectarian Oak Woods. Like many mob funerals, Colosimo's was spectacular. Expensive floral tributes sur-

---

[161] *Portrait and Biographical Record of Hancock, McDonough and Henderson Counties, Illinois : Containing Biographical Sketches of Prominent and Representative Citizens of the County* (Chicago: Lake City Pub. Co., 1894), Internet Archive, http://archive.org/details/portraitbiograph01lake.

rounded a bronze coffin. The 53 pallbearers included judges and Congressmen. One thousand First Ward Democrats[162] marched in the funeral procession to Oak Woods accompanied by two brass bands.

Bernie Epton (1921–1987) is buried nearby. As candidate for mayor in 1983, he waged the most successful Republican campaign for mayor of Chicago in decades, losing by only 40,000 votes to Harold Washington.

A recently-installed monument commemorates a man who died one hundred years before. In 2002, the Chicago office of the U.S. Secret Service placed a ledger stone to honor **William Craig** (1855–1902), an agent who was killed in a railway crash while protecting President Theodore Roosevelt. Roosevelt later stated that he was "fond" of Craig and praised him "for his loyalty and his faithfulness." Two star-shaped emblems are affixed to his marker, the elaborate Victorian-style insignia of the Secret Service in 1902 and the simplified modern version of 2002.

A number of large and impressive monuments stand on the eastern shore of Symphony Lake, largest of Oak Woods' four manmade lakes. Near the south end is the monument of **Marcus A. Farwell** (1827–1894), eclectic in style, with eight short columns supporting the cross-gabled capital. Farwell, owner of the land that became Oak Woods,[163] served as the cemetery's first treasurer.

Behind Farwell's plot is the cemetery's tallest monument, a grey granite obelisk surrounded with ledger stones. Republican **William Hale Thompson** (1869–1944) was the most bizarre and corrupt of Chicago's mayors. "Big Bill" was first elected mayor in 1915 and saw the mayor's office as a gateway to the presidency. He was linked to Johnny Torrio and Al Capone, who both reportedly made generous contributions to his campaign. When war was declared, Thompson supported Germany and declared he'd like to punch the British King George V in the face, earning him the derisive nickname "Kaiser Bill." As the scandals grew, he realized he could not win election

---

[162] See "Calvary Catholic Cemetery" entry for more on the First Ward's leaders Hinky Dink and Bathhouse John.

[163] John Moses and Joseph Kirkland, *History of Chicago, Illinois, Volume 2* (Chicago & New York: Munsell & Company, 1895).

to a third term and withdrew his candidacy in the 1923 election. Democrat William Dever, a reformer, was elected mayor.[164]

To keep himself in public view, Thompson organized a "scientific" expedition to search for tree-climbing fish in the South Seas: "I have strong reason to believe that there are fish that come out of the water, can live on land, will jump three feet to catch a grasshopper, and will actually climb trees." The yacht *Big Bill* got as far south as New Orleans, but Thompson had already jumped ship—even the pretense of research was too much like real work for his tastes.

Thompson ran again for mayor in 1927, promising to re-open taverns that Dever had shut down. He staged a mock debate in which two white rats stood in for his opponents. He won re-election, and once again was tied to organized crime by the press. Theatrics could not win him a fourth term; he was defeated by Anton Cermak in 1931. In part due to the power of the Democratic machine, in part due to Thompson's reputation as a buffoon, since 1931 Chicago has never had another Republican mayor.

A smaller obelisk on the shore commemorates another Chicago mayor, **Monroe Heath** (1827–1894). Heath is remembered today mainly for the bizarre circumstances that brought him to the office of mayor. In 1875, the Chicago city council voted to change the date of the mayor's election from November to April to be in compliance with state law, but neglected to specify whether the term of then-mayor Harvey Colvin would be extended. That November, neither Republicans nor Democrats nominated a candidate, and an independent named Thomas Hoyne ran for the position. Colvin refused to step aside, and Hoyne was unable to take office. A judge threw out the result and called for a special election the following July, which Monroe Heath won.[165]

Between these two mayoral obelisks is the cemetery's best-known grave site, marked with a star on their visitor's map, that of **Harold Washington** (1922–1987), first African-American mayor of Chica-

---

[164] June Skinner Sawyers, *Chicago Portraits : Biographies of 250 Famous Chicagoans* (Chicago: Loyola University Press, 1991), 251–252. Dever is buried in Calvary Cemetery in Evanston.

165 Colvin and Hoyne are buried at Rosehill.

go. Born in Cook County Hospital, Washington served in the Army in World War II and enrolled in Roosevelt College after his discharge. After earning a law degree from Northwestern University, he worked for and organized with the Democratic Party, eventually being elected to the Illinois legislature, then in 1980 to Congress.

In 1983 Washington defeated incumbent mayor Jane Byrne in the Democratic primary. In this three-way race, the white vote was split between Byrne and challenger Richard M. Daley. Washington then went on to defeat Republican challenger Bernie Epton. His first term in office was rough, as the city council opposed him in what became known as "Council Wars," refusing to enact his legislation or confirm his appointees. Eventually, he gained the upper hand, as redistricting reduced the number of aldermen in opposition. In 1987 he won a second term in office, again defeating former mayor Byrne in the primary, and Ed Vrdolyak—leader of Washington's city council adversaries—in the general election.

A few months into his second term, however, Washington collapsed at his desk in City Hall, and was rushed to the hospital, where he was pronounced dead, victim of a heart attack brought on by excess weight and other conditions. He was entombed in a grey granite mausoleum in the most prestigious section of the cemetery with a paved walkway leading from the road to his door. On the front of the mausoleum, alongside a list of his accomplishments, are his words: *Remember me as one who tried to be fair.*

Across the road to the east are some intriguing monuments. One of these consists of two pairs of marble Doric columns, each pair connected by a beam on which faint lettering can be seen. Between the two gates thus formed is a marble ledger. The inscriptions on the beams and on the ledger have worn away, leaving only a few letters legible and the identity of the person buried here a mystery. Further south is the monument of **Daniel Van Degrift** (1870–1946), which looks remarkably like Potter Palmer's grand tomb at Graceland. Though much smaller, containing one sarcophagus rather than two, and different in the rendering of the details, all the same design elements are present, including the Ionic columns, the entablature, and the elaborate floral garlands and inverted torches on the sarcophagus. Degrift, a dentist, was a major donor to the Art Institute of Chicago, leaving them over a half-million dollars upon his death in 1946.[166]

Paul Cornell (1822–1904), a lawyer and real estate investor, is buried at the north end of Symphony Lake. Cornell founded the town of Hyde Park—now a Chicago neighborhood that includes the University of Chicago and the home of President Barack Obama. He purchased land south of the city, then exchanged a parcel of it to the Illinois Central Railroad in exchange for building a station with a guarantee of frequent stops there, an act which improved the value of his remaining land tremendously. Cornell was also instrumental in the creation of Oak Woods Cemetery, serving as its first secretary.

The "white bronze" monument of Paul Cornell, founder of Hyde Park, founding secretary of Oak Woods Cemetery, and president of the American White Bronze Company, is the largest of its kind. The two bottom tiers seen here, deformed by the weight of the monument, were recently removed.

Additionally, Cornell was president of the American White Bronze Company, which manufactured cemetery monuments from zinc. Cornell's own monument, placed here 16 years before his death,[167] is one of the largest of this material to be found anywhere. About 15 feet tall, it was cast in the form of a multi-tiered pedestal. On one side of the monument, a relief portrait of Cornell is framed with pilasters (columns built into the surface) supporting a triangular pediment. At the very top is a massive funerary urn, draped with cloth. Like all white bronze

---

[166] "Dentist's Will Leaves Art Institute $531,988," *Chicago Tribune*, May 24, 1947.

[167] Carol A. Grissom, *Zinc Sculpture in America, 1850–1950* (Newark, DE: University of Delaware, 2009), 572.

monuments, it is hollow. Photos from 2004 and earlier show that the metal at the base was deforming from the weight of the monument above, sagging in the center and cracking at the corners. This led the caretakers to recently take the drastic step of cutting off the two damaged bottom layers and re-mounting the monument on a sturdy concrete base.[168]

Athlete **Jesse Owens** (1913–1980) is buried next to Cornell in a shady spot on the lake shore. His red granite monument includes a center tablet describing him as *Olympic Champion 1936*, flanked with two smaller pieces that feature the five-ring Olympic symbol. The 1936 games, held in Berlin, were intended to be a showcase for the ascendant Nazi party and its doctrine of Aryan supremacy. Owens, an African American, won four gold medals in sprinting and long jump events, making him the most decorated athlete of those games. The infuriated Chancellor Hitler refused to shake his hand.

Further south along this lake shore is the simple headstone of

Jesse Owens, winner of four gold medals in the Berlin Olympics of 1936, embarrassed the Nazi regime by disproving their claims of Aryan superiority.

---

[168] As evidenced by recent photos on Flickr and other websites. The two segments below the name "Cornell" are now gone. The work happened between 2004 and 2008.

Ida Wells-Barnett (1862–1931), another African-American hero. Born the daughter of slaves one year before the Emancipation Proclamation, Ida Wells attended a university for freedmen but dropped out to support her siblings after their parents' deaths. Working as a teacher, she became noted for her writings and activism for women's rights. In 1884, she refused to give up her seat on a train for a white person—as did Rosa Parks, decades later—and, after being ejected from the train, successfully sued the railway, though this was reversed on appeal.

Wells became a newspaper writer, editor, and owner. After an angry mob destroyed her newspaper offices in Memphis, Wells moved to Chicago and continued her writings against lynching and segregation. Together with Frederick Douglass, she published a pamphlet condemning the exclusion of African Americans from the World's Columbian Exhibition. She married newspaper publisher Ferdinand Barnett and, in a break with custom, kept her own surname.

The large open-air tomb of **George A. Fuller** (1851–1900) is nearby. The structure is a pergola (a structure with an open roof), consisting of limestone columns supporting three levels of horizontal beams, symbolizing steel, stone, and wood. Fuller, an architect and builder, is noted for originating the contracting system used for building construction. His firm built the Monadnock Building and Rookery in Chicago and the famed Flatiron in New York, originally called the Fuller Building. Fuller in died in 1900 at the age of 49 from amyotrophic lateral sclerosis (ALS, Lou Gehrig's disease). His monument was designed by Bruce Price, a noted New York–based architect.[169]

Another nearby tomb gained national attention in 2009, having been featured in countless television news stories, newspaper articles, and blogs. When **Roland Burris** (1937–?)was appointed to fill the Senate seat left vacant by President Obama, pundits and commentators noticed that, though living, he had already prepared his own mausoleum, one that—by modern standards, at least—is large and imposing. Consisting of twin granite sarcophagi and a shaded walkway, the tomb features large panels listing Burris's accomplish-

---

[169] Sinkevitch, *AIA Guide to Chicago*, 469.

ments, even before his Senate appointment. Beneath the seal of the state of Illinois are the words *Trail Blazer* and a list of Burris's accomplishments as first African-American comptroller and attorney general of Illinois.

At the northern edge of the cemetery is Chicago's tallest mausoleum, the **Tower of Memories**. This six-story community mausoleum features a sleek facade of beige marble blocks rising six stories, its reflection visible in the Lake of Memories. Above the door, the figure of a man rises, bare-chested and triumphant, over the words of Psalm 123: *Unto Thee I lift up mine eyes, O Thou that dwellest in the Heavens.* Inside, the cool marble walls and crypts are softened by an abundance of greenery, flowers, and vines spilling out from vases and bowls. A bas-relief sculpture on one wall depicts the Fates, Clotho, Lachesis, and Atropos, measuring out the thread of a human life.

Entombed in a first-floor crypt is **Thomas A. Dorsey** (1899–1993), the "Father of Black Gospel Music." Born in Georgia in 1899 to a minister and a piano teacher, he played blues under the stage name "Georgia Tom." The death of his son prompted him to write his best-known work, "Precious Lord, Take My Hand," which became a favorite of Dr. Martin Luther King and President Lyndon Johnson, at whose funeral it played. His "Peace in the Valley" was another hit. Dorsey's songs were performed by a number of notable artists, including Mahalia Jackson, Elvis Presley, Johnny Cash, and Aretha Franklin, among others.

This mausoleum was also the scene of two of Chicago's most bizarre entombments, later commemorated in a song by Stevie Ray Vaughn entitled "Willie the Wimp." Heroin dealer **Willie Stokes Jr.** (~1955–1984) was shot to death in 1984. At his wake, he was propped upright in a casket decorated to resemble a Cadillac, with headlights, grille, and hood ornament, a floral wreath for a steering wheel and wheels with spoked hubcaps underneath.[170] His father, **"Flukey" Stokes** (d. 1986), who followed the same profession, met a similar end two years later and was buried with a mobile phone in his hands—an uncommon item in the mid-1980s—in a glass-topped

---

[170] Johanna Stoyva, "Cemetery Makes Best of the Past Come Alive," *Chicago Tribune*, May 20, 1987.

mahogany casket[171] so large that the shelf above his crypt had to be moved upwards to make room.[172]

Continuing west past the Tower of Memories, behind the immense **Borden** family mausoleum, one finds the Trumbull family plot, featuring a simple granite monument and white marble headstones. Holder of a wide variety of public offices, **Lyman Trumbull** (1813–1896) was an Illinois state legislator, Illinois secretary of state, state supreme court justice, and finally United States senator. As senator, he co-authored the Thirteenth Amendment, which put an end to slavery, only to lose re-election after becoming one of seven Republicans to vote for acquittal in the impeachment proceedings of President Johnson.

Also nearby are the graves of congressman and Chicago mayor **James Hutchinson Woodworth** (1804–1869), and **Jonathan Young Scammon** (1812–1890), first president of Oak Woods Cemetery. At the **Soldiers' Home** lot, a statue of a soldier, flanked by four cannons, stands watch over the rows of headstones. Further west on this road, a bronze figure of Abraham Lincoln, one arm upraised in an oratorical flourish, adorns the lot of the **Grand Army of the Republic**.

In the southwest corner of the cemetery, next to the Lake of Reverence, stands a garden crypt building, one of several found on the grounds. Nearby is the monument of **Charles S. Deneen** (1863–1940), governor of Illinois and United States senator. Before his two terms as governor, Deneen led the prosecution of sausage-maker Adolph Luetgert for the murder of his wife. Luetgert was convicted on the basis of bones and a ring found in a grinder in Luetgert's sausage factory, a discovery that caused a noticeable decline in sausage consumption in Chicago for years after.

Across the Lake of Reverence is a 46-foot granite shaft, on which a bronze figure of a soldier stands. Unlike most such monuments, this soldier's pose is more sorrowful than heroic, for this plot com-

---

[171] "Thousands Pay Respect to Slain Reputed Drug Kingpin," Associated Press, November 22, 1986.

[172] Barbara Brotman, "Under All the Trappings There Lies a Dope Dealer," *Chicago Tribune*, November 23, 1986.

memorates prisoners of war—at least 4,275 of them, buried in concentric trenches, soldiers of the Confederate States of America.

Senator Stephen Douglas, a Chicago landowner who had been recently defeated for the presidency by fellow Illinoisan Abraham Lincoln, died in June of 1861, less than two months after the attack on Fort Sumter in South Carolina, the first engagement of the Civil War. Chicago was swept with fervor for the war, and a training camp for the hordes of enlistees was hastily constructed near the late senator's estate, four miles north of Oak Woods, partially on Douglas's property. In February 1862, the capture of Fort Donelson in Tennessee brought a need to house more than 12,000 captured Confederates, and Camp Douglas was selected to receive a large portion of these. The proposal was at first seen as a joke due to the lax security at the site.[173] Nevertheless, Camp Douglas was converted to a prison camp, and Colonel James Mulligan[174] appointed its commander.

As with any prison camp of the era, overcrowding and harsh conditions led to a high mortality rate. No provision had been made for a cemetery, and the handling of the prisoners' remains was repeatedly bungled. Victims of a smallpox outbreak in 1864 were buried on a site near the camp, and another 3,000 men were buried in City Cemetery.[175] Chicago undertaker C. H. Jordan was given the contract to bury all who died at the camp, as well as the responsibility for procuring coffins and grave sites, at a price of $4.75 per burial. Though this was a fair and adequate amount, Jordan kept his expenses down by choosing the pauper's section at City Cemetery, described as a "sand waste" with constantly shifting ridges.[176] By 1866, only 1,400 of these graves could still be identified. Then came the order to close City Cemetery and relocate the bodies elsewhere.

Rosehill, first proposed as the site of the re-interment, refused to accept the Confederate dead.[177] Oak Woods was selected instead. A year before, Oak Woods had provided for the reburials of the 655 small-

[173] George Levy, *To Die in Chicago: Confederate Prisoners at Camp Douglas, 1862–1865* (Evanston, IL: Evanston Publishing, 1994), 9.

[174] Colonel Mulligan is buried at Calvary Cemetery, Evanston.

[175] Levy, *To Die in Chicago*, 289.

[176] Levy, *To Die in Chicago*, 291.

[177] Levy, *To Die in Chicago*, 295.

pox victims when the tiny cemetery next to Camp Douglas had been removed. Now, it would receive the remaining Confederates as well.

The lot at Oak Woods was little better, consisting of low, swampy ground, about six feet below the typical elevation of the cemetery. The job of disinterring the remains and providing new coffins was given to two aldermen with connections to the quarter-

The "Confederate Mound" features a large central monument of Georgia granite, with individual headstones nearby commemorating 12 Union soldiers, though their bodies are in unknown locations. Originally low and swampy, this section was covered with an additional six feet of earth in 1902, covering the hundreds of original wooden markers.

master department, M. O'Sullivan and James J. O'Sullivan, at $1.98 per burial. This work was done in an even more slipshod manner than the original burials. Those few numbered headboards at City Cemetery that remained intact were tossed aside carelessly. Bodies were reburied with numbers corresponding to the original burial numbers at City Cemetery, which had no records associating these numbers with names. Witnesses reported that a large number of coffins seemed to be empty. Neither the Army nor the cemetery office supervised the burials.[178]

By the 1880s the condition of the "Soldiers Lot" had deteriorated, leading to complaints and government investigations. Graves were sunken, markers were missing, and part of the lot had become a road. A monument was finally installed in 1893, paid for by donations from former Confederate soldiers and other

---

[178] Levy, *To Die in Chicago*, 297.

Atop the monument, a bronze statue of a disarmed Confederate soldier looks sorrowfully down at his fallen comrades, buried in enemy territory.

Southern sympathizers. President Grover Cleveland spoke at the dedication in 1895, at which a magnolia tree from Louisiana was planted there in soil from Mississippi battlefields. This did nothing to improve the condition of the lot, however, as it continued to suffer drainage problems. In 1902, the monument was removed and six feet of earth placed on top of the lot, concealing the markers and walkways that had been on the surface.[179]

The monument is a tall four-sided shaft of grey granite from Georgia. At the top, a soldier stands, one leg forward, his arms crossed, looking down on the graves of his comrades. Below the shaft is a pedestal with bronze artwork on each side. At the bottom is a sloping red granite base, installed in 1912, with four tablets on each side, inscribed with the names and home states of the 4,275 soldiers thought to be buried here. Nearby, 12 military-style headstones commemorate the twelve Union soldiers buried in unknown locations here, guards at Camp Douglas who were buried with their prisoners. A cannon and pyramids of cannonballs decorate the lot.

Frederick Rueckheim (1846–1934) and **Louis Rueckheim** (1849–1927), the brothers who created "Cracker Jack," are buried nearby, as is **Henry Eckstein** (1860–1935), their business partner who created the "Eckstein Triple Proof Package" that ensured the product's freshness. Eckstein also created Gold Dust Washing Pow-

---

[179] Levy, *To Die in Chicago*, 299.

der. A grandson of Frederick Rueckheim, Robert, inspired the "Sailor Jack" mascot on the package. Robert died at the age of seven and was buried in St. Henry's Cemetery.[180]

Bishop **Louis Henry Ford** (1914–1995) is buried under a black granite ledger, next to a large monument featuring the logo of the Church of God in Christ, a bundle of harvested wheat enclosed in a circle. As bishop of the Illinois jurisdiction of the predominantly African-American church, Ford rose to national prominence when he delivered the funeral sermon of Emmett Till, a Chicago teenager who was murdered in Mississippi in 1955 merely for speaking to a white woman.[181] In 1990, Bishop Ford became leader of the national denomination, which he led from 1990 to 1995 with a motto of "Back to Basic Holiness." One year after his death, the former Calumet Expressway was renamed the Bishop Ford Freeway in his honor.

Nestled inside the south wall of Oak Woods is a distinctly differ-

The Jewish cemetery at Oak Woods is of a distinctly different character than the main nonsectarian cemetery, resembling a small slice of Waldheim with monuments closely packed together. The brick building in the background is a bet tahara.

---

[180] Charles Panati, *Panati's Extraordinary Origins of Everyday Things* (New York: Perennial Library, 1989), 324. See also St. Henry's Cemetery entry.
[181] See Burr Oak Cemetery entry.

ent cemetery, separated from the main cemetery by a battered and leaning iron fence. Adolph Strauch's careful landscaping is nowhere to be seen here. Instead, graves are tightly packed, with little space given to paths or to lawn. Tall monuments stand only inches apart, some of them noticeably leaning or covered with vines. Inscriptions are in English and Hebrew. "Jewish Oak Woods" was owned and operated by three synagogues,[182] separated from the non-sectarian cemetery by a fence as required by tradition.

In one corner is a small, red brick building, a *bet tahara*, where bodies were ritually cleansed before burial.[183] Constructed in 1930, the building is now disused and padlocked, with shades drawn and wire mesh covering the windows. An inset concrete panel on one side indicates that the building was given by **Selig** (d. 1931) and **Bessie Morris** (unknown), whose white granite mausoleum faces the building across the path. It is the only mausoleum in this section. Morris, a Russian immigrant,[184] was a scrap metal dealer and refiner, owner of S. Morris & Co. on South Canal Street.[185]

One outstanding monument in Jewish Oak Woods is that of **Wolf and Hattie Goldstein**, a large arched gateway. Red granite columns support an ornate limestone lintel (horizontal member), inscribed with *Family W. Goldstein*, the year *1917*, and its equivalent on the Hebrew calendar, *5677*. Atop the lintel are carved antefixes, or corner pieces, and a sphere inscribed with Hebrew lettering. Hattie Goldstein died in 1917, followed by her husband in 1935.

Oak Woods was featured in the 1999 film *Stir of Echoes*, starring Kevin Bacon. The main character's wife and young son are shown walking along the stretch of original brick wall on the north side of the cemetery, over which a fantastic—and entirely fictional—monument of a cloaked figure can be seen. They then observe a police funeral, but, not wishing to disrupt it, wander toward the Jewish section. The boy, Jake, shouts, "Whoa, this place is cool!" as he explores.

---

[182] Stoyva, "Cemetery Makes Best of the Past Come Alive."

[183] Marilyn Yalom, *The American Resting Place: Four Hundred Years of History Through our Cemeteries and Burial Grounds* (Boston: Houghton Mifflin Co., 2008), 172.

[184] "Million in Cash Left by Savings Believer," *The Pittsburgh Press*, December 31, 1931.

[185] *The Iron Age, Vol. XCIV*, July–December, 1914, (New York: David Williams Company, 1914), 1459.

As they speak with a policeman from the funeral, the Goldstein arch is clearly visible nearby.

During the twentieth century, the neighborhood around Oak Woods became predominantly African-American, as many whites left the South Side. The cemetery's management resisted this change, not wishing to alienate their traditional clients. Beginning in the 1920s, the cemetery's salesmen would refuse to sell lots to black customers, though blacks could still be buried at Oak Woods if the sale had been made previously, or if a white person owned the lot.[186] Around 1960 this policy was discontinued, and persons of all races were welcomed once again—as evidenced by the burial of prominent African Americans such as Mayor Washington and Jesse Owens.

Thus expanding its clientele, the cemetery has adapted successfully to a changing city, while still preserving within itself splendid relics of the Gilded Age.

ZIRNGIBL GRAVE

9331 South Ewing Avenue, Chicago
Established 1855

At this tiny graveyard near the mouth of the Calumet River, visitors must be accompanied by an escort and wear a hard hat at all times. **Andreas von Zirngibl** (1797–1855), occupant of the only visible grave, is buried in the middle of an operating scrap yard. And there he shall remain, his right to stay guaranteed by a decision of the Illinois Supreme Court.

During his lifetime, the location was not so industrialized; it was a marshy, rural area, purchased by Zirngibl for his family home. Andreas von Zirngibl was born in Bavaria on March 30, 1797. His father was a baron and a friend of Emperor Frederick Wilhelm IV, according to an interview given by Andreas's widow in 1897.[187] At the

[186] Stoyva, "Cemetery Makes Best of the Past Come Alive."
[187] "Squatter's Grave Is His Legal Fortress," *Chicago Daily Tribune*, May 30, 1897.

age of 18, von Zirngibl enlisted in the Prussian army, serving under Marshal Gebhard von Blucher against Napoleon's *Grande Armée*. At Waterloo, the tyrant was defeated, but in that battle the young soldier lost an arm.[188]

He lived most of his remaining years in Bavaria, with exclusive fishing rights along a two-mile stretch of the Danube. In 1854, with his wife **Monika** (1812–1898) and children Franz, Jacob, George, Theresa, and Henry, he emigrated the Chicago area, settling first in Whiting, Indiana. Within a year, Zirngibl is said to have purchased the land next to the Calumet River for $160 in gold, buying it from a neighbor known variously as Dutch Charley or Dutch John, performing the transaction in the local post office and having it certified by the justice of the peace.[189]

His happiness in his new home was to be short-lived. Two months after setting up his shack next to the Calumet, Andreas was struck down by a fever. As he lay dying, he asked his wife and children to bury him on his own land, and they gave him his last wish. His grave was marked with a headboard of white pine and enclosed in a picket fence. On his marker was written, *Hier Ruhet in Gott den Herrn, Der Wohlgeboren Andreas Zirngibl, geboren Mar. 30, 1797, gestorben Aug. 21, 1855. Hier Ruhet Seine Asche AMEN* ("Here rests in God, the Lord, the well-born Andreas Zirngibl…here rest his ashes").[190]

The family soon moved to the city of Chicago, then some miles to the north. Monika Zirngibl asked a neighbor, Frank Degman, to tend to the property. Monika and her children returned regularly to visit the solitary grave for decades to come. Sons Franz and George would return several times a year to fish and do maintenance on the fence and the shack. Degman left, but was replaced as caretaker by August Magaritz, who lived rent-free in the old Zirngibl shack in

---

[188] Sean Callahan, "Eternal Rust: Soldier's Bones Lie in a Scrap Yard Graveyard," *Chicago Tribune*, May 31, 1999.

[189] Supreme Court of Illinois, "Zirngibl et al. v. Calumet & C. Canal & Dock Co. et al., Oct. 30, 1895." *The Northeastern Reporter*, Volume 42, 1896.

[190] Hollis W. Field, "How a Lone Squatter's Grave in South Chicago Holds Out Against a $700,000 Real Estate Deal" *Chicago Daily Tribune*, October 4, 1908. The original article quotes the monument as saying "*Der Wohlge borne*," which is nonsense; probably this was *Wohlgeboren*. Justice Baker quotes it as "well-born" in his decision.

Next to a pile of steel scrap and surrounded by concrete barriers, this is the
replacement monument at the solitary grave of Andreas von Zirngibl.

exchange for keeping an eye on the land. They posted a sign, *No tres-
passing on this ground. Orders by Zirngibl Brothers*, though this was
destroyed about 1873. The Zirngibl brothers visited the site about
two or three times each year in the 1870s.

As the swampy, rural area became more industrialized and valuable, another claimant to the land arose: the Calumet & Chicago
Canal & Dock Company, which had purchased the 40-acre site from
the Federal Government after no one had paid taxes on it in decades.
In 1885 Zirngibl's widow and children, by then middle-aged, sought
to assert their ownership by filing suit against the canal and dock
company. To support their claim, their attorney found several elderly
residents and former residents of South Chicago, to attest that the
Zirngibls had purchased the land and regularly visited it.

The Zirngibl family could produce no documentation, however.
They stated that all proof of ownership had been lost in the Great
Chicago Fire—including the deed, the recording of the deed, the
physical description of the property, and the true name of "Dutch
Charley" or "Dutch John," from whom it had been purchased. Le-

gally, the Canal & Dock Company had a stronger claim, with documentation that they had purchased the land and had been paying taxes on it ever since.

After a long-fought struggle and multiple appeals, a final verdict was handed down by Illinois Supreme Court Justice David Jewett Baker, Jr.[191] in October 1895. Baker wrote that the Zirngibls had been "hunted up" by a lawyer with a "personal antagonism to the said Calumet & Chicago Canal & Dock Company." He believed their claims of having posted a sign at the site were false, and that the witnesses who claimed the Zirngibls had bought the land in 1854 were unbelievable.

Justice Baker stated that Zirngibl probably died at Whiting, Indiana, and was taken from there to the area near the mouth of the Calumet, then known as Ainsworth, and buried there in a cemetery operated by a Mr. Culver, where up to several hundred people were also buried. Elderly citizens of the area had testified that there were other graves on the site, though their simple wooden markers had long since vanished.

Justice Baker ruled that the Zirngibl family's tending of the grave for 30 years was "adverse possession," protected by law, though by occupying such a small fraction of the property in dispute they had no claim to the property as a whole. Therefore, he upheld the appellate court's ruling, finding the Canal & Dock Company the rightful owners of the site, with one exception:

The exception is this: Appellants established a bar and title by limitation to the grave of their ancestor, Andreas Zirngibl, and to the ground within the inclosure around it. The decree is so modified as to award to the widow and heirs the grave and the ground within the fence that incloses it, with right of access to and egress from it. In all other respects the decree is affirmed.[192]

The struggle to preserve the grave resonated with the public, which generally saw the ruling as a victory for the common man over

---

[191] Son of the U.S. Senator of the same name, who is buried in Alton City Cemetery. After leaving the Supreme Court, Justice Baker (1834–1899) dropped dead in his law office while conversing with his son. He was buried at Mount Greenwood.

[192] "Zirngibl et al v. Calumet & C. Canal & Dock Co. et al."

the faceless corporation—even though the Zirngibls had, for the most part, lost their case, and no longer had use of the part of the land that was worth any money. An 1897 *Tribune* article is full of sentimental prose about "brave squatter days" and the visits of the 86-year-old widow to the grave, and captions an illustration of Franz Zirngibl with "one of the heroes."[193]

The Calumet and Chicago Canal and Dock Company made the Zirngibl family an offer of $10,000 to allow relocation of Andreas's remains to Oak Woods. They refused, perhaps bitter after being accused of fraud by Justice Baker. Monika Zirngibl died on March 11, 1898, and was buried in St. Boniface.[194] Two of her children, George and Jacob, had died before the supreme court verdict. In the next few years, more Zirngibl children and grandchildren would go to their rest at St. Boniface and Graceland.

Unable to make use of the site due to the presence of the grave, yet unwilling to give it up, the company let the land remain idle and barren, with a "For Sale" sign on the Ewing Avenue side of the property. With an estimated value of $700,000 in 1908, the 40-acre site had been rendered useless by a 32-square-foot grave worth $16.[195] The pine headboard and picket fence remained, occasionally given a fresh coat of white paint and the letters of the epitaph re-inked in black, an incongruous sight in an area dominated by heavy industry.

The site remained vacant for more than 30 years. Passersby on Ewing Avenue could see the grave, and wrote in to the newspapers frequently to ask why it was there. Columnists would retell the story every five years or so, sometimes injecting a bit of humor or poetry. In 1928, a photo of the grave appeared in the *Tribune*, with heavy equipment in the background. The picket fence and wooden marker with a cross on top were still present, and the German epitaph was readable.[196]

Nevertheless, pieces of the land were sold off, and the vacant lot

[193] "Squatter's Grave is His Legal Fortress," *Chicago Daily Tribune*, May 30, 1897.

[194] *Cook County, Illinois, Deaths Index, 1878–1922.* Listed as "Zirngible."

[195] Field, "How a Lone Squatter's Grave." The assessment of the property as "idle" agrees with the 1897 article, saying it "is put to no use whatever."

[196] "Why This Lone Grave?" *Chicago Daily Tribune*, March 4, 1928.

containing the soldier's lonely grave shrunk to 7.5 acres. In January, 1933, this last troublesome parcel was finally sold to the Universal Atlas Cement Company, a subsidiary of U.S. Steel, with the stipulation that the grave remain inviolate and passage to it be permitted.[197] The land was then used for the loading of cement onto riverboats. A 1940 photo shows the grave, still intact, dwarfed by a nearby cement mixing drum.[198] By 1952 the industrial yard was the property of the Material Service Corporation, and the Zirngibl family had stopped visiting. The company knew to leave well enough alone, however, and had a hands-off policy with regards to the grave.

But accidents will happen. A truck backed into the grave in 1956, smashing the fence into so much kindling. The fence was immediately rebuilt.[199] A protective concrete curb was then erected around the grave, about two feet from the fence, as shown in a 1974 *Tribune* photo.[200] The site passed through a number of owners, becoming a metal recycling scrap yard. Mountains of junked cars, old appliances, and other broken and twisted metal objects rose up around Zirngibl's lonely grave as gigantic material-handling machines daily trundled by. The owners of the yard put up a fence around their property, blocking view of the grave from Ewing Avenue, and it largely disappeared from the public consciousness.

By 1987, the grave was in such poor condition that major efforts were needed to preserve it. The Southeast Historical Society stepped in, working with the cooperation of a Zirngibl descendant, Henry Zirngibl. They covered the entire grave with a concrete slab, with stout steel posts at each corner, linked by chains. On the ground next to the slab, at each corner, an enormous concrete block was placed, to prevent vehicles from approaching. A new monument, this one a heavy rectangle of grey granite, was placed at the head of the grave, with an inscription commemorating Zirngibl's service at Waterloo, though the date of the battle is wrong:

[197] Al Chase, "$250,000 Deal Keeps Soldier's Grave Sacred," *Chicago Daily Tribune*, January 31, 1933.

[198] "East Side Landmarks: Andreas von Zirngibl Gravesite," Northeastern Illinois University, http://www.neiu.edu/~reseller/esstvonzgrblgrv.html.

[199] "Grave of City Pioneer to Get New Fencing," *Chicago Daily Tribune*, August 25, 1956.

[200] "Action Line," *Chicago Tribune*, December 17, 1974.

In Memoriam – Andreas von Zirngibl
Born Mar 30 1797 – Died Aug 21 1855
A Veteran of 1816 – Battle of Waterloo

Even this wasn't indestructible. In 1999 a crane operator briefly lost control of the end of his boom, and the heavy electromagnet struck the granite monument and shattered it.[201] It was replaced with an identical stone. This monument survives, though stained by oil drippings from the junked cars and random machinery regularly hoisted through Andreas von Zirngibl's tiny sliver of airspace, a persistent reminder of Chicago's pioneer era in the middle of an industrial zone.

MOUNT GREENWOOD CEMETERY
2900 West 111th Street, Chicago
Established 1880

A tree-lined ridge 14 miles south of the Loop inspired cemetery and community founder George Waite to choose the name Mount Greenwood, both for his cemetery and for the adjacent town, now a community area within the city of Chicago.[202] This high ground, 70 feet above the level of Lake Michigan, provided such excellent drainage that three cemeteries were soon established on the ridge, all with names fit for lofty places: Mount Greenwood, oldest and northernmost of the three, was incorporated in 1879 and performed its first burial on April 28, 1880.[203] Mount Olivet, a Catholic cemetery immediately south of Mount Greenwood, was consecrated in 1885.[204]

---

[201] Callahan, "Eternal Rust."

[202] Clinton E. Stockwell, "Mount Greenwood," Encyclopedia of Chicago, http://www.encyclopedia.chicagohistory.org/pages/848.html. The town was annexed in 1927.

[203] Simon, *Chicago, the Garden City*, 155.

[204] "Mount Olivet Catholic Cemetery," Catholic Cemeteries, Archdiocese of Chicago, http://www.catholiccemeterieschicago.org/locations.php?id=12.

Mount Hope, the southernmost, opened for business in 1888.[205]

In addition to the three cemeteries on the ridge, the neighborhood of Mount Greenwood is bordered on the south by Oak Hill, Beverly, and Lincoln cemeteries, and on the west by Saint Casimir. This profusion of boneyards led the community to be nicknamed "Seven Holy Tombs." Mount Greenwood native John R. Powers (1945–2013) popularized this name in his novels about growing up Catholic on the South Side. In *The Last Catholic in America*, he wrote "We children of Seven Holy Tombs believed that the edge of the earth lay two blocks beyond the cemeteries."[206]

Mount Greenwood Cemetery was designed as a "park cemetery," part of the nineteenth-century movement to make cemeteries part of the natural setting. Naturally abundant with white oak trees, the cemetery was laid out with gently curving roads that followed the contours of the landscape. The cemetery was constructed next to the Grand Trunk Railroad, with a station at 111th Street, at the southwest corner of the cemetery.[207] In the early years of Mount Greenwood, this railroad would have been the primary means by which mourners reached Mount Greenwood and the other nearby cemeteries, and these were well-served by the taverns and restaurants next to the station.[208]

Today, the railroad station is gone, though traces of it may still be seen in the faint outline of a path in the southwest corner. The main entrance is on 111th Street at the center of the south face of the cemetery, directly opposite the gates of Mount Olivet Cemetery. The entrance consists of three columns of yellow limestone connected by swinging iron gates, providing for two separate lanes of traffic to enter and exit. The cemetery office, a simple, modern one-story building, stands on the site of the original office, a now-vanished ivy-covered structure

---

[205] Jo Ellen Johnson, ed., *An Inventory of Cemeteries in South Cook County*, Vol. 3, South Suburban Genealogical and Historical Society Research Series (South Holland, Illinois: South Suburban Genealogical and Historical Society, 1991), 81.

[206] Maureen O'Donnell, "John R. Powers, 67, Wrote *Do Black Patent Leather Shoes Really Reflect Up?*" *Chicago Sun-Times*, January 19, 2013.

[207] Simon, *Chicago, the Garden City*.

[208] Stockwell, "Mount Greenwood."

that had been built of wood with the bark still visible.[209]

Directly inside the entrance is "The Little Chapel," as the bronze plaque on the facade denotes it. Built of limestone blocks, similar to those used for the cemetery gate, the chapel consists of a nave with peaked grey-shingled roof and a small octagonal steeple, and in front a carriage-porch of the

The "Little Chapel" was originally a receiving vault with 500 crypts for temporary storage of coffins during winter. In 1937 it was converted to a chapel and dedicated to the memory of cemetery president Willis Rudd.

same material. First erected in 1892[210] as a receiving vault, the structure was initially filled with shelves for the temporary storage of the remains of the winter's newly dead, awaiting burial when the ground had thawed.[211] It could hold about 500 coffins.[212] Having fallen into disuse with the advent of modern earth-moving equipment, it was refitted as a chapel in 1937. The following year, the new chapel became the regular meeting place of the Mount Greenwood Mission of the Church of God, a congregation that had met in a real estate office until one member suggested that they approach the cemetery board for permission to use the chapel for their Sunday services.[213]

Upon its reconstruction the chapel was dedicated in honor of cemetery president **Willis Nathaniel Rudd** (1860–1925). In January,

[209] Simon described this in 1893, stating the entrance was "flanked on the right-hand side by the cemetery office," which seems to indicate the same location as the modern office.

[210] Date 1892 given on bronze plaque affixed to chapel facade.

[211] "Quiet Meeting Place Found by Mission Group: Hold Sunday Services in Cemetery Chapel," *Chicago Daily Tribune*, June 21, 1942.

[212] Simon, *Chicago, the Garden City*.

[213] "Quiet Meeting Place Found by Mission Group."

1890, Rudd, then Mount Greenwood's secretary and superintendent, was involved in a minor dispute in the *Chicago Daily Tribune's* letters column. An African-American citizen had written to that paper, complaining that he had been forced to wait several hours in the cold before his son's funeral was conducted, while white funeral parties were given priority.[214] Rudd's reply to the editor a few days later assured readers that funerals were strictly scheduled by the availability of the funeral train, and that "the question of color is not in any way allowed to influence the treatment of visitors."[215]

By 1910 Rudd had become the cemetery president as well as organizer and first president of the Illinois Association of Cemeteries.[216] Not only a prominent cemeterian, Rudd was a champion horticulturist, growing and exhibiting award-winning flowers, with Mount Greenwood Cemetery taking a number of prizes at Horticultural Society of Chicago exhibitions.[217] He served as president of the Society of American Florists and the American Carnation Society.[218] Willis Rudd died suddenly at his home in south suburban Blue Island in November 1925.[219]

Mount Greenwood's most widely-recognized monument stands just west of the chapel, on a small rise dotted with simple headstones. There atop a granite pedestal stood a life-sized "white bronze" statue of an elk, its head held high, bearing a full set of antlers. On the pedestal is written *The faults of our BROTHERS we will write upon the sands,* motto of the **Benevolent & Protective Order of Elks.** Known as Elks Rest, the plot belongs to B.P.O.E. Chicago Lodge No. 4. In May 1882 the lodge advertised their annual benefit, with "Proceeds to be applied to the erection of a Monument in the

---

[214] "No Civil Rights at the Grave," *Chicago Daily Tribune,* January 14, 1890.

[215] "Voice of the People—No Color Line at Mount Greenwood.," *Chicago Daily Tribune,* January 17, 1890.

[216] "Mount Greenwood, The Silent City," *The Reform Advocate: America's Jewish Journal,* Volume 39, March 26 1910, 249.

[217] "Flower Show in Bloom: Chrysanthemums Have an Opening at the Auditorium," *Chicago Daily Tribune,* November 8, 1899.

[218] "Mount Greenwood, The Silent City."

[219] "W.N. Rudd Dies Suddenly; Was Expert of Flowers," *Chicago Daily Tribune,* November 28, 1925.

Elk's Rest at Mount Greenwood Cemetery."[220] On August 13 of that same year the monument was dedicated, with a "Grand Excursion" of Elks proceeding to Mount Greenwood by special train for an afternoon of speeches, prayer, and the unveiling, accompanied by an orchestra.[221] As of 2013, the majestic statue is unfortunately no longer present. A smaller bronze elk was recently installed in its place. Mount Greenwood abounds with the symbols of fraternal orders. On several family monuments, the double-headed eagle of Scottish Rite Masonry appears, as do the Masons' square and compass and the cross and crown of the Knights Templar. Lodges of several fraternal orders maintain

Carl and Johanna Uhlich, hotel owners and philanthropists, are memorialized with this statue of Hope at Mount Greenwood.

plots with impressive central monuments. **Aldine Lodge No. 129, Knights of Pythias**, erected a grey granite obelisk on their plot in 1899. On its side is a relief carving of a knight, with two halberds across his torso and, perched atop his helmet, a falcon. The Pythian **DeMolay Lodge** provided a plot for their members as well.

A large section was reserved for **Freemasons**, and at its center stands the grandest monument in the cemetery, a towering column, rich in Masonic symbolism. Described as "the most beautiful and costly Masonic monument in America" in a 1918 cemetery trade magazine,[222] the monument is a 60-foot tall granite Corinthian col-

---

[220] "Haverly's Theatre. Elks' Benefit! Sunday Evening, May 28, 1882" (classified ad), *Chicago Daily Tribune*, May 14, 1882.

[221] "Grand Excursion by Chicago Lodge No. 4, B.P.O. Elks" (classified ad), *Chicago Daily Tribune*, August 13, 1882.

[222] R.J. Haight, "From the Cemetery Rule Books," *Park and Cemetery and Landscape Gar-*

umn standing on a pedestal, with a brazier at the top, over which a flame is rendered in granite. Masonic symbols and intricate foliate designs decorate all sides of the base, over the initialism *A.F. & A.M* (Ancient Free and Accepted Masons). Between 1910 and about 1918, while the monument was under construction, fifteen percent of the cost of burial in the Masonic plot was set aside for the monument, and for two much smaller Ionic and Doric columns.[223]

Some individual monuments, too, possess exceptional beauty. The monument of pioneers and philanthropists **Carl Gottfried Uhlich** (1781–1867) and **Johanna Sophia Uhlich** (1796–1867), 33 feet tall, is a pedestal supporting a statue of a woman, one hand on her chest, the other holding an anchor, symbolizing Hope.[224] Owners of Uhlich's Hotel at State and 22nd, the Uhlichs donated a large tract of property just north of the Loop in 1867 to endow the German Orphan Home, intended to house orphans of German-American casualties of the Civil War. The facility was renamed the Uhlich Children's Home in their honor, and today continues as UCAN (Uhlich Children's Advantage Network), a ministry of the United Church of Christ that provides a variety of services to children in need.[225]

Of roughly similar design is the monument of **James W. Brockway** (1837–1895) and **Mary Adelaide Smith Brockway** (1841–1875),

The base of the Masonic monument, detailed with Masonic symbols and slogans on all sides. The column, the tallest monument in the cemetery, rises to a granite tripod and flame.

dening, Vol. XXVIII, No. 3 (Chicago: Allied Arts Publishing Company, May 1918).
[223] "Mount Greenwood, The Silent City."
[224] Simon, *Chicago, the Garden City*.
[225] "History," UCAN, http://archive.org/details/pressclubofchicago00pres.

though its substance is very different: The Brockway monument is a hollow, ornately detailed pedestal of white bronze. At the top stands another allegorical figure, a woman clutching a book and pointing heavenward—Faith. This depiction of Faith was one of the most popular white bronze castings, and the Brockway monument appeared in the 1891 catalogue of its maker, the American Bronze Company.[226] James Brockway was president of Mount Greenwood Cemetery in 1885 when the cemetery sent a strongly-worded correction to the *Tribune*. It seems that, a few days earlier, that paper had published an announcement of Mount Hope's opening that incorrectly claimed the latter was the only cemetery situated on the Blue Island Ridge. Suitably chastened by Mr. Brockway, the paper published a glowing review of the fine qualities of the already-operating Mount Greenwood.[227] Cast in several pieces, Brockway's memorial is one of the largest and most elaborate white bronze monuments in Illinois.

Though smaller, the monument of **William Bromstedt** similarly features a depiction of Faith. **Herman Vanderbelt**'s monument surrounds a red granite column with a pedestal and capital of white marble. The **Clair** plot is beautifully landscaped, with hedges echoing the design of the monument, in which benches flank a pair of columns supporting an entablature over a funerary urn.

In June of 1924, 75 Boy Scouts descended on the cemetery for the unveiling of the monument of one of their own, **Gerald Coursen** (~1907–1923), a scout who had died the previous August at the age of 16.[228] The boy was memorialized with a statue, now missing; only the boots remain.

Famed Pony Express Rider is written across a simple granite headstone, that of **Robert Haslam** (1840–1912). The young men who carried sacks of mail on horseback from Missouri to California in 1860 to 1861 were expected to make the run in 10 days. But when given a copy of Lincoln's inaugural address to deliver, Haslam did it

---

[226] Carol A. Grissom, *Zinc Sculpture in America, 1850–1950* (Newark, DE: University of Delaware, 2009), 575.

[227] "Mount Greenwood Cemetery. Doesn't Want to Be Left Out," *Chicago Daily Tribune*, October 11, 1885.

[228] "Boy Scouts Pray While Youth's Statue Is Unveiled," *Chicago Daily Tribune*, June 17, 1924.

in just under eight days, the fastest Pony Express run ever made—and he did it while wounded, shot through the jaw with an arrow. Though he died in poverty, his grave at Mount Greenwood was paid for by a friend—Buffalo Bill Cody.

MOUNT OLIVET CATHOLIC CEMETERY

2755 West 111th Street, Chicago
www.catholiccemeterieschicago.org
Consecrated 1885

Catherine O'Leary (~1827–1895), as in Mrs. O'Leary, cow owner, was recently and officially thanked by the city for letting her cow burn down the town in 1871. The mayor and other fans of post-fire Chicago credit the Great Fire with furnishing a clean slate for the city's ingenious planners. The heroic O'Leary is buried in this well-designed cemetery with husband **Patrick** (~1819–1894) and son **James "Big Jim" O'Leary** (1869–1925), a notorious gambling boss.

Established by Chicago's South Side Irish in 1885, Mount Olivet was the first of the South Side Catholic cemeteries, and features the tree-lined landscape and curving roads popularized by the rural cemetery movement that was then in flourish. Purchased under the guidance of Archbishop Patrick Feehan a year before its opening, the expanse instantly provided a more geographically practical alternative to burial at Calvary, far north in suburban Evanston.

In addition to the O'Leary plot, other Celtic highlights at Mount Olivet include the **Irish Nationalist Society** obelisk and an 1897 monument to the **Ancient Order of Hibernians**. Designed by sculptor John Moore and financed by fund-raising picnics, the latter structure is a 30-foot tower embellished with traditional symbols: a wolfhound, a harp, and a Celtic cross. An unusual red brick mausoleum can also be found here. And, standing in two adjacent plots are life-sized statues of

The Great Chicago Fire of 1871 started in the South Side barn of Patrick O'Leary (1824–1894) and Catherine O'Leary (1827–1895). Though their cow has long taken the blame, a newspaperman later confessed to having concocted the story. The true cause remains unknown.

This life-sized statue depicts a soldier of World War I, Private Daniel E. Carey, who died in July 1918.

A view of monuments from 111th Street. Local legend has it that the cemetery has a "hungry fence" that hypnotizes passing motorists into crashing their cars.

soldiers of the Spanish-American War and World War I, shown with their uniforms, weapons, and equipment fully detailed.

Still in place too at Mount Olivet is the monument marking the original grave of **Alphonse Capone** (1899–1947), whose body was relocated to Mount Carmel Cemetery in Hillside because of the family's fear of grave robbers.

MOUNT HOPE CEMETERY
11500 South Fairfield Avenue, Chicago
mthope-cemetery.com
Established 1885

For their *park cemetery* burial grounds, designed in the same philosophy as Oak Woods, the founders of Mount Hope Cemetery chose the highest land in southern Cook County, a glacial ridge west of the Morgan Park neighborhood, elevated one hundred feet above the level of Lake Michigan.[229] The 304-acre cemetery extends south from 115th Street, across from Mount Olivet to its north, bordered on east and west by railroad lines, and was, as author Andreas Simon put it in 1893, "empathetically the best selection that could have been made."[230]

As much as the elevation—which allowed for excellent drainage—the presence of the railroads made this a prime location, and featured heavily in the cemetery's early advertising. Organized under the authority of the State of Illinois in 1885, Mount Hope maintained offices in the cemetery itself and in the Old Colony Building in the Loop. The Grand Trunk Railway line bordered the cemetery on the west, and a free trolley conveyed passengers to the Chicago & Southern Traction Company lines in the east.[231]

---

[229] "Mount Hope Cemetery" (advertising booklet), undated but prior to 1906, author's collection. The booklet claimed this was the highest point in Cook County, but that point is actually in the vicinity of Elgin.

[230] Simon, *Chicago, the Garden City*, 159.

[231] "Mount Hope Cemetery" (advertising booklet).

Hillside mausoleums at Mount Hope. With the Chicago area generally flat, this is a relatively rare sight.

Though the cemetery is now entered from the north, it was due to the Grand Trunk line that Mount Hope's original main entrance was on the west side. There, passengers would arrive at a dedicated "Mount Hope Station" on the cemetery grounds.[232] A map published by the cemetery association in 1903 shows the path from the west entrance forking as it entered the cemetery, leading to either side of a magnificent depot, chapel, and office building. This structure included an open Doric colonnade with *Mount Hope* in large letters affixed to the entablature. Twin buildings with triangular pediments stood at the north and south ends of the colonnade, housing the chapel, waiting rooms, and office. Beyond this structure was a formally arranged flower garden and a large pond with a fountain.[233] All of this is now gone, demolished—the west entrance closed off, the forked path grown over with grass, the pond filled in, and only a barren patch of land where the chapel and colonnade once stood.[234]

The other great structure at Mount Hope was a public vault, located north of a roundabout in the northwest corner. The vault contained 160 iron compartments[235] behind an ivy-covered wall with

[232] "Mount Hope Cemetery" (advertising booklet).

[233] "Mount Hope Cemetery Association of Chicago" (advertising booklet), 1903, author's collection.

[234] Satellite photos on Google Earth from as early as 1999 show yellowish earth there, though the rest of the cemetery is lush and green.

[235] Simon, *Chicago, the Garden City*, 159.

twin arched doors. For no charge, the cemetery association allowed all customers to temporarily store their family members' remains in these "numerous compartments, each properly secured, carefully numbered and registered,"[236] until the permanent graves were ready. But this, too, has vanished, as modern earth-moving equipment has obviated the need for such temporary disposition.

Though the chapel and vault are no more, Mount Hope remains a pleasantly landscaped park, filled with winding roads, rolling hills, and fine monuments and mausoleums. Established about 20 years after Chicago's other rural or park cemeteries, Mount Hope's monuments are almost entirely of granite, the softer marble and limestone having by then fallen out of fashion. East of the old chapel's location, a group of private mausoleums are built into the side of a hill, their rear walls almost completely buried. A rare sight in the generally flat terrain around Chicago, such mausoleums often feature unusually thick walls, barrel-vaulted ceilings, and rooftops level with the terrain at the rear.[237]

Atop the hill, the **Matthews** mausoleum shows an Egyptian style in its column capitals and its overall shape, resembling that of a *mastaba* tomb, an ancient design with sloping sides that pre-dates the pyramids. The **Veeder** tomb is severely geometrical, almost a cube, but with fluted rectangular columns across the front. Further along the ridge, the **Arquilla** mausoleum is octagonal in plan, with smooth walls of red granite. Downslope, a sculpted granite flame stands over the grave of Lieutenant **Donald W. Yarrow** (1924–1945), who at the age of 20 fell in battle at the Rhine River.

Near the hillside mausoleums, one may see a variety of monuments of fine quality. The **Jocelyn** crypt, built principally of granite, has a set of white marble doors that have acquired a delightful green patina from the copper hinges. The **Jouris** family monument includes a surrogate mourner, a granite statue of a woman, her head resting on one hand as she looks down in sorrow. **John Alexander Cooper** (1850–1935) and **Martha Eleanor Cooper** (1845–1906) have a

---

[236] "Mount Hope Cemetery" (advertising booklet).
[237] Forest Home Cemetery and Bluff City Cemetery have comparable hillside mausoleum groups.

monument depicting a hardback book, partially opened with its spine facing up, resembling a tent. The **Collins** monument is one of few here not made of granite; it is a marble baptismal font, standing atop an ornate column capital.

John Edward Kernott (1865–1928), wealthy landowner and investor, is entombed in a large Art Deco influenced mausoleum. The mausoleum of **Charles G. Blake**, though sleek and modern in style, has a nod to Classical architecture in the Ionic volutes over the doorway, the same curved decorative elements used on column capitals.[238]

Most remarkable of all in this part of the cemetery is an upright slab from which emerges a carved head and torso of an androgynous youth, hair swept back, eyes gazing slightly upward, one hand upraised. The figure is surrounded by a swirl of cloth. Below are the words, *The best is yet to be, the last of life, for which the first was made*, from the poem by Robert Browning. Nearby are the headstones of Georgia Clark Norton (1850–1937) and Lillian Norton Hoit (1871–1912), mother and daughter. Lillian was married to Lowell S. Hoit (1869–1912), a grain merchant and vice-president at the Chicago Board of trade. Though he likely had a hand in choosing this beautiful and sentimental monument, he remarried after his young wife's death, and was buried elsewhere.

The largest tomb here belongs to meat-packer **Gustavus Franklin Swift** (1839–1903). Swift pioneered the use of ice-cooled railroad cars to ship meat products across the country. Though the railroads resisted, fearing loss of business from the local meat dealers Swift was now competing with, he found ways to get his cars into his target mar-

---

[238] There was a maker of cemetery monuments in Chicago in the 1950s by the name "Charles G. Blake." I have not yet determined whether this is his mausoleum.

kets, and died an immensely wealthy man. Swift's mausoleum is of Classical design, with four Doric columns supporting an entablature and pediment. Windows in the side walls light the spacious interior, and planters stand on twin pedestals in the tomb's front yard.

A weathered sandstone obelisk, erected in 1892, stands at the **Press Club of Chicago** plot. On the front of the shaft is their intricate logo, the initials PCC entwined with a quill pen thrust at an angle through the loop of the "P." Organized in 1880, the club was intended to foster good relations among newspaper and literary professionals "and to provide them with comfortable club rooms."[239] Like many fraternal and professional organizations of the day, it extended to members benefits of help in times of disability and burial in a group plot. The club's 1907 booklet offers its members "a final resting place beneath the Press Club monument in Mount Hope cemetery."

Veterans of the Civil War have a special place at Mount Hope, in a section purchased by the **George G. Meade Post 444** of the **Grand Army of the Republic**. This veterans' organization, which originated in Decatur, Illinois, had chapters throughout the country until its ultimate dissolution in 1956 on the death of the last Union veteran. In 1905, the Englewood-based Post 444 placed a white bronze (zinc) monument in Mount Hope. Cast as one with the pedestal on which he stands, a soldier wearing a cloak and long overcoat stands solemnly, his hands gripping the barrel of his rifle—though most of the gun is now missing. As white bronze is a durable material, all the detail of the statue is in fine condition, the lettering on the pedestal still crisp and readable. Nearby, about 30 marble headstones are visible, of the standard design provided by the government for soldiers' graves. Before and after patriotic holidays, each is usually decorated with a tiny American flag.

Mount Hope's most celebrated grave site is the **Rotary International** plot. This elaborately landscaped plot in the south part of the cemetery features a long walkway of alternating octagonal and square bricks between two rows of hedges, leading to a large grey granite

---

[239] *The Press Club of Chicago: Its Past, Present and Future* (Chicago: Press Club of Chicago, 1907). Archived in the Lawrence J. Gutter Collection of Chicagoana, Internet Archive, http://archive.org.

The Rotary International plot, with founders Harris and Schiele buried next to other prominent Rotarians.

monument in the shape of the Rotary logo, a six-spoked gear wheel with 24 cogs around the circumference and a keyhole at the center.[240]

The Rotary Club began in Chicago in 1905 when attorney **Paul Percy Harris** (1868–1947) proposed that businessmen meet "in fellowship and friendship" regularly, "rotating" between locations. The first such meeting was hosted in the office of coal merchant **Sylvester Schiele** (1870–1945) on Dearborn Street. Harris and Schiele are both buried here, on either side of the central monument and walkway. **Dr. Cedric A. Pope** (1926–1990), the Rotary district governor who organized this memorial, is buried at the rear of the plot; his monument bears a smaller version of the Rotary logo. The Rotary plot is such a point of pride to the cemetery that the Rotary logo also appears on the fence of the cemetery, next to the entrance on 115th Street.

The **Lions Club** is similarly honored with a logo at the cemetery entrance, for their founder **Melvin Jones** (1879–1961) is buried here as well. Jones, who owned an insurance company, proposed in 1917 that successful men should work to improve their communities, thereby forming the first Lions Club. As the organization grew to be international in scope, Jones left his business behind to work full-time with the Lions. Melvin Jones's grave is comparatively modest: a serpentine-top rectangular granite monument with the epitaph, *Founder, Lions International*, and the logo of the Lions carved into its surface.

---

[240] "History of the Rotary Logo," Rotary Global History Fellowship, http://www.rotary-first100.org/history/history/wheel/.

As a park cemetery, Mount Hope differs from older cemeteries in that an open space, free from visual clutter, was a guiding principle of its design. Each spacious plot contains a single monument, of whatever style its owners preferred and the best quality they could afford, of the most durable material, granite. In the sections laid out in this design, there are no individual headstones to clutter the view. Flat or beveled markers only surround the family monument. Iron railings and stone copings around plots were forbidden from the outset. Though its greatest architectural glory, the chapel at the west entrance, has fallen to the ravages of modernization, Mount Hope remains what it was intended to be, a park cemetery allowing for individual expression within a carefully sculpted landscape.

MATERIAL CONSIDERATIONS

Almost as diverse as the contents of the graves they mark are the elements used in the creation of funerary monuments.

Early in the history of the Midwest, limestone was the preferred medium. Quarried in a number of areas, Bedford, Indiana, limestone offered the greatest ease of carving, and sculptors often demanded it. In Chicago and environs, the limestone quarried in Lemont, southwest of the city limits, found its way to the graves of thousands, its buttery hue and rough grain still easily distinguishable from the sleek granite and marble creations of later days. Lemont limestone was favored by architects as well, whose preferences are evidenced in the Chicago Water Tower and Pumping Station and in the elaborately arched and castellated entry gates of a number of area burial grounds. Some Chicago residents believe that the reported haunting of a number of local graves and cemeteries has something to do with the Lemont limestone used in their monuments and entry gates. Such believers hint at the existence of a special energy or other conductive quality inherent in the stone. Coincidence, however, seems a likelier explanation.

When limestone was beyond geographical or financial reach, other media were considered, namely, wood or wrought iron, which were often fashioned into fences that ran, decoratively and protectively, around gravesites. Sandstone, slate, and marble were also used, though granite was and is the most durable of monument materials. Adding to the array were local foundries, which were sometimes commissioned to create bronze detailing or portraiture for the embellishment of tombs.

A more affordable alternative was pot metal, which was used in the design of an increasing number of monuments. Later, some designers discovered concrete, which could be enhanced considerably by pressing seashells, colored glass, stones, or broken tiles into the fresh pouring.

ST. CASIMIR CATHOLIC CEMETERY

4401 West 111th Street, Chicago
www.catholiccemeterieschicago.org
Consecrated 1903

This stunning Lithuanian Roman Catholic cemetery is perhaps the most artistically progressive in the Chicago area. Though the earlier graves are marked by typically Catholic stones and monuments, the markers over post-World War II plots are both huge and sensationally unconventional, combining novel images with unexpected materials, such as fiberglass and steel, to create singular and often pleasing effects. Spacing, too, is unusual at St. Casmir's: The ample,

The St. Casimir Memorial Bell monument is considered the cemetery's principal monument. Designed by Ramojus Mozoliauskas and Bert J. Gast and erected in 1969, this 28-foot structure houses the bell that, from 1913 onward, announced the arrival of funeral processions at the cemetery.

Though noted for contemporary sculpture, the cemetery's older sections include many fine examples of traditional marble statuary, most with a religious theme.

manicured lots provide plenty of breathing room for the exquisite monuments, resulting in the overall effect of a sculpture garden.

St. Casimir was the subject of a coffee table book, *A Lithuanian Cemetery*, published in 1976, lavishly illustrated with black and white photos of the monuments and their artistic motifs. The text, in both English and Lithuanian, describes Lithuanian funeral customs as well as the history of the cemetery itself.

St. Casimir's Cemetery is noted for having many highly individualistic monuments in the modern artistic style. Crosses are an omnipresent motif.

Buried around this crucifixion group are founders of the Sisters of St. Casimir, including Father Antanas Staniukynas (1865–1918) and Mother Maria Kaupas (1880–1940). The order began in 1907 to nurture the faith of Lithuanian immigrants.

Shrine section dedicated to Saint Casimir, patron of Lithuania. The fifteenth-century prince, son of the King of Poland, and Grand Duke of Lithuania, was known for his charity and piety before his death of illness at the age of 25. Saint Casimir's popularity amongst Lithuanian Catholics ensured that the cemetery could not possibly be called anything else. The lily in his hand symbolizes purity; at his feet is a royal crown.

SUBURBAN
CEMETERIES

Nebel monument at Forest Home.

METRO NORTH

The cemetery near Shermer and Willow in Northbrook, at the northern edge of
Cook County, is a former churchyard. St. Peter's United Evangelical Reformed
Church stood on this site until it was destroyed by fire in 1961. The congregation
built their new church elsewhere, but continue to care for the cemetery at the
original location.

CALVARY CATHOLIC CEMETERY

301 Chicago Avenue, Evanston
www.catholiccemeterieschicago.org
Consecrated 1859

Chicago's preeminent historic Catholic cemetery lies a few blocks north of the city limits in the suburb of Evanston, stretching from Chicago Avenue and CTA's Purple line elevated track on the west to Sheridan Road and the lake shore on the east.

At the center of Calvary's western edge is a magnificent gate of yellow Lemont limestone, one of the finest entrances of any Illinois cemetery, and one of few such structures to survive to the present day. Designed by architect James J. Egan, the gate forms a triple arch, with smaller pedestrian entrances flanking the carriage entrance. Over the center arch is a triangular portion, forming the shape of a capital "A" (*alpha*), while the arch itself resembles the Greek letter *omega*. These first and last letters of the Greek alphabet are a traditional symbol of the perfection of God. Smaller omegas appear above each side arch. Around the main arch is inscribed the text, *Blessed are they that mourn, for they shall be comforted.*[241] From this grand entrance, a wide avenue runs the entire length of the cemetery, connecting to Sheridan Road, only a few yards from the lake shore.

Architect James J. Egan designed the cemetery's main entrance, incorporating the shapes of the letters Alpha and Omega, symbolizing the fullness of God as the beginning and the end.

---

[241] Matthew 5:4.

The oldest archdiocesan Catholic cemetery, Calvary was commissioned in 1859 as efforts were underway to remove the old lakefront cemeteries located at the south end of present day Lincoln Park. There, the Catholic cemetery was located just south of North Avenue, across from the archbishop's residence.[242] Louis Leonhart of Evanston and Lake View florist Edgar Saunder provided the initial design for Calvary's western 50 acres; the eastern half was initially undeveloped and reserved for later expansion.[243] Though the east side of the cemetery, with its unsurpassed view of Lake Michigan, might be considered a prime location today, in 1859 this land would have been marshy and far less desirable. The location of the railroad line, too, demanded that the west side of the cemetery be chosen for the Egan's glorious main entrance; trains from the Chicago & Northwestern Railway and the Chicago, Milwaukee & St. Paul Railroad stopped there regularly.[244] On All Souls Day, 1859, Bishop James Duggan and 15 priests consecrated the new cemetery.[245]

The 120 acres of Chicago's premier Catholic cemetery were quickly filled. By 1900, with 10 to 20 burials taking place every day, and over 160,000 graves already occupied, few lots remained available for purchase. The diocesan authorities announced that the cemetery would be closed to new burials.[246] As a replacement for Calvary, a new cemetery was offered—Mount Carmel, to be twice the size of Calvary, at the western edge of Cook County.[247]

This was not, however, the end of Calvary. Burials continued in lots that had already been sold prior to the closure. Landscaping work made more space available. Most dramatically, the pond in the western portion of the cemetery was filled in, and shrines to St. Peter and St. John the Baptist erected in the reclaimed land. In 1960, the appearance of Calvary changed again, as Dutch elm disease wiped out most of the cemetery's ancient trees.

The administration building and chapel is immediately inside and

[242] "Calvary Cemetery: Anecdotal Information," document available in cemetery office.
[243] *Chicago Press-Tribune*, August 23, 1859.
[244] Simon, *Chicago, the Garden City*, 136.
[245] *The Daily Times*, November 3, 1859.
[246] "Calvary Soon to Be Closed," *Chicago Daily Tribune*, March 25, 1900.
[247] "Soon to Seal Calvary," *Chicago Daily Tribune*, March 21, 1900.

north of the entrance, on a spot formerly occupied by greenhouses and a ladies' waiting room.[248] Here, one may obtain a map and list of historic points of interest. Century-old photos on the wall of the office show the cemetery as it once was, including some features that are now vanished, such as the lakes that have since been filled in, and the cemetery's original office—located opposite the present one, south of the main gate. A statue of St. Patrick occupies the ground where the original office stood.

Cater-corner from the office, a tall Celtic cross stands atop a pedestal on which is carved the face of a mustachioed man surrounded by a laurel wreath. This monument of **Colonel James A. Mulligan** (1829–1864), prominently situated, is one of the first sights to greet a visitor walking through the entrance. An attorney in his civilian life, Mulligan raised a volunteer infantry regiment in 1861, the 23rd Illinois, colloquially known as the "Irish Brigade." Defeated and captured at the Battle of Lexington, Missouri, Mulligan so impressed his Confederate opponent, Major General Price, that he was granted safe passage back to the Union lines. In 1862 he was appointed commander of Camp Douglas, a prison camp on Chicago's South Side.[249] Reassigned to combat duty and placed in command of a reorganized 23rd Illinois, Colonel Mulligan was mortally wounded in Kernstown, Virginia, in July of 1864. As he was carried from the battlefield, he ordered his rescuers to "lay me down and save the flag." This became his epitaph.

As with most Catholic cemeteries, the place of honor is given to priests. Calvary's main road proceeds directly east from the entrance only for a short distance, then splits and flows to either side of

Seen here through Egan's entrance arch is the monument of Colonel James A. Mulligan.

---

[248] Simon, *Chicago, the Garden City*, 135.
[249] See Oak Woods Cemetery entry for more on Camp Douglas.

a circular section dominated by a towering granite crucifix with art-fully arranged flowers and bushes at its base. Surrounding the cruci-fix are concentric circles of monuments, most of them cross-shaped, some decorated with vestments and Eucharistic chalices and hosts.

The section south of the priests' circle includes a pair of ledger stones. Buried beneath these are **Edward Fitzsimmons Dunne** (1853–1937) and **Elizabeth Kelly Dunne** (1862–1928). Edward Dunne was the only man to serve as both mayor of Chicago, a single two-year term ending in 1907, and governor of Illinois, which he did from 1913 to 1917. Dunne was also United States commissioner to the Chicago's World's Fair of 1933, the *Century of Progress*, as not-ed on his monument. In this section are also the graves of **Patrick Crowley** (1911–1974) and **Patricia Caron Crowley** (1913–2005),[250] originators of the Christian Family Movement, a national network of discussion and support groups meeting in members' homes.[251]

On the western edge of the cemetery is the mausoleum of **Charles Comiskey** (1859–1931), four Doric columns across its front. Comis-key was owner of the Chicago White Sox and the man for whom Comiskey Park was named. A notorious skinflint, Comiskey paid his players considerably less than other owners, at one point even benching a player who was a few runs away from qualifying for a large bonus that they had earlier agreed upon. The players' frustra-tion at the low wages is said to have prompted some to accept bribes, leading to the "Black Sox Scandal," in which the Sox intentionally lost the 1919 World Series. Nearby is the striking black granite marker of **T. Emmet O'Neill** (1929–1993), advertising executive and later adviser and chief of staff to senators Alan Dixon and Carol Moseley-Braun.[252]

The section immediately north of the priests' circle has a high con-centration of private mausoleums. Many of these are richly carved, with Classical or Gothic architectural styles, several with statues or crosses atop the pediments. One especially handsome mausoleum is

[250] "Patricia Caron Crowley—Obituary," *Chicago Sun-Times*, November 27, 2005.

[251] "About CFM," Christian Family Movement USA, http://www.cfm.org/aboutcfm.html.

[252] Art Barnum, "Emmet O'Neill, Adviser to Prominent Politicians," *Chicago Tribune*, March 21, 1993.

the tomb of **John Powers** (1852–1930), a Chicago alderman of 38 years called "dean of the city council."[253] Built in the Art Deco style, this sleek octagonal structure of grey granite blocks towers over its neighbors. A bronze name-plate over the intricate grillwork door is flanked with bas-relief urns.

At the eastern edge of the section is the ornate **Sexton** mausoleum, a limestone structure built in the Gothic style, with a cross atop its pyramidal roof. The front of the mausoleum is reminiscent of Egan's entrance arch, with shared de-

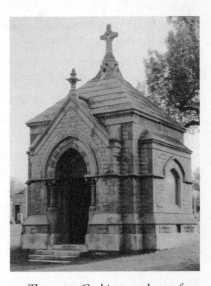

sign elements including a gently pointed arch set into a triangular wall above short columns, and an inscription following the curve of the arch: *Thy Kingdom Come, Thy Will Be Done.* **Patrick J. Sexton** (1846–1903) was a millionaire contractor and president of the Chicago Brick Company,[254] dying in 1903 after falling ill on a trip to London. Rumors soon spread that he had displayed symptoms of arsenic poisoning, prompting his widow and sons to order an autopsy. No evidence of poison was found.[255] In recent years a small tree has been seen growing from the roof of his tomb, having taken root between the stones.

Nearby is a modern **Pieta** monument, featuring a relief carving of the Virgin Mary cra-

The ornate Gothic mausoleum of brick company owner Patrick Sexton, wrongly thought to have died of arsenic poisoning. Stylistically, it is very similar to the cemetery's main entrance. Note the short columns on either side of the doorway, the shape of the arch, and the words inscribed along the curve of the arch.

---

[253] "John Powers, Noted Council Figure, Dies," *Chicago Daily Tribune*, May 20, 1930.

[254] Todd Kendall, "The Arena," The Chicago Crime Scenes Project, http://chicagocrimes-cenes.blogspot.com/2008/12/arena.html.

[255] "Autopsy on Sexton," *Chicago Daily Tribune*, October 30, 1903. The article goes on to say that interment will be at Calvary "where, a few years ago, Mr. Sexton built a costly mausoleum."

dling the body of Christ. From there one can see **Peter Smith's** mausoleum, or at least the top of it—it rises only a few feet from the earth, most of it underground, the stairs leading to the door long since filled in. The mausoleum of **Thomas Mathews** (d. ~1878) is composed of huge limestone blocks, with a facade wider than the rest of the building, with inset panels of marble inscribed with the names of those within. Huge quarter-circle pieces decorate the corners of the roof, and the door is of solid stone. The tomb gives an overall impression of immense weight and solidity.[256]

The **Cuneo** mausoleum, largest at Calvary, stands alone on an island in the road. This Art Deco mausoleum features a tall rectangular portion in the center with smaller chambers on either side. The door is of bronze and glass, and one may look within to view the two-story atrium. The faces of a woman and five bearded men are cast in bronze above the door. A few hundred feet directly north, close to the north wall of the cemetery, is another Cuneo mausoleum, this one in a more Gothic style, resembling a small church, with busts of a man and woman on either side of the door. **Frank Cuneo** (~1862–1942) was a produce merchant, who in 1888 organized the first fruit auction in Chicago, and in 1907 founded the Italian Chamber of Commerce.[257] In memory of his wife **Amelia Cuneo** (1870–1891) he endowed the Cuneo Hospital in the Uptown neighborhood (it now stands vacant, threatened with demolition). Their son **John F. Cuneo** (1884–1977) purchased the Henneberry Printing Company, renaming it Cuneo Press and making it into Chicago's second largest printer.[258]

Proceeding east from the older Cuneo mausoleum, one finds another memorial set into the roadway. Surrounded by a low, gently curving granite wall on all sides, the rhomboid-shaped plot features

---

[256] The receiving vault mentioned in the 1864 city directory was said to have had walls three feet thick, and this mausoleum certainly matches this description. Could that vault have been sold to Mr. Mathews when it outlived its original purpose? Or does that description refer to a now-demolished structure?

[257] "Frank Cuneo, 80, Pioneer Produce Merchant, Dies," *Chicago Daily Tribune*, September 18, 1942.

[258] "Printing," Encyclopedia of Chicago, http://encyclopedia.chicagohistory.org/pages/1010.html.

a large central monument, on top of which is a statue of a woman holding a Bible, her eyes gazing straight ahead. Next to her, a girl kneels, her face pressed into the woman's lap. An entrance is cut into the curbing, with angels on either side, their arms at their chest and heads bowed. This impressive plot belongs to the family of **John A. Lynch** (1878–1963), founder of the National Bank of the Republic.[259]

John F. Cuneo, owner of Cuneo Press, is entombed in this two-story mausoleum, largest in the cemetery.

Nearby, a granite statue of a girl sits atop a tall pedestal, a drooping lily dangling from one hand. The name *LILY* appears beneath her bare feet; the pedestal identifies her as **Nelly May Bryne**, who died in 1880 at the age of 17. A classical mausoleum holds the remains of **John Cudahy** (1843–1915), who with his brothers operated a meat-packing company active throughout the Midwest.

To the east, one can see what looks like a pile of rough white stones. Viewed from the other side, it becomes a grotto in which two small boys sit, their faces all but worn away by a century of weathering. *Artie and Willie* reads the inscription below the statues. In much smaller print, mostly worn away, they are identified as *Children of John F. and Mary E. Walsh.*[260] **Arthur Kenneth Walsh**, or *Artie, 4 years 3 months*, died April 3 1879. His brother **William F. Walsh**, or *Willie, 2 years 5 months*, died ten days later.[261]

---

[259] "Obituaries—John A. Lynch," *Chicago Daily Tribune*, October 6, 1938.

[260] While searching for the death notices for Artie and Willie I came across an odd coincidence—the *Chicago Tribune*'s death notices for November 5, 1876, include the deaths of two *other* Walsh brothers on subsequent days from scarlet fever—Eddy M., 2, and Franky J., 7, children of Michael and Maggie Walsh, also with burial in Calvary. The dual obituary was accompanied by the verse: "Dearest children, you have left us, And your loss we deeply feel; But 'tis God that has bereft us, He can all our sorrows heal."

[261] *Cook County, Illinois, Deaths Index, 1878–1922*. The entries do not list the parents' names, but give the boys' ages as 4 and 2, matching the monument's inscription, and both indicate burial at Calvary.

A favorite with visitors is this marble grotto enclosing the statues of brothers Artie and Willie Walsh, who died ten days apart in 1879. Their monument originally stood on the shore of a small pond, which was filled in after the cemetery ran out of burial space.

Artie and Willie's view was once much different. The section towards which they face was originally a pond, spanned by a bridge. Photos of it as it once was are on display in the administrative office. Rather than facing uniformly in one direction, the graves on the edge of this section follow the old shoreline. After the pond was filled in, statues of St. Peter and St. John the Baptist were placed on small landscaped hills, and the newly formed land sold as graves, organized neatly into parallel rows and marked with flat markers.

Behind the Walsh boys, the classically-style mausoleum with Ionic columns on all sides is the tomb of **Patrick J. Healy** (1840–1905), founder of Lyon & Healy, a world-renowned manufacturer of harps.

On the south side of the main road, several mausoleums stand on the former lake shore. One of these belongs to **Edward J. Kelly** (1876–1950), mayor of Chicago from 1933 to 1947, who is noted both for massive reductions to the city's debt and for establishing a powerful political machine. He was succeeded as mayor by **Martin H. Kennelly** (1887–1961), who campaigned as a reformer. Kennelly has a simple granite headstone located just north of the main road, to the east, near a new columbarium structure.

In the same section as Mayor Kelly's monument, a marble statue of a young man stands atop a pedestal, his head crowned with flowers. One hand rests on a harp, the other holds a palm frond, symbolic of victory. The inscription on the monument, entirely in Latin, tells of the life of *Reverendissimus* **Thaddeus J. Butler** (1844–1897).

Father Butler was a parish priest in Chicago when he was selected to become bishop of Concordia, Kansas.[262] He traveled to Rome to be consecrated as bishop, but died while there before the ceremony could take place. His monument thus describes him as *Episcopus Electus Concordiae*, Bishop-Elect of Concordia.

Continuing east along the central road, the visitor will encounter a robed and haloed figure, the Virgin Mary, the deep blue-green patina of the bronze statue staining the white stone of the plinth. A round plaque on the front commemorates **Father S. Morelli**, and the Latin words at the base, *Ossa et cineres Fratrum Ordinis Servorum BMV*, mean "bones and ashes of the Friars of the Order of the Blessed Virgin Mary." About 60 religious brothers are laid out in neat rows in front of the statue, each with a flat marker in the shape of a cross. A few rows east, a towering cross rises from a rectangular base at the grave of Chicago mayor **John Patrick Hopkins** (1858–1918). Hopkins was elected in 1893 to finish the term of the assassinated mayor Carter Henry Harrison, defeating interim mayor George Swift. However, Swift would then go on to defeat Hopkins two years later.[263]

This marble statue honors Most Reverend Thaddeus J. Butler, a Chicago priest appointed bishop of Concordia, Kansas. Traveling to Rome for his consecration, he died before ever setting foot in his new diocese.

Four large mausoleums stand on the corner opposite Mayor

---

[262] "History," Catholic Diocese of Salina, http://salinadiocese.org/about-us/history.

[263] "Chicago Mayors, 1837–2007" (table), Encyclopedia of Chicago, http://encyclopedia. chicagohistory.org/pages/1443.html. Harrison is buried in Graceland and Swift in Rosehill.

Hopkins, with styles ranging from Gothic to modern. The largest of these belongs to candy–bar manufacturer **Joseph B. Galli** (~1871–1935), president of the Peanut Specialty Company,[264] and features a door with exceptionally intricate metalwork depicting the crucifixion of Christ. North of this group of mausoleums, architect **James J. Egan** (1839–1914) is buried next to a limestone Celtic cross. Egan, a noted builder of churches in Chicago, San Francisco, and Pittsburgh, designed Calvary's main entrance. Next to Egan's plot, a robed and hooded figure of St. Scholastica holds a dove, looking over the graves of the Benedictine Sisters.[265]

Crossed baseball bats decorate the monument of **Robert Figg** (1872–1926) in the cemetery's northeast corner, their handles up and barrels pointed downward in mourning. A granite baseball, now missing, once rested on a small pedestal in front of his monument.[266] The tall and heavyset Figg, ironically called "Little Bob," was an avid baseball supporter, acting as umpire

Our friend, your friend, everybody's friend, 'Little Bob Figg'. A heavyset civil servant, Figg was an enthusiastic backer of amateur baseball. When he died in a fall, his friends called for donations to erect this monument, with crossed baseball bats pointed downward in mourning. A large granite baseball originally sat in the socket in front.

---

[264] "$50,000 Estate Goes to Joseph B. Galli's Widow," *Chicago Daily Tribune*, September 8, 1935.

[265] It is worth noting here that "Section Y" is actually two sections, on either side of the main road, and that odd-numbered rows are north of the road while even-numbered rows are on the south. Not only did this cause me some confusion while trying to locate Mr. Egan's grave, but it also confused a pair of visitors I spoke with later that day, seeking a relative's plot on the wrong side of the road.

[266] "Baseball Memorials," *Chicago Daily Tribune*, September 30, 1947. The article indicates that Bob Figg's baseball was almost two feet in diameter, and was "safely anchored to prevent removal." The stone baseball disappeared before 1994.

and announcer at games. He worked for the Cook County clerk and treasurer and unsuccessfully campaigned for a job as Cook County commissioner.[267] In 1926 he fainted while on a stairway at City Hall, toppled over a railing, and fell five floors to his death.[268] His epitaph: *Our friend, your friend, everybody's friend, 'Little Bob Figg.'*

Perhaps Calvary's finest monument is the "boy in the box," **Joseph A. Lyon** (1882–1891). This dapper young gentleman stands behind a glass door, within a cylindrical enclosure of rusticated stone. Sculpted in marble, "Josie" wears a jacket and big floppy bow tie as he casually stands, one leg crossed in front of the other, his elbow resting on a sculpted tree stump, a finger marking his place in his book. Aged nine years old, Joseph died at his South Canal Street residence in December 1891 of diphtheria.[269] Simple flat markers on either side of Josie's monument mark his parents' graves.

Josie Lyon, the "boy in the box," died at the age of nine.

In a granite shelter south of the main road stands a sad-eyed statue of Christ, crowned with thorns, his hands bound with rope, holding a reed in mocking parody of a scepter. At its base are the words *Ecce Homo* ("behold the man"), the words spoken by Pontius Pilate that became the traditional name of this artistic motif. **Thomas Gahan** (1847–1905), owner of a general contracting business, held many posts including police captain, alderman, chairman of the Cook County Democratic Central Committee, and delegate to multiple

267 Rogers Park/West Ridge Historical Society, "Robert W. 'Little Bob' Figg," http://www.rp-wrhs.org/index.php?option=com_content&view=article&id=91:robert-w-qlittle-bobq-figg&catid=24:people-and-personalities&Itemid=27.

268 "Robert Figg Falls to Death in City Hall," *Chicago Daily Tribune*, February 25, 1926.

269 "Deaths," *Chicago Daily Tribune*, December 6, 1891.

Democratic National Conventions.[270] His funeral was disrupted when union and non-union drivers clashed, causing a "runaway and smashup" on Michigan Avenue.[271] Look west from here to see an exceptionally beautiful and decidedly feminine marble angel, rising from a cloud and clutching a handful of flowers. **Paul Richard Morgan** died in 1918 at the age of 21, most likely a casualty of the Great War.

Mayor William Dever (1862–1929) is memorialized with an intricately carved Celtic cross, east of the boy in the box. Celtic knot

A superbly detailed angel honors a soldier of the Great War, Paul Richard Morgan.

work covers most of its surface, and the arms of the cross are decorated with symbols including the Star of David, Maltese Cross, and Chi Rho. Dever ran as a reform candidate against the spectacularly corrupt William Hale Thompson,[272] winning election in 1923 and waging war against Capone and his bootleggers. In the next plot east, the intriguing **Mary O'Brien** (1851–1915) monument includes a granite bust depicting a mature woman, protected by a canopy.

A mausoleum across the road is labeled *A.D. Hannah – David Hogg*, and contains the crypts of partners in the liquor business. **Alexander Hannah** (1846–1913) and **David Hogg** (1842–1933) are as close in death as they were in life. The two Scottish immigrants were not only in business together, but were brothers-in-law, having married a pair of sisters and eventually building mansions next to one another.[273]

[270] *Centennial History of the City of Chicago. Its Men and Institutions. Biographical Sketches of Leading Citizens* (Chicago: Chicago Inter Ocean, 1905).

[271] "Carriage in Gahan Funeral Procession Wrecked in Strike Blockade," *Chicago Daily Tribune*, May 4, 1905.

[272] See Oak Woods Cemetery entry.

[273] "Chicago Company Profiles," Chicago Billiard Museum, http://www.chicagobilliardmu-

In the same row as the distillers, a few hundred feet south, is the disappointingly plain headstone of **Michael "Hinky Dink" Kenna** (1858–1946). One of early twentieth century Chicago's most powerful politicians, the diminutive Hinky Dink was one of two aldermen from the First Ward, along with the obese and equally corrupt **"Bathhouse" John Coughlin** (1860–1938). Together, they were known as "Lords of the Levee," for the notorious red light district in their ward. They consorted regularly with pimps, gamblers, and gangsters, as well as "respectable" society. Their annual First Ward Ball, held in the Chicago Coliseum, raked in more than $50,000 a year until it was shut down by the city. Upon his death at age 91, Kenna left one million dollars to his family, with instructions to spend $33,000 to build him a mausoleum. They ignored his wishes and bought a simple $85 flat marker. "Bathhouse" John Coughlin's equally colorful nickname stemmed from his former job giving scrubs in a public bath. Coughlin, who died a few years before his partner, had been a bit more successful at getting into a mausoleum—he is entombed near Calvary's main entrance, only a few feet from the Priests' Circle.

This part of the cemetery includes a unique monument made from petrified wood—a slice of ancient tree, nearly two feet long, with bark still intact, is the monument of **Margaret M. Grosch** (1890–1932). Two nearly identical monuments here commemorate soldiers of the Spanish-American War, both privates in the 1st Illinois Volunteer Infantry who died in Cuba in 1898. **Eugene A. Hussey** (1876–1898) of Company A died near Santiago,[274] and **John E. "Jack" Fallon** (1878–1898) of Company H died at Siboney. Their monuments each depict a wide-brimmed hat resting on a carelessly heaped scabbard and gun belt. Fallon's bears the motto *non sibi sed patriae* ("not for self, but for country").

Next to Private Fallon's grave, a sculpted fireman's helmet sits atop a tree trunk, both carved from the same piece of limestone, commemorating another who died *non sibi*. **Thomas Dillon** (1870–

---

seum.org/chicago_billiard_companies.html.

[274] "Signal Corps at Home," *Chicago Daily Tribune*, September 29, 1898; and "Four of the First Buried—Bodies of Infantrymen who Died in Cuba Honored by Colonel Turner's Men," *Chicago Daily Tribune*, November 16, 1898.

1898), a truckman with the Chicago Fire Department, was one of four firefighters to die when a wall collapsed on them at the Palace Livery Stable in December, 1898.[275]

Bishop James Duggan (1825–1899), who presided at the consecration of Calvary in 1859, began to exhibit signs of mental illness in 1866. In 1869 he was institutionalized at a Catholic-run insane asylum in St. Louis, though still nominally Bishop of Chicago. It was 11 years before a successor was appointed. Upon his death in 1899 he was buried in Calvary and remained there for over a century even as the remains of other early Chicago bishops were relocated to the Bishop's Mausoleum in Mount Carmel, an omission generally held to be due to the stigma of mental illness. In 2001, with attitudes changing, the body of Bishop Duggan was finally disinterred and relocated to Mount Carmel.[276]

One of Calvary's better works of art is in this section—a life-sized granite statue of a woman stands in front of a cross atop three steps, one foot extended as if stepping down. Her hair is sculpted in a 1920s style, large curls on either side, and she wears a pearl necklace. One arm holds a bundle of roses against her side; the other hand, extended, offers a single rose. **Anna C. Spahn**, age 20, sister of an Illinois state representative, died in November 1922, after having been hospitalized for several months.[277]

Thomas Cusack (1858–1926) is buried next to the main

This life-sized granite statue portrays Anna Spahn, aged 20.

[275] "Firefighter Record," Illinois Fire Service Institute, http://www.fsi.illinois.edu/content/library/iflodd/search/Firefighter.cfm?ID=582.

[276] "Final Chapter, Final Rest: Chicago's Fourth Bishop 'Home' After 102 Years," *The Catholic New World*, April 1, 2001.

[277] "The Right Rev. Pigeas Will Be Buried Today," *Chicago Tribune*, November 21, 1922; and "Obituary 2," *Chicago Tribune*, November 21, 1922.

road here. The Irish-born "Billboard Baron" ran a successful sign-painting and outdoor advertising business, and was known as a kind and generous employer. A public education booster, Cusack served on Mayor Washburne's staff before being elected to a single term in Congress.

On the opposite side of the central road, the towering monument of **Richard Sanders** (1834–1892) boasts three statues of idealized women symbolizing Christian virtues. On the left side, facing outward, a seated woman holding an anchor represents Hope. On the right side, also facing outward, a seated woman with a baby in her lap represents Love. Between them, on a pedestal higher than the others, a woman stands with one arm upraised, the other holding a cross entwined with flowers. She symbolizes Faith. Of Blue Westerly granite, the monument was created by the Smith Granite Company and delivered in 1894 at a cost of $8,113. Eleven years earlier, the same company had delivered a similar monument for William Hoyt at Graceland. Though of the same basic design, each was hand-carved and differ slightly in the details.[278]

The large and costly statue group in Richard Sanders's plot represents the Christian virtues of Faith (center), Hope (left), and Love (right). Similar statue groups can be found in other Victorian-era cemeteries, Catholic and Protestant alike. An almost identical monument exists at Graceland.

In 1859, only the western half of Calvary was part of the initial design. The eastern sections were reserved for future expansion,[279] and the layout of this half of the cemetery shows long, straight rows on a regular grid, rather

---

[278] "Westerly Granite in Illinois: Calvary Cemetery: Sanders," Babcock-Smith House Museum, http://www.babcock-smithhouse.com/GraniteIndustry/MapUS/IL/Sanders.html.
[279] *Chicago Press-Tribune*, August 23, 1859.

than the curving *rural cemetery* design of the western half. The east-
ernmost sections were remote—being furthest from the railroad
line—and likely unpleasant and marshy. Today, however, these sections are dry, airy, and beautiful—there is nothing like this view in
any Chicago cemetery, as no other is so close to Lake Michigan.[280]
Across Sheridan Road, boulders placed by the City of Evanston protect the lake shore from erosion. Joggers and bicyclists are ever-present. These eastern sections are filled with some of the finest mausoleums and monuments to be found in the cemetery.

The northeast corner contains a most unusual depiction of the
Crucifixion, showing only the disembodied head and hands of Christ
emerging from a slab of granite. Illinois Supreme Court justice **William G. Clark** (1924–2001) is buried here. Simple flat markers further south denote the plot of congressman and would-be senator
William Lorimer (1861–1934). Appointed to the U.S. Senate by
the Illinois House in 1909—this was before senators were elected
directly by the citizens—it was discovered by the *Chicago Tribune*
that Lorimer had bribed at least one representative to vote for him.
He was then ejected from the Senate and his election ruled invalid,
three years into his term.

A number of stately Latin crosses, 15 feet high or more, line the
Sheridan Road fence. The **Doyle** monument, an exedra—that is, a
semicircular monument with curving benches on either side—provides a pleasant place to sit and enjoy the breeze. Faces of cherubs
decorate its sides. Another unusual monument here is the **Hogan**
stone, depicting a church window. The stone is pierced, with four
openings surrounding a cross-shaped central portion.

Dr. John Benjamin Murphy (1867–1916) is entombed in an
ornate lakeside mausoleum, with richly decorated Ionic pilasters
flanking the door and twin planters on pedestals beside the steps. A
pioneer in nineteenth-century surgery, Murphy was president of the
American Medical Association, and lent his name to several medical
techniques and instruments still in use today.

A markedly overweight angel stands before a cross next near the

---

[280] In Lake County, however, Waukegan's Oak Woods and St. Mary cemeteries have a lake
view that's nearly as good.

The east entrance of Calvary, a few feet from the shore of Lake Michigan, is the site of a ghost story. It is through these gates that a drowned pilot was said to crawl, seeking rest.

east entrance. **William A. Lydon** (1863–1918) was co-owner of the Great Lakes Dredge and Dock Company and namesake of the WWI patrol craft *USS Lydonia*, which had been Lydon's personal yacht before being purchased by the United States Navy.[281]

A short distance behind the rotund angel, next to a mausoleum, an upright stele (tall, slender slab) of red granite, streaked with black and decorated with a radiant bronze cross identifies Calvary's other senator, **James Michael Slattery** (1878–1948). Slattery, an attorney and law school professor, served in several Cook County and state-wide appointed positions before being selected to take the place of Senator James Lewis, who had died. Senator Slattery represented Illinois in the Senate for 19 months, but failed to keep hold of the office at the next election.[282]

At the southeast corner of the cemetery, a tall, square-sided shaft holds a granite brazier high above the fence, providing a dramatic sight to motorists a few feet away. Further west, along the fence, a seemingly ordinary monument reveals a highly detailed relief carving of an angel when viewed from the other side.

The Classical mausoleum of **R. Philip Gormully** (1847–1900) stands a few feet from the cemetery's south wall. In the last decade, it has acquired a new backdrop. Where beyond the wall there was open

[281] "USS Lydonia (SP-700)," Wikipedia, http://www.wikipedia.org/wiki/USS_Lydonia_(SP-700).

[282] "James Michael Slattery," Biographical Directory of the United States Congress, http://bioguide.congress.gov/scripts/biodisplay.pl?index=S000478.

space in the 1990s, a huge, modern apartment building has now been constructed, with black metal balconies that overlook the cemetery projecting from its red brick wall. Gormully was partner in Gormully and Jeffery Manufacturing Company, creators of the Rambler brand of bicycle.[283] After Gormully's death the company expanded into automobiles, also sold under the Rambler name.

The east entrance of Calvary, not so beautiful or architecturally significant as the west, nevertheless boasts its own claim to fame—it is reputed to be haunted. Multiple witnesses have reported seeing a man drowning in the lake, struggling to remain afloat before finally sinking below the surface. What followed next was even more shocking: The figure would then emerge from the water, crawl across Sheridan road, and then slip into the cemetery, only to vanish within. Thought to be an unnamed World War II aviator who had crashed into the lake during a training exercise, the apparition—known locally as "Seaweed Charlie"—was reported numerous times between the 1940s and 1960s, until ultimately the reports stopped. As the legend has it, after the cemetery gates were inadvertently left open one night, the ghost was never seen again.[284]

Charlie could not have made a better choice. Calvary is unsurpassed among Chicago's Catholic cemeteries in its beauty and its historical value.

[283] "Gormully and Jeffery Manufacturing," Route 66 Rambler, http://timeline.route66rambler.com/gnj.html.

[284] Ursula Bielski, *Chicago Haunts: Ghostly Lore of the Windy City* (Chicago, IL: Lake Claremont Press, 1997), 25–27.

THE REMAINS OF THE DAY: THE CRASH SITE OF FLIGHT 191

Chicago is a professional mourner. Counted among her tragedies is the worst single building fire in American history (the Iroquois Theatre Fire, December 30, 1903), the deadliest disaster in inland maritime history (the *Eastland* disaster, July 1915), and the deadliest commercial airlines crash in American history. In Chicago, a city forever focused on the future, the powers that be do not like to remember the negative events of the past. And so, all of these disasters have faced a hard road in our efforts to memorialize them.

The shocking crash of Flight 191 on Friday, May 25, 1979, at O'Hare Airport, remained unmemorialized for more than 30 years until, in 2011, a memorial was finally erected to the memory of the victims of the "Crash of '79." Typically, the memorial was set not by the City, but by an independent group. In this case, school children from the far North Side of Chicago.

The crash happened on Memorial Day weekend. In command of Flight 191 was Capt. Walter Lux, a pilot with 22,000 hours in flight behind him, who had flown the DC–10 nearly since it was introduced eight years earlier. Assisting him on the flight deck was First Officer James Dillard and Flight Engineer Alfred Udovich, who have 25,000 flying hours between them. At 2:50 p.m., N110AA was cleared to taxi to runway 32R at Chicago's O'Hare International Airport, and at 3:02 p.m. the flight was cleared for takeoff.

Moments after liftoff, 191 lost an engine, which flipped over the top of the left wing and landed on the runway. The pilot was able to retain control for a few moments, but lost contact with the tower. The aircraft began to lean in and rolled over in the air, going down only 4,600 feet from the runway, in a field next to a trailer park. All 271 passengers and crew members, as well as two persons on the ground, were killed.

Because of the September 11 attacks, most Americans are now aware of the rate of incineration that occurs when jet fuel is present. Indeed, because of the high heat of the fire achieved from the jet fuel, the fire that burned over the ground at the crash site of 191 vaporized everything. Dentists were the only forensics experts of any use in attempting to identify the victims in what most Chicago emergency and forensics workers still call the worst site they have ever encountered and the one scene they can never forget.

In October 2011, a memorial comprised of a two-foot high wall of bricks, each inscribed with a name of one of the victims, was dedicated in Des Plaines' Lake Park, located about two miles from the crash site. The memorial came to fruition from the efforts of sixth grade students at Chicago's Decatur Classical School, who were inspired to the project after learning that their assistant principal lost her parents in the crash.

But it is the crash site that is the real burial ground, and it is viewable from the Des Plaines Oasis along the Kennedy Expressway. To access the (unofficial and unmarked) viewing area, take the Kennedy Expressway (I-90) to the Des Plaines Oasis. The crash site is viewable from the oasis.

CHURCH OF THE HOLY COMFORTER

222 Kenilworth Avenue, Kenilworth
www.holycomforter.org
Established 1903 as a church, 1926 as a cemetery

Visitors making the trek to Calvary may continue further up the shore to the posh community of Kenilworth, where journalist and poet **Eugene Field** (1850–1895) rests in the courtyard of this community landmark. Upon his death from a heart attack at the age of 45, the "children's poet" was initially buried at Graceland with only a small headstone. Thirty years later, at a Christmas midnight service, Holy Comforter's rector Leland Danforth made the surprise announcement that the poet was to be reburied in the church's newly-completed cloister. Field's relocation took place with permission of his eldest daughter, Mrs. Englar, a member of the congregation and wife of the church's senior warden.[285]

Field was buried beneath a thick granite ledger at the cloister's center. In 1936 Reverend Danforth presided at the funeral of **Julia Comstock Field** (1856–1936), buried in the Kenilworth cloister alongside her husband,[286] and her name was added to the memorial.

At the rear of the courtyard is a limestone altar on which stands a cross. This was donated by Holy Comforter parishioner Herman A. Brassert in memory of his young son,[287] **Herman Brassert** (1904–1910). On either side of the Field graves are columbarium walls, set with granite-faced niches, housing the ashes of parishioners. Mounted high on the church wall, an angel statue keeps watch over all.

Another outdoor columbarium stands just across the street, the **Bowen Memorial Garden of Kenilworth Union Church.**

The grave of Eugene and Julia Field lies at the center of the cloistered garden of this serene Gothic-style church. At the rear, beneath the angel statue, the cremated remains of other North Shore Episcopalians are kept in a columbarium wall.

[285] "Eugene Field to Rest at Last in Fitting Spot: Church to House Bones of Children's Poet," *Chicago Daily Tribune*, December 25, 1925.

[286] "Eugene Field's Widow Buried in Kenilworth," *Chicago Daily Tribune*, June 13, 1936.

[287] "Eugene Field to Rest at Last in Fitting Spot," 1925.

FORT SHERIDAN POST CEMETERY

Vattner Road, Fort Sheridan
www.ftsheridancemetery.com
Established 1889

Situated just north of the Cook County border, this richly historic site nonetheless deserves inclusion in Chicago's cemetery inventory. Officially abandoned by the military in 1993, the National Historic District of Fort Sheridan was redeveloped as a residential community, becoming the Town of Fort Sheridan. The site continues to draw a steady stream of visitors to its impressive surroundings studded with the architecture of Holabird & Roche. The main attractions at the lakefront complex continue to be of the artistic and architectural variety, namely, the looming 150-foot brick-clad water tower and a glorious monument portraying fort namesake Philip Sheridan. Following closely in popularity is the fort's cemetery, which provides everlasting refuge for **Phillip Spinner**, **August Siefert**, and **John Hackett**, all of whom rode with Custer at Little Bighorn in 1876—and were among the few survivors.

Though most markers here are of the standard government-

This crucifixion group, a common sight in a Catholic cemetery, is surprising and out-of-place in this military cemetery. Monsignor Edward J. Vattman (1840–1919), a Major and U.S. Army Chaplain, designed the monument himself, receiving special permission from President Theodore Roosevelt to place it here. In recent years the monument has become badly damaged due to moisture seeping into the porous sandstone.

The entrance to Fort Sheridan Cemetery, with Major Vattman's monument in the foreground. In this photo, the flag flies at half-staff due to the then-recent death of President Reagan.

issue flavor, one is unusual enough to immediately draw the visitor's eye—a crucifixion scene, made of white-painted sandstone, more appropriate for a Catholic cemetery than a military one. **Major Monsignor Edward J. Vattman** (1840–1919), an Army chaplain stationed at Fort Sheridan, designed and installed his monument years before his death. President Theodore Roosevelt is said to have given special permission for the non-standard design. With the soft sandstone now crumbling, and repair estimates starting at $9,000, the monument has become a headache for the Army and Lake County Forest Preserve, both seeking to avoid the controversy of spending taxpayer money on repairing a religious symbol.[288]

Standard government-issue marble headstones mark most graves at the tiny post cemetery, though some graves feature privately-purchased markers instead.

[288] Susan Kuczka, "Fort Cemetery's Crumbling Monument Stirs Debate," *Chicago Tribune*, July 20, 2005.

NEW LIGHT CEMETERY
6807 North East Prairie Road, Lincolnwood
Established 1895

This two-acre Pratt Avenue site is amply served with a fine new chapel building, dedicated June 4, 2006, in a ceremony attended by more than 200 members of the Jewish community and Lincolnwood civic leaders. The interior of the Mander Chapel includes seven windows representing the branches of a menorah, and on the front wall, doors taken from the Holy Ark of the former Ezra-Habonim Congregation.[289] The new building, which also includes an apartment for a groundskeeper, replaced an earlier structure on the same site, that one built in 1914.

Chevra Or Chadash ("New Light Society") was established in 1895 to provide burial and religious services for its members. After the society was dissolved in 1926, the newly-formed New Light Cemetery Association took over ownership of the cemetery and continues to operate it on a not-for-profit basis today. In 2000, a Holocaust memorial was installed at the center of the cemetery. Bronze plaques listing the names of those memorialized are affixed directly to the ground, below a granite monument reading *In memory of Six Million Jewish Martyrs and Heroes.*

The cemetery's focal point is the Holocaust Memorial, installed in 2000. Plaques with the names of martyrs are affixed to tablets embedded in the earth.

---

[289] Al Gruen, "History of the New Light Cemetery," *Chicago Jewish History*, Summer 2009.

MEMORIAL PARK CEMETERY AND MAUSOLEUM

9900 Gross Point Road, Skokie
www.memparkcemetery.com
Established 1913

At a major intersection in the near north suburb of Skokie, thousands of drivers in the 1990s daily passed between the Old Orchard shopping center and a large billboard-like sign announcing the location of Memorial Park Cemetery. Circa 2000, this sign and the empty corner[290] of the cemetery in which it stood vanished, to be replaced with yet another prosaic shopping plaza.

That subtraction did not significantly diminish the cemetery. Memorial Park is a very large, well-kept, modern cemetery, with monuments of innovative contemporary design added in recent years. The

management takes particular pride in their greenhouses and landscaping capabilities, and many of the graves sport elaborate floral designs.[291] "The Beautiful North Shore Cemetery," as an early advertisement called it, was "nonsectarian," and operated by the Central

Main entrance of the Beaux Arts–style chapel. The ground in front has been extensively improved since this picture was taken in 2010.

---

[290] I was told by office staff that that portion of the land had never contained graves. Satellite photos from 1999 corroborate this. There were no monuments in that corner, only a small building with a peaked roof—possibly a disused caretaker's cottage or maintenance shed. The next available satellite pictures, in March 2002, show the shopping plaza.

[291] Memorial Park Cemetery, http://www.memparkcemetery.com/.

Cemetery Company of Illinois. It maintained an office in the Marquette Building in the Loop, as well as one in Evanston.[292]

Near the east entrance, on Gross Point Road, stands a tile-roofed office building and a series of greenhouses. Southwest of the greenhouses are a number of sections dedicated to Jewish congregations. The *Anshe Emet* section includes a monument for Rabbi **Solomon Goldman** (1833–1953), featuring an open book atop a pedestal, lauding him as *Beloved Leader of his People*. Born in Russia, Rabbi Goldman was nationally known as a leading Jewish scholar and lecturer, and led his synagogue for 24 years.[293] Nearby, at the north edge of the section is the family plot of *Chicago Sun-Times* columnist **Irv Kupcinet** (1912–2003). Kupcinet began his career as a sports writer with the *Chicago Daily Times* in 1935. He soon took over the "People" column, later retitled "Kup's Column," and remained active with the newspaper until his death at age 91. Kup is buried alongside his wife of 62 years, **Esther "Essee" Kupcient** (1915– 2001), and their daughter **Karyn**, or **"Cookie" Kupcinet** (1941–1963). Karyn was an actress who was found strangled in her West Hollywood apartment in 1963, only 22 years old. Her murder has never been solved.

In Section 6 of the annex southwest of the chapel is the grave of actor **Robert Reed** (1932–1992). Born John Robert Rietz in Highland Park,[294] Reed studied acting at Northwestern University and at London's Royal Academy of Dramatic Art.[295] He appeared as a guest on numerous TV series, and beginning in 1961 had a co-leading role in the controversial legal drama *The Defenders*.

In 1967, Reed acted in the Broadway production *Barefoot in the Park*, and was invited by Paramount to lead a television series adaptation. When the project was canceled, Reed instead accepted a role in a television pilot that, he thought, could not possibly be successful— a Sherwood Schwartz comedy series, *The Brady Bunch*. "I was absolutely horrified! I mean, it's *Gilligan* all over again, with just as much

---

[292] Advertising postcard, circa 1920s, author's collection.

[293] "Rabbi Goldman, Famous Jewish Scholar Dies," *Chicago Tribune*, May 15, 1953.

[294] IMDb, http://www.imdb.com/name/nm0001658/.

[295] Barry Williams, with Chris Kreski, *Growing Up Brady: I Was a Teenage Greg* (New York: HarperCollins, 1992), 36.

inanity...," he later wrote, but he took the job "...because there wasn't anything else for me to do. ...it'll never get off the ground, take the money and go."[296] When the pilot was picked up for a full series, Reed was appalled, but knew it would be unwise to break his contract.

The Brady Bunch lasted five seasons, 116 episodes, during which Reed frequently sparred with creator Sherwood Schwartz and the writers. Reed felt that the scripts he was given contained implausible situations and stylistically inappropriate material, which he later referred to as "this beyond-farce *Gilligan's Island*–level shit."[297] He demanded changes, writing to the producers and to the head of the network. Angered when his suggestions were ignored, at times he came to the set drunk.[298]

The final episode of the fifth season had a plot that Reed found particularly inane, in which one Brady son sells his brother a hair tonic that turned his hair bright orange. Reed sent the producers a memo in which he enumerated the genres of theater and explained how comedy and farce were entirely different and incompatible styles. He referred to several prior scenes and plots that clashed with a realistic comedy, and compared the hair tonic plot to the incongruity of Batman appearing in the operating room of *M*A*S*H*. "I can't play it," the letter concluded.[299]

Schwartz was furious. Filming was scheduled to start that day, and he had been given no time to make changes. Schwartz decided then that when the show returned, the character of Mike Brady would be written out—he would be killed off-camera, perhaps in a car crash, or sent overseas on an architectural project, never to return; and for the current episode, the lines intended for Reed would be given to the other actors.[300] The producer's decision to fire Reed was moot, however, as the show as not renewed for a sixth season.

In the years that followed, Reed remained active in television, appearing in *The Boy in the Plastic Bubble*, *Medical Center*, *Roots*, and other series and movies. Syndication brought new life to *The Brady*

---

[296] Williams, *Growing Up Brady*, 37, 54.
[297] Williams, *Growing Up Brady*, 53.
[298] Williams, *Growing Up Brady*, 57.
[299] Williams, *Growing Up Brady*, 118.
[300] Williams, *Growing Up Brady*, 113.

Bunch, and Reed willingly participated in several attempts to revive the franchise. He was enthusiastic about a short-lived *Brady* variety show in 1977, saying of the singing and dancing, "What fun! This'll be a hoot."[301] He came on board again for several specials and mini-series in the 1980s, and an ill-fated attempt at a *Brady* drama series in 1990.

Though he feuded with the producers, Reed was kind and generous to his fellow actors. Barry Williams ("Greg") wrote "Robert Reed may have detested *The Brady Bunch*, but he *adored* the six of us Brady kids. From day one, he was warm, and very supportive. His affection for us kids was genuine, and at times far beyond the call of duty."[302] One Christmas, Reed gave each of the six young actors a movie camera; he later took them all on a chartered fishing boat, and on another occasion a trip to London on the *Queen Elizabeth II*. Reed wrote the foreword to Barry Williams's 1992 memoir, *Growing Up Brady: I Was a Teenage Greg*, in which he described the difficulty of being a child actor and expressed his admiration for the kids he worked with.

Reed was married for two years, beginning in 1957. The marriage produced a daughter, who later made a guest appearance on *The Brady Bunch*. Fearing it would harm his career, Reed was reluctant to disclose his homosexuality to the public. "I knew since I was nine that he was gay," actress Susan Olsen (Cindy) said in a 2009 interview. "Bob would have liked very much to have come out of the closet but that was an era where ... they went 'oh, you're wonderful, you're so brave', and they'd never hire him again."[303] *The Brady Bunch Hour* head writer Carl Kleinschmitt said, "He was the most closeted guy you'd ever meet in your life. He was very nice, he was very sweet... His sexual orientation was of no interest to anyone."[304]

On May 16, 1992, Robert Reed died of colon lymphoma in a Pasadena hospital.[305] During his final illness, he spoke by phone from the hospital to his fellow *Brady* cast members. Maureen McCormick (Marcia) called "essentially to say goodbye" and told him that she

---

[301] Williams, *Growing Up Brady*, 151.

[302] Williams, *Growing Up Brady*, 108

[303] Susan Olsen video interview for Retroality.tv, produced by Chris Mann, July 2009.

[304] Ted Nichelson and Susan Olsen, *Love to Love You Bradys: The Bizarre Story of the Brady Bunch Variety Hour* (Toronot: ECW Press, 2009), 197.

[305] Certificate of Death, State of California, for John Robert Rietz.

loved him. She writes that "In a weak voice, Bob said the same to me: I love you, too."[306] Reed was cremated in California,[307] and his ashes were buried here in Skokie, next to his parents' graves. On his modest red granite headstone is a line from *Hamlet*: *Goodnight, Sweet Prince.*

A Shakespearean epitaph for a classically-trained actor who found himself unwillingly working on a TV sitcom: *Goodnight Sweet Prince.*

A short distance north stands the cemetery's most beautiful feature, a chapel and crematory building in the Beaux Arts style. The chapel features carriage porches on the east and west sides, a small mausoleum section in the rear, and a large dome covered with green copper tiles. On the west side, a stained glass window features an illustration of a *tholos*, or round temple, and the word *Resurrection*. On the opposite side, a similar window shows a fountain and the word *Life*. Over the rear door is the Latin phrase *Memento Mori* ("Remember you will die").

Nearby, a granite monument has a bronze plaque affixed showing a man's portrait, with an impressive list of fraternal organizations underneath. **Gustav A. J. Meyer** (1874–1939) is listed in county death records as an engraver by profession,[308] and was assignee of a patent for a "pocket seal press" for use by notaries.[309] His stationery shop, Meyer and Wenthe, supplied badges to the Chicago Police Department.

In 2011, the open space immediately north of the chapel was substantially improved with the creation of a formal garden. The earth was sculpted, raised, and encircled by a low stone wall, with a stairway leading up from the road in the north. Curving paths entwine about a central fountain amidst alternating areas of grass and

---

[306] Maureen McCormick, *Here's the Story: Surviving Marcia Brady and Finding My True Voice* (William Morrow, 2008), 198.

[307] The death certificate states that the disposition of the remains was CR/RES, cremated and released to a residence. The funeral home was Cabot & Sons.

[308] Illinois, Deaths and Stillbirths Index, 1916–1947, Gustav A.J. Meyer.

[309] http://www.prior-ip.com/patent/22221446/pocket-seal-press.

shrubbery, with benches provided for visitors to enjoy the landscape. The front door of the chapel is emphasized as the focal point of the composition. In an era when many cemeteries are tearing down or ignoring their vintage chapels and mausoleums, Memorial Park has instead, refreshingly, chosen to embrace and accentuate theirs.

Continuing north from the chapel garden, the road leads over a bridge that spans a long, sinuous pond, towards a Masonic monument, a tapering Ionic column supporting a large granite sphere. Just south of the bridge, two members of Congress are buried side by side. **Ralph Edwin Church** (1883–1950) was elected to the House as a Republican in 1935, losing his seat in 1941 after an unsuccessful run for senator. Church returned to Congress in 1943, remaining there until his death in 1950. His wife **Marguerite Stitt Church** (1892–1990) was then appointed in his place. Marguerite, a psychologist, then went on to win five terms of her own, leaving the House of Representatives in 1963.

On the opposite shore of the pond, a tall granite cross marks the grave of **Sheldon Munson Griswold** (1861–1930), Episcopal Bishop of Chicago. The base of his monument depicts a miter. A few plots east is the grave of **James Lewis Kraft** (1874–1953), who began selling cheese from a horse-drawn wagon in 1903. In 1914, J.L. Kraft & Bros. Company opened their first cheese-making plant in Stockton, Illinois. In 1916 Kraft obtained a patent for processed cheese—cheese mixed with other dairy products and emulsifiers to ensure a long shelf life and uniform melting—that continues to be produced today by the company that bears his name. In 1989, the owners of Kraft merged the company with General Foods, owners of the Chicago-based Oscar Mayer Company, whose namesake is buried at Rosehill. Kraft Foods is now the world's second largest food company.[310]

East of the chapel is a granite exedra, a large semicircular monument composed of an upright block at the rear from which two curved benches project. Carved into the center of the exedra is a coat of arms, surrounded by intricate mantling, over the Greek letters ΣAE. At the focal point is a granite ledger, with an additional bronze marker placed

---

[310] Kraft Foods 2009 Fact Sheet, http://www.kraftfoodscompany.com/assets/pdf/kraft_foods_fact_sheet.pdf, accessed July 2010, 3.

in front to give biographical detail. This elaborate monument commemorates **William Collin Levere** (1872–1927), who was initiated into Sigma Alpha Epsilon while a student at Northwestern University, then held several national positions within the fraternity, including "Supreme Archon." The coat of arms on the monument is that of ΣAE, and their symbols of Minerva and a lion appear on his ledger. While impressive enough in its own right, this is not Levere's only monument. The national headquarters of the fraternity, a church-like German Gothic structure located near Northwestern's campus, was named Levere Memorial Temple in his honor.

A pair of rectangular pools are located near the west entrance of Memorial Park, enhanced with a fountain that continuously sprays water into the air. A yellow brick building a few feet from the shore houses pumping equipment, and three rows east of this building is the simple granite headstone of landscape architect **Jens Jensen** (1860–1951). A Danish immigrant, Jensen studied the natural landscapes of his adopted home and applied his skills to create scenes of natural beauty within cities. He created Chicago's Columbus Park; redesigned Humboldt, Garfield, and Douglas parks; and landscaped parks in other Midwestern cities as well. He designed the grounds of private homes and cemetery plots, including the Vehon plot at Rosehill,[311] with its beautiful water nymph statue, and sections of Oak Ridge and Riverside cemeteries. The northern sections of Bohemian National Cemetery, with curving roads distinctly different from the rectangular design of the older section, are Jensen's work.[312] As general superintendent of Chicago's West Park Commission, he designed and orchestrated the construction in 1907 of the Garfield Park Conservatory, the "largest publicly owned conservatory under one roof in the world."[313] Considering his profession, Jensen's lot at Memorial Park is surprisingly ordinary, consisting of a simple slant-

---

[311] "The Architectural Drawings of Jens Jensen," Bentley Historical Library, University of Michigan, http://bentley.umich.edu/research/guides/architects/jensen/jensen_search.php?id=1737.

[312] "Information," Bohemian National Cemetery, http://www.bohemiannationalcemetery-chicago.org/information.html.

[313] "The Conservatory's Past, Present & Future," Garfield Park Conservatory, http://www.garfield-conservatory.org/history.htm

ed granite headstone with no special landscaping to distinguish it from its neighbors.

A short distance west of the pump building is a tall monument, showing a cross emerging from the rough granite, at its base a bronze plaque with an illustration of an airplane. **Richard Harold Tarrant** (~1908–1933) was the pilot of a United Airlines Boeing 247 propliner carrying cargo, three passengers, and a crew of four on the night of October 10, 1933, when it exploded in mid-air, broke into pieces, and crashed near Chesterton, Indiana, killing all aboard. An investigation led by the FBI's Melvin Purvis concluded that a nitroglycerin bomb had been hidden in the baggage compartment. The murderers were never identified, and the crime—the first-ever sabotage of a commercial flight—remains unsolved.

Nearby, an outdoor columbarium garden displays the sort of quality landscaping for which Memorial Park is acclaimed. Low walls of rough stone and granite benches surround a flagpole, with planted beds of flowers radiating from the center. A path leads between tall granite boxes, each housing niches for cremated remains.

Memorial Park's community mausoleum, operational since 1913, features a white marble exterior in a geometric style, all vertical and horizontal lines. Beneath the stair-step gable at the front, two eagles face opposite directions atop tall fluted pilasters. In front of the main

Main entrance of the mausoleum. Long after the mausoleum was constructed in 1913, a pavilion in a much more modern style was placed in front to welcome visitors.

A columbarium section on the mausoleum's upper level, showing a variety of urns in glass-faced niches. Surrounding it are more conventional stone-faced niches.

entrance, to soften the severity of the facade and invite entry, management more recently erected a modernistic white concrete canopy, its up-swept roof supported by four curved columns.

The main entrance leads to a non-denominational chapel with a soaring, elaborately painted ceiling. Beyond it are three levels of corridors and crypts, the walls dressed with marble of every color, with beautifully detailed stained glass windows showing religious scenes or natural landscapes. Columbarium sections include metal, wood, and stone urns behind panes of glass. On the east side of the ground floor is another chapel with ornate bronze candelabra and chandeliers; next to it is a room with two immense double sarcophagi.

West of the mausoleum, a metal frame holds aloft large white letters that read *Memorial Park Mausoleum*. Though a large bush is growing up and around the sign, it is still visible from Skokie Boulevard, drawing motorists' attention to one of north suburban Chicago's finest active cemeteries.

Grave of fraternity president William Levere, showing the fraternity's arms on the vertical monument, and its logo on the horizontal ledger.

50 (THOUSAND) WAYS TO LEAVE YOUR LOVED ONES: BURIAL CUSTOMS TO DIE FOR

Perhaps nothing says more about a person, or a culture, than funerary desires. From ancient pyres to electric crematoriums, from interment—whether underground burial, in a tomb, or in an urn—to burial at sea and the scattering of ashes, an individual may wish to be laid to rest with a cherished Chihuahua, in a glass coffin, seated behind the wheel of a beloved racing car, or lowered into a grave filled with rosebuds.

Though such whims run high on the list of influences, ethnicity and religion have always been the most common and uncompromising arbiters of burial arrangements. Consider, for example, the Medieval Chinese emperors who, upon their passing, took along their cookpots, as well as their soldiers and horses, to make the afterworld as homey as possible. Then there are the modern Indian Parsis who carry their corpses to a so-called tower of silence, where they are left to be eaten by carrion birds. The Bishnoi of Rajasthan dump their dead in unmarked trenches, covering the bodies with salt. Most Hindu Indians, however, are simply cremated according to religious dictates, and for a price of about $12.

Climate also has its say. Bereaved Russians may well leave their unembalmed beloved overnight in a chilly church to await the next day's funeral party. But the suffocating Pakistani heat insists on same-day services, even if relatives are away. And Americans are well-acquainted with the New Orleans practice of above-ground burial in whitewashed high rise tombs, owing to bad memories of heavy rains.

Cost, too, is forever a consideration. In China, one may take leave of this world for $50; in Japan, mourners might be allowed a few more tears, stuck as they often are with a funeral bill of nearly $32,000.

In industrialized countries, considerations become increasingly contemporary. In Britain, where 400,000 of the regions 640,000 yearly dead are cremated, environmental activists are up in arms over the burning of so many wooden caskets. Thus the birth of the Natural Death Centre, which offers burial in a cardboard casket as part of its Green Funeral plan. After burial, the plot is identified not by a headstone, but with a newly-planted tree.

Whether cardboard or 24-karat, the casket remains, in modernized nations, the most popular destination for embalmed corpses as well as ashes. Traditional graves or tombs, preceded by formal services, continue to be chosen by the great majority of funeral planners. In the positivistic intellectual climate of the West, it is perhaps surprising that millions consider the resultant cost of dying, in the U.S. $3,000 to $5,000 on average, a necessary expense. Yet, the carved and gilded casket, the lavish embalming services, one or two days of display at the local funeral home, and a custom marker over a scenic plot all continue to be touted, and ultimately included, as key components of a proper burial.

Though burial customs are among the slowest of all traditions to change, a shift might at last be coming. While the funeral industry is presently booming, their custom caskets and state-of-the-art embalming equipment may soon be gathering dust, as increasing numbers of would-be customers confess to a nagging feeling that the rituals propagated by the modern mortician are nothing short of morbid.

ST. ADALBERT CATHOLIC CEMETERY

6800 North Milwaukee Avenue, Niles
www.catholiccemeterieschicago.org
Consecrated 1872

By the last decade of the nineteenth century, five predominantly Polish neighborhoods had been established in Chicago, each in heavily industrialized areas: the Lower West Side, sheltering workers in the factories along the ship canal and the Burlington Railroad; the steel mill–centered community of South Chicago; Back-of-the-Yards on the Southwest Side, and the "Polish downtown" area just west of Goose Island. The latter of these was more than 85 percent Polish in 1898. In one precinct, the percentage actually reached 99.9, with only one non-Pole counted among its 2,500 residents. The churches in this area served more than 24,000 Polish immigrants and included two of the largest Roman Catholic parishes in the world, St. Stanislaw Kostka and Holy Trinity.

Along with worship, one of the main bases for community establishment for Poles, as with other ethnic groups, was the question of burial. Chicago's immigrants were understandably haunted by the prospect of dying far from their homeland, and the desperate desire to rest in peace prompted the formation of mutual aid societies. For the city's Poles, these societies primarily provided widows with the burial

St. Adalbert's features a large number of intricate hand-carved limestone memorials, such as these sorrowful angels. Note the dead bird below the feet of the statue in front.

fees needed upon the deaths of their blue-collar husbands. To this end, St. Adalbert Cemetery, perhaps the largest Polish cemetery in the metropolitan area, was established in nearby Niles in 1872. A modest site at first, the acreage grew tremendously as Polish and Bohemian parishes bought increasingly large portions of land to sell to their parishioners. Inseparable from St. Adalbert Cemetery is Przyblo's House of the White Eagle, a banquet hall that stands across the street from the cemetery gates on Milwaukee Avenue. Built on an old Polish picnic ground, Przyblo's plays host to hundreds of funeral parties each year, mourners pouring in to feast and drink after graveside services.

The war memorial, an obelisk surrounded by four bronze figures, unusually features a soldier of the Haller Army, a unit of the Polish army in World War I that included about 23,000 Polish-American recruits.

The majority of contemporary visitors to St. Adalbert's travel clear across the huge expanse from the Milwaukee Avenue gates to reach the newer section beyond the access road. A profusion of flowers and wreaths, fresh and artificial, flower boxes marked with peel-and-stick letters identifying the surnames of the dead, candles, musical greeting cards, toys, and other offerings covers the gently sloping area, and the entire modern section is overseen by the Shrine to **St. Maximillian Kolbe** (1894–1941), memorializing the Polish-born Franciscan friar, publisher, and missionary imprisoned in Auschwitz in 1941. While so confined, Father Kolbe begged his captors to take his own life in exchange for the life of another prisoner. They agreed, and Kolbe was slated for starvation. When his body neglected to give up after several weeks, officials became impatient, and the prisoner was given a lethal dose of carbolic acid, which Kolbe is remembered to have received cheerfully. His body was cremated, fulfilling his wish to use himself "completely up in the service of the Immaculata." Kolbe was canonized in 1982, not long before Chicago compatriots erected the local shrine to his memory.

St. Adalbert is also the final resting place of no less than six U.S. Congressmen, including **Chester Chesney** (1916–1986), **Leo Kocialkowski** (1882–1958), **William Link** (1884–1950), **Stanley Kunz** (1864–1946), **Anthony Michalek** (1878–1916), and the now infamous Dan Rostenkowski.

Daniel David Rostenkowski (1928–2010) was a United States representative from Illinois, serving from 1959 to 1995. He attended St. Stanislaus Kostka Catholic School as a boy growing up among the working class on the Northwest Side of Chicago, and from his youngest years, Rostenkowski was surrounded by politics. The son of an alderman, Rostenkowski's boyhood home was forever filled

Priests and brothers belonging to a religious order, the Congregation of the Resurrection of Our Lord Jesus Christ are buried in this spectacular mausoleum in the western part of the cemetery. The mausoleum features a below-ground portion with crypts on either side of an altar, stairs leading to the roof, and a high column with a figure of Christ at the top.

with other aldermen, precinct captains, and other movers and shakers of the Chicago Democratic machine. Winning the position as Democratic Ward Committeeman in the 32nd Ward, he went on to hold the position even through his Congressional years. Rostenkowski was a crucial force in creating many of the tax laws during the Reagan Administration, having found himself Chairman of the House Ways and Means Committee in 1981. He also played a key role in trade negotiations, social reforms, and other far-reaching policy, while at the same time securing billions of dollars for Chicago and Illinois. Rostenkowski was instrumental in neighborhood development and redevelopment efforts in Chicago, and is most remembered for his role in the erection of the housing and commercial development, Presidential Towers. It may have been launched in controversy, but it emerged as the dynamo behind the redevelopment and gentrification of the West Loop skid row district, and the settling in of many new West Side businesses, including Harpo Studios. Rostenkowski was also the key to saving the Chicago Theater from the wrecking ball. For his efforts both at home and in Washington, he has been called one of the most significant Chicago politicians of the twentieth century.

Sadly, Rostenkowski's image changed forever when in 1996 he was convicted of mail fraud and sentenced to 17 months in the penitentiary. After his release, Rostenkowski went on to teach at Northwestern and Loyola universities and died of lung cancer in 2010.

Arcade fans visiting St. Adalbert will want to stop at the grave of

A row of family
mausoleums on the east
side of St. Adalbert's.

inventor **Steve Kordek** (1911–2012), who designed more than one hundred pinball machines for Genco, Bally and Williams, and is credited with raising the pinball machine from mere arcade game to its highly sophisticated and competitive form. He died at the age of one hundred of natural causes.

Other notables buried at St. Adalbert are **Fredrak Fraske** (1874–1973), the last surviving veteran of the Indian Wars, and football icon and local hero **George "Papa Bear" Halas** (1895–1983). Halas narrowly escaped a much earlier death. Famously, he was late in arriving to the Western Electric Company's employee picnic on the morning of July 24, 1915, a cruise on board the *Eastland* steamer, which culminated in the capsizing of the vessel and the death of more than 830 passengers, the worst disaster in Great Lakes history.

The mausoleum of George Halas, of Chicago Bears fame.

Halas went on to establish himself as a baseball player, inventor, philanthropist, football player, and sports pioneer. But there was one role for which he is remembered fondly by millions of fans: the beloved creator, coach, and figurehead of the Chicago Bears. After one year of playing baseball professionally, Halas moved from Chicago to Decatur, Illinois, to work for a starch manufacturing company called the A.E. Staley Company, selling starch and coaching the company's football team. The "Staleys" began wearing orange and dark blue after Halas chose the colors of his own past collegiate team. One historic day, Halas went to Canton, Ohio, to represent the Staleys at the meeting that saw the formation of the American Professional Football Association (later, the National Football League). It was Halas who took the team to Chicago and established the Chicago Staleys, later taking the name of the Chicago Bears to honor the Chicago Cubs baseball team, which allowed the team to play their games at Wrigley Field.

Adoration of "Papa Bear" Halas is not misplaced. Fans well remember that this exemplary coach also played on the team, managed it, and even sold tickets. In 40 years, his team saw only six non-winning seasons. Off the field, Halas rose to the rank of lieutenant commander in the U.S. Navy and received the Bronze Star, as well as the Distinguished Public Service Medal, the Navy's highest civilian award. Halas was recognized by ESPN as one of the ten most influential people in sports in the twentieth century. Even now, the team jerseys of the Chicago Bears are embroidered with his initials, GSH, on the sleeves. One of his last acts as head of the Bears franchise was to appoint as coach one of his former players, Mike Ditka.

Halas died after a struggle with pancreatic cancer. At last visit, the doors of his crypt at St. Adalbert bore a worn orange and blue ribbon and a faded, typewritten copy of the words to the team's fight song, "Bear Down, Chicago Bears."

SUNSET MEMORIAL LAWNS

3100 Shermer Road, Northbrook
www.sunsetmemoriallawns.com
Established 1931[314]

This Northbrook site was opened in 1931 for North Shore blacks,[315] excluded from the white cemeteries by increasing Jim Crow attitudes, and geographically removed from the new black cemeteries located in the far southern reaches of Cook County. Today, other racial and ethnic groups are buried there as well. There is a **Torah Gardens** section for Jews, and in a rear corner of the cemetery stands a prominent "**Russian Jewish Family Memorial**" wall, designed by

[314] Based on first funeral notice found for this location.
[315] Helen A. Sclair, "Ethnic Cemeteries: Underground Rites," 630.

Entrance to Sunset Memorial Lawns.

architect Jerry Brim and installed in 1996.[316] Inscribed with thousands of names, this cenotaph honors relatives of Chicago-area immigrants buried abroad.

ALL SAINTS CATHOLIC CEMETERY
700 North River Road, Des Plaines
www.catholiccemeterieschicago.org
Consecrated 1923

Not to be confused with its definitively Polish, city cousin on Higgins Road, this Des Plaines site is Irish in origin, though currently home to many ethnic groups. The cemetery consists of two distinct sections, on opposite sides of River Road. The older section to the east, which opened in 1923,[317] features a wide neoclassical entrance of brick with limestone columns and pilasters. The newer section to the west, operating since 1954, has a fittingly modern entrance of its own, with swinging metal gates on either side of a pylon of limestone

---

[316] "Memorial Wall Honoring Russian Jews to Be Dedicated," *Chicago Tribune*, November 3, 1996.

[317] "All Saints Catholic Cemetery & Mausoleum," Catholic Cemeteries, Archdiocese of Chicago, http://www.catholiccemeterieschicago.org/locations.php?id=2.

Entrance to the older, eastern half of the cemetery, opened in 1923.

blocks and, at its summit, a slender cross.

The still-burgeoning burial ground rippled with sensationalism in the late 1990s when it opened its gates for the burial of nanny victim, **Matthew Eappen** (1996–1997, age 8 months). But cheerier visits are also to be made here. Along with thousands of common folk, All Saints provides eternal homes to **George Halas, Jr.** (1925–1979), Son of Papa Bear[318]; professional wrestler **Walter Palmer** (1912–1998); and baseball Hall of Famer, Cubs catcher **Charles "Gabby" Hartnett** (1900–1972). Yet it is another sports immortal that lately draws so many visitors to this sprawling ossuary. Since his death in 1998, **Harry Caray** (1914–1998), the beloved broadcaster of the Chicago Cubs, has rendered the confines of this cemetery decidedly friendlier.

With his signature glasses, unmistakable voice, and unswervable enthusiasm, Caray made going to a Cubs game a quintessentially

Harry Caray, Chicago Cubs announcer. Note the baseball depicted on the upper section of the monument. Harry's catch-phrase, *Holy Cow*, appears below his portrait on the base.

[318] Himself buried at St. Adalbert, Niles.

Chicago experience, particularly due to leading Wrigley Field's daily crop of diehards in singing "Take Me Out to the Ball Game" during his famed Seventh Inning Stretch. Years after his death, celebrity guests continue the charismatic Caray's tradition, offering their own varyingly vitriolic versions of the classic tune.

But not too loudly, please. Keeping unruly audience members under control was a specialty of **Andrew T. Frain** (1904–1964), "King of the Ushers," who now lies beneath one of the stately crosses in the eastern half of All Saints. Frain first became an usher as a teenager, when the

Andy Frain, "King of the Ushers," is finally at rest, near the entrance on the east side.

profession had a reputation for thuggishness and dishonesty. Instead of accepting bribes and getting in fights, Frain convinced a group of colleagues that, if they dressed smartly and acted ethically, they'd be better paid in the long run. It worked. "Andy Frain, Crowd Engineers" became a successful company, such that his name became synonymous with *usher* in Chicago for decades to come.[319]

In 2005, a man who did much to beautify Chicago cemeteries was laid to rest on the west side of All Saints. **Bert J. Gast** (1925–2005)[320] was one of a long line of sculptors at the family-operated Gast Monuments, a company that has designed and carved gravestones throughout the region for over 125 years.[321] Bert Gast and his wife Janice worked from a storefront opposite St. Boniface Cemetery, where this author (Hucke) had the pleasure of talking with them about their

---

[319] Rex Lardner, "The Crowd is Your Enemy," *Sports Illustrated*, October 2, 1961.
[320] "Obituaries: Gast, Bert J.," *Chicago Tribune*, October 9, 2005.
[321] "Our heritage as memorial designers," Gast Monuments, http://www.gastmonuments. com/. See also St. Boniface Cemetery and St. Henry Cemetery entries.

This section in the eastern part of All Saints resembles a forest of crosses, each different.

work in the late 1990s. Noted for his contemporary artistic style, Gast created many of the depictions of saints and religious scenes at the centers of "shrine sections" of Archdiocesan Catholic cemeteries, around which thousands of persons are buried beneath flush markers. His unique monument at All Saints consists of a grey granite base from which rises a three-sectioned tower of the same stone, interspersed with thin connecting pieces of black granite. Each section names and illustrates one of the Christian virtues of Faith, Hope, and Love, while a sinuous river winds through the background, from one segment to the next. Over the wedding rings on the lower portion appears the text, *The Greatest of These is Love.*

The western half of the cemetery opened in 1954. Public taste in architecture had changed enough in those 30 years that a completely different, sleeker, and simpler style was chosen for the second entrance.

SHALOM MEMORIAL PARK AND RANDHILL PARK CEMETERY

1700 West Rand Road, Arlington Heights
Randhill Park established 1924
Shalom Memorial Park established 1956

Though Shalom Memorial Park is now by far the larger of these two affiliated cemeteries, the non-sectarian Randhill Park Cemetery was first to be established on the 115-acre Rand Road site. Work began in 1924 on the new memorial park, designed by landscape architect Edson L. Nott, with chapel and entrance designed by Oman & Lillenthal.[322] Early advertisements for Randhill Park show that management prohibited "unsightly tombstones," allowing only lawn-level markers amidst the "full scenic value of Nature," in a cemetery advertised as "Strictly a Memorial Park."[323]

Most of Randhill was rededicated in 1956 as a Jewish cemetery, Shalom Memorial Park.[324] In keeping with Jewish custom, Shalom Memorial Park would be maintained as a separate cemetery, with

The Beth She'arim mausoleum, named for an ancient cemetery in Galilee. The mausoleum's courtyard features a cascading fountain and a replica of a second-century sarcophagus from its namesake cemetery, made from stone cut from Mount Carmel.

---

[322] "Work to Start at Once on Randhill Park Cemetery", *Chicago Daily Tribune*, December 21, 1924.

[323] "New Vogue—Randhill Park Cemetery" (display ad), *Chicago Daily Tribune*, April 30, 1935.

[324] "The Entire Jewish Community Is Invited to Attend the Inspiring Dedication and Consecration of the New Jewish Cemetery, Shalom Memorial Park" (display ad), *Chicago Daily Tribune*, May 3, 1956.

its own entrance and hours of operation different from Randhill. The new cemetery came about largely through the work of **Herschel Auerbach** (1918–2001), a U.S. Army major in Counter Intelligence, a World War II hero who had personally captured German rocket scientist Werner von Braun. After the war Auerbach led the first investigations into Nazi war crimes, and lobbied the Truman administration for the formation of the State of Israel. Auerbach managed both cemeteries for the next 29 years, rising to national prominence among cemetery directors and culminating in his 1979 election as president of the National Association of Cemeteries.

The centerpiece of Shalom Memorial Park is the **Tower of Remembrance**, one of the largest Holocaust memorials in the Midwest, stretching to an imposing 80 feet. Originally a feature of Randhill Park Cemetery, the monument's central shaft was topped with a statue of a robed woman holding a globe until 1958, when Auerbach ordered it removed, stating that it "has no significance whatever for

us."[325] A plywood box, lowered over the statue by helicopter, concealed it while work was under way on the replacement: a sculpted granite flame, ten feet high, covered with gold leaf.[326] At the base of the monument, mosaic tablets were installed with the symbols of the twelve tribes of Israel. Other six-foot tablets are wrapped in barbed wire and feature the names of concentration camps. Mounted on these tablets are bronze plaques bearing the names of Holocaust victims under the words *Remember That We Lived—Remember How We Perished.*

The Tower of Remembrance, its top a sculpted flame covered in gold leaf, rises above the trees.

---

[325] "Helicopter Used to Veil Statue Atop Tall Shaft," *Chicago Daily Tribune*, April 1, 1958.
[326] Ibid.

METRO WEST

Parkholm Cemetery began as the Covell family cemetery in 1846. Receiving a charter to operate as a commercial cemetery, it became Oak Hill in 1887, and eventually Parkholm. The cemetery is located next to a quiet stretch of woods in La Grange Park.

EDEN MEMORIAL PARK
9851 West Irving Park Road, Schiller Park
Established 1895

Eden Memorial Park was originally established in 1895 as *Evangelischer Gottesacker Verein* ("Evangelistic God's Acre Society"), by a group of German-speaking Evangelical churches in what is now the city of Chicago. In the earliest years of the cemetery's operation, horse-drawn bus service operated between Eden and Dunning Station, near Narragansett Avenue and Irving Park Road, where funeral-going wagons often became mired in the mud along the route.

The Kolze Family, one of the founding families of Schiller Park (originally named "Kolze"), has one of the most recognized plots in Eden. **Julia Marrenga**, wife of Albert Kolze, ran the Kolzes' famed White House Restaurant and Saloon at Irving Park Road and Narragansett Avenue and went on to become the first female mayor in the state of Illinois, serving from 1933 to 1935 as the mayor of Schiller Park.

Eden is also home to seven **victims of the *Eastland* disaster** of 1915, who perished when the *Eastland* steamer turned over on the Chicago River, taking more than 830 victims to their deaths. After the tragedy, funeral homes and cemeteries all over Chicago were

Eden's main entrance and matching administration building.

The older sections of Eden are similar in character to Concordia, German Waldheim, and St. Johannes. The cylindrical headstones seen here are very popular at German cemeteries and found almost nowhere else.

called upon to show mercy upon the destitute among the dead. Here at Eden, as elsewhere, room was made in the family plots of the compassionate living.

Four boxers rest at Eden, including **Oscar Nelson** (1882–1954), **Frank Gilchrist Sullivan**, **Marty Cutler**, and **John Dempsey**. Known as the "Durable Dane," Nelson once went 42 rounds with Jo Gans in Goldfield, Nevada, before taking the win.

Residents of Chicago's North Center neighborhood traveling out this way will recognize the name of Stauber on one of the family plots here from "Stauber's Ace Hardware," a store opened in 1972 at Lincoln Avenue and Bryon Street on Chicago's North Side. **William Stauber** saw that first shop grow into an empire of stores across the nation. The original store still thrives, serving the bustling neighborhood despite the prevalence of corporate home improvement giants today.

A new group of visitors has lately been making its way to Eden: the descendants and friends of the **displaced dead of St. Johannes Cemetery**, formerly located on the property of O'Hare Airport. For nearly a decade, the cemetery—burial ground of the congregants of St. John's Church—was locked in a brutal legal battle with the City of Chicago, who fought, successfully, to remove the cemetery to make way for a new runway as part of the O'Hare Expansion Project. The lawsuit, filed in 2007 against Bensenville's St. John (Johannes)'s Church (on whose property the cemetery resided) was won by the City of Chicago in 2010, and a price of $1.3 million settled on two years later, ending the court action. One by one, distraught family members have overseen the disinterment of their loved ones to area cemeteries. Eden was chosen by the congregation as the place for the "new" cemetery, actually called the "Old St. Johannes section." Though a number of graves were moved to other locations.

In 2011, members of St. John's Church chose Eden as the new site for the majority of burials from their cemetery near the airport. In addition to family monuments, the cross and stone that marked the former location of the church were moved here as well.

Visitors to Eden today, in these first days after the removal of a large number of the original burials, will be met by the shocking site of hundreds of graves reset in freshly turned earth, including scores of plots marked by flush stones indicating only *Unknown Adult previously resting at St. Johannes Cemetery* or *Unknown Child previously resting at St. Johannes Cemetery*. A few of the original stones have been moved here, some repaired. The great majority are new stones, likely commissioned with money from a City of Chicago settlement to the families. The resulting picture is a perplexing one indeed.

Ironically, the dead traded a burial site behind the FedEx hangar at O'Hare for one just a few dozen yards from the community pool and waterslide, which all of the new burials overlook. Both have been a long way from the solace offered by the original cemetery site, which was adjacent to the fruit orchards from which "Orchard Field" Airport took its name.

ST. JOSEPH CATHOLIC CEMETERY AND MAUSOLEUMS

3100 North Thatcher, River Grove
www.catholiccemeterieschicago.org
Consecrated 1904

As the North Side's St. Boniface Cemetery neared capacity, the German Angel Guardian Society sought a replacement, creating St. Joseph Cemetery here in River Grove in 1904.[327] Several affiliated priests are buried here, among them **Rev. John P. Schiffer** (1869–1927), whose headstone proclaims him "one of the founders of this cemetery," and **Rt. Rev. Msgr. George Eisenbacher** (1875–1950), rector of Angel Guardian Orphanage. Monsignor Eisenbacher's monument depicts an angel watching over two children, in the presence of a coiled snake, eternally poised ready to strike.

The monument of Rev. John P. Schiffer (1869–1927). As on every priest's headstone, the date of ordination is given equal weight to those of birth and death.

This west suburban graveyard features an ornate limestone-clad community mausoleum in the Gothic architectural style, with decorative spires atop the gables and the corners of the transepts, surrounding a copper steeple. Most extraordinary of all is the scene beneath an arched portico at the building's rear. On the front of an altar below a cruci-

[327] "St. Joseph Catholic Cemetery & Mausoleums," Catholic Cemeteries, Archdiocese of Chicago, http://www.catholiccemeterieschicago.org/locations.php?id=29.

In a departure from the typical images of afterlife usually shown at cemeteries, this bas-relief on the mausoleum at St. Joseph shows souls in torment, begging for mercy as they are consumed by flames.

fixion group—statues of the crucified Christ, flanked by the Virgin Mary and St. John—a marble inset panel presents a chilling depiction of the fires of Hell, complete with sinners writhing in agony, arms raised in supplication. Above the mausoleum door are the Latin words, *Memento homo quia pulvis es* ("Remember, man, that you are dust").

Even ultra-slippery gangster **"Baby Face" Nelson** (1908–1934) couldn't run from the reaper. During a pitched gun battle with FBI agents, popularly known as the "Battle of Barrington," the young bank robber was mortally wounded though he managed to escape the scene with the aid of his confederates. After he died in a safe house a few hours later, an anonymous

Within the mausoleum, a modern stained glass window shows a more joyful scene, as the angel at the tomb of Christ informs grieving women that "He has been raised."

telephone call led to the discovery of his blanket-wrapped body on the edge of St. Paul's Lutheran Cemetery in Niles Center (now Skokie). "Nelson" is buried here, under his real name, **Lester Gillis**.

The thug is memorialized with a simple flat headstone. Much more appealing is the mottled pink and grey granite monument of one who turned his skills to art rather than to murder. A bronze plaque on the latter monument describes the life's work of **Jules Berchem** (1855–1930), who worked with sculptors to reproduce their works as "colossal bronze statues." Among the bronzes cast by Berchem are the *Alma Mater* group at the University of Illinois, the equestrian statue of Saint Louis in the city of Saint Louis, the war memorials in Indianapolis and River Forest, and the great bronze lions at the entrance of the Art Institute of Chicago. To cemetery aficionados, the greatest work to emerge from Berchem's foundry may be found at Graceland Cemetery, Lorado Taft's *Eternal Silence*.[328] Born in France, Berchem went to work for the American Bronze Company, eventually becoming its superintendent.

Bronze foundry owner Jules Berchem (1855–1930) worked with sculptors such as Lorado Taft and Edward Kemeys, casting their works as magnificent bronze statues.

In 1904 he began his own foundry, the American Art Bronze Foundry Company, which operated until shutting down in World War II.[329]

Also notable here is the veterans section, featuring uniform rows of marble military headstones, next to which stands a monument with two sculpted eagles flanking a list of names. Nearby, a bronze

[328] "Smithsonian Institution: Search Results for Berchem Jules."

[329] Carol A. Grissom, *Zinc Sculpture in America, 1850–1950* (Newark, NJ: University of Delaware Press, 2009), 616.

plaque attached to a family monument serves as a cenotaph for a soldier buried in a United States military cemetery in the Netherlands: **P.F.C. William E. Glatt, Jr.** (1920–1945), gunner of the 741st Tank Battalion, was killed in action in Leipzig, Germany. Finally, the **Schmidt** monument, a rough-cut granite slab, has attached to one side a statue of a weeping woman at the base of a cross, her hand pressed to her face in sorrow.

ELMWOOD CEMETERY AND MAUSOLEUM

2905 Thatcher Avenue, River Grove
www.elmwoodcemeteryandmausoleum.com

One of two largely Greek-American cemeteries in the Chicago area (the other being Evergreen Cemetery on the South Side), this River Grove site is, on a fair night, something to behold. Hundreds of candles scattered throughout the cemetery set the darkness glimmering, reassuring passers-by of the brilliance of resurrection set against the blackness of death.

In addition to the Greek sections and those nearby, the cemetery also hosts gatherings of Germans, Swedes, Albanians, Russians, Ukrainians, Bulgarians, Macedonians, Romany, and others, whose mourners have easily traveled to Elmwood via railroad from its earliest days.

Comedian **John Belushi** (1949–1982), still deeply mourned by his sweet home Chicago, has a cenotaph at this cemetery,

Though most cemeteries begun before the twentieth century included a receiving vault, for temporary storage of remains in winter, few such structures are intact. Elmwood's vault is mostly underground, with only the facade visible.

although his remains lie elsewhere, on Martha's Vineyard, Massachusetts. The beloved Belushi, a veteran of influential local comedy company, The Second City, went on to help make a new television show, *Saturday Night Live*, the rage of a generation. But Belushi really distinguished himself as Chicago's own with the release of the Hollywood film, *The Blues Brothers*, in which he brought his singing, dancing, ex-convict character of Joliet Jake Blues to life on the streets of the city he loved. Though Chicago is today a filmmakers' town extraordinaire, *The Blues Brothers* was the first film to showcase the rich atmosphere and culture of the Windy City. In it, Chicagoans found a common ground and

Elmwood includes two Civil War memorials, by different posts of the Grand Army of the Republic. The larger of these, erected by U.S. Grant Post #28 in 1903, includes figures representing Infantry, Artillery, Cavalry, and Navy.

private jokes that have made the movie and its soundtrack, featuring a slew of rhythm and blues and soul masters, plus Belushi's wailing vocals, among Chicagoans' most sincerely valued pop-cultural treasures.

The obelisk of William Worthington Higgins (1867–1941) is perfectly situated to take advantage of the cemetery's reflecting pool.

STRONG AND SILENT: THE CATHOLIC CEMETERIES OF CHICAGO

With 44 sites currently under its jurisdiction, the Catholic cemeteries of the Archdiocese of Chicago continue to provide a solid and ever-increasing local front against the onslaught of the corporate cemetery.

At last count, Archdiocesan cemeteries held 2.5 million graves and 128,000 crypts and niches, spread among more than 3,000 acres and 27 community mausoleums. From single-acre churchyards to sprawling ossuaries burying over one thousand faithful a year, local Catholics have a dizzying array of funeral destinations to choose from. And they just keep coming.

The Archdiocese had a head start on the burial business— the oldest cemetery in the metropolitan area is the Catholic churchyard of St. James-Sag Bridge in Lemont. In use from the early 1830s and still in operation, St. James survives along with every one of the Catholic cemeteries opened since except the first Diocesan burial ground at North Avenue and Dearborn Street, whose burials were re-interred at Calvary Cemetery in Evanston upon the closing of the earliest city cemeteries during the 1860s.

The tremendous popularity of Chicago's Catholic cemeteries increased dramatically after the consolidation of their control under Francis Cardinal Meyer during the 1960s. With a central authority dictating burial policy, pricing, maintenance, and regulations, the sites presented an appealingly reliable destination for those contemplating their own inevitable demise. The manicured elegance and glossy brochures of the new cemetery system seemed to promise comfort and care for those worried about the future of many local, independent sites that seemed to be falling under mismanagement or, worse yet, going wild.

During the Cardinal Bernardin years, a full 90 percent of the Archdiocesan Catholic population utilized at least one of the system's cemeteries. Some credit the huge majority to the system's recent emphasis on ethnic identification of individual cemeteries or separate sections within them catering to specific cultural groups. Dutifully tracking the ethnicity of their burials, the Archdiocesan cemeteries have been quick to cater to cultural sensibilities, erecting monuments to specific heritages and creating instant ethnic mini-settlements.

FOREST HOME CEMETERY (INCLUDING GERMAN WALDHEIM)

863 South Desplaines Avenue, Forest Park
www.foresthomecemetery.net
Established 1873

"**B**lack Friday," they called it—November 11, 1887. Four men mounted the scaffold and were hanged for a crime they did not commit. A fifth had died the day before, committing suicide in his cell with a smuggled explosive; his dying agonies lasted six hours.[330] They were anarchists and radicals, victims of public hysteria, convicted on the basis of negligible evidence. Only one cemetery was willing to accept the bodies of such hated men: German Waldheim, now part of Forest Home.

Centuries before Chicago was settled by European-Americans, the site of Forest Home was a cemetery where the native Potawatomi people buried their dead beneath mounds of earth. The Black Hawk War, followed by the Treaty of Chicago in 1833, put an end to their long history at the site. The Potawatomi were banished from Illinois, forced to migrate to Nebraska. In 1839, French-Indian fur trapper

---

[330] "Lingg's Fearful Death," *Chicago Daily Tribune*, November 11, 1887.

North side of Mausoleum Ridge, with Ferdinand Haase's obelisk at left. Forest Home's original chapel, now demolished, stood at the west end of the ridge.

Leon Bourasea made his home near the ancient graveyard, having received the 160-acre property by a land grant personally signed by President Martin Van Buren.[331] He chose the spot at the request of his Potawatomi wife, it was said, so that she could watch over the graves of her ancestors.

The fur trader did not remain long, soon selling his land to a young Prussian immigrant, Ferdinand Haase, who set up a farm at the site. The Haase family graveyard, near one of the ancient burial mounds, received its first burial in 1854 with the death of bother-in-law Carl Zimmerman, the first non-native person to be interred at the future site of Forest Home.

Despite the presence of this small graveyard, Haase had other uses for the property in mind. In 1856, the natural beauty of the site prompted him to create a public picnic ground. "Haase's Park (near Harlem)" was advertised, especially to the German community, as "the most beautiful pleasure grounds in the vicinity of Chicago."[332] The pleasure park featured picnic areas and outdoor pastimes such as hunting and fishing, even a bowling alley, and could be reached by a spur line especially built for Haase by a railway company and paid

---

[331] Historical Society of Forest Park, "The Story of Forest Park's History," Village of Forest Park, http://www.forestpark.net/pdf/FPHistory.pdf.

[332] Historical Society of Oak Park and River Forest, *Nature's Choicest Spot: A Guide to Forest Home and German Waldheim Cemeteries* (Oak Park, Ill.: Historical Society of Oak Park and River Forest, 1998), 2.

for with gravel mined from Haase's land.

By the late 1860s Haase had little desire to continue running an amusement park. The crowds were larger and noisier than before, bringing complaints from the neighbors. Public health concerns and the rising value of land in downtown Chicago meant that new space was needed for cemeteries on the fringes of the city, and Haase's land with its railroad line was ideally situated. He first sold the northernmost part of his property to a Lutheran organization that created Concordia Cemetery there in 1872. The following year, a group of German fraternal lodges established German Waldheim Cemetery on another parcel of land purchased from Haase because Concordia would not permit lodge insignia on monuments. The remainder of the land, under the stewardship of Haase and other community leaders, became Forest Home Cemetery, designed to appeal to English-speaking persons. "Forest Home" is the English translation of "Waldheim."[333]

The new cemeteries were designed according to the principles of the rural cemetery movement. A departure from the grid-like layouts of city cemeteries, rural cemeteries feature winding roads, landscaping, and features designed to emphasize the natural beauty of the location. Already, the picnic grounds included numerous trees, glacial ridges, and the Des Plaines River. Haase and his colleagues visited Spring Grove Cemetery in Cincinnati for inspiration. Both German Waldheim and Forest Home erected elaborate stone entrance gates.

The two cemeteries were unified in 1968 after both were sold to a real estate developer. With the entire complex now known as Forest Home, both entrance gates were removed, the southern entrance closed entirely, the northern entrance—originally belonging to German Waldheim—enlarged, and land along the edges of the property sold for other uses. North of the apartment buildings on Des Plaines Avenue, a portion of the original wrought iron fence can still be found.[334]

---

[333] Historical Society of Oak Park and River Forest, *Nature's Choicest Spot*, 3.

[334] Discovered by cemetery explorer John Martine, who showed it to this author in September 2011.

WALDHEIM CEMETERY

The northeast corner of Forest Home was originally Waldheim, also called German Waldheim, a non-denominational cemetery. Established by a group of German Masonic lodges in 1872, it accepted persons of any ethnicity, a rarity at that time. Waldheim's original entrance on Des Plaines Avenue, a few steps from a branch of the Wisconsin Central Railroad, was a massive castle-like structure with a narrow pointed archway, incorporating a chapel on one side and the cemetery's office on the other. Ponds flanked the main road inside the entrance, and a receiving vault stood nearby.[335] These features are now gone, with the gate demolished and the entrance widened to permit easier access by vehicles, and the ponds filled in. At the modern administrative building here, visitors may request *Forest Home Cemetery Facts*, with a map and list of points of interest. Other books and pamphlets are usually available for purchase there, particularly about the Haymarket Monument and the history of the labor activists buried nearby.

Proceeding northwest from the entrance, one first encounters a set of large, modern granite monuments, elaborately decorated with religious statues and laser-etched portraits. These belong to Romany people, commonly called "Gypsies," who are well-known for the great importance they place on honoring their dead. These spectacular monuments clearly demonstrate this tradition. Throughout the cemetery, one may find Romany surnames like Ely, John, Nichols, and Ristick.

Continuing west, the visitor finds older monuments, most inscribed with Germanic surnames. There are statues, obelisks, and headstones of every type. On several monuments, the faces of husband and wife appear side by side, facing each other or facing outward, some carved into the granite shafts and some as a separate piece of marble, bolted to the side. To the north, a group of mausoleums stand side-by-side like houses on a city street. One is made of yellow limestone blocks, now blackened with age, with a prominent

---

[335] Simon, *Chicago, the Garden City*, 167. The book, now in the public domain and freely available online, contains a photo of Waldheim's original entrance.

Masonic square and compass over the door. A granite cross inscribed *King Steve John* perches on the roof of another; this is the tomb of the **"King of All Gypsies,"** who died in Detroit in 1926.[336]

Looming over this section is one of the largest private tombs in the Chicago area, a grand structure, more than 30 feet tall, with pairs of Ionic columns supporting a massive roof over a large open space, and carved lions on either side of the steps. No name or other text appears on the mausoleum, except the date: 1902. A stairway in back leads down to a basement, where one might expect to find burial crypts. But this is empty, with only leaves and mud below the sagging timbers that support the upper level.[337] This majestic mausoleum stands empty, but was not always so. Built for **Ernst J. Lehmann** (1849–1900), the mausoleum once held six bodies, and the Lehmann name appeared across the roof. Lehmann was owner of the Fair Store, a discount department store, so-called because it was "like a fair," offering many things for a good price. In 1920 the Lehmanns chose to relocate their deceased relatives to Graceland Cemetery, to a mausoleum of a more convention-al design, and the

A puzzle to most visitors, the cemetery's largest mausoleum stands empty, with nothing inscribed other than the date 1902. It belonged to the family of Fair Store owner Ernst Lehmann (1849–1900). Their bodies were later relocated to Graceland, leaving this tomb abandoned.

[336] "Gypsy King Dead; Successor in Brazil," *Associated Press*, March 1, 1926. The date on King Steve John's mausoleum is February 26, 1926, and both newspaper and mauso-leum give his age as 65. Confusingly, another King Steve John, aged 75, died in May of that same year in Springfield, Massachusetts, and newspapers indicate he was also buried in Chicago's Forest Home, in an elaborate jeweled coffin.

[337] The basement door has been open in the past but is presently locked.

Lehmann name was removed.[338] Their tomb at Forest Home has stood empty ever since, a curiosity to visitors. It also provided artistic inspiration for a now out-of-print card game, "Mausoleum: The Game of Unfortunate Mishaps," in which an illustration of this mausoleum decorated the reverse of every card.[339]

Continuing west from the empty mausoleum, one finds several sections that directly border the Eisenhower Expressway, separated only by a low concrete partition and a chain-link fence. The noise and stink of the traffic are ever-present here, with brightly colored advertising billboards looming over the highway, and there are relatively few trees, compared to the rest of the cemetery, to provide respite. In this section stands one of Forest Home's most unusual monuments. Atop a tall pedestal sits a robed man with a long, scraggly beard and drooping mustache. He gazes wistfully into the distance, one arm resting on his bent knee and supporting his head. His other hand grips a harp, the top of which is carved to depict the head of a child. On the front of the pedestal appear only the date 1888, the cryptic initials U.A.O.D, and a symbol of an eye in an inverted triangle. Surrounding the monument are concentric circles of limestone coping, carved like tree branches. This monument was erected by the **United Ancient Order of Druids**. These were not Druids in the religious sense, but members of a secret society and fraternal order founded in London in 1781, who cloaked themselves in

A fraternal order, the United Ancient Order of Druids adopted the imagery—if not the actual religion—of the ancient Celts.

---

[338] Historical Society of Oak Park and River Forest, *Nature's Choicest Spot*, 57.

[339] "Info," Mausoleum: The Game of Unfortunate Mishaps, http://www.studiohunty.com/sg/mausoleum/info.html. Game by R. Hunter Gough.

the symbolism of the legendary architects of Stonehenge and called their lodges "groves." A search of the cemetery records led to an 1875 warranty deed for the plot, handwritten in ornate lettering, listing three names as "Trustees of the Druids." At its peak, the U.A.O.D. had as many as 35,000 members, but eventually this secret society seems to have disappeared altogether.[340]

North of the Druid monument, near the expressway, a tree provides shade for the **Augusta Nebel** monument, a slender pyramid of rough-cut stone, crowned with a stone basket. Augusta died in 1889 at the age of 28, preceded in death by two of her children: Willie, six months, and Fritz, two. A figure of a small boy, wearing only a loincloth, his hand pressed to his forehead in sorrow, stands at one corner. Beneath Augusta's name appear the words *ruhe sanft* ("rest gently").

West of the Druid monument stands the figure of a woman atop a tall slender shaft, holding an anchor. This is the monument of another fraternal order, the **International Order of Odd Fellows,** which purchased group burial plots for their members in most of Chicago's finest cemeteries. Near the Odd Fellows monument is one of this author's favorite memorial sculptures—the figures of **Lars and Eddie Schmidt**.[341] Barely three feet tall, the soft white marble statues of these two children have been worn down by a century of rain and wind, smoothing their facial features into a haunting, skeletal appearance. Lars, age six, wears a sailor suit with a knotted cravat and a

Brothers Lars and Eddie Schmidt died two days apart in 1890. Gifts are regularly left at their tiny statues.

[340] John Rice, "Temple of the Tree People," *Forest Park Review*, October 27, 1993.

[341] A previous edition of this book, and the *graveyards.com* website, incorrectly identified the younger child as "Ruth" Schmidt. This error resulted from a misreading of the severely weathered inscription and conversations with other graveyard explorers who also believed the child to be a girl. I apologize for the error.

row of buttons down the front. Eddie, age two, sits on a box and wears a dress, as very young boys did in the 1880s. Below the dress, his feet are missing, broken away long ago. The brothers, children of a local undertaker, died of diphtheria in 1890, only two days apart.[342] Their parents, who died in 1935 and 1941, have a much larger, much simpler monument, a granite tablet.

Some distance behind is another monument to a child lost suddenly. On the side of a red granite shaft a large photographic portrait is affixed, showing a young girl standing. This is the grave of **"Baby" Sophia Gudehus**, age six, a victim of the Iroquois Theatre fire of 1903.

Turning back toward the entrance, but taking a more southerly route, the visitor will catch sight of the chapel in the distance. Near the chapel is Waldheim's most famous monument, visited by labor activists from around the world, site of May Day rallies, and a designated National Historic Landmark: **The Haymarket Martyrs' Monument**.

The "Haymarket Affair" or "Haymarket Riot" took place in downtown Chicago, at Haymarket Square near Randolph and Desplaines[343] streets on May 4, 1886. Three days before, 80,000 workers and supporters had marched on Michigan Avenue calling for enforcement of the existing laws limiting working hours to eight hours a day, a law regularly ignored by employers.[344]

The Haymarket Martyrs Monument, burial site of seven of the eight men convicted of inciting riot, features a heroic statue of Justice crowning the fallen worker.

---

[342] Historical Society of Oak Park and River Forest, *Nature's Choicest Spot*, 56.

343. Not the same Des Plaines Avenue on which this cemetery is located. The name is a coincidence.

[344] Joe Powers and Mark Rogovin, *The Day Will Come...: Stories of the Haymarket Martyrs and the Men and Women Buried Alongside the Monument* (Chicago: Charles H. Kerr Publishing Company, 1994).

As tensions escalated, Chicago police fired on striking workers at the McCormick Reaper Works on May 3, killing at least two of them. To protest the slayings, activist leaders—with the permission of Mayor Carter Henry Harrison—called for a public rally at Haymarket Square.

The meeting was poorly organized and sparsely attended. Mayor Harrison, seeing that it was peaceful, departed. As the event wound down, about 200 remained in attendance, surrounded by a similar number of armed police. During a speech by Sam Fielden, a Methodist lay preacher, the police attempted to forcibly disperse the audience, marching into the crowd wielding rifles and clubs. It was then that some person—unknown to this day—threw a homemade dynamite bomb at the line of police. Panicked, they began firing into the crowd, with some of their gunfire striking their fellow officers. One policeman died from the bombing; six more police, and four workers, died from the gunfire.[345]

The enraged public, and the *Chicago Tribune*, called for blood. **Samuel Fielden** (1847–1922), who was on stage at the time of the bombing, was arrested, as were **Albert Parsons** (1848–1887), organizer of the May Day protests, and **August Spies** (1855–1887), publisher of the *Chicagoer Arbeiter-Zeitung* ("Chicago Worker Newspaper"); **Michael Schwab** (1853–1898), a writer for that paper; **Adolph Fischer** (1858–1887), who had helped to plan the meeting; **George Engel** (1836–1887), who was not present at the meeting, but had spoken at the events leading up to it; **Oscar Neebe** (1850–1916), an organizer of brewery workers; and finally, **Louis Lingg** (1864–1887), a 22-year-old carpenter, who was fingered as the bomb-thrower, even though witnesses stated he wasn't at the rally at all. Eight men were tried, and all eight convicted, based on almost no evidence. Neebe was sentenced to 15 years and the others were sentenced to death. Intervention by Governor Oglesby spared Fielden and Schwab.

The day before the hangings, Louis Lingg bit down on a dynamite blasting cap that someone had smuggled into his jail cell, blowing off half his face. The following day, "Black Friday," the surviving four con-

---

[345] Powers and Rogovin, *The Day Will Come.*

demned—Spies, Fischer, Engel, and Parsons—were taken to the gallows. It was there that Spies spoke his famous last words: *The day will come when our silence will be more powerful than the voices you are throttling today.* It is these words that appear at the base of the monument.

The five bodies were brought to German Waldheim, the only cemetery willing to accept them, a cemetery that was open to all, where, in the words of its first president, "everyone could repose after his own fashion."[346] They were buried together in the same plot. In 1893, Governor John Peter Altgeld[347] pardoned the three surviving prisoners—an unpopular move that ended his own political career. Schwab and Neebe, thus pardoned, resumed their lives as free men and, upon their deaths, were buried alongside their martyred comrades. Of the eight, only Fielden is not buried at Waldheim.

The spectacular monument was designed by sculptor Albert Weinert.[348] A larger-than-life bronze figure of a woman symbolizing Justice is shown placing a wreath on the head of a fallen worker, his head tilted back and arms limp in death. Below them is the date 1887, when the hangings took place, and a smaller bronze piece, a cluster of palm leaves. This last piece is a reproduction of the original, stolen some time before the mid-1990s, but replaced with an exact replica just before the monument's re-dedication ceremony on May Day 2011.[349]

The Haymarket Monument became a place of pilgrimage for labor activists and socialists, and a number of them chose to be buried nearby, in a section that local graveyard enthusiasts jokingly refer to as "the Communist Plot." As many of them were cremated, they have small markers, spaced closely together. **Lucy Parsons** (1853–1942), wife of Haymarket martyr Albert Parsons, is buried in this section, only steps away from the husband she survived by over 50 years.

---

[346] Historical Society of Oak Park and River Forest, *Nature's Choicest Spot*, 3.

[347] See Graceland Cemetery entry for more on Altgeld.

[348] Historical Society of Oak Park and River Forest, *Nature's Choicest Spot*, 36.

[349] Matt Hucke had planned to attend the ceremony but was involved in a serious car crash the day before; John Martine (cemetery explorer and Forest Home expert) had also planned to be there but was attacked on the street and badly beaten two weeks before. We have thus concluded that some sort of curse was in effect, preventing our attendance—though we did successfully meet there the following September.

Born Lucy Gonzalez of mixed Native American, African, and Mexican ancestry, she was a socialist author and organizer and a tireless crusader for racial and women's equality.

Elizabeth Gurley Flynn (1890–1964), labor organizer, cofounder of the ACLU, and chair of the Communist Party USA, was given a state funeral upon her death in the Soviet Union. Her ashes are buried here. CPUSA presidential candidate **William Foster** (1881–1961); medical doctor and "King of the Hobos" **Ben Reitman** (1879–1943); Russian revolutionary **Boris Yelensky** (1889–1974); and union organizer **Jack Johnstone** (1881–1942) are also among the many buried here. Half of the ashes of International Workers of the World founder **"Big Bill" Haywood** (1869–1928), who fled to Russia after being convicted of sedition, were scattered here, with the remainder entombed in the Kremlin wall.[350] One activist, buried immediately adjacent to the Haymarket monument, has a special connection to the site: **Irving S. Abrams** (1891–1980), last survivor of the Pioneer Aid and Support Organization, did more than anyone to preserve and provide for the Haymarket monument and the labor leaders' graves nearby.

Perhaps the best-known of these activists is **Emma Goldman** (1869–1940), whom J. Edgar Hoover called one of "the most dangerous anarchists in the country." Eighteen years old when the Haymarket martyrs were hanged, the shocking event prompted the young Goldman to become an activist. Goldman traveled, wrote, and lectured in support of women's equality, workers' rights, and birth control. She was imprisoned several times for incitement to riot, for illegally distributing birth control information, and for inducing persons to not register for the draft—after which she was deported to her native Russia. Prohibited from re-entering the United States, she spent her later years traveling Europe and Canada, writing and lecturing. She died in Canada in 1940. At her request, her body was shipped to Chicago to be interred next to the Haymarket martyrs who had inspired her. Sculptor Jo Davidson created a bronze plaque

---

[350] Powers and Rogovin, *The Day Will Come*. The stories of many of the socialists and union activists buried in this section are told in this book, which this author purchased at the cemetery office.

with a portrait of Goldman that was affixed to the front of her monument. Irving Abrams gave her eulogy and provided funds for the maintenance of the grave. Due to a stone carver's error, the monument incorrectly gives the year of her death as 1939.[351]

An exceptional monument here is the life-size statue of **Minnie Hagemeister** (1864–1940). This realistic granite figure of a middle-aged woman depicts her standing, with one hand atop a column, the other hand apparently missing—when viewed from the front. However, her right hand may be seen by walking around the monument; it is behind her back, clutching a handkerchief.

FOREST HOME CEMETERY: WEST

West of the Des Plaines River lies a distinctly different part of Forest Home. This is a newer development, with more rectangular sections and simple granite monuments. This section has its own entrance in its southwest corner, along First Avenue, but may also be reached from the eastern part of Forest Home by driving across a bridge spanning the river. For some years, when safety concerns prompted one of the two bridges to be closed, the unusable bridge was blocked with a sign reading *May Your Crossing Be Blessed with Eternal Rest*. Later, the second bridge was closed, closing off the only route between the east and west sides of the cemetery. One would have to leave the cemetery and drive on the public streets to reach the other side. Both condemned bridges have been demolished and a single span now crosses the river in their place.

Several monuments of interest are in the sections nearest the river. Various trade unions have established plots for their members here. The monument of the **Cigar Makers' International Union** featured a bronze ornament depicting a tax stamp, now missing. Union organizer and AFL co-founder **Adolph Strasser** (1843–1939), a cigar-

---

[351] Irving S Abrams, *Haymarket Heritage : The Memoirs of Irving S Abrams* ([S.l.]: Small Press Distribution, 1989), 41.

maker, is buried in this plot.

Not far from the bridge is a simple stone for two brothers who died together in the Iroquois Theatre fire of 1903, along with over 600 other victims, mostly children. Among these were the brothers Barry Winder, age 12, and Paul Winder, age 7, whose monument reads *Lost in the Iroquois Fire.*[352]

The largest memorial on the west side of the cemetery is the mausoleum of Congressman **Adolph J. Sabath** (1866–1952). A Bohemian Jew, he was elected to Congress as a Democrat in 1907, first of an unprecedented 24 terms in office. From 1934 to his death he was considered Dean of the House of Representatives, a ceremonial title given to the longest-serving member, which Sabath held longer than any other congressman before or since.

At about 11:30 p.m. on the night of July 27, 1960, a Sikorsky S-58 helicopter operated by Chicago Helicopter Airways took off from Midway Airport on a routine 11-minute flight, carrying passengers who had arrived at Midway and needed to make connecting flights at O'Hare. Witnesses reported that it seemed to stop in mid-air, zigzag, and then plummet to the ground. It crashed in the western part of Forest Home Cemetery, killing all—two crewmen and 11 passengers. Firemen reported that the flames were so hot they could not approach the wreckage for nearly an hour.

FOREST HOME CEMETERY: EAST

The older part of Forest Home Cemetery stretches from the south edge of Waldheim to Roosevelt Road. While once it had its own entrance gate, a fortress-like structure with crenelated parapet and tower,[353] this was demolished after the 1968 merger of the cemeteries, and this part of Forest Home is now accessible only by the connecting bridge from the western half or by a narrow road at the rear

---

[352] See the Montrose Cemetery entry for more about the Iroquois Fire.
[353] Historical Society of Oak Park and River Forest, *Nature's Choicest Spot*, photo, 1.

of Waldheim. This secluded, picturesque cemetery has a stretch of road frontage only on its southern boundary. To the east, a series of seven-story apartment buildings block the view and much of the noise from Des Plaines Avenue. Two automobile dealerships stand between the cemetery and the street corner to the southeast. The cemetery is generously planted with trees, giving it an atmosphere of seclusion and solitude, peaceful yet sometimes eerie.

An unmarked grave in Forest Home may have contained the remains of **Belle Sorenson Gunness** (1859–1908?), notable both for the cruelty of her deeds and for being that rarest of notorious individuals, a female serial killer. Born Brynhild Paulsdatter Størset in Norway, she immigrated to America in 1881, Americanizing her given name to Belle and marrying a candyshop owner by the name of Mads Sorenson. By 1900, the candy shop had burned down, two of their four children had died with symptoms similar to poisoning—each event yielding an insurance payout—and Belle's husband himself died on the one day when two insurance policies overlapped, of what one doctor described as strychnine poisoning but the official records noted as heart failure.

Belle moved to La Porte, Indiana, purchased a farm with the insurance money, and remarried. Within a week she had dispatched her new husband's infant daughter. By the end of the year, Belle's husband, Peter Gunness, conveniently suffered a fatal accident—though his 14-year-old daughter Jennie claimed to her schoolmates that Belle had killed him with a meat cleaver. When Jennie refused to repeat this accusation at the coroner's inquest, Belle was free to kill again. Jennie vanished three years later (supposedly sent to boarding school in Los Angeles), and Belle began courting various men who answered her newspaper advertisements, convincing them to bring her large sums of cash, after which each of them mysteriously disappeared.

Belle's undoing came when her farmhand and accomplice Ray Lamphere, jealous of her many suitors, began threatening her, at the same time that the brother of one of her victims was making inquiries into his brother's disappearance. Belle told a lawyer that Lamphere had threatened to kill her and her children and burn their house down. And, on April 28, 1908, her prediction seemed to come true as her farmhouse burned to the ground. Four badly burned bodies, those of three children and a woman were found in the wreckage, but the woman's head could not be found. Moreover, the woman's corpse was much smaller than Belle, and the autopsy revealed traces of strychnine in her stomach. Belle, it seems, had faked her own death, substituting a headless corpse, and killing her stepchildren to give it plausibility.

Who, then, is buried alongside the murdered children in Belle Gunness's grave in Forest Home Cemetery? As the La Porte authorities searched Belle's property, they found a fragment of jaw that Belle's dentist identified as containing work that he had done for her. They also found portions of at least 12 other bodies, including three more children and numerous of Belle's suitors, buried on the part of the farm where Belle had fed her hogs. One of the children found buried was stepdaughter Jennie, who had recanted her accusation against Belle years before.

In 2007, a team of forensic scientists from the University of Indianapolis received permission to exhume the headless body from the Sorenson plot at Forest Home and perform DNA analysis. As the reference sample, an envelope supposedly licked by Belle, did not contain enough DNA for a comparison, the results were inconclusive, and the samples await further study.

In the corner of the cemetery next to busy Roosevelt Road, and only about ten feet from the steep bank of the Des Plaines River, stands another grand mausoleum. The brilliant white granite mausoleum is of classical design, with Ionic columns on all sides, pediment roof ornamented with palmette antefixes, and lion statues on either side of the path to the front door. Porches on the two sides of the mausoleum shelter statues—on the south, a male figure, bearing the caduceus and winged sandals of Hermes, labeled *The Spirit of Commerce*; and on the north, a female figure, wearing headphones and holding the palm frond that symbolizes Nike, goddess of victory, *The Spirit of Radio*. Over the front door is the name Grunow. **William Grunow** (1893–1951), a partner in the Grigsby-Grunow

Radio Corporation, was manufacturer of the Majestic brand of radios, phonographs, and other household appliances.

Nearby is the grave of **Samuel Fallows** (1835–1922), a brigadier general of the Civil War, and presiding bishop of the Reformed Episcopal Church. Fallows happened to be in the vicinity of the Iroquois Theatre when the fire took place, and assisted the firemen in rescuing those trapped within. He later commented that the carnage he saw that day exceeded any he had seen in the war.[354]

The Spirit of Radio, at the side of the Grunow mausoleum, is depicted as a classical Greek goddess—with the addition of headphones. William Grunow (1893–1951) manufactured radios under the trade name Majestic.

Another hero of the Iroquois tragedy is buried at Forest Home, **William Lancaster McLaughlin** (1885–1903). A university student and son of a Methodist minister, McLaughlin escaped the theater building when the fire began, but then rushed back in when it became clear that others were trapped. He stood on a fire escape, helping women and children climb towards a makeshift bridge on the roof that enabled them to escape safely to the roof of the neighboring building. Though he saved the lives of many, he himself was badly burned, dying in hospital the following day, at the age of 18.[355] On his monument is written his almost-final words, *I knew that I was following Christ, and I could not do otherwise.*

Visually, the dominant feature here is **"Mausoleum Ridge."** This naturally occurring sand ridge was part of the Oak Park Spit, a landmark for Native Americans and pioneers.[356] The highest point within Forest Home, it was the site of the cemetery's original chapel, no vis-

[354] "A Forgotten Victim of the Great Chicago Theater Fire of 1903," Examiner, http://www.examiner.com/article/a-forgotten-victim-of-the-great-chicago-iroquois-theater-fire-of-1903.

[355] "A Memento of the Iroquois Fire," *The Missionary Review of the World*, Funk & Wagnalls, Volume 29, 1906, 382. Thanks to John Martine for informing me of this story.

[356] Historical Society of Oak Park and River Forest, *Nature's Choicest Spot*, 38.

ible trace of which remains. On either side of the ridge are hillside vaults, the largest such collection in the Chicago area. Generally of similar design to free-standing mausoleums, these tombs are partly buried in the sloping sides of the ridge, with their fronts fully exposed but their rear walls partially or wholly underground. A visitor might walk up the gentle slope at one end of the ridge and stand on the roofs of these tombs, for a panoramic view of the cemetery landscape.

East of the ridge is the family plot of **Ferdinand Haase** (1871– 1928), founder of Forest Home. His monument is a tall obelisk with an ornate pedestal, the edges forming curves sweeping down

The obelisk at the end of Mausoleum Ridge stands over the grave of Ferdinand Haase (1826–1911), cemetery founder and original owner of the land. His house stood just outside the gates.

from the Ionic volutes at its upper corners. Haase's plot is well maintained, featuring a variety of shrubs and flowers of all colors.

In the middle of section 10, north of Haase's towering monument, are the simple markers of **Dr. Clarence Hemingway** (1871–1928) and opera singer **Grace Hall Hemingway** (1872–1951), parents of Ernest Hemingway. Ernest spent the early part of his life in Oak Park, but, finding it dull, sought adventure elsewhere. No fan of the Chicago area, the esteemed author is buried in the small Idaho town where he took his life.

Also nearby is the plot of **Henry Warren Austin** (1828–1889), businessman and state legislator, for whom the town of Austin (now part of Chicago) was named.[357] It is not Mr. Austin's grave here that catches the visitor's eye, rather it is that of his eight-year-old daugh-

---

[357] "Austin, Chicago," Wikipedia, http://en.wikipedia.org/wiki/Austin,_Chicago.

ter, **Hannah Austin**, who died on Christmas Eve 1879. Her monument is a hip-roofed granite sarcophagus in the general shape of a coffin. It was said her father "could not bear the thought of his little girl buried under the cold earth."[358] Henry Austin died ten years after his daughter, to the day.

Two legs of stone stand, side by side, on the same base. Nearby, fragments on the ground are all that remain of the arch that once joined them. Across the base is written *The Rev. Morrill Twins.* Identical twins **Horace Morrill** (1867–1902) and **Herbert Morrill** (1867–1927) entered the ministry together and built a church in the shape of a ship on Chicago's Near West Side. They called their church, "The Gospel Ship," wore naval uniforms, and preached with a nautical theme. Horace died at the age of thirty-four, and a newspaper photograph at that time shows Herbert sitting sadly by Horace's open coffin.[359]

At the eastern edge of the cemetery, surrounded only by trees and open air, is the **Indian Trail Marker**. This pink granite boulder, placed in 1942, has an inscription carved on one side that tells the story of the ancient trail that passed this spot, through the wild plum groves to the Des Plaines River. Next to the text, the stern face of a Native American man stares from the boulder. His headband, and the stone sloping back above his brow, suggest the feathered headdress of a chieftain.

Frank Sinatra sang that Chicago was "the town that Billy

Modeled after a church window, this is the monument of baseball player turned preacher Billy Sunday (1862–1935).

[358] "The Austin Obelisk," Greenline Wheels, http://www.greenlinewheels.com/poi/austinobelisk.

[359] Photos and articles are in the collection of John Martine.

Sunday couldn't shut down," and, true enough, the town survives long after his death. **William Ashley Sunday** (1862–1935) was born with a name fit for a preacher, but it was not until his twenties that he became a religious man. A natural athlete, he was discovered by "Cap" Anson[360] and recruited for the Chicago White Stockings baseball team, becoming known as the fastest runner in the league. About 1886 or 1887, Sunday was attracted to a service of the Pacific Garden Mission when he overheard the hymns, and he thereafter began attending services regularly. He became a Christian, renouncing his habits of gambling and drinking. In 1891 he left baseball to work as a preacher at a small fraction of his former salary.

Sunday traveled throughout Illinois and Iowa, preaching first in churches, then in large tents as his popularity grew. He preached temperance, personal discipline, and self-reliance, and spoke out against the capitalists exploiting the working man. It was his crusade against liquor that brought him lasting fame, immortalized by Sinatra. Sunday's monument takes the form of a church window, rendered in granite, inscribed with a verse from the book of Timothy: *I Have Kept the Faith.*

Considered by many to be the cemetery's most beautiful work of funerary art, the monument commemorating real estate developer **Edmund A. Cummings** (1842–1922) is rich in detail. A veteran of the Civil War, Cummings operated E.A. Cummings & Co., one of Chicago's preeminent real estate firms, whose motto was "We Welcome All Who Would a Home Acquire." He was also in-

The monument of Edmund Cummings, designed by the firm of Louis Tiffany, is one of the most highly regarded works of art in the cemetery.

---

[360] See Oak Woods Cemetery entry for biography of Cap Anson.

strumental in the expansion of several towns in the vicinity, including Ridgeland and River Forest, and co-founded the Cicero & Proviso Street Railway Company.[361]

Edmund Cummings's monument was created by the firm of artist Louis Comfort Tiffany. The general shape is that of a tall, tapering stele, similar to the royal monuments of Axum in Ethiopia. At the top is a Celtic cross, each arm of which bears a three-lobed Celtic knot symbolizing the Trinity. A wicker-like pattern is carved into all sides of the stele. On the front, an angel stands, its wings upright, its feet on an eight-spoked wheel. The Cummings plot was once elaborately landscaped to complement the design of the monument, with a multitude of colorful plants forming the shape of a wheel, one spoke broken as a symbol of death, echoing the wheel that appears beneath the angel's feet.[362]

South of Mausoleum Ridge is another beautiful and secluded part of the cemetery. Here, mysterious voices may occasionally be heard, saying words that are not quite intelligible, even when no other visitors are present. These are, in fact, simply announcements from loudspeakers at the two car dealerships on the corner.

Visible here is a remnant of the original Potawatomi cemetery. Atop a gentle earthen mound stands a granite shaft, one face covered with text, with several flat markers embedded in the surrounding soil. The monument, erected in 1941, depicts a Native man astride a horse, and tells of the ancient people who inhabited the site, and how they buried their dead on this spot; how the land passed to Leon

An earthen mound in the south part of Forest Home is a remnant of the ancient Potawatomi cemetery on the site. Relatives of Haase were buried here as well, predating the land's use as a public cemetery. In the distant background, one of Jewish Waldheim's many brick archways can be seen.

[361] Historical Society of Oak Park and River Forest, *Nature's Choicest Spot*, 9.
[362] Historical Society of Oak Park and River Forest, *Nature's Choicest Spot*, 9.

MODERN WOODMEN OF AMERICA

The Modern Woodmen were founded in the 1880s by Iowan Joseph Cullen Root, whose vision of a self-governing society fed by nationwide camps was realized in the formation of a fraternal benefit society. Not associated with forestry, logging, or other such professions, the group's misleading name was inspired by a sermon heard by Root, in which his minister evoked a spiritual analogy involving pioneer woodmen clearing away a forest. Aiming to help members clear their financial responsibilities before death, Root seized upon the image and christened his society "Modern Woodmen," later adding "of America" to include the patriotic bent of the group's membership.

The public became acquainted with the Woodmen during the 1904 World's Fair at St. Louis, when the Modern Woodmen Foresters, an axe-wielding drill team, dazzled audiences with their colorful garb and clever performances. The team's popularity continued to grow, with local appearances in parades and competitions across the country leading to a presidential audience with Herbert Hoover. Unfortunately, World War I resulted in the dissolution of the Foresters. They would never reassemble again.

Despite their retreat from the public spotlight, the Woodmen continued to shine. From 1909 to 1947, the fraternity operated a tuberculosis sanitarium in the Rocky Mountain foothills outside of Colorado Springs with tremendous success. More than 12,000 members were treated during those years, more than 70 percent of whom recovered. The treatment? The era's recommended medicine of clean air and exercise.

Bourasea, and thence to Ferdinand Haase; and concludes:

Thus, many years ago, Ferdinand Haase and his sons re-established and dedicated to sepulcher the ancient forest home of the Pottawatomie to become the present Forest Home of the white man.

WALDHEIM JEWISH CEMETERIES

1800 South Harlem Avenue, Forest Park
www.waldheimcemetery.com
Established 1873

When Chicago's Jewish population began its westward movement, some may have anticipated that the western suburbs would ultimately become a prime destination for Jewish migrants from Chicago. Yet, though the concentration of Jews in the old Maxwell Street ghetto rapidly thinned, transplanted to neighborhoods like Lawndale, Austin, Douglas, and Garfield Park, points further west never became a popular target. One reason was the already huge populations of a number of these western suburbs. Due to their proximity to the city center, many of these villages, like Maywood and Oak Park, had already hosted significant prewar settlement, leaving little room for new mass migrations. Additionally, places like Berwyn and Cicero were overwhelm-

Within the eastern portion of Waldheim, many of the gates are intact, identifying the cemeteries belonging to congregations, fraternal orders, or benevolent societies.

ingly blue-collar towns.

Even today, a mere 15,000 Jews live in the western suburbs, yet the largest of the 13 Jewish cemeteries in the Chicago area is here in Forest Park, part of the sprawling burial ground known vaguely as Waldheim. Jewish Waldheim was founded during the second wave of Jewish immigration to Chicago in the mid- to late–nineteenth century. While the first group of settlers had been Germanic, quickly conforming to

The photo on the monument of David G. Henner (1898–1925) shows the botanist and sculptor at work at the Field Museum, crafting a model of a plant. Henner drowned near the Indiana Dunes at the age of 27.

American ways, the second migration was comprised of Eastern European Jews, who were typically more conservative and less eager to be assimilated into American culture. Insisting on their own cemeteries, congregations eagerly purchased the plots offered by their synagogues, opting for burial in places like Waldheim, which was never a single cemetery but rather a gathering of the communal plots of more than 300 congregations, *Vereins*, and *Landsmanschaften*, at one time rigidly divided by gated fences, some of which remain. Initially intriguing for this sectionalization, the thousands of monuments spanning many ethnicities, and the *Bet-Taharas* once used for the preparation of bodies in the days before burial vaults, the cemetery is ultimately valued

Largest in the cemetery, the Egyptian-styled Balaban mausoleum was built by architects Cornelius and George Rapp, who designed numerous theaters and movie palaces for the Balaban and Katz company.

Operated by a fraternal order, the Free Sons of Israel Cemetery, at the southern tip of Waldheim, is distinctly different in character from the rest of the cemetery, resembling a Victorian rural cemetery more than the European appearance of the rest of Waldheim.

as a treasure cache of Chicago's Jewish history.

Waldheim's first interment was held in 1875. At that time, funeral parties and visitors faced a day-long excursion from the Maxwell Street neighborhood to the graves of their loved ones. In 1914, however, the Metropolitan Elevated began running a funeral route to Waldheim that operated successfully for two decades.

One of the most famous graves among the nearly 175,000 at this site is that of 18-year-old marine **Samuel Meisenberg** (d. 1914), the first American to be killed during the American military landings at Vera Cruz, Mexico. Meisenberg received the Purple Heart for his actions 75 years after his death.

Infinitely less deserved is the fame of another Jewish Wald-

This white bronze angel was erected by grieving parents after the deaths of brothers Abel Abraham Levin (1878–1901) and George William Levin (1875–1901). Along with two friends, they drowned when their skiff capsized in Lake Michigamme in Michigan's Upper Peninsula. Their bodies were not recovered.

heim plot: the grave of **Albert Weinshank** (1893–1929), who had been the newest member of Bugs Moran's gang when he was shot to death with six others in the St. Valentine's Day Massacre.

Upon leaving Jewish Waldheim, note the cemetery gates, which are made from columns taken from the old County Building, demolished in 1908.

With each congregation or benevolent society needing to fit their members into a small cemetery, monuments in the older section of Waldheim are packed closely together. Many have inscriptions in both English and Hebrew, some entirely in Hebrew.

WOODLAWN MEMORIAL PARK

7750 West Cermak Road, Forest Park
www.woodlawncemeteryofchicago.com
Established 1912

This Forest Park burial ground is a hit with children—just ask them about the elephants in the cemetery.

Showmen's Rest, Woodlawn's biggest drawing card, is maintained by the Showmen's League of America for the burial of circus performers. Included among its resurrection-bound residents are 50 performers and crew members killed in a wreck of the Hagenbeck-Wallace Circus train near Hammond, Indi-

Established for members of a trade organization, the Showmen's League of America, Showmen's Rest soon became famous when victims of a horrific train crash were buried here.

The monument of cemetery designer Svend Lollesgard (1860–1934), a larger boulder balanced on three smaller stones, paraphrases the famous epitaph of Sir Christopher Wren: *If you want to see his memorial look around* you.

ana, in June 1918. Most of the headstones are marked with only nicknames, like *The Fat Man* or *Baldy*, or with *Unknown* designations. Drawing the curious to this spot are five spectacularly somber stone elephants, their trunks lowered as if in mourning, testimony to an unfounded legend that tells of the animals rescuing victims from the deadly fire that consumed most of the train wreck's victims.

Across Des Plaines Avenue from the rest of the cemetery, the community mausoleum stretches along the banks of the river. Opened in 1964, the building includes several courtyards surrounded by crypts.

Also buried here is **Ervin Dusak** (1920–1994), who played for the Pittsburgh Pirates in the 1950s.

Burned beyond recognition, most of the victims of the Hagenbeck-Wallace train crash were buried as *Unknown Female* or *Unknown Male*.

CONCORDIA CEMETERY

www.ingodsarms.com
7900 Madison Street,
Forest Park
Established 1872

This monument features a cross above three steps, representing the virtues of Faith, Hope, and Charity, along with a surrogate mourner. This popular motif may be found in several Chicago-area cemeteries, both Catholic and Lutheran.

The first of the Forest Park community of burial grounds to be carved out of Ferdinand Haase's property, Concordia Cemetery was established in 1872 by a group of seven Lutheran churches, six of which continue as the Concordia Association today. Wanting the cemetery to remain strictly religious in character, the management prohibited the insignia of fraternal orders on monuments—a prohibition which led to the establishment of German Waldheim on neighboring land to the south the following year. Between the cemeteries was a 60-foot wide right-of-way used by the Chicago Aurora and Elgin Railroad, on which trains equipped with special funeral cars would bring coffins and mourners to the cemeteries.

An elaborate 55-foot tall entrance arch on Madison Street also housed administrative offices and a 400-coffin receiving vault. This was demolished about 1931, when the new administration building was constructed. Designed by the architectural firm of Miller & Wallace, the golden Ohio sandstone building houses a carillon that delights visitors with the sound of chimes.

The railroad's 60-foot wide strip between Concordia and Waldheim proved insufficient for the construction of the Congress Street

Super-Highway, now known as the Eisenhower Expressway. In 1953, Cook County authorities began proceedings to condemn and seize land from both Forest Home and Concordia to provide for the new highway and for the relocation of the railroad line. The plan called for the removal of an estimated 3,150 graves, more than two-thirds of them on the Concordia side. Though the county superintendent proposed a 2,000-foot long elevated road span over the cemetery, this idea never got off the ground—the state's attorney instead proceeded with the original plan to sue the cemeteries to force removal of the bodies, at a cost of $500 each. The courts ruled in favor of the county, but also mandated the notification of relatives, which delayed the onset of the project by several years. The actual work of removal began in August of 1955 at Forest Home and June 1957 at Concordia.

Half a century after this unwanted incursion, Concordia is today a beautiful place for quiet contemplation and remembrance. The impeccable surroundings are made even more elegant by the rare carillon and a beautiful limestone grapevine and marker commemorating a pair of victims of the 1915 *Eastland* disaster. The high concentration of obelisks, in places seeming as thick as the trees of a forest, also provides for some splendid views.

Older sections of the cemetery resemble a forest of obelisks, many of them draped with cloth as a symbol of mourning. The angel shown here holds a palm frond to represent victory over death.

ALTENHEIM CEMETERY

7824 Madison Street, Forest Park
thealtenheim.com
Established circa 1895

Tucked away behind the German Old People's Home is this quiet little cemetery, provided for burials of the home's residents. The home opened in 1885 on grounds designed by landscape architect Herman J. DeVry, superintendent of Lincoln Park, with the picturesque main building having an initial capacity of 75 residents, which would increase as additions were made to the building.[363] Those residents who were able to work were asked to do so, and they performed various chores in the kitchens and gardens for the good of the community.

Most grave markers at Altenheim are cast in concrete, with *Hier ruht* ("here rests") over the names and dates. In a few cases, families provided for a more conventional granite headstone. The obelisks and tall pedestal tombs of Concordia Cemetery can be seen behind the fence in the distance.

According to those stones still readable, the first burials took place in 1895.[364] The rows are arranged by date, not by surname, for there are no family plots here. Little variety may be found here in the way of grave decoration; the simple concrete

[363] Altenheim, http://thealtenheim.com.
[364] *The Cemetery at Altenheim, Forest Park, Illinois* (Chicago: Chicago Genealogical Society, 1991).

markers seem rather to strive together for uniformity. Like at many other institutional cemeteries, the markers were made by residents themselves, pouring concrete into molds into which movable letters had been placed.

Superintendent **Karl Mueller** (1893–1950) is a notable exception to the uniformity, given pride of place in a little section set apart from the rest, with concrete letters spelling out *ALTENHEIM* embedded in the ground nearby.

Just over the fence on the west side is Concordia Cemetery, with its obelisks and statues, providing a drastically different appearance.

MOUNT AUBURN CEMETERY

4101 South Oak Park Avenue, Stickney
www.mountauburnmemorial.com
Established 1897

In 1895, the indefatigable Ossian Cole Simonds began work on a new cemetery in suburban Stickney. Mount Auburn would open for business in 1897 as the first Chicago area cemetery with entire sections designated for flush markers only, providing for a park-like appearance.[365] Customers aren't restricted to that option alone, however. Other sections in the cemetery have the traditional upright monuments, and there are a scattering of mausoleums as well.

The Chinese temple altar includes two ovens for the burning of offerings. Numerous Chinese are buried nearby.

---

[365] According to a sign on the cemetery grounds.

The community mausoleum at Mount Auburn.

Mount Auburn is a destination of choice for the Chinese-American population of Chicago, due to the construction of a temple altar by the Chinese Consolidated Benevolent Association, which leases a section of the cemetery. This monument, with elaborate green and gold roof and an inset panel of granite inscribed with Chinese characters, features two soot-blackened ovens where visitors have burnt offerings. Though initially surrounded exclusively by flush markers, with Chinese lettering being the only indication of the owners' heritage, as reported in the first edition of this book, the cemetery has since allowed for upright monuments to be installed. These granite memorials, some of them featuring Oriental design flourishes such as pagoda roofs, illustrations of dragons, and stone lanterns, have names, dates, and epitaphs in the Chinese script, with the characters inked in colors that vividly contrast with the stone.

Another notable monument here is called **The Living Lord.**

The face of Christ is carved as a negative image in "The Living Lord," recessed into the stone. The effect is that, from almost any angle, he appears to be looking directly at the viewer.

The face of Christ is sculpted as a negative—that is, features that would ordinarily be closest to the viewer are instead furthest away, as if a face had been pressed into the stone leaving an impression behind. The resulting effect is that the face seems to always be looking toward the audience when viewed from any direction, an optical illusion unique among Chicago cemeteries.

MOUNT EMBLEM CEMETERY
510 West Grand Avenue, Elmhurst
www.mountemblem.com
Established 1925

Long before the Mount Emblem Cemetery Association began landscaping the 75-acre site on County Line Road, its most cherished and celebrated manmade feature was already present. The **Fischer Windmill**, predating the cemetery by 60 years, came to be the unmistakable emblem of Mount Emblem, granting a unique charm to the site, though its lack of maintenance and vulnerability to storm damage has led to considerable headaches for the administration and frequent costly repairs.

The Dutch smock mill, the oldest of its kind still standing in Illinois, was built by landowner Henry Frederick Fischer using structural and mechanical parts manufactured to his specifica-

The Fischer windmill, seen here in the 1990s before a storm tore off the original sails.

The principal monument of Mount Emblem, from which the cemetery takes its name, is a small hill with three columns at its summit, each supporting a Masonic symbol—plumb, square, and level. In front of each stands a marble statue of a personified virtue—Faith, Charity, and Hope.

tions in Holland, then shipped piece-by-piece to Chicago. Construction began in 1865 and was complete by 1867.[366] Built on a stone foundation, the mill rises to a height of 51 feet and originally boasted a sail span of 74 feet, facing southwest to catch the wind. The mill could grind 40 barrels of grain a day, providing roughly one-third of the flour needed by the city's population and industry. After ten years, Fischer sold the mill to Edward Ehlers, who continued to operate it until his death in 1916. In 1925 Caroline Ehlers, his widow, sold the windmill and its surrounding land to the newly-formed Mount Emblem Cemetery Association.[367]

"Watch for the opening of Mount Emblem Cemetery," read a 1924 display ad in the *Chicago Daily Tribune*, "Devoted Exclusively to Masons and their Families."[368] Led by its president, Emil H. Ahrbecker, the association sought to create a beautifully landscaped burying ground of the lawn cemetery design, with only flat markers permitted, on grounds adorned with planned features of the cemetery board's choosing.

Masonic tradition and symbolism were of paramount importance to the new cemetery's planners. An early advertising booklet tells how "Freemasons, from time immemorial, have buried their dead

[366] Tom Haskell, "Fischer Windmill, Old Dutch Mill, Mount Emblem Mill, Ehlers' Mill," Illinois Windmills, http://www.illinoiswindmills.org/index_files/Fischer.htm, 2012. The cemetery's advertising material, from 1926 to the present, gives a construction date of 1850 for the windmill, but Haskell's research supports the 1865–1867 date.

[367] Haskell, "Fischer Windmill."

[368] "A Line o' Type or Two," *Chicago Daily Tribune*, June 18, 1924.

with rites and ceremonies peculiar to the craft," going on to describe the need for burial places exclusive to the Masonic order. "Masons live and labor together in life; in death it is fitting that they rest together in peaceful surroundings amid those creations of Nature which they have been taught to contemplate and adore."[369]

To create these peaceful surroundings, the association hired the "foremost landscape architects of the country, Simonds & West"[370]— this Simonds, of course, being Ossian Cole Simonds, long-time superintendent of Graceland Cemetery, who had in 1925 promoted employee James Roy West to partner in his landscaping firm.

Though initially intending to demolish the disused windmill, the cemetery association instead decided to make it a centerpiece of the new design, and allow the mill to remain open as a museum. They hired Henry and Franklyn Ehlers, sons of the mill's previous owners and owners of a general contracting firm, to renovate the decrepit structure. In 1925, the mill had been neglected for nearly a decade, and two of its four sails were missing. The Ehlers brothers replaced these, as well as the shingles, windows, and exterior trim. They removed part of the mill's gearing to allow visitors a better view of the mechanism, and rotated the cap and sails to face northeast, towards the cemetery's main entrance. The sails were turned to form a St. Andrew's Cross, or "X," the traditional configuration of a mill in a "long rest."[371]

In front of the mill, the landscape architects took advantage of an existing creek, widening it to form Lake Emblem. They installed curving roads throughout the cemetery and planted numerous shrubs and trees. One wing of the mill was demolished to make way for an administration building designed in the English Gothic style, a style chosen in recognition of the medieval and northern European origins of Freemasonry.[372] The building was constructed of courses of stone blocks of varying sizes, now covered with a thick coat of ivy,

---

[369] "Without the Gates of the City," Mount Emblem Cemetery, no date given but probably 1928. Photos within are dated October 1927. Author's collection.

[370] "Without the Gates of the City."

[371] Haskell, "Fischer Windmill."

[372] "Without the Gates of the City"

The administration building, constructed in 1925 as part of the original cemetery design, was built in the English Gothic style in recognition of the Northern European origin of Masonry.

rising to a steep grey-shingled roof in several sections, punctuated with dormers and a cupola.

The cemetery's main entrance, in the northeast corner, is of the same architectural style as the administration building. A stone wall stands on either side of a swinging metal gate, with pedestrian archways on either side of the main road, and a copper roof over each arch. The left side of the gate also features an octagonal turret. Carved on either side of each arch is a head of a bearded medieval king, four in total, a detail that continues to delight visitors who take the time to study the entrance rather than simply driving through it. The artist's depiction of the gate in the 1920s advertising booklet also included a conical roof on the turret, and a small building to the north, probably a waiting room, similar in design to the administration building. If this was constructed at all it has long since been lost.

The cemetery's other principal feature, apart from the windmill that came with the land by happenstance, is "Mount Emblem" itself.[373] The Mount is a small artificial hill on the west side of the cemetery with a winding staircase on its east face. At the summit are

---

[373] From "Without the Gates of the City": "Rising from a mount or a mound denominated Mount Emblem are three majestic columns..."

three 40-foot columns of red granite, each with a life-sized Carrera marble statue at its base. Atop each column is a sculpture of a Masonic symbol: plumb, square, and level. The statues, all female, depict the virtues of Faith, Hope, and Charity. On the left is Faith, clutching to her chest the *Volume of Sacred Law*. At right is Hope, one hand holding an anchor, the other arm upraised; and in the center is Charity, greatest of these virtues, holding an offering bowl.

After a decade of landscaping work, the cemetery was dedicated in June 1936—though as early as 1927, it seems to have been providing burials, as "Interment Mount Emblem" began appearing in obituaries.[374] As a lawn park cemetery, Mount Emblem was intended to have only flush markers, without upright individual or family monuments. For the most part, this plan was carried out. The cemetery is open and park-like and uncluttered, with only granite benches and the occasional small mausoleum visible above the level grass. The cemetery also offers entombment in a modern community mausoleum. Nearby is a gleaming white flame sculpture, surrounded by a columbarium wall. In a few sections, particularly near the lake, family monuments were permitted, and one full-sized mausoleum stands near the shore.

The white granite mausoleum of **Dr. Allan Hruby** (~1890–1939) has simple, modern lines overall, but an elaborate bronze door depicting a hooded figure surrounded by flowers. The superintendent of the Chicago Municipal Tuberculosis Sanitarium, Dr. Hruby was recognized as a national leader in the fight against the disease. Through his efforts, all schoolchildren in Chicago were tested for tuberculosis.[375] Dr. Hruby died from pneumonia at age 49. He was entombed in a mausoleum bearing the symbol of his profession, the caduceus.

The decision in 1925 to permanently rotate the cap of the windmill, though providing a stunning view from the entrance across the lake, resulted in repeated damage to the mill itself. The prevailing winds in the Chicago area come from the southwest, and while operational the mill had faced that direction, and could be rotated

---

[374] "Death Notices—Hartman," *Chicago Daily Tribune*, February 17, 1927.

[375] "Dr. Hruby Dies; Leader in Fight on Tuberculosis," *Chicago Daily Tribune*, November 19, 1939.

when the direction changed. When the Ehlers brothers locked the cap with the sails on the northeast side, and dismantled part of the gear mechanism, the mill was exposed to stresses it had never been designed to withstand—tailwinds. In the years that followed, three of the original sails were broken and replaced.[376]

Since 1990, the mill has been battered by one severe storm after another. In the winter of 1990–91 the force of the wind was so great that the sails began to turn, even though the brake had been applied, and the shaft and wheels were twisted apart. The cap broke free of the tower and teetered dangerously forward. The damage was repaired, but the mill, now considered structurally unsafe, was permanently closed to the public.

The replacement sails, though looking fine to a casual observer, were non-functional fakes, and the shaft was permanently bolted into a fixed position. Another storm, in 1998, broke off the top two sails; the damage was once again repaired. In 2004 a severe storm tore the entire sail and shaft assembly away; it lay on the ground for months. The replacement was a greatly simplified light-weight aluminum assembly, only two-thirds the span of the original.[377]

ARLINGTON CEMETERY

401 East Lake Street, Elmhurst
arlington-cemetery.com
Established 1901

In its zeal to punish rebel General Robert E. Lee, the United States Government seized his Virginia plantation, converting his home to a military hospital and the grounds to a cemetery. Lee's home had been called "Arlington House," and the repurposed land forever preserves this heritage as "Arlington National Cemetery," burial place of presidents, chief justices, astronauts, and the revered

---

[376] Haskell, "Fischer Windmill."
[377] Haskell, "Fischer Windmill."

Tomb of the Unknowns.

That storied Virginia site inspired the names of other cemeteries throughout the nation, one of them in Elmhurst at the eastern edge of DuPage County. Chicago's Arlington Cemetery is a familiar sight to motorists on the nearby Tri-State Tollway, who for decades saw the name of the cemetery spelled out in two-foot-high individual letters mounted on poles (until their recent removal).

The pleasantly wooded burial ground lies between the expressway's frontage road on the east side, where a high wall separates it from the traffic, and Elm Lawn Cemetery to its west. Inside the granite and iron entrance is a small brick Greek Orthodox chapel devoted to Saint John, its interior richly decorated with icons and hanging candles in red glass sleeves. Greek names predominate in the section nearest the chapel, where similar candleholders stand before the headstones. Many of these graves are additionally enhanced with small semicircular gardens immediately in front of the headstone, enclosed with brick edging, filled with flowers and decorative pebbles.

At the southeast corner of the cemetery, almost in the shadow of the elevated highway, is the plot of **Wm. McKinley Camp No. 6, United Spanish War Veterans.** About 130 soldiers of the Spanish-American War are buried around the flagpole, each with a standard-issue headstone listing his rank and unit. Nearby, first lady Ida McKinley similarly lent her name to the plot of the **Ida McKinley Auxiliary No. 3, United Spanish War Veterans.**

The plot of the United Spanish War Veterans, Wm. McKinley Camp No. 6, in the southeast corner of the cemetery. The elevated road in the background, above and behind the cemetery's wall, is Interstate 294.

In this corner of the cemetery one also finds lots of three organizations whose members kept turn-of-the-century Chicagoans well fed: the **Chicago Waiters Association**, the **Bartenders and Beverage Dispensers Union (Local 278)**, and Chicago Branch No. 6 of the **International Geneva Association**, an association of hotel and restaurant employees founded in the Swiss city in 1877.[378]

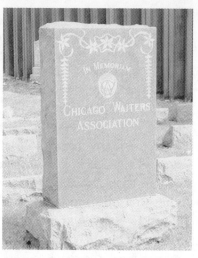

The Chicago Waiters Association is one of several trade associations with plots at Arlington.

The north part of Arlington contains a Shi'a Muslim cemetery, which, together with a section at neighboring Elm Lawn Cemetery, are operated as the **Valley of Peace**.[379] On the flat markers in the **Ahl-al-Bayt Islamic Cemetery**[380] one can find English, Arabic, and Urdu writing. This writing does not, however, include verses from the Qur'an, which are forbidden lest a visitor thoughtlessly step on the sacred words.[381] Against the fence, an upright wood and glass enclosure protects a black slab inscribed in white Arabic writing, with a transliteration below in Roman lettering, *Ziyarat-E-Ahle Quboor* ("visiting a grave").

Notables buried at Arlington include Illinois Attorney General **William J. Scott** (1926–1986), who brought environmental activism to his office, suing companies and cities that flouted the laws

---

[378] Walter Hermann, "International Geneva Association," *Cornell Hospitality Quarterly*, Vol. 10 No. 3, November 1969.

[379] "About Us," Valley of Peace, http://valleyofpeaceus.com/valley_of_peace_us/about_us.html.

[380] "Ahl-al-Bayt Section Grave Search," Valley of Peace, *http://valleyofpeaceus.com/cemetery_database/* provides this name for the Arlington section.

[381] Joanne von Alroth, "Grave Concerns—Tombstone Buffs Dig Into the Past," *Chicago Tribune*, July 10, 1994; and Helen Sclair lecture.

against pollution,[382] and Muslim scholar **Fazlur Rahman Malik** (1919–1988), professor at the University of Chicago, who argued for an adaptable interpretation of the Qur'an, and was called "one of the most prominent Islamic liberal reformers of the present generation" by a colleague.[383] In 1991, the ashes of famed jazz cornetist **Jimmy Dugald McPartland** (1907–1991) were scattered here, on his mother's grave.[384]

Near the center of the cemetery stands a red granite column with a sphere on top, dedicated to the **Ladies of the Grand Army of the Republic**. Affixed to the front of the shaft is the bronze insignia of the GAR, an eagle over a five-pointed star, and at the base, a bronze medallion showing the profile of Abraham Lincoln.

Equally impressive is the **Modern Woodmen of America** monument near the cemetery's northeast corner. Atop a tall pedestal stands a young man, simply dressed in workingman's clothes, looking straight ahead with a humble and thoughtful expression on his face. One hand rests on the axe at his side, the other holds a tall-crowned boater hat at his chest. The front of the monument shows the emblem of the Woodmen, and a dedication from the *Camps of Cook County Illinois* on June 1913.

Today, Arlington Cemetery and the adjacent Elm Lawn Cem-

The Modern Woodmen of America have one of the cemetery's more impressive monuments, with a statue of a young man atop a tall shaft.

---

[382] "Candidate: William J. Scott," Our Campaigns, http://www.ourcampaigns.com/CandidateDetail.html?CandidateID=76201.

[383] Andrew Herrmann, "Fazlur Rahman—]U. of C. Prof Was Leading Moslem Scholar," *Chicago Sun-Times*, July 27, 1988. The quoted colleague was Rashid Kalidi.

[384] Irv Kupcinet, "Kup's Column," *Chicago Sun-Times*, April 3, 1991.

etery are a part of Troost Cemeteries, Inc., owned by descendants of
the founders of the Peter Troost Monument Company,[385] the largest
privately-owned monument company in the United States.[386]

ELM LAWN MEMORIAL PARK

401 East Lake Street, Elmhurst
elmlawnmemorialpark.com
Established 1905

Immediately west of Arlington Cemetery on Lake Street in Elmhurst is Elm Lawn, another park cemetery of the same era, both now
operated by the same company, Troost Cemeteries, Inc.[387] Near the
entrance stands a chapel of a soaring modern design, with the strong
vertical lines of the windows and sweeping angles of the roof all di-
recting the visitor's gaze upwards. On either side, the walls are lined
with garden crypts, fronted with reddish-brown granite.

This is the second community mausoleum at Elm Lawn. The
original, still intact, stands a short distance to the west. Constructed
in 1915, the classically inspired **Elm Lawn Abbey** was designed by
prolific mausoleum architect Cecil E. Bryan, who created numerous
community mausoleums throughout Illinois and the Midwest—including those in Beecher, Woodstock, Waukegan, Morris, and Mazon, among others.[388] The mausoleum front features steps leading
up to bronze doors, with columns on either side supporting an arch.
Above the door is a stained glass window depicting an urn on which

[385] Joan Giangrasse Kates, "Robert Troost: 1937–2010: Cemetery Owner Helped Families Deal With Grief," *Chicago Tribune*, July 4, 2010.

[386] "Company History," Troost Monument Company, http://www.troost.com/Template. cfm?PageName=history.

[387] As shown by Internet domain name registration records, https://www.troost.com/about/history.

[388] "Cecil E. Bryan," http://www.cecilebryan.com, and personal communication with Cheryl Koch Bryan. Cecil Bryan's community mausoleums in Waukegan, Mazon, and Morris have been destroyed. Beecher and Woodstock are still intact as of 2012.

Elm Lawn Abbey, a community mausoleum in the classical style by architect Cecil Bryan.

two doves are perched; over them is a wreath. Truncated bases on either side of the entryway show that urns may have once been present. This is a regular design motif of Cecil Bryan mausoleums.

Inscriptions on the facade quote the Bible in both English, *I am the Resurrection and the Life...*, and German, *Ob ich schon wanderte im finstern Thal...*("though I walk through the darkest valley..."). At the top of the mausoleum, a metal chimney rises, with a mesh filter at the top, revealing that this is a crematorium as well. The mausoleum's basement contains a retort, a gas-powered cremation furnace.

As with the adjoining Arlington Cemetery, a section has been reserved for the burial of faithful Muslims. Near the south fence is a sign identifying the **Valley of Peace Cemetery**, maintained by an organization that coordinates with local mosques to provide for traditional Muslim burials.[389]

Several beautiful monuments stand in the sections nearest the main entrance, many with Germanic surnames. The **Balgemann** and **Behrens** families, related by marriage, have adjacent plots with similar monuments, rusticated grey granite monoliths with a partial entablature and a single Ionic column emerging at one corner, entwined with vegetation. The monuments represent a work unfinished, or may be alternately read as chaos and order, nature and human artifice, inseparable. Other monuments nearby repeat this theme, such as the **Fischer** monument, where roughly half is presented as a finished work, the other half left completely rough—as if the sculptor

---

[389] Valley of Peace, http://valleyofpeaceus.com/valley_of_peace_us/.

Greater love hath no man
reads the monument of
police chief Harry Magers
(1894–1920), who was
ambushed upon arriving
at the scene of an armed
robbery.

had walked away—and the **Fred and Anna Wandschneider** stone,
again with just one column appearing in a rough and unfinished work,
but with the bizarre addition of a dove perched on top.

Visitors cannot help but ponder the short but heroic life of **Harry
Magers** (1894–1920), whose monument proclaims that *Greater love
hath no man than this, that a man lay down his life for his friends.*[390]
A three-year veteran of the United States Navy, Magers re-enlisted
when America entered the Great War, this time choosing the Army.
Returning home in 1919, he was appointed Chief of Police in Elmhurst, though only 25 years old.

In the wee hours of Sunday, October 31, 1920, Chief Harry Magers rushed on his motorcycle to Elmhurst's new Masonic temple,
where a gang of robbers had attacked participants at the temple's
dedication ceremony. As he arrived at the corner of York Street and
St. Charles Road, the bandits surrounded and ambushed him.[391]
They fired upon the policeman, gravely wounding him, but Magers returned fire even as he fell, wounding one of his assailants. As
the robbers fled, the word spread among the citizens of Elmhurst,
who armed themselves, barricaded the roads leading from the village, and searched any cars that sought to pass. The wounded robber
was found and apprehended the following day, a trail of blood having
led detectives to his accomplices' house.[392] That day was also Harry
Magers's twenty-sixth birthday. He spent it lying in hospital, gut-
shot, dying slowly. He succumbed to his wound the following day.[393]

[390] John 15:13.
[391] "Return Suspect Today in Slaying of 17 Years Ago," *Chicago Daily Tribune*, May 6, 1937.
[392] "3 die, 2 dying, 4 shot in day of gun fights," *Chicago Daily Tribune*, November 1, 1920.
[393] "Elmhurst Chief of Police, Shot by Robber, Dies," *Chicago Daily Tribune*, November 3, 1920.

The murderer who had been wounded in the gunfight was sentenced to life in Joliet Prison. One of his confederates evaded capture for 17 years before being apprehended in West Virginia in 1937.[394] The second suspect was convicted, not of murder, but only of robbery, as the witnesses were unsure that he had actually shot the police chief.[395]

The monument of **John Langguth** (1840–1922) and **Sophia Langguth** (1839–1913) features a sculpted granite angel, clutching flowers to its chest and looking downward in sorrow. **William J. and Bertha Ross**, too, have an angel looking sorrowfully down at their monument, this one pleasantly shaded by evergreen trees on either side.

In 2009 a large granite monument was placed here by the **Biological Resource Center of Illinois**, depicting that organization's logo in crisp detail below a quote from Winston Churchill: *We make a living by what we get, but we make a life by what we give.* In this shared plot are the cremated remains of organ and tissue donors who have requested burial here. A ceremony takes place each April as new remains are interred, with each donor's name added to the monument.[396]

Another unusual feature is the cemetery's Zoroastrian section, where most of the markers display the likeness of the creator, *Ahura-Mazda.* Located towards the northwest corner of the cemetery, the section is not readily apparent from the road, as there are only flush markers with no upright monument, but a visitor on foot will see the depiction of a winged man on each stone or bronze marker, accom-

One of many bronze markers in the Zoroastrian section, with the ancient words meaning "Good Thoughts, Good Words, Good Deeds," around a symbolic representation of Ahura Mazda.

[394] "Return Suspect Today in Slaying of 17 Years Ago," *Chicago Daily Tribune*, May 6, 1937.
[395] "Sought 17 Years as Slayer; Gets Robbery Term," *Chicago Daily Tribune*, July 3, 1937.
[396] "Memorial Garden," Biological Resource Center of Illinois, http://www.brcil.org.

Elm Lawn includes "Pet Lawn," a section of the grounds where animals can be buried next to their human companions.

panied by the words *Humata, Hukhta, Hvarshta* –"Good Thoughts, Good Words, Good Deeds," in the ancient Avestan tongue.

Animal lovers will appreciate a peculiar burial custom at this cemetery: the interment of pets with their owners. For the slightly less eccentric, separate pet burial is available here as well, in a "Pet Lawn" section at the end of a long road, north of the main part of the cemetery. Pet Lawn is cheerfully decorated with statues, depicting dogs of several breeds, cats, even a goose. Next to these stand several figures of Saint Francis, friend and patron of animals. The tiny headstones here are often carved with depictions of the species of each grave's occupant. Dogs and cats dominate, of course, but there are birds and lizards too.

OAKRIDGE GLEN OAK CEMETERIES

4301 West Roosevelt Road, Hillside
www.ohicemetery.com
Established circa 1899

Formed by the merger of two adjacent cemeteries—Oakridge (the western half) and Glen Oak (the eastern half), this site unusually includes two community mausoleums. **Oakridge Abbey**, an ornate neoclassical structure at the top of a hill with wide steps leading up

Community mausoleum of Glen Oak Cemetery, one of two mausoleums in the combined cemetery.

to its front door, is a sight not to be missed. Entombed within is **Harold Lincoln Gray** (1894–1968), local suburban boy and creator of Li'l Orphan Annie, who established his hollow-eyed heroine on the pages of the *Chicago Tribune*.

But "Annie" isn't the only orphanage resident associated with the site. In September 1937, a cemetery visitor heard some crying behind a hedge and there found an abandoned baby girl inside a brown paper shopping bag. About two weeks old, the baby was healthy but hungry. Hillside police placed the baby at St. Vincent's Orphanage.[397] Days later, a search of hospital records led police to the mother, who had left the child there at the insistence of her shiftless husband.[398]

Guitar and harmonica adorn the monument of "Howlin' Wolf." The blues singer's monument is the most popular at the cemetery, with visitors leaving pebbles, coins, and other mementos.

And **"Howlin' Wolf"** (1910–1976), born Chester A. Burnett, was laid to rest here in 1976, after nearly 70 years of exceptionally hard living. Hailing from Mis-

---

[397] "Finds Abandoned Baby in Sack in Cemetery Hedge," *Chicago Daily Tribune*, September 20, 1937.
[398] "Mothers of Two Deserted Babies Blame Husbands," *Chicago Daily Tribune*, September 21, 1937.

sissippi, Howlin' Wolf's earliest form of musical expression involved singing in church on Sunday. At the age of 18, though, he was given a guitar by his father. Almost simultaneously, Chester met a man named Charley Patton, a Delta Blues pioneer who took Chester under his wing and taught the youngster according to his own unique style. For several years, Chester honed his skills for patrons of the local weekly fish fries, spending his days farming with his family. After moving to Arkansas, Chester met another Delta Blues performer, Sonny Boy Williamson, who taught him the harmonica. Not long after, Chester quit farming and took his show on the road. After several years of wayfaring and another four in the service, he returned to farming, only to abandon it once again to form his own band and return to the road. Though Chester gained a solid following in Mississippi and Arkansas, it wasn't until he was 38 years old that he landed the radio spot in West Memphis which made him a sensation and led to a recording contract with Chicago's Chess Records in 1950 for his cut, "How Many More Years" and "Moanin' at Midnight." After the record sold a whopping 60,000 copies, RPM began competing with Chess for Wolf's recordings. Chess won. And Chess, Chester, and the Chicago Blues became thoroughly entwined.

At 6 feet, 6 inches and nearly 300 pounds, with an earth-shaking voice punctuated by gut-wrenching moans and wails, Chester Burnett had become a performer known for scaring audiences out of their wits. In the years since his debut, he has been credited by

The Chicago branch of the Show Folks of America maintained this plot from at least 1947, installing a monument about 1954, according to announcements in *Billboard*.

The magnificent Oakridge Abbey mausoleum, built on elevated ground for a commanding view of the cemetery, was designed by Joseph J. Nadherny and dedicated in 1928.

hundreds of musicians, representing countless countries and musical styles, as a major influence on their work.

Chester continued his popular performances throughout his later years of kidney trouble, receiving dialysis before beginning his engagements. He died in Chicago, the town that loved him well, on January 10, 1976.

"Mason's Rest," on the west side of Oakridge, includes two columns supporting spheres, representing the pillars Jachin and Boaz in the Temple of Solomon, with the globes representing Earth and heaven.

MOUNT CARMEL CATHOLIC CEMETERY

1400 South Wolf Road, Hillside
www.catholiccemeterieschicago.org
Consecrated 1901

Located in the near western suburb of Hillside, this lavishly decorated, predominantly Italian cemetery contains perhaps the most eclectic slate of personalities to be found in the Chicago metropolitan area.

Not many Chicagoans had ever seen the inside of the **Bishops Mausoleum** at Mt. Carmel until the death of **Joseph Cardinal Bernardin** (1928–1996) in the fall of 1996. The mosaic-encrusted interior of the hilltop structure became home to the body of Chicago's Archbishop after his much-publicized battle with pancreatic cancer. Throughout his illness, Bernardin won the acclaim of countless observers from all walks of life, writing and speaking on his struggle to accept his imminent death and emphasizing the need for reconciliation and faith in attaining the peace and joy he had found on the threshold of that death.

At the center of the cemetery is the Bishops Mausoleum, burial site of most of Chicago's archbishops. The last to be entombed here was Joseph Cardinal Bernardin, in 1996.

After his passing, Bernardin lay in state for three days in Holy Name Cathedral, as 100,000 mourners lined up around the block to pay their last respects to this remarkable leader.

Though guards at this wake began their watch in trying to keep mournful hands from touching the casket and body, they soon abandoned their duty after the throngs persisted in their efforts. The result was a symbolically soiled casket, well suited to the funeral procession, which would travel, not swiftly over the expressways, but laboriously through the streets of Chicago, as the Cardinal had insisted.

After much dignified but down-to-earth fanfare, Bernardin was interred with other Catholic dignitaries, including **Bishop Quarter** (1806–1848), **Archbishops Feehan** (1829–1902) and **Quigley** (1854–1915), and predecessor **Joseph Cardinal Cody** (1907–1982), in Mt. Carmel's Bishop's Mausoleum, drawing thousands to the site during the winter of 1996–97, when the cemetery extended the hours for public viewing due to the Bernardin burial. The interior of the Mausoleum is still open on Sundays several months of the year; the exterior is always accessible during regular cemetery visitation hours.

Also popular at Mt. Carmel is the grave of a young mother named **Julia Buccola Petta** (1892–1921), locally known as "The Italian Bride." After dying in childbirth, Buccola was buried with her baby. Dreams of Julia haunted her mother, however, who often envisioned her daughter begging to be disinterred. After seven years, the woman finally gave in to her nightmares and had Julia's coffin unearthed. Upon its opening, all were shocked to discover that, although the baby was completely decomposed, Julia remained perfectly intact. To commemorate the supposed miracle, the family had two porcelain portraits added to Julia's marker: one of the girl in life, the other of Julia lying in her casket, seven years after her death.

The monument of Julia Buccola Petta, called "The Italian Bride," was based on one of the young woman's wedding photos, affixed below the statue.

The "incorrupt" Julia Buccola Petta, seen here in her coffin, seven years after death.

Mt. Carmel serves not only as the slumber-ground of saints but as a last hideout of some of the most notorious characters in gangland history, among them, **Alphonse Capone** (1899–1947). Capone was born in Brooklyn, the fourth of nine children of Italian immigrants. He abandoned his education in sixth grade when he received a beating from the school principal for thrashing his own tutor. He joined up with the James Street Gang, a bunch of adolescent thugs headed by John Torrio, who would later become the first of the Chicago bootleggers. Torrio put Al to work as a bouncer for a brothel and bar in their home borough. Here, he tangled with a punk named Frank Galluccio, who slashed Capone's left cheek, gaining him the immortal identification of Scarface.

Capone fled arrest to Chicago to reunite with Torrio, who was up in arms about his uncle, gangster head Jim Colosimo, who was reluctant to involve himself in the business of bootlegging. Capone and Torrio had Big Jim killed by a team of New York hit men.

Torrio and Capone took over the Chicago Outfit, presenting a solid front of murder to any local gang that wouldn't recognize their ultimate authority. It was Dion O'Banion's gang, in particular, that put up the toughest fight against the partnership and at last landed Torrio himself in the hospital. Torrio recovered and moved back to New York, leaving his boyhood friend with full command of the Chicago Mob.

Capone was 26 years old.

After making a fortune through bootlegging, prostitution, and gambling rackets and orchestrating countless murders of uncooperative or disloyal colleagues and rivals, Capone was finally sent to

Visitors regularly leave mementos of cigars, whiskey, and coins at the grave of of Al Capone (1899–1947). At least twice, the mobster's headstone has been stolen. The current version is permanently bonded to a heavy concrete base.

prison for tax evasion. He split his sentence between the federal penitentiary in Atlanta and Alcatraz Island, where he suffered a number of attempts on his life, including efforts of his co-convicts to strangle, poison, and stab him to death. But it was Al's own life that finally killed him. An early bout with syphilis spread to his brain and rendered him utterly helpless during his final days. He died in the same Florida home where he had been when his men carried out the St. Valentine's Day Massacre of 1929.

Capone's simple grave marker has been stolen at least twice—at 125 pounds, that's a risky and weighty souvenir. But don't blame any of the other underworld denizens also buried here, who are, these days, as inactive as old Al.

The **Genna Family** tree produced an abundant harvest of ne'er-do-wells—the "Terrible Gennas"—including **Pete** (d. 1948), **Sam** (d. 1951), **Vincenzo "Jim"** (unknown), **Bloody Angelo** (d. 1929), **Tony The Gentleman** (d. 1925), and **Mike The Devil** (d. 1925), who made the rounds of gangster circles before ending up here at Mt. Carmel. None of the Gennas had known birth dates.

Also here to stay is choir boy and florist **Dion "Deanie" O'Banion** (1892–1924), who moved swiftly from the Little Hell district (bounded by Chicago Avenue, Wells Street, Division Street, and the Chicago River) of North Side Chicago into infamy. As a kid, O'Banion spent his nights in brothels and bars, eventually landing jobs as a singing waiter in the Near North hovels along Erie and Clark streets, moaning weepy Irish folk songs and picking the pockets of his drunken listeners. Supplementing his income by mugging pedestrians after closing time, O'Banion was arrested in 1909, spending several months in prison. A couple of years later, he was arrested for the second and last time for concealment of a weapon. After this final stint, Dion stuck to the Chicago system of avoiding arrest for his crimes, regularly paying off the local authorities to ensure his future freedom.

O'Banion's reformed life brought him a job manhandling newspaper vendors for the *Chicago Tribune*, encouraging hawkers to push the local daily, for their own good. While working the same racket for the Hearst newspaper group, Charlie Reiser took the fragile youngster under his wing, teaching him the art of safecracking.

But it was Prohibition that really nurtured Dion's dormant talents. Emerging as the head honcho of the so-called North Siders, O'Banion led a motley crew, including such low-life luminaries as Bugs Moran. Together they hijacked shipments of alcohol produced by bootlegger John Torrio, rerouting them to the burgeoning speakeasies. When demand outgrew their supply, the North Siders seized a number of local breweries, but continued to steal Torrio's turnout. The bootlegger grew increasingly incensed.

Suddenly, O'Banion offered to sell Torrio the local Sieben Brewery for a half million clams and to leave him to do business in peace. Stunned, Torrio practically

After a lavish funeral, murdered mobster Dean O'Banion (1892–1924) was buried in a silver coffin under a huge monument with angel wings and the inscription *My Sweetheart*. Cemetery authorities demanded its removal; it was replaced with a simple obelisk.

threw the money at Dion, after which the Feds stormed the brewery and charged the bewildered businessman with violation of Prohibition laws. When he discovered that O'Banion had known about the Feds' plan to seize the business, and had turned it into a moneymaking scheme to his own benefit, Torrio began to think of revenge.

That revenge came one fall morning while O'Banion was busy at his flower shop on North State Street, a legitimate front from which he filled orders for gangland funerals. Three men arrived to pick up an arrangement for the funeral of mobster Mike Merlo and, while O'Banion was graciously shaking hands with one of them, the remaining two shot him six times. It was payback time for Torrio and the end of O'Banion's reign.

A key colleague of O'Banion was a Polish immigrant named Earl Wajciechowski. After their arrival in Chicago, the family changed their name to Weiss and began to make a life in their new city. Son Earl soon met up with the teenaged Dion, and together hooligan O'Banion and **Hymie Weiss** (1898–1926) pulled off numerous car thefts and burglaries before moving on to more legitimate paid jobs muscling newspaper vendors.

As O'Banion's closest associate, Weiss took over leadership of the North Siders after his boss's murder by Torrio's henchmen. At barely 28 years old, his primary order of business was to avenge O'Banion by rubbing out those he felt were responsible: John Torrio and Al Capone. After two unsuccessful attempts on Torrio's life and numerous failures to rub out Capone, Weiss was killed by a sniper who opened fire from the window over O'Banion's old flower shop. Weiss is buried at Mt. Carmel with his boyhood chum.

Joining O'Banion and Weiss in the cemetery is a rival mobster: the fastest gun in Chicago history, **"Machine Gun" Jack McGurn.** Born and raised **James Vincenzo DeMora** (1904–1936), the young Chicago native was an upstanding family man until the Genna gang killed his father **Angelo DeMora** (d. 1923) for selling bootleg alcohol behind their backs. According to a local legend, James drenched his hands in the blood of his father and became obsessed with avenging his murder. After self-instruction in marksmanship and training as a boxer, the contender known as Battling Jack McGurn' joined Capone's gang.

McGurn's expertise in handling the so-called Tommy gun earned him a high place among Capone's cronies. Al chose him often for his biggest hit jobs and, in time, Jack would number among his 25 commissioned homicides six members of the Genna gang. When he did away with the Gennas, McGurn placed in each of their stiffening hands a five-cent piece, identifying them as lousy nickel and dimers. Yet though the death of the Gennas satisfied his deep personal vendetta, it was his role in the St. Valentine's Day Massacre that made McGurn a legend. Rumored to have been the lead gunman and orchestrator of the massacre, McGurn was arrested in connection with the operation, but cleared by the testimony of girlfriend Louise Rolfe who furnished an alibi. When Rolfe's story was disproved, McGurn was charged with perjury, then prevented Rolfe from testifying against him by marrying her before the trial.

Left on his own after Capone went off to prison, McGurn unwisely turned to narcotics trafficking and was gunned down in a bowling alley by two strangers on the night before Valentine's Day, 1936. Authorities found a nickel pressed into his palm and, beside his body, a grotesque valentine reading

> *You've lost your job,*
> *You've lost your dough,*
> *Your jewels and handsome houses.*
> *But things could be worse, you know,*
> *At least you have your trousers.*

The conflicting clues embedded in the jingle left police baffled. Was the culprit seeking remorse for the Genna deaths, as suggested by the palmed nickel? Or was the grisly valentine a token from someone determined to pay back McGurn for his role in the February 14th massacre? The puzzle remains unsolved.

Despite his rise and fall in the pages of gangland history, James DeMora did achieve some legitimate success, which continues to this day. While Machine Gun Jack McGurn became a legend owing to

This water tower, decorated with crosses, loomed over the cemetery's west side until its removal in 2007. Many such structures were removed in recent years as various cemeteries, once isolated in the countryside, became connected to city water supplies.

A marble statue of a woman, collapsed in utter grief, is a fitting memorial for the tragedies that befell the Salerno family. Exactly one year and a day after insurance agent John Salerno (1899–1926) died at the age of 27, his father Samuel Salerno (1868–1927) was shot to death in a robbery at his grocery store. Decades later, nephew Todd Salvatore Salerno (1921–1944) gave his life in the Army Air Corps.

his strong-armed exploits, he has been beloved by local nightclubbers for decades. DeMora's real job involved ownership of a string of cabarets, among them the still-stompin' Uptown fixture, The Green Mill.

Rounding out the roster at Mt. Carmel are gangland loveables **John May** (d. 1929), **Frank "The Enforcer" Nitti** (1884–1943), **Roger Touhy** (1898–1959), Capone advisor **Antonio "The Scourge" Lombardo** (1892–1928), and **Sam Mooney Giancana** (1908–1975), ruthless successor to the notorious Tony Accardo, longtime boss of Chicago's Mafia.

Still not enough to sate your quest for infamy? No problem—simply cross the street to Queen of Heaven Cemetery.

Most intriguing of Mount Carmel's monuments is this intricately detailed group statue at the graves of Angelo Di Salvo (1869–1932) and Rosa Di Salvo (1872–1927). Remarkable enough for its attention to detail and for being a rare group portrait, the monument has a unique feature—it rotates on its base and, without much effort, can be made to face any direction.

The lifelike marble monument of Francisco Salerno (1914–1921) was based on a photograph of the boy, located next to his feet, showing exactly the same pose.

Resembling houses on a crowded city street, these are some of the over 400 private mausoleums at Mount Carmel, a greater number in any Illinois cemetery.

South entrance of Mount Carmel, opposite the Queen of Heaven gates. Originally, the "front" of the cemetery was the north, until the office there was closed after administrative functions were transferred to Queen of Heaven.

QUEEN OF HEAVEN CATHOLIC CEMETERY

1400 South Wolf Road, Hillside
www.catholiccemeterieschicago.org
Consecrated 1947

Here you'll find the plots of such sterling citizens as Mob boss, **Sam Battaglia** (1908–1973), a teddy bear compared to his predecessor, Giancana. Queen of Heaven is also the dead end for another Capone cohort, **Paul "The Waiter" Ricca** (1897–1972). Ricca began his mob life in high style by murdering his sister's ex-boyfriend, Emilio Perillo, when Perillo's family openly disapproved of the Ricca clan. Imprisoned for the deed, Ricca emerged from stir two years later and immediately demonstrated his remorse by killing Vencenzo Capasso, the eyewitness that had put Ricca behind bars.

After emigrating from Naples to the United States via a careful route of escape through France, Ricca traveled to Chicago and began working as a waiter for "Diamond Joe" Esposito. A Mob hangout, Esposito's restaurant was a fine place to be for a young go-getter like Paul. He soon became friends with a select group of patrons and left Esposito's to run the World Playhouse, a venue owned by Al Capone. The Mob boss and his new charge became fast and lasting friends, so much so that, when Ricca was married in 1927, Capone served as his best man.

Though Ricca was involved in many of the Mob's Chicago plans, he spent much of his time on the East Coast, serving as something of an ambassador for Al Capone. He made the national spotlight in the 1940s, however, for his involvement in the so-called Hollywood Extortion Case, in which Ricca and others had been found blackmailing the motion picture studios by threatening the striking of the Mob-controlled Projectionists Union if the studios didn't pay off big. When two of the extortionists were charged, they squealed on the others. Paul Ricca and others were indicted. But when Frank Nitti, then head of the Chicago Mob, killed himself over the consequences, Ricca found himself the new leader of the local Outfit.

Ricca's reign was a short one. Found guilty of extortion, he was sent to Leavenworth for ten years. Next in line for the Chicago throne was Tony Accardo.

After serving only three years and four months, during which time he communicated constantly with Accardo, Ricca was paroled. Because he could not associate with known gangsters due to parole restrictions, Ricca was officially out of the Mob. Though his exploits went undercover, he was finally nabbed for his first crime when Immigration and Naturalization Services exposed Ricca as Italian fugitive, Felice DeLucia. Ricca was issued a deportation order after having his citizenship revoked, but he struggled to remain in the United States. After many tactics, both shady and solid, he succeeded in having the order dropped. "The Waiter" passed away in the early 1970s from natural causes and joined his cohorts in a plot at Queen of Heaven.

But neither Battaglia nor Ricca can hold a candle to the legacy of one **Antonio Accardo** (1906–1992), the original "Big Tuna," otherwise known as "Joe Batters."

Antonio Leonardo Accardo grew up in Chicago's Little Sicily, his parents having immigrated around the turn of the century. When Antonio failed to show progress in the classroom, Mom and Dad filed a delayed birth record affidavit, placing his birth in 1904 rather than 1906 and rendering him fit to legally drop out of school. Not two years later, Accardo was arrested for a motor vehicle violation. His life of crime had begun.

The next year, Tony was fined for disorderly conduct at a pool hall and joined the Circus Cafe Gang, where he mixed with such members as Claude Maddox and James DeMora. Like many would-be gangland greats, Accardo started out pickpocketing and jumping passers-by, moving on to armed robbery, jewel and car theft, and other specialties. Then real opportunities came with the advent of Prohibition, when the delivery boy began using his truck to deliver booze from Sicilian family stills to Chicago's speakeasies. Finally, Accardo got his big break when boyhood buddy DeMora, who had since been picked up as a hit man for Al Capone, put in a good word for Tony at the office.

Capone called Accardo to his office at the South Loop's Metropole Hotel, leading him in swearing the oath which would make him an official member of the Chicago Mob.

Capone's eyes shone at the loyalty of the new recruit. During Hymie Weiss's siege of Capone's Hawthorn Inn in Cicero, Accardo pulled his boss to the ground, lying on top of him to protect him from the thousands of rounds of machine gun fire that were showering the building. After this impressive display of devotion, Accardo could often be seen in the lobby of the Hawthorn, armed and awaiting any further attempts on the life of his leader.

Accardo continued to win the esteem of his boss in equally unorthodox ways. In fact, the plucky underling earned his most famous nickname when sponsor Jack McGurn reported to Capone that Tony had ruthlessly smashed the skulls of two adversaries with a baseball bat, prompting the boss to comment that Accardo was a real Joe Batters.

Accardo made bona fide history when he was ordered to storm the SMC Cartage Company garage on North Clark Street on Valentine's Day of 1929 and with the help of three associates do away with Bugs Moran and a key portion of his gang. Disguised as police officers, Al's four delegates entered the garage, spraying the seven men

Queen of Heaven Mausoleum, opened in 1957, is the largest Catholic mausoleum in the world, with 30,000 crypts and nearly a mile of corridors on three floors.

there with machine gun fire. Though Moran himself had been running late to the rendezvous and thus eluded his fate, six of his men died immediately. The seventh miraculously survived long enough to reach the hospital, where he died without squealing on his assailants.

The Big Tuna continued to distinguish himself as a mobster's mobster, remaining faithful to his boss, Capone, throughout the leader's prison term, carrying out assignments and stepping in as gangland leader when circumstances called for his authority.

When Accardo at last tired of Mob rule and heat from the IRS, he petitioned for an out and got it. Officially handing the family reigns to Sam Giancana, Joe Batters publicly retired into the consulting business, but lived his last years still overseeing the Chicago Mob. Upon his death from heart disease, Accardo was buried at Mt. Carmel, in proper Italian style.

But don't be fooled by the few bad seeds at this handsomely landscaped headquarters of Chicago's Archdiocesan Cemeteries. The innocent easily outnumber the guilty.

In fact, this is the site of **The Shrine of the Holy Innocents**, a section reserved for the burials of children. Many visitors travel to the shrine to offer their prayers at the **Our Lady of the Angels Memorial** dedicated to the victims of one of the worst tragedies in Chicago's history, the 1958 school fire which took the lives of 92 children and three nuns. The bodies of 25 of these children rest at this special site, a triangular portion of land marked by a striking monument bearing the

Nearly half of those who died in the 1958 fire at Our Lady of Angels School were buried here at Queen of Heaven. On either side of the monument by sculptor Corrado Parducci are tablets listing the names and burial locations of all 95 victims.

The central tower
of Queen of Heaven
Mausoleum is adorned
with spires in the Gothic
Revival style, an unusual
choice for a 1950s
structure.

names of all the fire's victims.

Queen of Heaven is also host to the more than 20,000 souls interred in its **Community Mausoleum**. One of the largest in the United States, the enormous crypt is also a stunning gallery, filled with panes of beautiful stained glass.

Though mourners are plentiful at this sacred and spacious burial site, the most frequent visitors come not to spend a quiet moment at a loved one's plot, but to take part in a curious phenomenon that has centered on the cemetery for well over a decade: the Marian apparitions reported by retired railroad employee, Joseph Reinholtz.

In 1987, the widowed Reinholtz made a pilgrimage to the town of Medjugorje, Bosnia-Herzegovina, to pray at the site where six young people had been claiming visions of the Blessed Virgin. During his time in Medjugorje, one of the seers prayed over Reinholtz and, upon his return to the Chicago area, Joseph's failing sight returned suddenly when he beheld in his home a small statue of Mary weeping tears.

Returning to Bosnia in 1989, the visionary that had prayed over Reinholtz gave the American pilgrim a mission: Joseph was to return home and search for a crucifix next to a three-branched tree. There, he should pray.

Back in Hillside, Illinois, Reinholtz found the spot in nearby Queen of Heaven Cemetery. He immediately began a determined vigil. Approximately one year after beginning his prayer at the **Trinity Tree**, Joseph experienced his first apparition of the Blessed Virgin. Several months later, she returned to the site accompanied by the archangel, St. Michael.

Blissful, Joseph enthusiastically spread the news of his visions, and soon large numbers of pilgrims were joining him in his daily prayers at the site. Almost immediately, reports of strange phenomena began to issue from these gatherings. Visitors reported photographs containing vivid images of Mary and of angels, the strong scent of roses at the wintry cemetery site, secret conversations with heavenly beings, and other marvels. As evidence of the visions, they displayed their once battered and multicolored rosaries that had turned a glittering gold after visiting Queen of Heaven.

It was at this crucifix that Joseph Reinholtz experienced visions of the Virgin Mary in the early 1990s. With a large number of pilgrims coming to pray at the site, the cross was moved to a plaza in a corner of the cemetery.

Soon, the Archdiocese of Chicago was called on to issue a statement regarding the apparitions. Though officials refrained from declaring the reality of the apparitions, the local Church continued to allow Reinholtz to visit the site, though placing on him a restriction of obedience forbidding visitation on Tuesdays. Joseph continued his almost daily visits to the crucifix and continued to receive monthly messages from the Blessed Virgin until he suffered a stroke in 1995. Reinholtz reported visitations from the Blessed Virgin while hospitalized, and died in 1996. He is buried in his family plot at Queen of Heaven.

For lighter relief, along with the cemetery's would-be saints and dreadful sinners are comedian **George Kirby** (1925–1995), who settled in here after his last laugh, and Chicago Bear **William Wightkin** (1927–1997).

Adjacent to Queen of Heaven is Our Lady of Sorrows Cemetery, established for Slovak Catholics in 1923.

Visitors should note the adjacent **Our Lady of Sorrows Cemetery** on this property, which is now under the care of the larger Queen of Heaven complex. Our Lady of Sorrows was consecrated in 1923, having been championed by Monsignor Victor Blahunka, former pastor of Sacred Heart Slovak Parish. The cemetery continues to serve the Slovakian Catholic community.

CHAPEL HILL GARDENS WEST CEMETERY

17W201 Roosevelt Road, Oakbrook Terrace
www.chapelhillgardenswestcemetery.com
Established before 1926

Like its South Side counterpart, this cemetery underwent a name change when it became part of Chapel Hill Gardens, Inc. in the 1940s. It had previously been known as Green Ridge Cemetery.[399] That seems only appropriate for a cemetery located in Oakbrook Terrace, a town that also changed its name for commercial reasons—it was Utopia before 1958, then becoming Oakbrook Terrace to capitalize on the popularity of a nearby shopping mall.[400]

---

[399] "Our Town: Brief Bits of Friendly, Interesting News About the Neighbors," *Chicago Daily Tribune*, March 4, 1928.

[400] Margaret Franson Pruter, "Oakbrook Terrace, IL," Encyclopedia of Chicago, http://en-

The cemetery is noted for the **Hippach Chapel**, a breathtakingly beautiful square-towered Gothic design by sculptor Richard W. Bock, built in 1926. In front of the sandstone chapel is a five-foot-tall bronze urn, depicting the life of man "from the cradle to the grave," world events of the 1920s, and portraits of religious leaders. So intricate is the urn that, according to Bock, he spent more than a year working just on that one piece.[401] Human figures are carved into the tower, peeking out over the parapet at each corner. The chapel was commissioned by Louis Hippach and dedicated to his parents,[402] **Franz Joseph Hippach** (1830–1908) and **Lena Everling Hippach** (1833–1922).[403]

A wealthy manufacturer of plate glass and window glass, **Louis Albert Hippach** (1864–1935) had ample cause to erect such a grand memorial, which cost more than one million dollars in 1920s currency,[404] for his family was touched with tragedy on multiple occasions. Two of Hippach's three sons, Robert and Archie, died at ages 14 and 12 in the Iroquois Theatre Fire of 1903.[405] His remaining son, Howard, died in a car crash in 1914.[406] Louis's wife Ida and daughter Jean, however, were more fortunate. In the early morning hours of April 15, 1912, they were rescued from a lifeboat in the North Atlantic, having survived the sinking of *Titanic*.[407]

Though Louis Hippach died less than ten years after building this splendid chapel, he was not buried at Chapel Hill. Instead, Louis, and later Ida and Jean, joined the boys they'd lost in the Iroquois fire and the car crash, at their family plot in Rosehill.

Apart from the chapel, Chapel Hill Gardens West looks much

---

cyclopedia.chicagohistory.org/pages/918.html.

[401] "Louis Hippach Family Chapel – Oakbrook Terrace, IL," Waymarking, http://www. waymarking.com/waymarks/WMBWGH_Louis_Hippach_Family_Chapel_Oakbrook_ Terrace_IL.

[402] "Our Town: Brief Bits."

[403] Originally buried at Forest Home. The headstones behind the chapel seem to hint that they were later reburied here.

[404] "Our Town: Brief Bits."

[405] "Day Given Over to Burial Rites," *Chicago Daily Tribune*, January 4, 1904.

[406] *Chicago Daily Tribune*, October 31, 1914.

[407] "Miss Jean Gertrude Hippach," *Encyclopedia Titanica*, http://www.encyclopedia-titanica. org/titanic-survivor/jean-gertrude-hippach.html.

like its Oak Lawn cousin, with flat markers surrounding cemetery-provided central monuments. It has a Masonic section, nearly identical to the one on the South Side, except that the main altar is granite instead of brick. In 2004 the cemetery hosted the traveling Vietnam Wall Memorial, allowing Chicagoans a rare opportunity to visit a replica of the famous Washington, DC, landmark.

HINSDALE ANIMAL CEMETERY AND CREMATORY

6400 South Bentley Avenue, Willowbrook
www.petcemetery.org
Established 1926

The same Biblical quote that appears on Police Chief Magers's monument at Elm Lawn—*Greater love hath no man*—appears again on the cenotaph of a different sort of hero at this unique suburban site. **Arap**, a canine of mixed shepherd and retriever ancestry, lived with the Stankowicz family in Russia. In 1921, his frantic barking alerted the family that the Communist militia were approaching their home. They fled, never to return, but in their haste had to leave their beloved protector behind.[408]

This view shows typical monuments at Hinsdale, most less than two feet high, a substantial number of them including ceramic photographs. Heart-shaped stones are a popular choice.

[408] Louise Hutchinson, "Animals Given an Undisturbed Haven in Death," *Chicago Daily Tribune*, January 25, 1953.

In 1930, John Stankowicz, who had immigrated to the United States after Arap's vigilance saved his life, purchased the Hinsdale Animal Cemetery, set in a rural landscape in what was then Clarendon Hills.[409] The cemetery had already been operating since 1926, the same year Illinois Pet Cemetery opened in northern DuPage County; these were the first pet cemeteries in Illinois.

The new owner erected a life-sized statue of his lost Arap on the grounds. Alert and vigilant, with head held high, the iron dog stands on a concrete base inscribed with *He gave up his life that a human might live. Greater love hath no man.* This monument has been the symbol of the cemetery ever since, proudly displayed on their signs and literature to this day. In 1950, John Stankowicz sold the cemetery to his friend George Remkus and Remkus's father-in-law William Dykema.[410] The cemetery continues to be operated by the Remkus family, now in its fourth generation.[411]

The symbol of Hinsdale Animal Cemetery, the statue of Arap commemorates the dog who alerted his owners of approaching Communist soldiers. The family fled to America, later purchasing this cemetery.

This intriguing expanse provides rest for more than dogs and cats. Grieving owners can pay their respects to cherished birds, prized horses, loved monkeys, and other gone-but-not-forgotten pets from across the metropolitan area. The heartfelt expressions of grief on the monuments make this space as dramatic as any human cemetery. Many plots here hold the remains of successive pets, companions to the same human owner, interred side-by-side as the years progressed.

409 "Hinsdale Animal Cemetery," Local History from Darien, Willowbrook, and Burr Ridge, http://ippl.info/localhistory/?page_id=1136.

410 Ibid.

411 *Hinsdale Animal Cemetery and Crematory* (informational DVD).

Though most pet cemeteries consist mainly of flush markers, the majority of monuments at Hinsdale are upright, typically of the size used for human children, some even the sort of full-sized monuments used on adult graves. Though slant markers dominate, heart-shaped monuments are more common here than any other area cemetery. To many of these are affixed oval porcelain photographs, of the sort popular in Jewish or Italian cemeteries, but here displaying color portraits of dogs and cats instead.

Simple yet imaginative names appear at the top of each stone: *Duke. Brownie. Trixie. Cheech & Chong. Fluffy. Sir Koko. Rex* (more than once). *Tiny. Ginger. Lucky.* In a strange case of life imitating art that will delight fans of *The Simpsons*, **Snowball I** and **Snowball II** share a mausoleum crypt above **Lisa.**

Those companion animals who practiced a particularly noble profession are given special recognition: *Seeing Eye Dog* appears on several monuments. Author and lecturer Bernice Clifton (1901–1985),[412] one of the first Chicagoans to use a guide dog, began employing a German Shepherd named **Karla** (1936–1952) shortly after she was blinded in a 1938 accident.[413] Her autobiography *None So Blind* described how she learned of The Seeing Eye school in New Jersey where such dogs were trained, sold homemade jams to raise the money needed for a dog, then acted as an ambassador for the program.[414] Karla ac-

Bernice Clifton employed four Seeing Eye dogs, all named Karla, all buried here. The first Karla was celebrated as a Doctor of Canine Intelligence.

---

[412] Location of burial unknown.

[413] June Geserick, "Girl Discovers New Life Thru Her Blindness," *Chicago Tribune*, June 24, 1946.

[414] "Bernice Clifton; Pioneer in the Use of Guide Dogs," *Chicago Tribune*, May 1, 1985.

companied her mistress to lectures and media appearances and on Clifton's volunteer activities for the Red Cross, greeting and cooking for servicemen returning from the war. Acclaimed as the oldest Seeing Eye dog in service,[415] and awarded a "Doctor of Canine Intelligence" from an Ohio music college,[416] Karla lived almost to the age of 16. Her funeral at Hinsdale, coming only a year after she had been made famous by Bernice's book *Sight Unseen: How Bernice Clifton Discovered the Value of a Handicap*, was said to have been attended by 3,000 people.[417] A Baptist minister presided at the service.[418] Karla's epitaph: *Have a Good Rest My Karla*.

After Dr. Karla's death, Clifton gained a new companion, **Karla II** (1951–1965), who shares the same monument with her predecessor, and was buried with the words *Sleep Tight My Karla*. **Karla III** (1964–1977) received a separate headstone close by, eulogized with *You Are My Good Karla Baby*. Clifton's final companion was **Karla IV** (1975–1989), who survived Bernice by four years. The last Karla shares a monument with the first two, her portrait placed at the very top and her epitaph at the bottom: *Sleep Tight Little Sweetheart*.

Effusive praise is given to Ch. Ring's **Fraulein Von Oakbrook** (1969–1978), described on her monument as *The only dog ever—anywhere in the world of any breed—living or dead, to hold five national and*

Fraulein von Oakbrook, a champion show dog, is celebrated with one of the cemetery's largest monuments.

[415] Lucy Key Miller, "Front Views & Profiles: Karla and I," *Chicago Tribune*, March 18, 1952.
[416] "Bernice Clifton."
[417] "Hinsdale Animal Cemetery."
[418] "Animals Given an Undisturbed Haven in Death."

international awards for heroism and courage. The German Shepherd's pink granite monument, with her portrait flanked by praying cherubs, is one of the largest in the cemetery. The awards won by Fraulein appear after her name: *CDX*, for Companion Dog Excellent, and *TD*, for Tracking Dog, in the system of the American Kennel Club.[419]

A marble headstone topped with a lamb and cross, of the type normally used for children, here memorializes a beloved cat **Colonel (Pookie)**, (1929–1944). Laser-etched black granite portrays dogs **Laine** (1976–?), **Herman** (1970–1990), **Molly** (1993–2006), and a feline named **Itty Bitty Kitty** (1985–1998), eulogized as *The First, The Best.* One portrait, that of **Brother Uncle Damien** (1984–2000), shows a dog strapped to a wheelchair-like device, while the picture of **B. Cake** (1973–1994) and **Chia** (1972–1989) shows a dog and cat snuggling together.

The marble headstone of Colonel (Pookie), a feline, is of a style often found at the graves of children in other cemeteries.

Though two species dominate the landscape, others are represented here as well. **Kelly** (1991–1995), *Our Gentle Boy*, was clearly a rooster, strutting proudly in a vivid color photo. **Big Boy** (~1901–1940), was a turtle of advanced years, killed by a dog. Near Arap's monument, a curious monument only a foot tall looks just like a chess piece: An iron horse's head, mounted to a concrete base, at the grave of five-gaited saddle horse **Admiral Togo** (1902–1937). The monument was originally marked off by chains and included a pickle

[419] "AKC Titles and Abbreviations," American Kennel Club, http://www.akc.org/events/titles.cfm?page=2.

jar with a photo of the horse inside, now missing.[420]

And one more unexpected species is present—*Homo sapiens*. According to the management, more than 30 persons have chosen to be buried here, alongside their beloved companions.[421] Their comparatively long lifespans, as well as the porcelain photographs affixed to their monuments, make such graves readily identifiable to those who know where to look.

But burials represent a tiny fraction of those animals who are brought to this cemetery. Cremation is by far the more popular choice. The cemetery offers two levels of this service. With "memorial cremation"—usually arranged through a veterinarian's office—groups of pets are cremated together, their intermingled ashes then scattered on the cemetery grounds. Those owners seeking a permanent memorial may purchase a nameplate to be affixed to one of four granite monuments on the property.[422]

The other option is private cremation, and it was this service that this author (Hucke) chose for **Cat #1** (1995–2009), a black-and-white short-haired "tuxedo cat" who had been suffering from ulcerated breast cancer. The day after her euthanasia in a veterinary office, we drove to Hinsdale Animal Cemetery for a private cremation. With this level of service, the animal is cremated separately, in one of the same models of cremation furnace used elsewhere for human remains. Afterward, the client may take the remains home. At every step of the way, the body, the furnace, and the containers used to carry the cremated remains are carefully labeled. Even if the client is not present, there is absolutely no doubt as to the identity of the final pulverized remains: the client will receive their own pet's "ashes."

In the case of my own feline companion, I elected to watch the process. Her body was gently placed in the retort by Stewart, the crematory operator, and the door was shut, after which I wandered through the peaceful grounds for about 30 minutes until being summoned to return. What remained was softly glowing bone frag-

---

[420] "Photostream," Indian Prairie Public Library, http://flickr.com/photos/ipplinfo.

[421] *Hinsdale Animal Cemetery and Crematory* (informational DVD).

[422] "Cremation Services," Hinsdale Animal Cemetery, http://www.petcemetery.org/services/cremation.php.

ments, which were then raked into a metal box, name tag already attached, then ground to a uniform consistency in a device much like an industrial dough mixer. The resulting cremated remains, not ash but charred bone, had the appearance and weight of sand. The particles were swept into a plastic bag, which was then tied shut, tagged with Cat's name and mine once again, placed into a white plastic box, labeled a final time, then given to me to take home.

Some weeks later, an elegant wooden box arrived in the mail, the top etched with Cat's name and years of birth and death. I had ordered this at the cemetery office before the cremation, choosing it from a collection of sample urns that were on display. My "gritty kitty" was then placed inside, there to remain for years to come.

In 2011, the cemetery added a specially-designed horse crematory, the first of its kind.[423] Due to their size, horses are especially difficult to transport and cremate, with the process generally undignified and (for the owner) traumatic. Other facilities generally treat the bodies of horses as medical waste, incinerating them in large drums. Hinsdale's new crematory, with its extra-large opening, allows horses to be placed inside, intact, offering their owners unparalleled peace of mind.

Though some may flinch at the technical details of cremation or burial, clients of Hinsdale Animal Cemetery can be as involved in the process—or not—as they wish. Those who choose to accompany their pets on their final journeys may watch, from a windowed booth adjoining the cremation room, or simply walk the grounds until the process is concluded. Or, private cremation may take place without the witnesses present. Most veterinary offices in the area are willing to make the arrangements and ship the bodies to the crematory; the cremated remains are then sent back to the doctor's office for pickup by the owners. Either way, the staff are willing to accommodate the client's preferences, for cremation or burial. They understand the intensity of the feelings humans have for the creatures who share our homes. This entire site is a testament to the depth of that love.

---

[423] Bridget Doyle, "In End, Humanity for Horses," *Chicago Tribune*, August 22, 2011.

ILLINOIS PET CEMETERY

6N347 County Farm Road, Hanover Park
illinoispetcemetery.com
Established 1926

The first pet cemetery in the United States opened in 1896 in Hartsdale, New York, when a veterinarian agreed to bury a client's dog, providing a grave on his own rural property. He later told the story of what he'd done while having lunch with a friend who happened to be a newspaper reporter. The resulting publicity resulted in the kindly doctor being bombarded with requests for burials.[424] Thir-

At the center of the cemetery, almost hidden in the bushes, is the cenotaph of founder Michael Bloze (1899–1930).

ty years later, pet cemeteries came to Illinois. In that year, 1926, two of them opened for business: Illinois Pet Cemetery in Hanover Park and Hinsdale Animal Cemetery in Clarendon Hills.

Illinois Pet Cemetery, the oldest pet cemetery in Illinois,[425] was founded in 1926 by Michael Joseph Bloze (1899–1930), a fraternal organizer and a veteran of World War I, who saw pet cemeteries while serving in France and brought the idea home.[426] In July of that year Bloze purchased a six-and-a-half-acre plot and applied to the city health department for a permit to bury animals, announcing his intent to convey ani-

---

[424] "Pet Cemeteries Help Recognize Pet Bereavement," Aurora Casket Company, http://www.auroracasketcompany.com/.

[425] Illinois Pet Cemetery, http://illinoispetcemetery.com.

[426] Anne Ford, "Gary Bloze, Owner, Illinois Pet Cemetery," *Chicago Reader*, August 30, 2011.

Typical monuments at the cemetery, almost every one of them with a photo affixed to the front.

mals of all sorts to their graves in a "miniature hearse," and to provide certificates of burial to the owners.[427]

A devoted animal lover, Bloze also ran a pet newspaper and animal ambulance service. Sadly, his life was cut short at the age of 30, when he was impaled on his car's steering column while driving through Evanston to sell a headstone.[428] Bloze was buried at St. Casimir's,[429] but a cenotaph was placed at the pet cemetery as well—a granite obelisk, given a place of pride at the center of the cemetery.

The cemetery has been owned and operated by the Bloze family ever since. Michael's widow Marie, who gave birth to a son two weeks after her husband's fatal crash, devoted her life to the cemetery, and her children and grandchildren carried on the family business after her.[430] Marie died in 1973; a bronze plaque affixed to the entrance honors her memory.

The cemetery is a pleasantly wooded space on the side of a hill in northern DuPage County, not far from Schaumburg, set comfortably apart from the city noise. Upright monuments of granite are almost all decorated with photographs. Planters, birdbaths, and statues of St. Francis, protector of animals, are scattered throughout the shady grounds.

---

[427] "Chicago Cemetery Planned Where Pets May Rest in Peace," *Chicago Daily Tribune*, July 4, 1926. The original article describes an intention to purchase five acres near Hawthorne Race Track, but the site chosen seems to be somewhat further from the city.

[428] Ford, "Gary Bloze."

[429] *Illinois, Deaths and Stillbirths Index, 1916–1947.*

[430] Ford, "Gary Bloze."

The majority of burials are dogs and cats, of course, as at other pet cemeteries, but Illinois Pet Cemetery is home to other creatures as well. **Precious Pepi**, a yellow canary, is *always in our heart*. Another of that species, **Jenny Lind** (d. 1962), named for the Swedish opera singer, is lauded with *The more I see of men, the more I admire birds* on her tiny granite marker.[431] Rabbits, ferrets, birds, and monkeys share the space, along with a rooster named **Big Boy** who was buried with red nail polish on his claws.[432] And

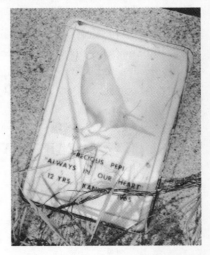

Precious Pepi, a 12-year-old yellow canary, is Always in our Heart.

there's at least one turtle—**Rufus**, bought at the 1933 Century of Progress exposition and buried a few short years later in a jewel box.[433]

Clients return to the site, year after year, to bury successive generations of pets. A row of six identical headstones, each with a photograph, memorialize the **Kalberg** dogs, spanning the 1940s to the 1990s. The three **Shapiro** cats share one stone, marked *with our girls forever*. And the monument to **Schwer's Pets** (*Always Remembered*) lists no fewer than 25 names, with room left for more.

Funerals are occasionally elaborate. Ministers have performed services here, and musicians played a violin concerto at a Great Dane's funeral.[434] A ring-tailed monkey named **Monty** was buried after a three-day wake, after which four neighborhood children served as pallbearers. **Queenie**, a 14-year-old Spitz, went to her grave in style,

[431] Illinois graveyard explorers will also recognize Jenny Lind as the namesake of the chapel in the Lutheran cemetery in Andover, Henry County.

[432] Kermit Holt, "This Cemetery Has Place for All But People," *Chicago Daily Tribune*, September 8, 1949.

[433] "Dogs and Cats, Even a Turtle, Lie in Cemetery," *Chicago Daily Tribune*, November 24, 1940,

[434] Michael Sneed, "Cemetery Offers Final Resting Place for Pets," *Chicago Daily Tribune*, February 16, 1969.

placed in a silk and plush casket, driven by a black limousine, followed by a procession of 14 cars carrying 14 floral tributes.[435]

Unlike the pet cemeteries at Elm Lawn and Hinsdale, one species is notably absent: humans. Though many have requested burial at the site, Marie Bloze gave them all "a firm 'no'."[436]

BLUFF CITY CEMETERY
945 Bluff City Boulevard, Elgin
www.cityofelgin.org
Established 1889

This aptly named site, with its scenic dips and climbs, opened in 1889, when overcrowding became a problem at Elgin's earlier cemetery on Channing Street, where Channing Elementary School stands today. Over the years, burials from the original site were reinterred at Bluff City, though skeletal remains were reportedly found during the

The hilly terrain within the cemetery allows for hillside mausoleums, generally a rare sight in northern Illinois.

---

[435] Holt, "This Cemetery Has Place."
[436] Sneed, "Cemetery Offers Final Resting Place."

breaking of ground for the school foundation.

The picturesque location is home to many military heroes, including Civil War Congressional Medal of Honor Recipient **Andrew O. Apple** (1845–1890). Hailing from Pennsylvania, Apple served in West Virginia's Volunteer Infantry during the American Civil War, and rose to the rank of Corporal. He received the Congressional Medal of Honor for his participation in the Union assaults at Petersburg, Virginia, in April of 1865, particularly the capture of Fort Gregg, the defining action of the Petersburg victory. After the war, Apple relocated to Elgin, Illinois, esteeming himself again as the city's fire marshal.

Appropriately, one of the most celebrated aspects of Bluff City is the **Avenue of Flags** erected each Memorial Day weekend. The

The Hendee-Brown monument, still remarkably crisp in detail, belongs to a family descended from Miles Standish of the Mayflower. Huldah Washburn (1792–1874) married Homer Hendee (1790–1865). Their daughter was Annette Hendee Brown (1825–1903). The statue of an angel holding a cross is of such superb quality that, shortly after it was made, it was shown at an art exhibition in Paris.

stunning display was initiated by Marvin Schmidt, who served as superintendent for most of his 25 years at Bluff City from the 1960s to the 1980s. The display, which has steadily grown from several dozen to more than 500 full-size flags, includes hundreds of flags presented to family members at the funerals of their veteran spouses, parents, and children. Schmidt and his secretary began the project by sending letters to about 700 military families asking for donations of the flags given to them after their loved ones' deaths. Many of these made their way to Schmidt's hands, and he has also purchased many additional flags with donations made by living veterans and family members seeking to honor American service men and women.

Besides the Avenue of Flags and the Memorial Day service held each year, Bluff City also draws much attention each fall when the annual **Cemetery Walk** is held on the grounds. Created by the Elgin Historical Society in 1987, the popular event features costumed narrators who present a "living history" of Elgin by delivering short monologues at the graves of some of Elgin's most prominent dearly departed.

Elgin pioneer Benjamin Burritt (1796–1880) built a log cabin in 1837, then worked as a stonemason. At his grave is a stone replica of his cabin, in miniature, moved here from the old city cemetery.

At the base of a hill, painted white, is the cemetery's receiving vault, one of few such structures still surviving in the area.

METRO SOUTH

St. Michael stands at the center of the Mausoleum of the Archangels at Holy
Sepulchre.

RESURRECTION CATHOLIC CEMETERY & MAUSOLEUMS

7201 Archer Avenue, Justice
www.catholiccemeterieschicago.org
Consecrated 1904

Search all you want for the most famous grave at this enormous graveyard just southwest of Chicago in the village of Justice. The freewheeling phantom known as **Resurrection Mary** has been traced to a half dozen occupants of this cemetery, all young accident victims buried in the 1930s, and all named Mary. The easily frustrated opted instead for years to examine the front gates on Archer Avenue.

In the 1970s, a young woman clutching the bars from the inside was seen by a passing motorist. The driver called the police, who found no one trapped in the cemetery. However, the bars had been bent apart and seared with the imprint of two small hands. Though the cemetery administration had the bars removed and repaired, it seemed the damaged areas did not remain unmarred for long. Two generations of curiosity-seekers made the trek to Resurrection from around the world to view the two strips of burned metal where the handprints once had been until, sometime around 2010, the Archdiocese refurbished the entire front gate area. No trace of the spot

Standing in a cloud and surrounded by cherubs, the Virgin Mary is offered a crown as Queen of Heaven on this superb monument.

Conrad Pickel Studio designed the faceted stained glass window walls of Resurrection Mausoleum, constructed in 1969. About 22,000 square feet, wrapping the two-story building on all sides, this is recognized by Guinness as the world's largest stained-glass installation.

remains where Mary is said to have once left her mark.

Fittingly, the man who brought the story of Resurrection Mary out of the stockyards—and to the world—was interred here with his favorite girl after his death in 2012 of pancreatic cancer. **Richard T. Crowe** (1948–2012), known by generations as "Chicago's Original Ghost Hunter," began the world's first ghost tour company, offering the first haunted tours on earth in the early 1970s, when he was teaching at DePaul University. The inaugural tour, organized as a student event, reportedly had a waiting list of more than 200 curious customers. His Chicago Supernatural Tours grew to a bona fide business, and Crowe went on to thrill countless thousands of fans with his mellow voice and engaging storytelling, which he also shared on late night radio each Halloween with longtime broadcaster, Eddie Schwartz. Crowe is credited by Chicago researchers with creating the original framework for the city's supernatural folklore, and for uncovering some of Chicago's most beloved ghost stories.

This relatively modern cemetery boasts two mausoleums, a massive, traditional structure and an open air variety. The original **Resurrection Cemetery Mausoleum**, completed in 1969 and designed by the Detroit firm of Harley, Ellington, Cowin, & Stirton, is a breathtaking example of the style called New Formalism, part of the Greek and Roman Revivalist movement. Located just north of the cemetery gates, the mausoleum contains the world's largest stained glass window, the Dalle de Verre (faceted glass) comprised of 2,448 panels and

Karol Cardinal Wojtyla, Archbishop of Krakow, visited Resurrection Cemetery in 1969 to bless the Millennium Shrine, celebrating 1,000 years of Polish Christianity. In 1983 this 275-crypt mausoleum opened, dedicated to that esteemed visitor, who had by then become Pope John Paul II.

measuring out at 22,381 square feet. Visitors to the mausoleum can enjoy a full three floors of stained glass and murals, following their brilliant path of Biblical stories around the circumference of the building. The building's glass is notable for its dramatic interpretations, showing Bible characters fully and passionately engaged in the stories they tell—a far cry from the static tableaux of most earlier religious glass. The entrance window also depicts some fully unique offerings, including dinosaurs in the Garden of Eden, Chicago's "L" train, planes, a satellite dish and—soberingly—a mushroom cloud. The forward-reaching and humanitarian feel extends also to the mausoleum's murals, depicting Polish notables like Marie Curie, working in her laboratory.

Across Archer Road from the cemetery is Chet's Melody Lounge, long associated with the "Resurrection Mary" legend and a popular drinking spot for ghost tour participants.

Sports fans will want to seek out the graves of major league outfielder, **John Ostrowski** (1917–1992)—who played for both the Cubs and the White Sox—and **Tony Piet** (1906–

1981) and **Chick Naleway** (1902–1949), also players for the Sox, as well as third baseman **Raymond Jablonski** (1926–1985), whose 21 home runs and 112 RBI in 1953 stood as Cardinal rookie records until 2001. Also interred at Resurrection are football players **Ted Lapka** (1920–2011) and **Joe Krupa, Sr.** (1933–2011).

Eugene Record (1940–2005), lead singer of arguably Chicago's dearest soul group, the Chi-Lites, rests eternally at Resurrection, after making an indelible mark on music lovers. The group's hits, including "Have You Seen Her" and "Oh Girl," won Record and his group a permanent place in the hearts of generations of fans. Not one to be forgotten, Resurrection resident **Eddie Blazonczyk, Sr.** (1940–2005), the "Polka King," received no less than a National Endowment for the Arts Heritage Fellowship for his tireless devotion to polka music. His band, The Versatones, formed in 1962 and revolutionized the polka style by combining it with rock and roll, Cajun and zydeco elements, and country music flair. He received more than a dozen Grammy nominations and was inducted into the Polka Music Hall of Fame in the 1980s. A stroke in 2001 led to his retirement, and Blazoncyzk died of natural causes at the age of 70.

BETHANIA CEMETERY
7701 South Archer Avenue, Justice
www.bethaniacemetery.com
Established 1894

Adjacent to Resurrection is this lovingly-maintained Lutheran cemetery, its many German inscriptions revealing the heritage of the interred. Its name, too, is evocative of Resurrection, for Bethania was the Biblical home of Lazarus, whom Christ raised from the dead.

On March 20, 1894, the Bethania Cemetery Association, a group of Lutheran congregations, received from the Town of Lyons a permit to operate a cemetery at the site, and to "pass with its funeral

The monument of grocer Alexander Kathmann (1835–1916), depicting a woman at a well, is an artistic highlight of the cemetery.

Monuments feature German-language epitaphs and traditional "blackletter" script.

Bethania's picturesque administrative building houses the original cemetery bell from 1894, still tolled when a procession passes through the gates.

processions without hindrance or interruption over any street or alley within the limits of the Town of Lyons."[437] Later, a street car line was installed on Archer Avenue, with a special all-black funeral car bringing mourners from the city.[438]

The original cemetery bell from 1894 survives in the historic stone administration building, tolling as present-day funeral processions enter the gates.[439]

A highlight of Bethania is the **Kathmann Monument** near the entrance. This intricately detailed stone, depicting a woman kneeling before a well, is expertly carved and exceptionally well preserved.

LITHUANIAN NATIONAL CEMETERY

8201 South Kean Road, Justice
Established 1911

This fiercely patriotic site boasts monuments to national heroes and national tragedies, burials of many area immigrants, and a constant scattering of gold, green, and red flags.

Secluded and serene, the cemetery is also home to the curious

The cemetery's front entrance and administration building, dating to the founding in 1911.

---

[437] "Original Township Permit to Operate a Cemetery," *100th Anniversary 1894–1994,* Bethania Association.

[438] *100th Anniversary 1894–1994.*

[439] Bethania Cemetery, http://www.bethaniacemetery.com.

memorial commemorating the life of **Albert Vaitis Carter** (1915–1987). Born on the Fourth of July, the eccentric Carter would celebrate his birthday in historic places like Plymouth Rock and Gettysburg and ten separate towns named Independence. His monument bears witness to Carter's self-conscious achievements: all four sides of the stone are inscribed with details of his life's activities, from his occupation as *PERCUSSIONIST (DRUMMER TO YOU)*, to the historic trails he traveled, to the events and attractions at which he was the first paying customer, among them, the Gateway Arch in St. Louis and Chicago's Sears Tower. Carter is no restless spirit, however. Though his gravestone attests to the fact that he *ENJOYED LIVING, AND IT WAS CONTAGIOUS*, it also makes perfectly clear that the buoyant wayfarer is now *AT REST – FINALLY*.

A former head of state buried in a foreign country is a rarity—but this cemetery once housed the remains of **Dr. Kazys V. Grinius** (1866–1950), President of Lithuania. A medical doctor, Grinius was also active in politics during and after Lithuania's occupation by Russia. When the nation gained its independence in 1918, he served as member of the national assembly, then Prime Minister, then was elected president in 1926. Deposed in a military coup after only six months, Dr. Grinius was placed under house arrest and pressured to resign. In 1941 the former president fled his country to escape the Nazis. He died in Chicago in 1950 and was buried here, at Lithuanian National Cemetery.[440]

This burial was, from the

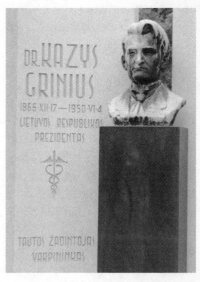

Dr. Kazys Grinius (1866–1950), President of Lithuania, lived his later life in Chicago after being illegally deposed from office. His remains were repatriated to Lithuania in 1994.

---

[440] "Obituary: Dr. Kazys V. Grinius," *Chicago Daily Tribune*, June 8, 1950.

start, intended to be only temporary. At the time of Dr. Grinius's
death, Lithuania was a Soviet
Socialist Republic, and remind-
ers of its past as an independent
republic were not welcome. For
more than 40 years, this former
president was buried on the out-
skirts of Chicago, until in 1990
the collapse of the Soviet Union
restored Lithuania's independence. In October 1994, the cremated remains of Dr. Grinius
were removed from this cemetery
and returned to his home town
in Lithuania, there to be embedded within a newly constructed
memorial,[441] featuring a life-sized
statue of the handsome president
in white granite.

Dr. Jonas Sliupas (1861–1944), offered
the Lithuanian presidency during the
coup that removed President Grinius,
turned it down out of loyalty to his
friend and respect for the law. After
dying in Berlin his ashes were sent to
Chicago for burial.

Another prominent na-
tional figure, **Dr. Jonas Sliupas**
(1861–1944), was nearly caught
up in the coup of 1926. Before
deposing President Grinius, the military officers who orchestrated
the coup approached Sliupas, a university professor, with an unusual suggestion—that Dr. Sliupas be installed as president. Out of
friendship for Kazys Grinius and respect for the democratic process,
Sliupas refused; the conspirators found another figurehead and went
ahead with the plan anyway. Later serving as mayor of the city of
Palanga, he was forced out of that office by the Germans. He died

---

[441] http://www.spaudos.lt/Knygnesiu_paminklai/knygnesiai/kazys_grinius.html. Web page
is in Lithuanian, but Google provides the following machine-generated translation:
"Approaching the second Soviet occupation, fled to the west. He died in the U.S. in
1950. June 4. In 1994. October 8. Urn with his remains were sent from the United States
and solemnly re-buried at his native village."

in exile in Berlin, and his ashes were sent to relatives in Chicago for burial at Lithuanian National Cemetery.[442]

The ordinary citizens of Lithuania, too, suffered greatly at the hands of the German and Russian occupiers, and to their memory is dedicated one of the cemetery's most unusual monuments: a slender iron shaft with two square platforms near the top, forming a Patriarchal cross when viewed from any direction. The work of sculptor **Julius Pakalka** (1915–2002), who is buried nearby, it commemorates 300,000 Lithuanians deported to Siberia between 1941 and 1953.

This lifelike granite statue commemorates Helen Kasperitis Sudent (1909–1932), young wife of Peter Sudent (1897–1960). The broken column symbolizes a life cut short.

MOUNT GLENWOOD MEMORY GARDENS, WEST
8301 Kean Ave, Willow Springs
Established 1920

Still called "Archer Woods Cemetery" by most local burial-ground and ghost-lore aficionados, this site was given the unwieldy moniker "Mount Glenwood Memory Gardens, West" by the new management a few years ago. Except for the large etched-granite sign out front, it didn't change anything. One of two Kean Road cemeteries,

---

[442] "Jonas Sliupas—The Man Who Declined the Presidency," VilNews—The Voice of International Lithuania, http://vilnews.com/?p=1858.

Archer Woods is known as the unsettling burial ground next to Lithuanian National Cemetery.

With good reason.

Visitors to this enclosure, set in a forested area off the main thoroughfares, are often uncomfortably treated to the sight of concrete burial vaults stacked up by the side of the road. Adding to the effect is the local legend of a weeping woman said to haunt Archer Woods, as well as old-timers' memories of the honky-tonk bars that used to stand along Kean Road.

Despite the negative popular impression, the rustic feel and varied markers of Archer Woods offers a pleasant tour.

Built in 1925, the narrow Kean mausoleum stands only a few feet away from Kean Avenue.

A shady, wooded section in a corner of the cemetery.

EVERGREEN CEMETERY
3401 West 87th Street, Evergreen Park
www.evergreencemetery-illinois.com
Established 1910

This sprawling Evergreen Park ossuary provides repose for a number of cultural groups, including Greeks, Ukrainians, Palestinians, and Jews. The cemetery was created in 1910 by Max Guthman and Jacob Rothschild, who had studied cemetery management under the great Ossian Cole

Evergreen's unique main entrance was lost in 2004 when the northeast corner of the cemetery was sold, becoming a drab, uninteresting shopping plaza.

Simonds, designer and superintendent of Graceland. Doing business as the LaSalle Sales Organization, the two hired landscape architect

Typical monuments, many with Greek names and epitaphs, are widely spaced in accordance with the lawn-park cemetery design.

Svend Lollesgard to lay out the site as a flush-marker cemetery, intending to showcase the natural beauty of the location. Over the years the rules were relaxed to allow upright monuments as well, though the emphasis on the natural landscape remained.[443]

A favorite destination is the grave of **Ray Schalk** (1892–1970), Chicago White Sox catcher and Hall of Famer.

ST. MARY CATHOLIC CEMETERY & MAUSOLEUMS

87th Street & Hamlin Avenue, Evergreen Park
www.catholiccemeterieschicago.org
Consecrated 1888

Several large Mexican-American sections have joined the earlier ethnic gatherings at this Evergreen Park site, established by South Side Germans in 1888. Mourners of many cultures join to keep an enchanting grotto aglow with glimmering votives.

Two sports figures are buried here: popular Chicago Bears running back, **Brian Piccolo** (1943–1970), and **Edward C. Gaedel** (1925–1961), onetime midget baseball sensation.

Baseball showman Bill Veeck hired the diminutive athlete to play for the St. Louis Browns against the Detroit Tigers in the

Michael Anthony Bilandic (1923–2002) was mayor of Chicago from 1976 to 1979, appointed acting mayor upon Richard Daley's death and then winning election in his own right. In 1984 he was elected appellate court judge, and in 1990 became a Justice of the Supreme Court of Illinois. For two years he was Chief Justice of Illinois.

[443] "History of Evergreen Cemetery," Evergreen Cemetery, http://www.evergreeencemetery-illinois.com/dm20/en_US/locations/03/0304/history.page.

This grotto is a popular place for devotional offerings, with hundreds of votive candles flickering on the table next to the statue of the Blessed Virgin.

second game of a 1951 double-header. Between the games, the fun-loving Veeck had sponsored a 50th-anniversary extravaganza in honor of the American League, parading acrobats, antique cars, and a huge celebration cake—from which Gaedel emerged, sporting a Browns jersey bearing the number "1/8" and delighting the crowd.

Dismissing Gaedel as a charming stunt, fans went wild when he was announced as a pinch hitter in the second game's first inning. Unknown to even the umpires, Gaedel had actually been signed by the Browns several days earlier. Though Detroit's manager was infuriated, umpire

The St. Elisabeth monument was erected by cemetery founders Heinrich and Maria Wischemeyer, dedicated to the German Catholic Sisters of Chicago.

Ed Hurley let Gaedel face the pitcher. Though he had been warned by Veeck against swinging, the 3-foot, 7-inch Gaedel couldn't resist. Reaching first base, Gaedel would recall he felt like Babe Ruth.

After the game, enraged American League president Will Harridge had Gaedel's name removed from the records and, in a scathing letter to Bill Veeck, officially banned *midgets* from playing in future AL games.

CEDAR PARK CEMETERY

12540 South Halsted Street, Calumet Park
Established circa 1924

Tucked between Blue Island and Chicago, this cozy Calumet Park cemetery serves both as the end of the road for race car driver **James L. Snyder** (1909–1939), and as home plate for Chicago White Sox infielder **Donald M. Kolloway, Sr.** (1918–1994). In recent years, it has also gained attention for the variety of wildlife on the grounds, including a herd of at least 20 deer.

Originally a Masonic cemetery, Cedar Park is much like Acacia Park in appearance, complete with an obelisk bearing the square and compass emblem of Masonry perched atop a small hill. A plaque at the base of the obelisk—now obscured by bushes planted in front— reads *Dedicated to the Memory of Departed Masons MCMXXIV*; save for the date, this is identical in design and wording to those at Acacia

The entrance and administrative building of Cedar Park Cemetery, built of mortared stones of various colors, with obelisk-shaped posts beside each driveway.

A herd of deer have made their home on the cemetery grounds, delighting visitors.

Park. Elsewhere on the grounds, a fountain is likewise dedicated to *Departed Members of the Order of the Eastern Star, MCMXXX*. Unlike Acacia Park, where markers are set on top of the ground, Cedar Park permits only flush markers, set into the ground. The cemetery also includes a garden crypt mausoleum, and several statues adorn the grounds.

At the time of the Burr Oak scandal in 2009, Cedar Park had been owned by Perpetua Inc., the same company that owned Burr Oak. Perpetua filed for bankruptcy after the incident. Both cemeteries were sold at a public auction in 2010, with court approval, and both purchased by a partnership of local African-American cemetery and funeral home owners, unconnected to the horrific events.[444]

The splendid entrance avenue includes an eternal flame and a sculptural group, leading to the obelisk.

---

[444] Julianne Malfeaux, "Burr Oak, Cedar Park Cemeteries Sold," *Chicago Defender*, April 27, 2010.

FREEZE! A CHILLING ALTERNATIVE TO CHECKING OUT

If the high price of dying is getting you down, take heart: Even in these days of outrageous funeral costs, burial is still a downright bargain compared to the cost of sticking around. Cryonics providers, in the business of freezing folks at the moment of death in hopes of revival and survival in a later, more medically advanced age, are currently charging about $200,000 for a full-body freeze, which includes indefinite storage at -320 degrees Fahrenheit in liquid nitrogen.

Though the fee seems whopping, it's rather necessary for business: only about 300 people are currently in cryonic suspension and these divided among four cryonics firms in California, Michigan, and Arizona. Combining business operating costs with freezing fees, and adding on the burden of storage for perhaps hundreds of years, cryonics companies could feasibly be called struggling. For these outfits, it is hoped another less expensive process will boost future income. Neurosuspension, the freezing of only the head (and storage in a cookpot of liquid nitrogen), is a relative steal—the going rate is a mere $80,000.

LINCOLN CEMETERY

12300 South Kedzie Avenue, Blue Island
www.lincolncemeterychicago.com
Established 1911

One of two African-American cemeteries opened during Chicago's pre-World War I years in response to discriminatory policies of their white counterparts, Blue Island's Lincoln Cemetery was founded in 1911 by a cooperative organization supported by fraternal lodges, on land that was initially an undeveloped portion of the neighboring Swedish cemetery, Oak Hill.[445]

Jazz immortals, **Lil Hardin Armstrong** (1898–1971), one of the most outstanding women of early jazz, and **Jimmy Reed** (1925–1976), whose guitar-embossed stone marks the resting place of *The Boss Man of the Blues*, are buried at Lincoln.

Memphis-born Hardin was first invited to play with Sugar Johnny's Creole Orchestra while working as a pianist/demonstrator at a Chicago music store. She then went on to lead her own band at Chicago's Dreamland. In the 1920s, Hardin hooked up with King Oliver. Then, in New Orleans, she met Louis Armstrong and became his second wife.

Though Moorish Science Temple founder Drew Ali (1886–1929) was buried under a simple flat headstone at Burr Oak, his name appears on a mausoleum at Lincoln as Prophet Drew Ali Reincarnated. The mausoleum houses the remains of Ali's follower John Givens-El, who claimed to be a reincarnation of the prophet shortly after the original Drew Ali's death.

Some historians credit Hardin with the bulk of Armstrong's success; she is often cited as the driving force behind his emergence as a great musician. Leaning on Louis to be more aggressive toward his own goals, Lil was a relentless, one-woman pep squad. It is said that, under her influence, Armstrong found the confidence to leave King Oliver's band and begin his own.

Lil maintained strong support of her husband's career, but she also followed her own star. Though she contributed greatly to some of Armstrong's Hot Five and Hot Seven recordings, Lil led a number of

---

[445] "History," Lincoln Cemetery, http://www.lincolncemeterychicago.com/dm20/en_US/locations/62/6241/history.page.

her own groups, including Lil's Hot Shots, and was featured in more than one Broadway production. After splitting with her husband in the late 1930s, Lil worked for Decca records as a swing vocalist and pianist, recording more than a dozen cuts before returning to Chicago and the nightclub circuit. She died while performing "St. Louis Blues," a month after Louis's death, at a memorial concert in Chicago.

Like Lil Hardin Armstrong, Jimmy Reed was a native Southerner. Born in Dunleith, Mississippi, the blues singer wrote his own songs, accompanying them with guitar and harmonica. As a teenager, Reed left school to find work, at first taking up farming jobs around the state. When World War II made Northern jobs more plentiful, he traveled to Chicago where he was promptly drafted into the Navy. After his discharge, he returned to Chicago to work in the steel mills and spent his free hours playing music with Willie Joe Duncan, who played the Diddley-bow (one-string guitar). But Reed's real joy was in playing with old friend, guitarist Eddie Taylor, a Dunleith chum who had also moved north for work.

In the mid-1950s, Reed scored a contract with VeeJay Records. His recording, "You Don't Have to Go" was a smash, and he followed it up with a string of hits, including "Ain't That Lovin' You Baby," "You Got Me Dizzy," "Big Boss Man," and "Bright Lights, Big City." Taylor added much to Reed's recordings, and together they put 14 hits on the R&B charts in the ten years after their debut.

Despite phenomenal success, Reed was plagued with problems. An epileptic and alcoholic, he constantly struggled for the physical stability necessary for his work. In later years, he became notorious for performing drunk, and his failing health led to an early death in 1976 from respiratory failure.

Another Lincoln notable is **Bessie Coleman** (1896–1926). She is remembered primarily as the first African-American woman to gain a pilot's license, but in life she really soared as a stunt pilot.

Born in Texas in the early 1890s, Coleman's childhood was filled with helping her abandoned mother raise her 12 siblings. Picking cotton and doing laundry didn't leave much time for bettering herself, but Bessie had an unusual drive to achieve and dedicated her scarce free time to reading. Thanks to the traveling library that passed through her home-town of Atlanta on occasion, Coleman was able to finish high school and, with the aid of the money she made taking in washing, pay for a semester of college. Frustrated by her financial situation, Bessie did not abandon her quest for schooling, but turned to even higher education. Determined to become a pilot, she was turned away from every flying school she approached because of both her race and her sex. Undiscouraged, Coleman appealed to an editor of the *Chicago Weekly Defender*,

On the monument of Bessie Coleman, the first African-American pilot, a hand-tinted photo shows her ready for flight.

who helped her learn French, after which she obtained entrance to a French aviation school, paying her tuition with the money she made as a manicurist and working in a chili parlor. Bessie earned her pilot's license in 1921, two years before Amelia Earhart, becoming the only licensed black pilot in the world.

Progressing still further into aerobatics, Coleman received stunt training in Europe and then returned home to tour the United States, staging exhibition flights and lecturing on the promises of flight and racial progress. After five short years of stunt-flying, Coleman's World War I Jenny nose-dived during a barnstorming run in Florida. She was thrown from the plane and killed.

Another African-American pioneer rests at Lincoln: **Andrew "Rube" Foster** (1879–1930), eulogized upon his death in 1930 as the father of Negro baseball.

Born in Texas in September of 1879, Foster began as a 17-year-old pitcher on the road with the Waco Yellow Jackets. His strong arm led him north to the mounds of some of the most successful black ball clubs of the time, among them the Philadelphia Giants and the Chicago Union Giants. He was given the nickname "Rube" after the pitcher Rube Waddell, whose Hall of Fame skill was bested by Foster at a 1902 exhibition game. The next year, fans cheered Foster through four straight wins of the so-called Colored World Series.

Foster's playing days laid the groundwork for his years of retirement from the game. He became a manager and entrepreneur, forming the Chicago American Giants in 1911 and going on to organize the Negro League in 1920, serving as its first president. Traveling in high style with his superstar Chicago team, Foster brought organized black baseball to an eager nation, and sensational fame to a black organization in a time when African-American celebrity was non-existent.

Despite a great and long career, Rube Foster could not elude the mental illness that overtook him in 1926, forcing him to quit baseball. After his death in an Illinois asylum four years later, he was mourned by millions who recognized early the pioneering spirit that, more than 50 years later, gained Foster election to the Baseball Hall of Fame.

BEVERLY CEMETERY

12000 South Kedzie Avenue, Blue Island
www.beverlycemetery.com
Established 1920

A few years after Lincoln Cemetery was carved out of Oak Hill, a third cemetery opened across the street. The Beverly Cemetery Company, under the leadership of Dr. Franklin Porter,[446] laid out a modern, non-denominational lawn park cemetery with pleasant landscaping, including a fountain and an impressive entrance gate. The site includes Masonic and Jewish sections with sizable central monuments.

---

[446] "Beverly Cemetery: History," Dignity Memorial, http://www.dignitymemorial.com/beverly-cemetery/en-us/history.page.

CEME-PRAIRIES: THE SILVER LINING OF ABANDONMENT

While cemetery lovers and survivors bemoan the declining state of ancient, local burial places, naturalists are urging the further under-maintenance of these often tiny, largely untended sites.

Increasingly, biologists are discovering that abandoned, or near-abandoned, cemetery grounds are sheltering rare plants and animals too often sacrificed to the strict landscaping rules proscribed by larger sites under centralized management. In Will County, scientists inspecting more than 150 obsolete graveyards have literally hit pay dirt time and again; a large number retain even their original soil structure. In addition, a number of endangered prairie species have been found flourishing within the untouched confines of these rural retreats.

Desperate to keep these treasures safe from the hands of well-meaning individuals and groups set on cleaning up their local cemeteries, several states, including Ohio, Indiana, and Illinois, have joined The Nature Conservancy in managing a number of local graveyards. Volunteers shun the mower, instead spending tedious hours hand-pulling overgrown grass and keeping trees in check with controlled fires.

Despite their loving attendance to these difficult duties, however, naturalists admit to being frustrated by one seemingly insurmountable obstacle: the unswerving determination of a minority of bereaved to keep the weeds off Grandma's grave.

OAK HILL CEMETERY

11900 South Kedzie Avenue, Blue Island
www.oakhillcemeterychicago.com
Established 1902

This Blue Island site was founded in 1902 by Swedes hailing from Chicago's South Side.[447] The vast acreage was originally designed for many years of service to the ethnic population of the surrounding area, but when Scandinavians began leaving the vicinity soon after the cemetery's founding, sections of the land were sold off for establishment as an African-American cemetery—Lincoln Cemetery, in 1911.

Oak Hill Cemetery features a neoclassical chapel-mausoleum, designed by architect Conny Ramberg and erected in 1921.[448] The frieze depicts a funeral of the ancient Mediterranean. A crowd of mourners of all ages are gathered, one of them carrying an urn. Their eyes are downcast and they cling together in their sorrow. Torchbearers bring up the rear of the procession, as the sun sets between hills in the distance. Over the door appear the words:

May this Temple Ever Proclaim Liberality in Religion –
the Existence of an Omnipresent God:
the Immortality of the Soul.

The original mausoleum at Oak Hill, built in 1921. A funeral scene of the ancient world appears in bas-relief over the door.

---

[447] "About Oak Hill Cemetery II," Oak Hill Cemetery, http://www.oakhillcemeterychicago.com/dm20/en_US/locations/62/6240/overview.page?.

[448] The name of the architect and construction dates of the mausoleum are on a bronze plaque on the mausoleum exterior.

A typical scene at Oak Hill, with a winding road between widely-spaced granite monuments.

Baptist preacher **Carl Gustaf Lagergren** (1846–1941) is buried under a stately granite monument in the shape of a church window. A pastor in Sweden, Lagergren edited a religious magazine, gave lectures in support of temperance and religious freedom, and established a school for lay preachers before immigrating to the United States in 1889, called to lead the Swedish seminary in America. He continued his own studies, earning a doctorate, all the while publishing numerous papers and books and serving as pastor of Englewood Church. From 1889 until his retirement in 1922, Dr. Lagergren was Dean of Swedish Baptist Theological Seminary of America, the longest-serving dean of that institution. Under his stewardship the seminary merged with Minnesota-based Bethel Academy, relocating to St. Paul. The institution continues today as Bethel University.[449] After retirement, Dr. Lagergren enjoyed a long life, dying at the age of 95.

Carl A. Carlson (1850–1923) is memorialized with a rough-hewn shaft of granite with a bronze plaque mounted on one side, which proclaims *He Had a Good True Heart Within* over an Odd Fellows logo.

Most intriguing of all is the unique monument of **Dr. John Alfred Enander** (1842–1910). Sixteen feet tall and six feet wide, the monument is a large granite stele with a rough surface, tapering as it rises, higher on one side than the other, looking like an ancient standing stone. Above Dr. Enander's name and vital statistics is set a round

[449] "Carl Gustaf Lagergren 1889–1922," Bethel University, http://www.bethel.edu/bgc-archives/leaders/seminary/carl-lagergren.

bronze medallion bearing his portrait. Almost every other inch of the front of the monument is covered by a carving of a double-headed dragon with a long, sinuous body, entwined with itself in a half-knot. From each of the two heads come a barbed tongue and tendrils of vapor, twisting about to fill all of the available space. Swedish text is written on the reptile's body.

A dragon entwines around the bronze portrait of Dr. John Enander (1842–1910), on a monument funded by public subscription.

John Enander trained as a minister in his native Sweden, coming to America when appointed a pastor in Paxton, Illinois. After becoming editor and later owner of his church newspaper, Enander was appointed minister to Denmark by President Benjamin Harrison, but had to resign due to poor health. He then became a professor of Swedish literature at Augustana College, and wrote several books including a *History of the United States*.[450] Initially, his gravestone was modest; but it was in recognition of his work to preserve and promote Swedish culture in America that, five years after his death, a call went out in the *Swedish American Press* for contributions to erect a suitable monument.[451] The public subscription was an overwhelming success. The monument, designed by Carl J. Nilsson, was unveiled with great ceremony on May 22, 1921, on what would have been Dr. Enander's seventy-ninth birthday.[452]

---

[450] "Swedish Writer Who Died Here," *Chicago Daily Tribune*, September 10 1910.

[451] "Foreign Language Press Survey: A Call to Swedish Americans," The Newberry, http://flps.newberry.org/article/5423404_3_1034.

[452] "Monument to Dr. Enander Will Be Unveiled Today," *Chicago Daily Tribune*, May 22, 1921.

HOLY SEPULCHRE CATHOLIC CEMETERY & MAUSOLEUM

6001 West 111th Street, Alsip
www.catholiccemeterieschicago.org
Consecrated 1923

At the start of the twentieth century, on a good day, thousands of Chicagoans would travel by rail to this south suburban site, walk through the gates, and take their seats, eager with anticipation. They had not come to pay respects to the dead—for no one was buried here yet—they had come to have a good time, a few beers, and perhaps win some money. Not yet a cemetery, the future site of Holy Sepulchre was, beginning in 1901, a place for horses, jockeys, and grandstands full of cheering spectators—the Worth Race Track.[453]

By 1910, however, Cook County Sheriff Christopher Strassheim was vigorously prosecuting bookmaking operations, and the race track shut down.[454] For the next decade or so, the shuttered track was used as a military training ground and as a stockyard.[455] By 1923, the property had been acquired by the Catholic Archdiocese for a new cemetery to supplement the rapidly-filling Mount Olivet.

Chicago's first Catholic cemetery to open after the Great War, Holy Sepulchre incorporated the latest trends in cemetery designs. Flush markers would be standard in most sections, though upright monuments were permitted in others, and graves were priced with future care costs included.[456]

The main entrance is on the north edge of the cemetery, consisting of bronze gates between two copper-roofed limestone buildings with understated neoclassical features. On one side, a tower rises, into which is carved the words of 2 Maccabees: *A Holy and Whole-*

---

[453] Ken O'Brien, "The Stars Aligned, and There Was Worth," *Chicago Tribune*, September 6, 1998.

[454] "New Racing Plan; Ponies at Worth?" *Chicago Daily Tribune*, July 10, 1910.

[455] O'Brien, "The Stars Aligned."

[456] "Holy Sepulchre Catholic Cemetery & Mausoleum," Catholic Cemeteries, Archdiocese of Chicago, http://www.catholiccemeterieschicago.org/locations.php?id=9.

some Thought to Pray for the Dead That They May Be Released from Their Sins. Inside, the main road widens, then branches out in seven directions. Here, at the focal point of the cemetery, is buried its most famed resident, quintessential machine politician **Richard J. Daley** (1902–1976), who joined thousands of his constituents at this site after a remarkable life that included 21 years as Chicago mayor.

Leader of the Cook County Democratic party for 23 years and mayor for a whopping six terms, Daley evolved from figurehead of an organized, local force into a bona fide national presence, commanding the attention, and even subservience, of national political personalities.

Richard J. Daley (1902–1976), for 21 years mayor of Chicago, popularly called "Da Mare," "Hizzoner," and "Boss."

Equally legendary dead or alive, the late Richard J. Daley continues to haunt the political life of his city, as well as the everyday life of his former neighbors. On the city's South Side, Daley's lifelong home, a typical Chicago-style bungalow in the prototypical working-class neighborhood of Bridgeport, was still guarded round the clock by a squad car posted out front during his son's multiple terms as mayor.

Despite Daley's sensational legacy, most of the crowds flocking to Holy Sepulchre are not seeking to honor "Hizzoner," but to say a silent prayer at the grave of an enigmatic little girl.

Mary Alice Quinn (1920–1935) died at the age of 14, after a short but intensely pious life of devotion. Following the example of Saint Theresa of Lisieux, who found the key to devotion in her "Little Way" of everyday charity, Quinn won the faith and affection of

At the grave of "Miracle Child" Mary Alice Quinn (1920–1935), visitors seeking the help of the pious child's spirit have left religious statues, toys, candles, and other mementos.

scores of followers who believed her to have the stuff of sainthood. After her death, pilgrims gravitated to her gravesite, offering prayers, pleading for intercession in their needs, and even taking handfuls of soil as sacred souvenirs. In recognition of their faith, visitors are said to be treated to an overwhelming odor of roses, even in wintertime, a phenomenon reminiscent of St. Theresa's promise to send a shower of roses to assure the faithful of her constant intercession for them.

And torch singer **Helen Morgan** (1900–1941) took her final bow and exited to a plot here, after wooing the world with such famous cuts as "Can't Help Lovin' Dat Man," "Bill," "Frankie and Johnny," and other favorites.

In 1993 a spectacular addition was made to the cemetery, the **Mausoleum of the Archangels**, located in the southwest corner, an impressive sight from nearby Interstate 294. A garden-crypt mausoleum, in which the crypts are on the outside walls, this mausoleum is a huge, sprawling structure, one of the largest and most splendid of its kind. Using statues of archangels Michael, Gabriel, and Raphael taken from Queen of Heaven Cemetery, where they had previously stood next to the Gothic-style mausoleum there,[457] the architects placed two of them in decorative gardens between rows of crypts. The statue of St. Michael was placed at the mausoleum's front and center, with soaring metallic beams meeting overhead, forming a majestic space of air and light and awe.

---

[457] Jenny Floro-Khalaf and Cynthia Savaglio, *Mount Carmel and Queen of Heaven Cemeteries* (Mount Pleasant, SC: Arcadia Publishing, 2006), 50.

Visitors to Holy Sepulchre will note the contrast between this cemetery's varied landscape and the overwhelmingly flat Chapel Hill Gardens South, directly across Central Avenue, whose burials are marked almost exclusively by flush stones.

CHAPEL HILL GARDENS SOUTH CEMETERY

11333 South Central Avenue, Oak Lawn
www.chapelhillgardenssouthcemetery.com
Established 1927

When this cemetery opened a few years after neighboring Holy Sepulchre, it had a very different and much more evocative name, Sleepy Hollow Cemetery.[458] In their 1920s newspaper advertisements, the Sleepy Hollow Cemetery Company offered "Death in Sunshine," entombment in "daylight crypts" in the Sleepy Hollow Abbey mausoleum, "infinitely more tranquil and more beautiful... than ground burial."[459] Though it was the focus of early advertising efforts, the mausoleum is a tiny one; the vast majority of the land was used for in-ground burial.

By about 1948[460] the Hollow had become a Hill, as the cemetery was renamed to match its DuPage County counterpart, Chapel Hill Gardens West, when both were joined under the ownership of Chapel Hill Gardens, Inc. The west suburban cemetery had previously been known as Green Ridge.

The two Chapel Hill Gardens cemeteries are visually similar, being of the "memorial park" type. Though there are a few rare exceptions, for the most part graves are marked exclusively with lawn-level markers, flush with the ground.

---

[458] Chapel Hill Gardens South Cemetery, http://www.chapelhillgardenssouthcemetery. com.

[459] "Death in Sunshine" (display ad), *Chicago Daily Tribune*, December 19, 1927.

[460] The first obituary to mention the cemetery's new name was in September 1948.

In 1958 the policy of permitting only flush markers led to a lawsuit against the cemetery company by a group of Chicago monument dealers, alleging conspiracy to violate antitrust law by limiting the types of monuments that could be installed. The James H. Matthews company of Pittsburgh, a leading manufacturer of bronze grave markers, was named as co-defendant.[461] Ultimately, the attempt to compel the cemeteries to change their policies was unsuccessful, as a quick survey of the grounds will demonstrate—the headstones are still flat.

But that's not to say the landscape is entirely featureless. Both Chapel Hills include various cemetery-owned monuments, generally of a Christian theme, placed at the centers of sections, often surrounded by bushes planted in creative geometric patterns. There are a few private mausoleums and above-ground granite crypts, and a scattering of granite benches placed by individual lot-owners.

And, both cemeteries include nearly-identical Masonic sections, each with three marble chairs, laid out as in a Masonic lodge. In the east, on a raised concrete platform with three steps, is the seat of the Worshipful Master. On the back of the chair is inscribed the "Jewel" of that office, a square—that is, the instrument used by masons and carpenters to produce right angles. To the west, a two-step platform supports the seat of the Senior Warden, on which is carved a level. And, a one-step platform in the south holds the Junior Warden's seat, marked with a plumb-line. At the center of this arrangement is an altar on which rests an open book, the *Volume of Sacred Law*.

RESTVALE CEMETERY

11700 South Laramie Avenue, Alsip
Established circa 1930

Reminisce for a moment at the grave of **Nathaniel Sweetwater Clifton** (1926–1990), famed Harlem Globetrotter and DuSable

---

[461] "Grave Marker Monopoly Suit Seeks $1,500,000," *Chicago Daily Tribune*, September 10, 1958.

Restvale Cemetery's
entrance.

*The Mojo Is Gone—
the Master Has Won.*
Better known as
"Muddy Waters,"
McKinley Morganfield
(1913–1983) is one of
several prominent blues
musicians at Restvale.

High School basketball immortal. Or tour the plots of ten—count
'em—noted musicians, including the incomparable **Muddy Waters**
(1915–1981). Also at Restvale are blues buddies Samuel G. Maghett,
otherwise known as **Magic Sam** (1936–1969), and King of the Blues
Harmonica, **Walter Horton** (1918–1981).

Rounding out the cemetery's musical theme is a rare type of monument: an appropriately whimsical stone organ, just waiting for the
ethereal fingers of Restvale's talented residents.

HAZELGREEN CEMETERY
115th & Laramie, Alsip
Established circa 1852

Across the road from Restvale is a tiny Victorian graveyard, seemingly out of place in a town full of large modern cemeteries. Less than two acres in size, Hazelgreen Cemetery includes a variety of monuments in the typical styles of the era, providing a welcome visual relief from the uniformity of the nearby flat-marker cemeteries. Square-sided shafts dominate the landscape, alternating with thick granite tablets. Pedestals taller than a man hold aloft stone urns, some draped with sculpted cloth. One monument features two circular bases that may have once supported twin columns, perhaps an arch, now missing. Surrounding all are slanted or flat headstones. In the northwest corner stands an old cast-iron hand pump, rust visible beneath the green paint, rising from a bed of flowers.

DeWitt Lane (1805–1852) purchased the land occupied by the

At the center of the cemetery, looking towards the Lane family plot. DeWitt Lane (1805–1852) was the original owner of the land that became Hazelgreen, as well as the village of Worth.

modern village of Worth in 1836, calling the settlement "Lane's Island."[462] Hazelgreen Cemetery, where Lane and his descendants lie, was built on the Lane family farm, east of downtown Worth. Near the pump stood a wood-frame schoolhouse, demolished when a new Hazelgreen School was built across the street. The land where the school stood was then donated to the cemetery and used for burials.[463] Members of the Lane family continue to be involved in the cemetery management to the present day, and provided information to the South Suburban Genealogical and Historical Society, which published an index of the cemetery in 1990.

This pump, at the corner of the cemetery, is on the site of the former school, torn down when a new school was built across the street.

BURR OAK CEMETERY

4400 West 127th Street, Alsip
theburroakcemetery.com
Established 1927

It's been several years now since the headlines in Chicago—and around the world—revealed that four workers at suburban Burr Oak Cemetery had dug up more than 200 graves, disposing of the corpses

---

[462] "History," Village of Worth, http://www.villageofworth.com/Worth/history.htm.

[463] South Suburban Genealogical and Historical Society, *Hazelgreen Cemetery—Alsip—Cook County, Illinois* (South Holland, Illinois: South Suburban Genealogical and Historical Society, 1990).

The original cemetery entrance. Due to the construction of expressway on-ramps nearby, this entrance was closed off and made inaccessible.

in a dumping ground on the property and reselling the plots for cash to unknowing, grieving families of the newly deceased. In July 2009, the Burr Oak scandal, one of the worst in American cemetery history, prompted Sheriff Tom Dart and the Cook County Sheriff's Office to shutter the enclosure, declaring it a crime scene and arresting the cemetery manager and three groundskeepers. Head of the operation, manager Carolyn Towns, was sentenced to 12 years in prison. Backhoe operator Maurice Dailey, foreman Keith Nicks, and dump truck operator Terrence Nicks are, at this writing, still awaiting trial.

In the wake of the gruesome and heartbreaking announcements, more than 5,000 family members and friends filed class-action lawsuits against the owners of Burr Oak. The sheriff's office worked on photographing undisturbed headstones and setting up a searchable online database, including the salvageable records from the chaotic listings on hand. After examining the records, it was disclosed that, although between 140,190 and 147,568 bodies were interred at Burr Oak, the cemetery is mapped for a maximum of 130,000 graves. Even more shocking is the fact that even some of these areas had no burial records at all. When burials resumed in the fall of 2009, workers breaking ground for new burials in supposedly unused areas were routinely finding totally unidentifiable and unrecorded remains. Included in the desecrated sections was the area known as "Babyland," a part of the cemetery set aside for children and infants. The Cook County Sheriff went on record as having spoken to numerous mothers who could not find the graves of their children.

In January of 2010, inspired by the Burr Oak scandal, Illinois governor Pat Quinn signed the Illinois Cemetery Act, which mandated greater monitoring of cemeteries by local authorities. The new regulations will require cemetery owners, managers, and customer-service employees to be licensed and undergo continuing education courses. Cemeteries will be required to keep burial maps, which will be stored in a database maintained by the Illinois Department of Financial and Professional Regulation. The department also will be able to conduct audits and issue fines of up to $10,000 for violations ranging from poor grounds upkeep or other conduct deemed unprofessional. Because the department has the ability to look into past practices, director Brent Adams said that means the state could close Burr Oak.

In May of 2011, during bankruptcy proceedings, a federal judge approved a plan to place the cemetery into a trust that will use about a quarter of the $7 million insurance settlement to overhaul and manage Burr Oak. In the decision, the judgment included $50,000 for a memorial to those whose graves were desecrated. Sickeningly, those with loved ones at Burr Oak received an average settlement of $100, these litigants made up of the thousands who agreed to walk away from the mess. Each would have had to file individual suits, the costs into the thousands of dollars per party. For many of the economically strapped in question, it wasn't even a consideration to try. Others forfeited their payments, giving them up to a proposed

Administration building at Burr Oak Cemetery.

memorial fund. A third group, a little over 350, were the worst hit by obvious desecration, and their settlements were larger, but confidential. Still, the total dispersal to more than 350 persons was a scant 1.2 million dollars, or a little over $3,000 per case.

The Burr Oak scandal reminds us that, among the well-known or "celebrity" individuals buried at any given cemetery are the thousands upon thousands of the "ordinary" interred—the daily grinders, the husbands and wives, mothers and fathers, children and grandchildren, friends and colleagues: the citizens that make up our families, neighborhoods, and cities and, ultimately, our lives. We think that we lay them to rest once and for all. Until Burr Oak, it was—for many of those left behind—one of the only sure things in life.

Still, among the heartbroken "ordinary" mourners who will forever suffer the scandal at Burr Oak, there are, indeed, the mourners and rememberers of some of Chicago's most esteemed history-makers. And so the general public expressed horror beyond simple human reaction to the misdeeds at Burr Oak. A large part of Chicago—and American—history was disturbed in sync with the physical destruction of this overwhelmingly African-American burial ground.

Harlem Globetrotter **Inman Jackson** (1907–1973) slam-dunked himself into a plot at this Alsip site, where he keeps heavenly company with a host of more traditional Chicago sports superstars, including world heavyweight boxing champion **Ezzard Charles** (1921–1975), **J. Mayo Williams** (1894–1980), one of the first black players in the National Football League, and no less than four Negro League baseball players, **Jimmie Crutchfield** (1910–1993), **Ted "High Pockets" Trent** (d. 1944), Hall of Famer **Pete Hill** (1882–1951), and **James A. "Candy" Jim Taylor** (1884–1948).

Along with sports pioneers, Burr Oak is home to a staggering treasure trove of African-American jazz and blues talent, including blues musician **James Kokomo Arnold** (1901–1968), **George "Sonny" Cohn** (1925–2006), bandleader who died with ten members of his band in the Rhythm Nightclub Fire, and the woman who came to be known as "Queen of the Blues," Dinah Washington.

Dinah Washington (1924–1963) laid herself down at Burr Oak

Ruth Jones, known by her stage name of Dinah Washington (1924–1963), was called "Queen of the Blues."

at the age of 39, after devouring seven husbands and an endless stream of alcohol and drugs. As a legend among the many fans she left behind, however, her short life made no difference to her brilliance; she is as immortal as they come.

Born Ruth Jones in August 1924, the Tuscaloosa, Alabama, choir girl was hired by Lionel Hampton in 1943. Dinah sang with Hampton's band for three years, recording such smashes as "Evil Gal Blues" and "Salty Papa Blues."

After leaving the group, Washington turned to rhythm and blues, meeting with increased success and proving herself a versatile and talented artist. Later, her performances began to include hints of jazz, blues, and pop music, rounded out with favorite standards of the era. She also experimented with the new soul sound, becoming one of its most prominent early stars. Dinah recorded a string of hits in a number of vocal styles, including her most famous, "What a Difference a Day Makes."

Washington's broad appeal and obvious talent won her legions of fans and a fortune unknown to most black artists of the day. Reveling in her wealth, Dinah blossomed on a steady diet of jewels and furs, drugs and drinks—and men. As her career and confidence thrived, the beloved singer felt no need to ease up on her excess. At the age of 39, however, by all appearances content with both her public and personal lives, Dinah Washington died after overdosing on diet pills and liquor. She was buried with many tears at this suburban site.

Burr Oak shelters the remains of two other jazz legends, **Willie Dixon** (1915–1992) and **Otis Spann** (1930–1970).

A monumental presence at Chess Records, Dixon composed music, played bass on countless cuts, led the label's studio band, and arranged and produced the majority of the Chess blues blockbusters. After accompanying Chess on its way to major success, Dixon ducked out of the company to build up the new Cobra label on Chicago's West Side. Cobra immediately took off after Dixon's work with Otis Rush ("I Can't Quit You, Baby"). Willie stayed on to bolster the fledgling careers of artists like Buddy Guy and Magic Sam. As the '60s dawned, however, financial discord sent Dixon back across town to grateful Chess.

Another Chess mainstay, pianist Spann distinguished himself in the 1960s as a solo artist. He is best remembered, however, as the man at the keyboard in the Muddy Waters Band.

Celebrity hounds will want to make one final visit—to the grave of actor **Lexie Bigham** (1968–1995), whose movie credits included *Boyz in the Hood*, *Dave*, *Seven*, *South Central*, and *High School High*.

Despite all the joy to be found in the lives of the majority of Burr Oak's most famous residents, one grave leads many to tears: that of Emmett Till, victim of one of the most publicized instances of racial violence in civil rights history.

Emmett Louis Till (1941–1955) was an African-American Chicago child of 14 who was murdered in Mississippi while staying with relatives in the Delta. During his time there, Till reportedly flirted with Carolyn Bryant, a white, married woman, prompting Bryant's husband and his half-brother to seek revenge. The two abducted Till, beat him, and gouged out one of his eyes, finally shooting him in the head. They weighted his body and dumped his body in the Tallahatchie River, where it was found several days later and returned to his mother.

Before the burial at Burr Oak, Till's mother displayed her son in a glass-faced casket, to show the world the full brutality of Emmett's death. Spectators numbering in the tens of thousands came to view the corpse, and photographs of Till's body were published in newspa-

The murder of Emmett L. Till (1941–1955), beaten, shot, and dumped in a river when he innocently flirted with a white woman in Mississippi, was a major event in the Civil Rights movement, sparking national outrage. In 2005 his body was exhumed and autopsied as part of a recently reopened investigation.

pers and magazines around the world. The killers were acquitted of their crimes, but after the trial (and safe via double jeopardy) admitted to them in an interview.

Problems identifying Till affected the trial, partially leading to Bryant's and Milam's acquittals, and in 2004 the case was officially reopened by the Department of Justice, who ordered Till's casket opened in order to attempt a positive identification. After the exhumation of his grave in June 2005, Till had been reburied in a new casket, which is typical in exhumations. The original casket was to be held in safekeeping to be used as an exhibit at a memorial site. According to sources, the cemetery manager extorted the donated funds and removed the casket to a rundown shed on the cemetery property.

After the scandal of 2009, Till's glass-faced casket was found at Burr Oak during the Sheriff's investigation. The casket, in its dilapidated state, was given into the care of the Smithsonian's National Museum of African American History and Culture.

ST. BENEDICT CATHOLIC CEMETERY

4600 West 135th Street, Crestwood
www.catholiccemeterieschicago.org
Consecrated 1885

This modest site, managed by the office of St. Casimir, shelters many members of the Mantellate Sisters, Servants of Mary, including **Reverend Mother Louis Pedrini** (1875–1938), founder of the order's American congregation.

BACHELORS GROVE CEMETERY

Everdon Woods, Midlothian Turnpike & 143rd Street,
Unincorporated Bremen Township
Established circa 1844

This enigmatic site has been a thorn in the side of southwest suburban officials since the closing of the old Midlothian Turnpike in the 1960s, which barred the one-acre cemetery from vehicle traffic and simultaneously created the most legendary lovers lane in the metropolitan area. Even before this, vandals had begun to desecrate and dismantle the now-infamous site.

Part of Everdon Woods, across from the larger Rubio Woods Forest Preserve, Bachelors Grove (also known as Batchelor Grove, Old Bachelor's Grove, Bachelder's Grove, Batchelor's Grove, English Bachelor's Grove, Old Smith's, and others) was founded in the mid–nineteenth century as Everdon's Cemetery, hosting its first burial when Eliza Scott was interred in November of 1844, though evidence exists that the first burial—that of William B. Nobles—took place in 1838. For many years a placid place where families picnicked on Sundays and fished in the site's quarry pond, the burial ground began its aesthetic decline in the 1950s and '60s, when teenagers enjoying the surrounding woods initiated reports of mysterious flashing lights and a "magic house" that would appear and disappear from a clearing in the forest.

Since these earliest reports of a haunted Bachelors Grove, myriad tales have taken root in the area's fertile soil, which is credited as the place of origin of a number of popular modern American folktales. For example, these woods are supposed to have been the site where the original "Hooked Maniac" of urban leg-

The cemetery gate, seen here battered and torn in the 1990s, was never much of a deterrent to visitors, with plenty of gaps wide enough to step through.

end preyed on lovelorn victims after escaping from a mental institution. In addition, numerous other phantoms have joined the magic house in haunting the grove, including a two-headed man, a woman in white called "The Madonna of Bachelors Grove," ominous, darkly-hooded figures, and a man in a yellow suit who is reputed to appear and disappear in a shower of sparks.

Fueling the imaginative fire here are the ongoing reports of satanic worship alleged to have occurred at Bachelors Grove since the 1960s. Far from unfounded, such reports were authenticated with some frequency during the '70s, when hooligans in search of kicks routinely dug up graves and rearranged tombstones, some leaving animal remains and other grisly tokens as calling cards.

Though Bachelors Grove is still largely a heart-wrenching mess of a place these days, a growing frustration with the neglect—and bourgeoning appreciation of the site—has inspired a renewed effort to restore to the cemetery some its former dignity.

Originally settled in the early 1830s by British migrants from New England, a second influx of German settlers traveled to the

Bachelors Grove area during the 1840s. Though local popular history traces the site's name to four single men who migrated to these woods during the first phase of settlement, resulting in the designation as "Bachelors" Grove, local researchers now believe that the true spelling of the place name was Batchelder, and that the Grove was named for the family that had settled in the area in 1845. Still, the popular name of Bachelors Grove persists, despite the more common historical use of the hybrid "Batchelor" Grove name, among others. The last known burial of a body at Bachelors Grove took place in 1965; the last burial of ashes was recorded in 1989.

Burials after 1950 are rare, and some remains have been disinterred and moved from Bachelors Grove throughout the century as a result of the migration of families, the need for larger plots, and, later, the horror of families at the desecration of the grounds. Still, a search for the origins of the region should begin by walking the few hundred feet down the weed-choked road to the grove, where many of the area's earliest and most influential settlers have, in recent decades, endured a less than peaceful sleep.

Though anywhere from 150 to 200 persons are estimated to have been buried in this tiny enclosure, fewer than 20 headstones remain. Pilgrims to the infamous site are drawn to a few stones among the scant offerings, first among them the **"Fulton stone,"** a highly recognized feature of the cemetery. The largest stone still standing, the Fulton stone marks a substantial family plot in a small clearing near the entrance to the quarry pond. The stone stands over the graves of

The largest monument in the cemetery, the Fulton monument has proven impervious to vandals, being one of a very few to remain in its original location. Some of the cemetery's more sentimental visitors often leave toys, coins, or other gifts around the *Infant Daughter* headstone.

John Fulton (1838–1922) and **Hulda Fulton** (1849–1919), prominent early settlers of Tinley Park, and several of their children and grandchildren. An attendant stone reading *Infant Daughter* marks the grave of a grandchild, **Marcia May Fulton** (1914–1914), and is a popular site for visitors to place candy, coins, small toys, and other "grave goods" meant as gifts to the dead. Another infant, **Emma Fulton** (1867–1867), is also interred here, but her stone was given into the care of the Tinley Park Historical Society after being recovered from vandals. One wonders if the apparition known as the Madonna of Bachelors Grove (sometimes called "Mrs. Rogers") is that of Emma's older sister, **Louella Fulton Rogers** (1879–1944), who was struck by a hit and run driver and died of her injuries, or of Katherine Vogt, mother of Marcia May Fulton. Though Marcia May rests under the "Infant Daughter" stone at Bachelors Grove, her mother is buried in town at Zion Cemetery. Could she be here in spirit form, tormented because of the separation from her daughter? Also interred in the Fulton plot is **"Emma 2"**—a daughter born in 1868, the year after infant Emma's death. The second Emma's life wasn't much longer. She died in 1876, a mere eight years old. Some confusion tends to arise because a "memorial" marker was erected in town at Zion Cemetery near other burials of the Fulton family, listing these same Bachelors Grove burials. No bodies were ever moved, however, from the Grove. They remain at the Fulton Stone.

Near the entrance to the cemetery are two prominent markers. The base of the **Moss monument**, the top of which was once dragged to the gate by vandals, today stands safely at the entrance to the Tinley Park Historical Society. Buried at the plot

A gap torn in the fence on the north side of the cemetery allows for easy access to the pond, where vandals are thought to have deposited many of the headstones.

are **Richard Edmund Moss** and family. Near the Moss plot, at the base of a hallmark split tree, twin stones mark burials for Richard's daughter, **Laura (Moss) McGhee** (1887–1965) and husband **Robert McGhee** (1876–1939).

Also not far from the entrance is the celebrated **"quilted stone"**—a textured monument base—featured in a much-publicized photo taken during a visit by the Ghost Research Society in 1991, showing a woman in a long white gown perched on the stone in a placid pose. Like most of the stones in Bachelors Grove, the question of whether this base stands on the original grave site is unclear. Verifying whose stone was originally on this base is, at this time, impossible. Near the northwest corner and other points along the perimeter of the

The monument of Walter Patrick (~1817–1885), now detached from its base, has been moved a considerable distance from its original location.

cemetery, almost three dozen unsold plots remain empty, and set here and there in the wild brush of the central area, only a smattering of mysterious and often camouflaged stones and monument bases of a smattering of long-gone settlers remain. It's believed that a number of these missing stones may rest at the bottom of the quarry pond.

Fortunately, largely owing to the efforts of historian Brad L. Bettenhausen, a plat map was compiled in the mid-1990s based upon the original on display at the Tinley Park Historical Society, which was published along with background notes in the fall 1995 issue of the South Suburban Genealogical and Historical Society's journal, *Where the Trails Cross*. Gathering research from area maps, students of Bremen High School, and members of local historical societies, Bettenhausen matched up burial records and plot locations to create a picture of the true Bachelors Grove, despite the vandalism, missing stones, and waist-high foliage of recent years. The result is an intriguing tale of settlement and growth and, sadly, of decline.

For the past decade, the care of Bachelors Grove's physical grounds—and its complex history—has been primarily and lovingly tended to by volunteers, many of whom say they feel "called" to protect the area known to fans as simply "The Grove."

One of the greatest accomplishments of volunteers has been to map the cemetery and the trails surrounding it, trails which traverse past not only breathtaking pockets of flora and fauna, but the foundations of long-gone homes, silos, and other structures dating into the first part of the nineteenth century. On any given Sunday, sometimes hundreds of visitors pass quietly through the paths and navigate the woods to search for the hidden treasures of history, pursue their hobby of geocaching, and indulge their love of the past—and the paranormal. Over the last few years, the vignettes of years long gone have been sometimes spotted again: a couple sharing a bottle of wine and conversation, a casual picnic on a blanket spread over a stone, rock skippers on the banks of the quarry pond. Joining them are scenes the dead here wouldn't recognize: the ever presence of self-styled "ghost hunters," with cameras and recorders, patiently keeping vigil among the wildflowers and weeds.

The future of this, one of the most talked-about burial grounds on earth, remains uncertain. Clean up days are held by various volunteer groups several times a year to tend to the overgrowth of the surrounding woods, as volunteers wrestle weeds and dead trees for

A scattering of monuments at Bachelors Grove, looking west. This particular photo, posted to graveyards.com and Wikipedia, later was used as the basis of a widely distributed trading card.

burns headed by the Forest Preserve District. Talk continues of a possible draining of the quarry pond (rumored to have been a body dump for gangsters in the 1920s), the building of a new fence to replace the torn and tattered chain link enclosure, and the sale of the property itself to private interests. A constant tug of war continues between the powers that be (often largely elusive) and the powers that "wanna be": the passionate volunteers, followers, and fans of "the most haunted cemetery in the world."

Through it all, only time (and, ironically, the dead here) know the full history—and the end of the story—of Bachelors Grove.

ST. JAMES CATHOLIC CEMETERY
106th Street & Archer Avenue, Lemont
historicstjames.org
Consecrated 1837

More commonly known as "St. James at Sag Bridge," or simply "St. James, The Sag," this former Indian burial ground and French signal fort became a cemetery in 1837. Though St. Johannes Cemetery, one of the two burial sites at O'Hare International Airport, was also established that same year, burials at St. James were recorded before the official establishment of the cemetery, rendering it the Chicago area's oldest existing ossuary.

Downslope from the church, the cemetery has a separate entrance, with the name "Saint James— The Sag" on the gate.

As the oldest cemetery in the county, the cemetery has a fine collection of marble monuments in mid-nineteenth-century styles. The cross at right, at the graves of Hugh Ward (~1800–1877) and Catherine McManaman Ward (~1807–1877), is much admired by local taphophiles.

Located in Lemont Township, St. James-Sag takes its name both from the onsite Catholic church of St. James and for its location at Illinois Rte. 171 and the Calumet Sag Channel, but the church and its churchyard were established to serve Irish workers who dug another waterway, the Illinois and Michigan Canal, through the heavily wooded region along what is now Archer Avenue.

The construction of the I&M Canal provided a crucial link between the Great Lakes and the Illinois River, which had previously been separated by the so-called Chicago Portage, the low divide of prairie that frustrated explorers Marquette and Joliet in their travels north from the Mississippi via the Illinois and Des Plaines Rivers. In fact, it was Joliet who first introduced the idea of a canal, insisting that a minor one—of only half a league of prairie—would allow water traffic a clear shot from Lake Michigan to the Mississippi River and all points along its route. Ultimately, creating this crucial corridor would allow a much grander journey: a portage-free passage from New York to the Gulf of Mexico.

Joliet's vision went unheeded by the French Canadian government. Preoccupied with the fur trade, officials viewed a potential canal as a superfluity, as did the British government which took control of the portage region after the French and Indian War. After the American

The elevation drops sharply south of the church, high atop the river bluff. This land, too, was used for burials, with terraces, steps, and retaining walls installed on several levels.

Revolution, however, the establishment of military force became the priority, and the founding of Fort Dearborn, at the mouth of the Chicago River, began the trading boom that led to the re-emergence of talk about a canal. As always, talk was cheap. Though interest in a canal resurfaced in 1810, the necessary land was not secured for six more years, and it was another seven years before a Canal Commission was established by the state of Illinois.

The enormously slow pace of canal development kept steady. No money came to the commission, and the organization eventually folded. More than a decade passed before the forming of a new commission in 1835. Unlike its predecessor, the new body was empowered by the government to raise money toward its efforts and, finally, work on the Illinois & Michigan Canal was begun in the summer of 1836. The burst of energy and optimism that accompanied the onset of construction would prove short-lived, however. A relentless shortage of funding, made disastrous by the Panic of 1837, brought the sporadic work to an end in 1841. While the abandoned canal lay unfinished, investors were desperately sought by its commissioners, who struggled to secure funds from the east coast and even England. A full year later, the canalers took up their tools once more. At last, in 1848, 25 years after the establishment of the first Canal Commission, the locks were opened on the Illinois & Michigan Canal, and in April of that year, a cargo of sugar from New Orleans reached the docks at Buffalo, New York. American commerce would never be the same. Chicago itself was destined to become the very heart of that commerce, its population increasing an incredible 600 percent in the ten years after the dedication of the canal. But the success of the venture was not without a human cost.

The life of the canalers was often brutal, comprised of arduous, unsteady labor and uncertain and meager payment, underscored by a staggering communal disheartenment. Illness and death were among the inevitable byproducts of the project, and a number of Irish-American canalers were laid to rest near the site of construction, in the churchyard of St. James.

This bluffside burial ground would prove infinitely superior to the two cemeteries that had been established in 1835 in Chicago proper. Both city sites were located on the very banks of the lake; as a result, upkeep of the plots was difficult to impossible, and the shallow graves often became unearthed. Though St. James was, and is, surrounded by countless rivers, canals, minor lakes, and sloughs, its steep and sloping layout has brought it through more than 160 years of service.

At the highest point in the cemetery grounds is the church, built of local Lemont limestone beginning in 1853. Numerous improvements were made in later years, including addition of the steeple, buttresses, and stained glass windows.

MOUNT GLENWOOD MEMORY GARDENS

18301 East Glenwood-Thornton Road, Glenwood
Established 1908

In prewar Chicago, as elsewhere, African Americans attempting to form cooperative business ventures were usually in for disappointment. One of the only ways for a would-be business owner to gain any footing was by investing in a cemetery association. African Americans were constantly frustrated by efforts to be assimilated into the white cemeteries. For example, the March 4, 1910, edition of the *Chicago Weekly Defender* said that one white cemetery was running an advertisement specifying their grounds exclusively for the white race. And sliding price scales, adjusted according to the race of the customer, were so rampant among the white cemeteries that, in 1911, Edward Green, a black state legislator, pushed for passage of an amendment to the civil rights law forbidding lot sale discrimination.

While politicians like Green fought the good fight in their own arenas, black businessmen responded to discriminatory policies by founding cemeteries of their own. The first of these was Mount Glenwood, which opened in 1908, and which heralded itself as the only Chicago cemetery with a non-discriminatory clause in its charter.

Perhaps the most popular site here at Mount Glenwood is the

More things are wrought by prayer than this world dreams of, a line from Alfred Tennyson, graces the granite sign at the cemetery entrance.

One of several Masonic lodge plots, the Eureka Lodge monument proclaims a Prince Hall affiliation, an African-American branch of Freemasonry largely independent from the mainstream organization.

grave of Robert Poole. Born in Sandersville, Georgia, Poole became one of the first followers of Wallace Fard, who used the teachings of the Jehovah's Witnesses to dismember the theology of the Trinity and fully humanize the figure of Jesus Christ. His theory of racism, in which the white race was created by an evil black god, sparked tremendous controversy, but won Fard some important converts. Poole was the most fervent.

The son of a Baptist minister, Fard eventually changed Robert's name to the Muslim name of Kariem. Several years after Poole's conversion, Fard disappeared, and some accused his apprentice of foul play, claiming that Poole had his teacher murdered to make way for Poole's own leadership.

Taking the helm of the movement, Poole changed his name to **Elijah Muhammad** (1897–1975) and went on to convert the boxer Cassius Clay (Muhammed Ali) and another preacher's son, Malcolm

For 40 years, Elijah Muhammad (1897–1975) led the Nation of Islam. His marker is simple and modest, far smaller than the nearby red granite ledger purchased for his mother in 1958.

Little, who became Malcolm X.

Upon his death in 1975, Muhammad had headed the Nation of Islam for a full 40 years. Succeeding him was his son, Wallace D. Muhammad, who changed many of his father's doctrines to reflect a more orthodox Islam.

HOLY CROSS CATHOLIC CEMETERY & MAUSOLEUMS

801 Michigan City Road, Calumet City
www.catholiccemeterieschicago.org
Consecrated 1893

Legendary jazz drummer **Gene Krupa** (1909–1973) fidgets in his family plot at this Calumet City site.

A native Chicagoan, Krupa bought his first drum set with money earned from working as a window-washer and errand boy at the South Side Brown's Music Company. Though his passion for music eroded his grades, Krupa graduated high school and enrolled at Indiana's St. Joseph's College, where he studied under the classical guidance of Fr. Ildefonse Rapp. After less than a year of formal training, Krupa abandoned the classroom in favor of a career, spending the next years with commercial dance bands around Chicago. In

Behind the administrative building is a large garden crypt mausoleum complex, erected in several stages from 1983 to 1989, which includes walkways sheltered by glass roofs leading to courtyards with religious statuary.

the late '20s, Krupa found himself sitting through two musical shows a night at the local movie house, listening in rapt attention to a group of white jazz musicians called the Austin High Gang. It was the Gang's drummer, Dave Tough, who first took Krupa to see the legendary drummer, Baby Dodds. Krupa was instantly sold on black jazz, and he began modeling his own style on the patterns of Baby and other New Orleans drummers like Johnny Wells and Zutty Singleton. High on jam sessions with Bix Beiderbecke and Benny Goodman at the Three Deuces nightclub across from the Chicago Theater, Krupa finally recorded in 1927 with Austin High Gang members under the name

This striking figure mourns physician Robert Lenard (1874–1918), shot in the head in 1918 by a man who believed the doctor was having an affair with his wife. Dr. Lenard survived the shooting, but died of pneumonia six months later.

of McKenzie-Condon's Chicagoans. The session proved pioneering when Krupa insisted on using his entire set, against the wishes of producer Tommy Rockwell. The resulting driving beat set the

The J.B. Wyszynskich mausoleum, one of many such tombs at Holy Cross, includes the Polish word *rodzina* ("family") over the door.

standard for the Chicago sound in jazz.

Krupa was soon impressing the greatest musicians of his time, including the Gershwins during his work with the orchestra for their hit Broadway musical *Strike up the Band*. He went on to dazzling performances with Benny Goodman and Tommy Dorsey. By the late 1940s, however, Krupa needed to save his career, threatened as it was by a 1943 arrest for marijuana possession. He set about re-forming his own orchestra, brilliantly incorporating trends of the fledgling bebop movement.

Gene Krupa died in 1973 in Yonkers, New York, from heart failure during treatment for leukemia and emphysema. A requiem mass was held at local St. Dennis Roman Catholic Church, and his body returned to the Chicago that had raised him.

This particularly ornate example of a rustic monument, designed to resemble a tree trunk, includes a scroll with biographical details, lilies, ivy, a cross, and an alcove with a small marble statue of the Virgin Mary.

BURIALS
OUTSIDE OF
CEMETERIES

A bust of Senator Stephen Arnold Douglas (1813–1861) stands atop the sarcophagus housing the remains of the "Little Giant," within a monument designed by Leonard Wells Volk at 35th Street and Lake Shore Drive. The Illinois Historical Preservation Agency, which maintains the site, conducts annual celebrations on the Saturdays nearest his birth and death dates in April and June.

Aside from Ira Couch, whose Lincoln Park tomb still stands as it did when the area was City Cemetery, a number of other locals are interred in unconventional crannies, by choice or by circumstance.

One of the most notable is the tomb of **Stephen A. Douglas** (1813–1861), presidential opponent of Abraham Lincoln. The first state memorial to be erected in Illinois, the Douglas monument is the centerpiece of **Stephen A. Douglas Memorial Park** (35th Street & Lake Park Avenue, Chicago). Designed by renowned sculptor Leonard Volk,[464] the structure boasts a larger-than-life-sized likeness of the Little Giant.

Douglas became a leading figure in the Illinois Democratic Party and went on to debate Abraham Lincoln during a bid for the Illinois Senate and then the presidential election of 1860. After being defeated, Douglas supported the new president, lecturing in the border states on Lincoln's behalf.

Though his grave has been relocated, due in part to rampant vandalism, **Francis Stuyvesant Peabody** (1859–1922) continues to draw hundreds of teenagers a year to his Oak Brook estate, intrigued by the legends surrounding the late coal magnate.

When multimillionaire Peabody acquired nearly 850 acres of land in eastern Du Page County, he envisioned the site as an ideal home for him and his family. The resulting 39-room Tudor Gothic mansion emerged as the centerpiece of a lavish estate that included more than 12 acres of wetlands, nine acres of lakes and ponds, one-and-a-half acres of prairie, and nearly 70 acres of rolling lawns. Sadly, Peabody would not live to enjoy the site, which he christened **Mayslake** (Route 83 & 31st Street, Oak Brook) after his wife and daughter. Only three years after conceiving the project, Peabody was stricken with a heart attack while riding his horse on the estate grounds. Upon his death, Peabody's widow had her husband interred on the spot where he had died, and to mark the location she built over it a remarkable monument: the **Portiuncula Chapel**, an exact replica of the Chapel of St. Francis in Assisi, Italy.

The grieving Peabody family deserted the property after Francis's

---

[464] See Rosehill Cemetery entry for more of Volk's work.

death, and in the spring of 1924, the estate was sold to the Franciscan Order, who built a retreat house next to the mansion and a friary elsewhere on the grounds. Sometime after the change in title, the chapel was moved to its current location, facing Peabody's dream house.

Under cover of darkness, suburban curiosity-seekers have stolen upon the grounds of Mayslake for decades, undaunted by the monks who, until their move from the site in recent years, dealt with trespassers by apprehending them, taking them to the estate's little Portiuncula Chapel, and forcing them to pray through the night. The possibility of such punishment was worth the chance of finding the remains of the late Peabody, whose corpse was supposed to have been suspended in a glass casket filled with oil and interred somewhere on the estate.

Though Peabody's body was disinterred and relocated to one of the Archdiocesan cemeteries, the legend of Peabody's Tomb lives on, and there seems to be no end to the steady stream of believers determined to solve the Mayslake enigma.

Colonel Robert R. McCormick (1880–1955) rests on the grounds of his estate-turned-tourist attraction, **Cantigny** (1 South 151 Road, Wheaton). McCormick inherited the sprawling Red Oaks Farm from his grandfather, *Chicago Tribune* publisher Joseph Medill, who in the mid–1890s commissioned a country house from architect C.A. Collidge, designer of Chicago's Art Institute and public library. The resulting white frame colonial home was enlarged by McCormick in the 1930s when he added a bedroom wing, sitting rooms, servants' quarters, a new kitchen, an enormous library, and a private movie theater. By the time the building frenzy ended, Medill's 11-room country house had become a 35-room palace.

A World War I artillery officer in the First Division, McCormick renamed the estate Cantigny, after the division's 1918 battle— America's first major victory of the conflict. McCormick bequeathed the Cantigny estate to the people of Illinois, and five years after his death in 1955, the War Memorial of the First Division was opened to the public. Each year, Cantigny plays host to more than 100,000 visitors to its renowned museum and spacious gardens, and for tours

Beneath the white granite exedra on the grounds of Cantigny Estate in DuPage County are the graves of Amy Irwin McCormick (1880–1939) and Colonel Robert R. McCormick (1880–1955), publisher of the *Chicago Tribune*.

of the mansion and McCormick's placid garden tomb.

From **Clarence Darrow** (1857–1938) **Memorial Bridge** (approx. 58th Street, east of Cornell Avenue) in Jackson Park behind the Museum of Science and Industry, one may gaze across the lagoon where the attorney's ashes were deposited and reflect on Darrow's figurative and literal enrichment of the city's environment.

Wrigley Field (Clark Street & Addison Street) reportedly serves as the final resting place for numerous unofficial scatterings of cremains. Though such activities are officially disallowed, there was one exception who made the cut. **Charlie Grimm** (1898–1983), beloved manager of the Cubs, led the team to National League championships in 1932, 1935, and 1945. Born in St. Louis, Grimm first played for the Pittsburgh Pirates before being traded to the Cubs in 1945, with whom he would work for most of the rest of his life. Upon his death, Grimm's widow sanctioned the spreading of his ashes at Wrigley Field, which the park approved.

Grimm's cremains have some otherworldly company at Wrigley. **Steve Goodman** (1948–1984), prolific songwriter and die-hard

Cubs fan, who wrote several songs for his favorite team, including "Go Cubs Go" and "A Dying Cubs Fan's Last Request." Yet, he is most remembered for his American classic, "The City of New Orleans," which won singer Arlo Guthrie much acclaim.

Goodman himself was not fated to become an "old Cub fan," however. A year after the song was published, and only days before he was due to sing the national anthem at the Cubs' first post-season game since 1945, Steve Goodman died of leukemia at the age of 36. His friends sought to recreate the story of "A Dying Cubs Fan's Last Request," but the ballpark managers weren't too thrilled at the idea, and for three years the songwriter's ashes languished in a canister in a desk. Eventually, with the aid of a sympathetic security guard, Goodman's brother and friends smuggled a portion of the ashes into the park before a game. Though popular legend places the ashes beneath home plate, the clandestine funeral party instead stood in the bleachers, sang the song, and scattered the remains to the wind.[465]

---

[465] Eric Zorn, "Steve Goodman Rests in Little Pieces at Wrigley Field. Why Not Other Fans?" *Chicago Tribune*, October 2, 2007.

BURIALS
IN OUTLYING
SITES

Former grave of King Peter II Karadjordjevic (1923–1970) of Yugoslavia, who lived
in Illinois after being deposed in 1945. In early 2013 he was disinterred from the
church in Libertyville and repatriated to Serbia, where he was entombed in the royal
mausoleum.

Cemetery aficionados should note that in Illinois, as in any state, funerary intrigue extends outside the metropolitan area limits. The following are only a few of Illinois's many buried treasures.

A nineteenth-century cemetery takes up a half-acre of **Yorktown Shopping Center's parking lot** (Route 56/Butterfield Road & Highland Avenue, Lombard), having been established by William Boeger for the congregation of the Church of St. Paul, which once stood at Butterfield and Myers roads. Though the church closed its doors around the turn of the century, the cemetery remains, a pleasant peninsula in an ocean of automobiles.

Far south of the southernmost suburbs is the town of Metropolis whose **Masonic Cemetery** (R.R. #2) received the remains of **Robert Stroud** (1890–1963), the legendary "Birdman of Alcatraz." A pimp convicted for murder in Juneau, Alaska, Stroud was to spend 12 years imprisoned on McNeil Island for his crime, but was transferred to Leavenworth after attacking an orderly. There, just five years later, he stabbed a guard to death and was sentenced to be hanged. While he waited on death row, Stroud petitioned Mrs. Woodrow Wilson, begging for a lesser punishment. A week before his execution date, he was re-sentenced to life in prison.

With no chance of parole, Stroud had nothing but time, and he put it to good use. At Leavenworth, the convict had rescued a sickly bird, keeping it as a pet in his cell. Though this practice was not uncommon, Stroud's interest in his feathered friend grew into an obsession, and he eventually took in some 300 birds, caring for them in several cells that were allotted him by the prison administration. Far from an eccentric interest, Stroud's work with his birds was serious business. After

Robert Stroud (1890–1963) was buried in Metropolis in southernmost Illinois after spending most of his life in prison for two murders. A visitor has placed a tiny figure of a bird at the headstone of the famous "Birdman of Alcatraz."

engaging in formal research, the Birdman wrote two books: *Stroud's Digest on the Diseases of Birds* and *Diseases of Canaries*.

In 1942, Stroud was transferred to isolation in the notorious "D" block on Alcatraz, where his birds were barred. After ten years, the Birdman decided on a new project; he began to write the story of his life. Remarkably, Stroud's manuscript was published only a year after its completion, and Hollywood went wild for the story.

Stroud never saw his story played out on the silver screen. Like the chirping chums of his younger days, *The Birdman of Alcatraz*, with Burt Lancaster playing the title role, was banned from the infamous island, its subject left to a few more years of lonely reflection. He died in a prison hospital in 1963. His sister claimed the body and buried it in Metropolis, where she lived at the time. Stroud, during his lifetime, had never resided in Illinois.

Yugoslavia's last king was laid to rest in a Libertyville sanctum: **St. Sava Orthodox Monastery** (32377 North Milwaukee Avenue), headquarters of the Serbian Orthodox Diocese of the U.S. and Canada. The 11-year-old **Peter II Karadjordjevic (1923–1970)** took the throne in 1934, after the assassination of his father, Alexander I. Though he took official control six years later, he fled almost immediately afterward when the Germans invaded his kingdom and spent his self-imposed exile working at a savings and loan in California.

The grandson of Queen Victoria, Peter was destined to be buried with Victoria's own. When he died in 1970, however, the king was found to have specified in his will a burial at this Libertyville location. Interred in the monastery's onion-domed church, he became the only European monarch ever buried in the United States.

But nothing lasts forever. In January 2013, mere days ago as we write this, the body of King Peter was disinterred from St. Sava and flown to Belgrade, at the request of his son, Crown Prince Alexander. The king's body now lies, temporarily, in a chapel near the palace, while preparations are made for a state funeral to take place in May.[466]

St. Sava attracts a scattered population to its confines: Serbs from as far north as Milwaukee and as far south as Gary. Non-Serbs will

---

[466] Michael Holtz, "Remains of Yugoslavia's former king returned to Serbia from Libertyville," *Chicago Tribune*, January 22, 2013.

find ample evidence of the site's ethnic heritage: Like many Eastern European-Americans, St. Sava's Serbian visitors memorialize their dead with offerings of food and drink, left behind for the deceased after graveside picnics.

In the nearby town of Third Lake is another Serbian retreat: the **Monastery of the Most Holy Mother of God** (Route 45). Behind the monastery and gorgeous full-scale replica of a famed Medieval church stands a cemetery with row after row of black granite monuments, many inscribed with patriotic anotations. As a center of expatiate life, the site includes a playground and picnic facilities, only a few feet from the graveyard.

The **Elk Grove Cemetery** (under the off ramp for I-90 on Arlington Heights Road, Arlington Heights) boasts a wide range in age of markers, some dating to Colonial times. In fact, the cemetery shelters two veterans of the American Revolution.

Woodstock's **Oakland Cemetery** (Oakland Avenue & Jackson Street) cradles **Chester Gould** (1900–1985), creator of comic strip protagonist Dick Tracy. Born in Pawnee, Oklahoma, Gould dreamed of being a cartoonist, an aspiration lavishly supported by his newspaperman father, who published his seven-year-old son's drawings in the *Pawnee Courier Dispatch*. After going to the Oklahoma Agricultural and Mechanical College, Gould headed to Chicago with 50 dollars in his pocket. Over the next ten years, he worked at every paper in the city except the *Post*. In 1921, he returned to school to rethink his career.

By 1931, Gould had decided he was a failure. Struggling to support his wife, Edna, and their daughter, Gould threw his last artistic energies into a clinging hope: to sell a comic strip to the *Chicago Tribune–New York News* syndicate. After trying to sell them literally hundreds of ideas, he despondently sent off a few frames chronicling the adventures of a down-to-earth crime-fighter called "Plainclothes Tracy."

With Chicago in the grip of gangland rule, the concept of a heroic and honest detective proved golden. All *Tribune* publisher Joseph Medill required was a new name, and Gould furnished him with a beauty. Thus, "Dick" Tracy was born.

Near the westernmost point of Illinois, the tiny city of **Nauvoo** has a grave as its major tourist attraction: the above-ground crypt of **Joseph Smith** (1805–1844), Prophet of the Latter-Day Saints. As theocratic ruler of the Mormon settlement at Nauvoo, Smith had mobilized the city's militia—about 5,000 men—to shut down a newspaper critical of his regime. Charges of treason and incitement to riot were brought against Smith and his brother **Hyrum Smith** (1800–1844). The two were held at the county jail in nearby Carthage, awaiting trial. An angry mob stormed the jail, killing both Hyrum and Joseph. They now lie side-by-side, along with Joseph's first wife, **Emma Hale Smith** (1804–1879). Emma, who hadn't originally been keen on the idea of polygamy, seems to have fared a bit better than the other (estimated) 27 wives. As his only legally-recognized widow, she is the only one to share the crypt with the Smith brothers.

Actor and singer **Burl Ives** (1909–1995), narrator of holiday television classic *Rudolph the Red-Nosed Reindeer*, is buried under a black granite monument with a laser-etched portrait of himself in a pleasant churchyard on a hill in rural **Jasper County.** Activist and labor leader **"Mother" Mary Harris Jones** (1837–1930) rests in the **Union Miners' Cemetery** in Mount Olive, Macoupin County, surrounded by the miners for whom she marched and fought. Behind a modest house in **Galesburg**, Knox County, are the ashes of poet **Carl Sandburg** (1878–1967), under a granite boulder called "Remembrance Rock."

Two vice-presidents of the United States are buried in Illinois. Charles Dawes is, as previously mentioned, at Rosehill. The other is **Adlai Stevenson** (1835–1914), vice president under Grover Cleveland, buried in **Evergreen Memorial Cemetery** in Bloomington. In that same plot is his grandson, **Adlai Stevenson II** (1900–1965), governor of Illinois and two-time Democratic presidential candidate. The cemetery contains other notables as well: **David Davis** (1815–1886), senator from Illinois and associate justice of the U.S. Supreme Court, and **Dorothy Gage** (1898–1898), a five-month-old infant, whose sudden death inspired her uncle to write a book in her memory, naming the main character for her. Her uncle was Lyman Frank Baum. He called Dorothy's book *The Wonderful Wizard of Oz*.[467]

In **Alton City Cemetery**, on the river north of St. Louis, is one of the most spectacular monuments to be found in the state. At the cemetery's edge, a 93-foot column rises above a flight of steps, flanked by pedestals supporting bronze eagles. Atop the column is a 17-foot bronze statue of winged Victory, sounding a trumpet. The column is set on a raised terrace, surrounded by a semicircular granite wall. This monument honors the city's greatest hero, **Elijah Parish Lovejoy** (1802–1837). A newspaper editor, Lovejoy was an abolitionist in Southern Illinois, an area where a significant proportion of the population was aligned with the states that would soon form the Confederacy. He published the *Alton Observer*, a paper with a decidedly anti-slavery slant. Three times, mobs of Southern sympathizers attacked and destroyed Lovejoy's printing presses. On the fourth occasion, he had hidden the machinery in a warehouse, and was watching over it with armed guards. The mob fired guns at the warehouse and set it on fire. Lovejoy was shot with a shotgun, dying on the spot. The press was broken up and thrown into the Mississippi.

Lovejoy's body would rest in an unmarked grave in Alton City Cemetery until the political climate changed. In 1860, his grave was located and a marble ledger placed over it, with an iron fence surrounding the plot. Plans began for an awe-inspiring monument, though it would be more than 30 years before work began. In the 1890s, sculptor R. P. Bringhurst of St. Louis designed the monument, which would be built

Heroic monument of Elijah Lovejoy (1802–1837) at Alton City Cemetery, floodlit at night.

[467] "Our History," Evergreen Memorial Cemetery, http://www.evergreen-cemetery.com/our-history/.

The coffin of Abraham Lincoln (1809–1865), the only President of the United
States buried in Illinois, is under the floor of the tomb, parallel to this marble
sarcophagus and about a foot in front of it.

by Culver Stone Company of Springfield. The monument was dedicated in 1897,[468] and has been a symbol of the city ever since, appearing on postcards and souvenir plates and spoons.

And, of course, the second most-visited cemetery in the United
States[469] is in Central Illinois. In **Oak Ridge Cemetery**, northwest
of the state capital Springfield, is the magnificent tomb of **Abraham
Lincoln** (1809–1865), sixteenth President of the United States, the
first president to be assassinated, and the first to be embalmed. Daily,
busloads of tourists and schoolchildren arrive to rub the nose on the
bronze face of Lincoln mounted on a pedestal in the tomb's fore-
court, then proceed, usually quite boisterously, to enter the mausoleum. Once inside, the chill marble walls and the watchful eyes of
guides employed by the state are enough to quiet the visitors. As one
approaches the rear of the tomb through the interior corridor, the
sense of solemnity deepens.

---

[468] "Monument," Illinois Historic Preservation Agency, http://www.state.il.us/hpa/lovejoy/
monument.htm.
[469] Oak Ridge Cemetery, http://www.oakridgecemetery.org.

In a semicircular chamber, behind a velvet rope, surrounded by flags and wreaths, stands a six-foot-long sarcophagus of reddish-brown granite. The president is buried beneath the floor, parallel to the sarcophagus, a foot or two in front of it—his walnut-and-lead coffin was encased in reinforced concrete to deter grave-robbers.[470] Behind the wall on the opposite side of the corridor, First Lady **Mary Todd Lincoln** (1818–1882) and children **Edward** (1846–1850), **William** (1850–1862), and **Thomas** (1853–1871) are entombed. The only member of the president's immediate family not present is Robert Todd Lincoln (1843–1926), secretary of war under Garfield and later ambassador to the United Kingdom. He earned a place for himself at Arlington National Cemetery.

At the rear of the softly lit burial chamber, above the stained-glass window, are the words of Secretary of War Edwin Stanton, spoken in a Washington boarding house seconds after the horrifically wounded president breathed for the last time: *NOW HE BELONGS TO THE AGES.*

---

[470] See Graceland Cemetery chapter for more on the George Pullman story.

CEMETERY RESTORATION AND PRESERVATION

Contributed by Angie Johnson, *www.walkamongthedeadgirl.com*

I want to give hope to our cemeteries in Illinois. The idea of restoration and preservation is starting to spread across the state. There are a dozen or more cemeteries in each county that have fallen due to weathering and vandalism. I live in Piatt County in central Illinois. We are very fortunate that a gentleman by the name of John Heider has restored almost all of our older cemeteries.

If you are interested in learning to do restoration work, then I recommend seeking out our state's restoration programs. Familiarize yourself first with the **Illinois Historical Preservation Agency**. In Illinois a permit is needed to do work in an unregistered cemetery. The IHPA website (www.illinoishistory.gov/cemetery/) contains Illinois cemetery laws, information on restoration classes the state provides, and contact information.

The **Association for Gravestone Studies** (www.gravestonestudies.org) is a wonderful organization for cemetery enthusiasts. The Illinois chapter was started in the fall of 2011. We hold public education meetings throughout the year covering various topics in history, genealogy, and the preservation of cemeteries. Our chapter's goal is to expand our reach into all corners of the state, connect others with the resources in their own counties, and share the opportunities the national organization has to offer its members.

I have always been a firm believer that if you want something bad enough it will happen. If every county's interested volunteers came together, got trained, and started working, just think how many cemeteries could be conserved in the next 20 years, perhaps with plans for future maintenance.

I love the satisfaction of restoring cemeteries, but the greater gift for me is the joy a rejuvenated cemetery brings to the families who have loved ones buried there. Join me in my quest to spread the message of cemetery restoration and preservation so that when we too lay to rest, we can be assured that those who come after us will protect our final resting places.

—Angie Johnson, Illinois Chapter chairperson for the Association of Gravestone Studies

SELECTED BIBLIOGRAPHY

Bielski, Ursula. *Chicago Haunts: Ghostly Lore of the Windy City*. Chicago: Lake Claremont Press, 1997.

Bielski, Ursula. *More Chicago Haunts: Scenes from Myth and Memory*. Chicago: Lake Claremont Press, 2008.

Brown, John Gary. *Soul in the Stone: Cemetery Art from America's Heartland*. Lawrence, KS: University Press of Kansas, 1994.

Cutler, Irving. *The Jews of Chicago: From Shtetl to Suburb*. Urbana, IL: University of Illinois Press, 1996.

Floro-Khalaf, Jenny, and Cynthia Savaglio. *Mount Carmel and Queen of Heaven Cemeteries*. Charleston, SC: Arcadia Publishing, 2006.

Grissom, Carol A. *Zinc Sculpture in America, 1850–1950*. Newark, DE: University of Delaware Press, 2009.

Graf, John, and Steve Skorpad. *Chicago's Monuments, Markers, and Memorials*. Charleston, SC: Arcadia Publishing, 2006.

Historical Society of Oak Park and River Forest. *Nature's Choicest Spot: A Guide to Forest Home and German Waldheim Cemeteries*. Oak Park, IL: Historical Society of Oak Park and River Forest, 1998.

Jackson, Kenneth, and Camilo Jose Vergara. *Silent Cities: The Evolution of the American Cemetery*. New York: Princeton Architectural Press: 1989.

Kaczmarek, Dale. *Windy City Ghosts*. Oak Lawn, IL: Ghost Research Society Press, 2006.

Keister, Douglas. *Stories in Stone: A Field Guide to Cemetery Symbolism and Iconography*. Salt Lake City, Utah: Gibbs Smith, 2004.

Kezys, Algimantas, ed. *A Lithuanian Cemetery*. Chicago: Lithuanian Photo Library and Loyola University Press, 1976.

Lanctot, Barbara. *A Walk Through Graceland Cemetery*. Chicago: Chicago Architecture Foundation, 1988.

Markus, Scott. *Voices from the Chicago Grave: They're Calling. Will You Answer?* Holt, MI: Thunder Bay Press, 2008.

Sawyers, June Skinner. *Chicago Portraits: Biographies of 250 Famous Chicagoans*. Chicago: Loyola University Press, 1991.

Sclair, Helen. "Ethnic Cemeteries: Underground Rites," in *Ethnic Chicago: A Multicultural Portrait, Fourth Edition*, edited by Melvin G. Holli and Peter d'A. Jones. Grand Rapids, MI: William B. Eerdmans Publishing Company, 1995.

Sclair, Helen. *Greater Chicagoland Cemeteries: Based on the tour and mini-tour notes from the 1994 AGS Conference*. Worcester, MA: The Association for Gravestone Studies, 1994.

Simon, Andreas. *Chicago, the Garden City: Its Magnificent Parks, Boulevards, and Cemeteries*. Chicago: The Franz Gindele Printing Co, 1893.

Sinkevitch, Alice, and Laurie McGovern Petersen. *AIA Guide to Chicago*. Boston: Houghton Mifflin Harcourt, 2004.

Sloane, David Charles. *The Last Great Necessity: Cemeteries in American History*. Baltimore: The Johns Hopkins University Press, 1991.

Taylor, Troy, Mark Sceurman, and Mark Moran. *Weird Illinois*. New York: Barnes & Noble Books, 2005.

Vernon, Christopher. *Graceland Cemetery: A Design History*. Amherst, MA: University of Massachusetts Press, 2011.

INDEX

39–40
Grand Army of the Republic
  George G. Meade Post 444, 178
  Oak Woods lot, 153
Graves, Dexter, 33
graveyards.com, 2, 3, 9, 54, 254, 372
Gray, Harold Lincoln, 293
Greek cemeteries/cemetery sections.
  See Arlington Cemetery; Elmwood
  Cemetery and Mausoleum; Evergreen
  Cemetery
Green, Dwight, 79
Green, Edward, 377
green funerals, 223
Green Mill, the, 303
Green Ridge Cemetery, 312
Grimm, Charlie, 387
Grinius, Dr. Kazys V., 335–336
Griswold, Sheldon Munson, 218
Grosch, Margaret M., 201
Gruel, William & Johanna, 57
Gudehus, "Baby" Sophia, 255
Gunness, Belle Sorenson, 261–262
Gunsaulus, Rev. Frank, 27
Gusenberg, Frank, 118
Gusenberg, Peter, 188
Gypsies. *See* Romany cemetery sections

H

Haase, Ferdinand, 5, 249, 250, 264, 267,
  269, 274
Hackett, John, 210
Hagenback-Wallace Circus train, 272
Hagermeister, Minnie, 259
Halas, George ("Papa Bear"), 228–229
Halas, George, Jr., 231
Hannah, Alexander, 200
Harlem Globetrotters, 123, 359, 363
Harris, Eddie, 144
Harris, Paul Percy, 179
Harrison, Carter Henry, 40, 41, 197, 256
Harrison, Carter Henry, Jr., 40–41
Hartnett, Charles ("Gabby"), 231
Harvey, Patrick and Bertha Hirsch, 54
Haslam, Robert, 171
Hayes, Charles M. and Ella Mae, 120–121

"Haymarket Affair"/"Haymarket Riot," 32,
  255–258
Haymarket Martyrs' Monument, 255, 257,
  258
Haywood, "Big Bill" 258
Hazelgreen Cemetery, 359–360
Healy, Patrick J., 196
Heath, Monroe, 147
Hebrew Benevolent Cemetery. *See* Jewish
  Graceland and Hebrew Benevolent
  Cemeteries
Hebrew Benevolent Society of Chicago, 47,
  48, 49, 50, 52
Heider, John, 398
Hemingway, Dr. Clarence and Grace Hall,
  264
Hemingway, Ernest, 264
Hendee-Brown monument, 325
Henner, David G., 270
Herting, John, 67
Hesing, Anton C. and Louise Lamping,
  64–65
Hiker, 91
Hill, Pete, 363
Hinckley, Otis Ward, 80
Hinsdale Animal Cemetery and Crema-
  tory, 314–320
Hippach, Franz Joseph and Lena Everling,
  313
Hippach, Louis Albert, 313
Hippach Chapel, 313
Hogan stone, 204
Hogg, David, 200
Holabird & Roche, 23, 24, 210
Holocaust Memorial (New Light Cem-
  etery), 212
Holocaust memorial (Tower of Remem-
  brance), 235
Holy Cross Catholic Cemetery & Mausole-
  ums, 379–381
Holy Sepulchre Catholic Cemetery &
  Mausoleum, 327, 353–356
homestead graveyards, 5
"Hooked Maniac," 368
Hopkins, John Patrick, 197
Horner, Dilah Levy, 131
Horner, Henry (governor), 131

ACKNOWLEDGMENTS

The exploration of graveyards, it would seem, is a solitary endeavor. Grab a camera and a map, pick a destination, get in the car, and go—that is how I began, more than 16 years ago, having nothing more in mind than a pleasurable day surrounded by history and architecture. But in doing this I have encountered a number of people who educated, helped, and inspired me. *Graveyards of Chicago* would not exist if not for their support.

David Wendell, who in the 1990s was on-site historian at Rosehill, was of tremendous help to me in my earliest days of exploring Chicago graveyards. Not only did he drive with me around Rosehill, pointing out all the best monuments and telling their stories, but he was also eager to give advice on where else I should be exploring. He recommended a dozen graveyards that I had not yet been to, telling me what I'd find there and where to look for it. I still remember our first encounter, how I was frantically scribbling on the back of my map the names of mobsters and mayors, plutocrats and socialists, heroes and murderers, and how I absolutely had to go to Forest Home next. Later, he sent me the notes he had painstakingly accumulated, long before the time of Google and online archives, when research meant paging through ancient books or spending hours twisting the knobs of microfiche machines. His newspaper clippings and handwritten notes were invaluable in the writing of this book.

As I arrived at each location, I would stop in at the office, ask for a map and a list of historic points of interest (most sites didn't have the latter). I am in debt to the mostly anonymous authors of these documents, some of them clearly written decades before I first received one as a photocopy, their authors having long since departed.

I thank those who work in the cemetery offices for their willingness to perform lookups (sometimes, a quite lengthy list), to share what they know, and to offer recommendations on what monuments I'd likely find interesting. In particular, Tom Berry at Calvary provided me with a number of maps and clippings and described the history of the cemetery and how its terrain had changed over the years. Al Gruen, President of New Light Cemetery, invited me to the chapel dedication and provided historical information.

In their stone-carving studio next to St. Boniface, Jan Gast and the late Bert Gast gave me information on their company's history and some of the remarkable works of art they've created. Some years later, Seven Swinbank of Troost Monuments sent me a packet of valuable historical information, including a rare copy of Helen Sclair's conference guide book.

Other cemetery explorers have shared their knowledge, photos, and observations with me, as well as shared in the joy of discovery and awe. Several have provided websites that continue to be valuable tools in locating interesting graves and graveyards. Larry Kestenbaum's *Political Graveyard* named the burial sites of thousands of senators, governors, and congressmen; I used it as a "to-do list," seeking to visit the graves of major Illinois politicians, supplemented by Father John McNalis's list of Chicago mayor burial sites. Jim Tipton's *Find-a-Grave*, now approaching 100 million burial records, is a hugely useful database of common people as well as famous people. I used it not only to locate the famous burials in Chicago-area graveyards long ago, but, more recently, for fact-checking names and dates of birth and death for this book. Finally, the now-mothballed *City of the Silent* site of Joel Gazis-Sax was fascinating reading for me in the first year of graveyards.com's existence, the place where I first learned much about graveyards—and was inspired to create a website about graveyards.

John Martine, who knows every inch of Forest Home and Waldheim, showed me a few of the more obscure sights there, sent me copies of documents from his collection, and provided photos and personal memories of Helen Sclair.

Minda Powers-Douglas of Moline, author of the book on Chippiannock Cemetery, gave me a guided tour of her local graveyards.

Michael Kleen, expert on the ghosts of Charleston and Rockford, publishes the *Legends and Lore of Illinois* series, featuring, among other stories, the haunted legends about Chicago-area cemeteries.

David Habben, who has visited and photographed many of the same cemeteries as I have. I consulted his photos to view details that were missing or unclear in my own.

Troy Taylor, author and researcher, has written extensively on Illinois hauntings, many of which are associated with graveyards, as well as other aspects of the state's history. His books inspired me to visit a number of sites, and are a welcome alternative to the official histories.

Angie Johnson, graveyard explorer of central Illinois, accompanied me on a whirlwind five-county tour of her area, then came to Chicago to see Forest Home and Waldheim. As the Illinois State Coordinator for the Association for Gravestone Studies, Angie now organizes meetings of our fellow graveyard geeks, with presentations on history, research, and preservation.

Carol Slingo, Jim Kube, Gail Pepin, Alan Gornik, C.T. Thieme, Lynn Johansen, Susanne Frumin Peters, Rachel Black, Karl Kochmann, Bruce Cline, Jim Craig, and other Illinois taphophiles (graveyard enthusiasts, that is), have regularly shared stories of their expeditions and photographs, either by contributing to my website or posting to their own sites. Their fine work lets us visit cemeteries that aren't conveniently close, or revisit those we've already been to, seeing them from a different perspective.

And, going further afield, the work of such notable cemetery researchers and photographers as Beth Santore, John Thomas Grant, Ed Snyder, and Douglas Keister inspires us all.

Dale Kaczmarek, president of the Ghost Research Society, who has been researching supernatural phenomena in the Chicago area for almost 40 years, has generously shared his notes and graveyard photographs with me. He told me of an abandoned graveyard in the woods (Sauerbier-Burkhardt), and provided photos of early Bachelor's Grove before much of the vandalism took place.

Jim Graczyk, Stan Suho, John Cachel, Mark and Chris Wallbruch, Joey Tito, Nicole Tito, Lisa Krick, the late Dave Guss, and other members of the Ghost Research Society conducted investigations at a number of haunted sites, some of them graveyards. Together, we explored Bachelor's Grove, "Graveyard X" near Decatur, Crown Hill in Indianapolis, and, on a brutally hot June day, the graveyards of Woodstock.

Forever foremost among the Illinois taphophiles is Helen Sclair, who was the acknowledged expert on anything to do with Chicago cemeteries. Though we never met, we spoke on the phone when I was just getting started, and she gave me some tips on where to go. Helen told me of Bohemian National Cemetery's magnificent columbarium, of the colorful graves at St. Nicholas, and the Chinese burial practices at Mount Auburn. Much of our research began with Helen's written works and the newspaper articles that cited her; without her decades of hard work, much of Chicago's graveyard history would be lost.

I thank my friends, for tolerating my strange hobby and my habit of interjecting "He's buried at such-and-such cemetery" whenever a famous local corpse is mentioned. This includes my Monday night dinner crew: Rachael Bild, Craig Brozefsky, Cinnamon Cooper, Rebecca Epstein, Anna Goldberger, Jael Goldsmith-Weil, Rebeca Mojica, and Esther Verreau. Their recent gift of some old embalming fluid bottles (including the hard-to-find Frigid Junior bottle with the baby on the label!) is much appreciated. And, as well, Stephen Geis, Sandy Wood, Allison and Ashley Foxborn, Michael Balk, Kyle and Natalie Therriault, and Cindy Garland, all have patiently listened as I spoke about graveyards at every opportunity.

David Jones and Brandy Sargent, my friends and neighbors for ten years before moving to Portland, now accompany me on graveyard expeditions whenever I visit them or they visit me. Since the publication of the first edition, their two young daughters Kenna and Leila have joined us, eagerly hopping from one plot to the next, peering into broken mausoleum windows with a flashlight in the hopes of seeing a coffin, and listening in good spirits to my descriptions of tragedies like the Iroquois fire, and why mausoleum crypts need air vents.

And on each of my southern Illinois expeditions, my parents Bob and Sue Hucke of Millstadt would participate, traveling with me on day-long expeditions to such places as Calvary Cemetery in St. Louis, the famous Miles Mausoleum in Randolph County, Kaskaskia Island, Fort de Chartres, and more. Each of my visits home now includes a graveyard crawl of some sort, and their patience and understanding is much appreciated.

I thank my publisher, Sharon Woodhouse, who initially conceived of this project in 1998, who continued to keep it alive then in spite of my horrible procrastination habit, and who made a proper book out of our mess of documents and photos.

And, finally, I thank my co-author, Ursula Bielski, who has been a delight to work with. With the first edition, we did our parts separately, but in today's more connected world the second edition has been a much closer collaboration. Throughout the process, we were reading each other's work, offering comments, and choosing where to focus our energies next. I have thoroughly enjoyed the time we spent on this project.

—Matt Hucke

Despite all our work to revise it from its original form, this book is still far from comprehensive. In fact, it could be described most accurately as an introduction—an invitation to begin excavating the endless surprises buried with our bereaved urbanity. Such digging could go on forever; the determined have a staggering number of resources to exhaust in their quest for a comprehensive knowledge of Chicago's cemeteries. Just as this book is far from complete, so is the list of thanks to follow.

Attempting to acknowledge all who have contributed to this project would be as impossible as cataloging every grave in Cook County. We can only make a valiant effort, knowing the whole time that we are failing.

In this effort, however, I will start by thanking the one person who has done more for the cause of graveyards than anyone else: my co-author Matt Hucke, whose *Graveyards of Chicago* website provides an ever-growing cache of photos and information on cemeteries both dazzling and dilapidated. For his years of effort that can be described only as tireless and loving, I thank him for all the graveyard lovers who, less fortunate than us Chicagoans, have come to know our cemeteries through his beautiful photographs and companion research. He is a joy to work with. If everyone cared as much about what they do, it would be a wonderful world indeed.

Two of Chicago's most beloved researchers have left us since the first edition of this book. No one can ever take their places. Many Chicagoans knew local historian Helen Sclair as "The Cemetery Lady," owing to her longtime devotion to the discovery and dissemination of funerary facts. Sclair regularly shared her wealth of knowledge in formal seminars offered at Chicago's Newberry Library, and finished out her days actually living at Chicago's Bohemian National Cemetery, where she now rests. You'll find Matt's tribute to her in a sidebar in this volume.

My own lifelong hero, Richard T. Crowe, "Chicago's Original Ghost Hunter," passed through the gates of Resurrection Cemetery for the last time in June of 2012, where he now slumbers in his family's plot near his favorite girl, Resurrection Mary—known as Chicago's most famous ghost—whose name he brought out of the stockyards and taverns and to the world. Crowe did much in bringing life to the cemeteries of Chicago through his rich folk stories, and he often boldly included cemetery visits on his famed Chicago Supernatural Tours. Much of what Chicagoans know about their cemeteries are the tales they learned from Richard of Resurrection Mary on Archer Road, Julia Buccola and Al Capone at Mount Carmel, the children of Our Lady of Angels at Queen of Heaven, and the Miracle Child at Holy Sepulchre. His stories, his voice—and the voice he gave our dead—will be missed.

So many readily-available resources are too vast to mention by name; cemeteries themselves often provided maps and guides, and some even books or booklets detailing the achievements of their residents. A number of such titles are detailed at the back of this book. Branch libraries and archives, too, provided untold literary treasures, as well as historical documents invaluable for the independent cemetery historian. Local historical societies and associations often house libraries rife with books, plot maps, and burial records, and genealogical societies will often assist researchers in locating death records, obituaries, genealogies, and settlement information. Ethnic societies, too, maintain similar resources for use in documenting the settlement of their specific cultures; cemetery histories and records often make up a substantial part of their holdings. Readers are encouraged to explore these resources on their own. So much more information is out there to be discovered. In my own research, I am especially grateful to Brad Bettenhausen and the whole staff of the Tinley Park Historical Society, and to June Oulund and the other members of the Schiller Park Historical Society.

A number of online resources need recognition as well, including the aforementioned *Graveyards of Chicago* website; Cook County, IL GenWeb Research Resources—for expansive genealogical and general cemetery information; the site maintained by the Catholic Cemeteries of Chicago; and, for hours of fun, the intriguing *Find-a-Grave* site that efficiently traces the plots of thousands of notable and notorious personalities around the world. All provided much-needed clues and tips in piecing together this huge puzzle.

Owing to the staggering amount of information on the subject, my own scholarly tour of Chicago's cemeteries was certainly no cake walk. In addition to scouring the above resources for seemingly endless minutiae, I relied on a number of individuals for both scraps and heaping helpings of information and assistance in completing the final manuscript, among them Brandon Zamora, whose diligent research efforts brought so much life to the personalities remembered in these pages; Anne Fitzpatrick, who located for me a number of elusive personalities through her endless resourcefulness; Dagmar Bradac, who graciously procured and bravely loaned a precious volume of information on Bohemian National Cemetery; and Augie Alesky, who sent from his Centuries and Sleuths bookstore in Oak Park a guidebook on Forest Home and Waldheim Cemeteries to aid us in our cause. I must mention the remarkable Alfred Opitz and Daniel Pogorzelski, both walking, talking encyclopedias of Chicagoana; Dolores Bielski, who clipped dozens of newspaper and magazine articles, related to our subject and kindly shared her own books on Graceland Cemetery; and, most overwhelmingly, David Wendell, whose inexhaustible stores of information could fill at least a hundred volumes. I will never forget our many walks through Rosehill Cemetery, though so much time has slipped away.

Pamela Bannos and her *Hidden Truths* site about Chicago City Cemetery provided some of the most important updates for this volume, as did the information provided by Dunning Asylum researcher Silvija Klavins-Barshney; John Stephenson and Pete Crapia with their Bachelors Grove websites and gracious patience with many questions; and Linda Legnar Romano, who continues to find the most remarkable contacts at every turn and enthusiastically share them and her endless information.

One of the best parts of this book was getting to know Robinson Woods and its Indian Burial Ground with archaeologist Dan Melone and Robinson descendent Verlyn "Buzz" Spreeman. The many happy hours spent there together—and my stronger friendships with these incredibly knowledgeable and gracious men—were a true highlight of my research. I look forward to many more adventures to come as the Robinson story unfolds.

In preparing the finished tome, the usual suspects deserve every accolade: David Cowan, for his initial readings of the manuscript, Todd Petersen, for his design work, and of course, Sharon Woodhouse, whose skill in every aspect of publishing continues to astound me. Thanks, too, to Bruce Clorfene, Tim Kocher, and Brandon Zamora whose fine production work on the first edition helped make this second edition possible.

One of the best parts of life is the time spent at these cemeteries with those who love them too, and I am every day grateful for my fellow taphophiles, fellow enthusiasts, Len Dorman—and his patient wife, Gail Thomas; Dave and Kathy Wismer and their cool kids; Karl K.; Scott Markus; Mike Spudic and his wonderful wife, Wanda—the best friends anyone could have. And thanks, of course, to the cemeteries themselves, whose patient managements allow us to pursue our obsession with our many walks, rendezvous, picnics, and prolific picture-taking at their sites.

Finally, gratitude is eternally due to my late father, Adalbert S. Bielski, who—when I was ten years old—opened up a whole new world by giving me driving lessons in Graceland Cemetery.

—Ursula Bielski

ABOUT MATT HUCKE

Matt Hucke has explored and photographed over 1,100 graveyards, cemeteries, and mausoleums since 1995, most of them in Illinois. His website, *graveyards. com*, began in August 1996, with a mere 12 featured cemeteries, each with three to ten photos. As of 2013, the site now has over 10,000 photos, comprehensive listings of all known cemeteries in Illinois, and mapping tools used by genealogists, researchers, and taphophiles throughout the state.

Hucke grew up near St. Louis and moved to Chicago in 1993. He has lived for most of the time

Photo by Laurel Mellien.

since in Rogers Park, relocating to Logan Square in 2005. He works as a web developer and Linux sysadmin, using open-source tools and programming languages to build on-line shops and order fulfillment systems for a variety of small local companies.

His cemetery photography has appeared on numerous websites, in both editions of *Chicago Haunts*, in *More Chicago Haunts*, in the *Washington Post*, on the cover of a Faye Kellerman detective novel, on *Topps* trading cards, and has even inspired the design of a mausoleum-themed card game.

Matt's favorite Chicago-area graveyard is Forest Home, which he appreciates for its solitude and for the diversity of persons buried there.

He lives with cats named Harold and Maude.

ABOUT URSULA BIELSKI

Ursula Bielski is the author of the critically acclaimed *Chicago Haunts* book series, the founder of the award-winning Chicago Hauntings Ghost Tours, and the host of PBS's *The Hauntings of Chicago.* An historian by training, Bielski has been writing and lecturing about Chicago's supernatural folklore and the paranormal for nearly 25 years, and is recognized as a leading authority on the Chicago region's ghostlore and cemetery history.

Ursula's interests in Chicago ghost hunting began at a young age. She grew up in a haunted house on Chicago's North Side and received an early education in Chicago history from her father, a Chicago police officer, who introduced her to the ghosts at Graceland Cemetery, Montrose Point, and the old lockup at the storied Maxwell Street Police Station. Since that time Ursula has been involved in countless investigations of haunted sites in and around Chicago, including such notorious locales as Wrigley Field, the Congress Hotel, the Indiana Dunes, the Red Lion Pub, Hull House, Bachelors Grove Cemetery, Rose Hill Cemetery, haunted Archer Avenue, Chinatown, the Eastland disaster site, Death Alley, Dillinger's Alley, and the St. Valentine's Day Massacre site. Her paranormal travels have also led her to investigate sites as diverse and infamous as the Bell Witch Cave in Tennessee; the Oshkosh, Wisconsin, Opera House; New Orleans's House of the Rising Sun; the City Cemetery in Key West, Florida; and the Civil War Battlefield at Gettysburg, Pennsylvania.

Aside from her writing, Ursula has been featured on numerous television documentaries, including productions by the A&E Network, The History Channel, The Learning Channel, SyFy, The Travel Channel, and PBS. She's been a judge on *Paranormal Challenge* and a regular guest on *Ghost Adventures* and the *Maury Show*, as well as a regular on local Chicago television and radio. She lectures frequently at libraries, historical societies, and professional associations.

In addition to her books, Ursula is the author of numerous scholarly articles exploring the links between history and the paranormal, including articles published in the *International Journal of Parapsychology*. Ursula is a past editor of *PA News*, the quarterly newsletter of the Parapsychological Association, and a past president and board member of the Pi Gamma Chapter of Phi Alpha Theta, the national history honor society.

A graduate of St. Benedict High School in Chicago, Ursula holds a B.A. degree in history from Benedictine University and an M.A. in American cultural and intellectual history from Northeastern Illinois University. Her academic explorations include the Spiritualist movement of the nineteenth century and its transformation into psychical research and parapsychology, and the relationships among belief, experience, science, and religion.

In her spare time she is working with her fellow taphophiles and ghost hunters towards a permit to restore her favorite cemetery, Bachelors Grove, and still spends a lot of Saturdays watching Chicago's *Svengoolie* or horror movie marathons at the Portage Theater. She lives in Chicago with her two daughters. She also loves to cook, sing at church, and shop for dresses (which she notoriously even wears to graveyards).

Lake Claremont Press has been publishing books on the Chicago area and its history since 1994. Find us on Facebook, Twitter (@ChicagoPress), Pinterest, and at *www.lakeclaremont.com*. For special events and more information related to this book, visit *www.graveyardsofchicago.com*.

Selected Booklist

Oldest Chicago

Finding Your Chicago Ancestors

The Golden Age of Chicago Children's Television

Chicago TV Horror Movie Shows: From Shock Theatre *to* Svengoolie

Historic Bars of Chicago

A Chicago Tavern: A Goat, a Curse, and the American Dream

The Beat Cop's Guide to Chicago Eats

The Chicago River: A Natural and Unnatural History

The Chicago River Architecture Tour

Just Add Water: Making the City of Chicago (for kids)

The Politics of Place: A History of Zoning in Chicago

For Members Only: A History and Guide to Chicago's Oldest Private Clubs

Gold Coast Madam: The Secret Life of Rose Laws

Rule 53: Capturing Hippies, Spies, Politicians, and Murderers in an American Courtroom

What Would Jane Say? City-Building Women and a Tale of Two Chicagos

Wrigley Field's Last World Series: The Wartime Chicago Cubs and the Pennant of 1945

From Lumber Hookers to the Hooligan Fleet: A Treasury of Chicago Maritime History

Near West Side Stories: Struggles for Community in Chicago's Maxwell Street Neighborhood

I Am a Teamster: A Short, Fiery Story of Regina V. Polk, Her Hats, Her Pets, Sweet Love, and the Modern-Day Labor Movement